CRITICAL ECOLOGIES:
THE FRANKFURT SCHOOL AND CONTEMPORARY
ENVIRONMENTAL CRISES

Environmental movements are the subject of increasingly rigorous political theoretical study. Can the Frankfurt School's critical frameworks be used to address ecological issues, or do environmental conflicts remain part of the 'failed promise' of this group? *Critical Ecologies* aims to redeem the theories of major Frankfurt thinkers – Theodor Adorno, Max Horkheimer, and Herbert Marcuse, among others – by applying them to contemporary environmental crises.

Critical Ecologies argues that sustainability and critical social theory have many similar goals, including resistance to different forms of domination. Like the Frankfurt School itself, the essays in this volume reflect a spirit of interdisciplinarity and draw attention to intersections between environmental, sociopolitical, and philosophical issues. Offering textual analyses by leading scholars in both critical theory and environmental politics, *Critical Ecologies* underscores the continued relevance of the Frankfurt School's ideas for addressing contemporary issues.

ANDREW BIRO is the Canada Research Chair in Political Ecology and Environmental Political Theory and an associate professor in the Department of Political Science at Acadia University.

EDITED BY ANDREW BIRO

Critical Ecologies

The Frankfurt School and Contemporary Environmental Crises

UNIVERSITY OF TORONTO PRESS
Toronto Buffalo London

© University of Toronto Press Incorporated 2011
Toronto Buffalo London
www.utppublishing.com
Printed in Canada

ISBN 978-0-8020-9840-5 (cloth)
ISBN 978-0-8020-9565-7 (paper)

Library and Archives Canada Cataloguing in Publication

Critical ecologies : the Frankfurt School and contemporary environmental
crises / edited by Andrew Biro.

Includes bibliographical references and index.
ISBN 978-0-8020-9840-5 (bound). – ISBN 978-0-8020-9565-7 (pbk.)

1. Human ecology – Philosophy.   2. Social ecology.   3. Ecology –
Philosophy.   4. Critical theory.   I. Biro, Andrew, 1969–

GF21.C75 2011   304.2   C2011-900252-3

This book has been published with the help of a grant from the Canadian
Federation for the Humanities and Social Sciences, through the Aid to
Scholarly Publications Program, using funds provided by the Social
Sciences and Humanities Research Council of Canada.

University of Toronto Press acknowledges the financial assistance to its
publishing program of the Canada Council for the Arts and the Ontario
Arts Council.

 Canada Council   Conseil des Arts   ONTARIO ARTS COUNCIL
for the Arts   du Canada   CONSEIL DES ARTS DE L'ONTARIO

University of Toronto Press acknowledges the financial support of the
Government of Canada through the Canada Book Fund for its publishing
activities.

Contents

Acknowledgments

In many ways this book began with a workshop at Acadia University in the fall of 2006, where earlier versions of most of the chapters were discussed. Christopher Buck, Eli Meyerhoff, and Cate Mortimer-Sandilands contributed papers to the workshop but for various reasons weren't able to have chapters in this volume. Nevertheless, their contributions were helpful in moving this project forward. The workshop was also attended by students in my Environmental Political Theory seminar that semester: Zach Abugov, Johannah Black, Heather Chamberlin, Tyrone Clarke, Peter Eirikson, Colin Hoult, Jennifer Mark, Patrick Murphy, Emma Pullman, Nigel Tinker, Joel Turnbull, and Gordon Wadley. Tyrone and Peter provided assistance in organizing the workshop; Johannah, Heather, Tyrone, and Emma each bravely volunteered to chair panel sessions. Additional panel sessions were chaired by my colleagues at Acadia, Leo Elshof and Greg Pyrcz. Support for the workshop also came from the Social Sciences and Humanities Research Council of Canada and the Canada Research Chairs Program, as well as Acadia's Office of the Vice-President (Academic), Division of Research and Graduate Studies, Dean of Arts, and Department of Political Science. The idea for hosting such a workshop initially came from a conversation with Janice Drakich and Karen Grant.

Through the process of going from workshop to book, my colleagues at Acadia, both within and outside the Political Science department, have provided a supportive community in many ways. Additional intellectual inspiration, and confirmation that this kind of work is important, has consistently come from colleagues in the growing Environmental Political Theory section of the Western Political Science Association. Daniel Quinlan and other members of the editorial staff at the

University of Toronto Press helped shepherd the book to publication. Two anonymous reviewers solicited by the press provided generous and perceptive comments on the manuscript.

Finally, friends and family members have provided support of all kinds, encouragement, and an occasional welcome distraction. In particular, my partner, Lisa Speigel, has provided me with more than I can express. Our children, Kaela and Nathan, who continually teach me to see the world anew, are, for me, the ultimate reason for thinking about, and working on, the construction of a more humane and beautiful world.

CRITICAL ECOLOGIES:
THE FRANKFURT SCHOOL AND CONTEMPORARY
ENVIRONMENTAL CRISES

Introduction: The Paradoxes of Contemporary Environmental Crises and the Redemption of the Hopes of the Past

ANDREW BIRO

At the most general level, 'critical theory' can be described as knowledge that aims at reducing domination. In contrast to (social) science, which aims at a value-free, 'objective' view of the world, critical theory begins with the normative proposition that domination ought to be reduced or even eliminated, and pursues knowledge to that end. In a letter to Arnold Ruge, Karl Marx defined the task of the critical theorist: 'not to draw a sharp mental line between past and future but to *complete* the thought of the past ... the self-clarification (critical philosophy) of the struggles and wishes of the age.'[1] Thus while critical theory has a transcendent normative basis (the critique of domination), its specific prescriptive content must change with the particular historical circumstances.

Critical theory is often associated with Marx and his intellectual heirs, and more specifically with the mid-twentieth-century social theory of the Frankfurt School, particularly the most prominent of the 'first generation' of Frankfurt theorists: Theodor Adorno, Max Horkheimer, and Herbert Marcuse. For these thinkers, the historical and geographical circumstances of the mid-twentieth century's advanced capitalist societies provided a specific conundrum – one not anticipated by Marx. As Richard Wolin notes, by the 1930s 'objectively speaking prospects for radical change had become all but chimerical ... The Frankfurt School represented the first generation of critical theorists, going back to Marx's day, who were forced to grapple with the problem of not merely a temporary setback for the forces of class struggle, but rather the possibility of their *permanent eclipse*.'[2]

In some sense, the development of postmodern capitalism has confirmed this pessimistic diagnosis of the 'permanent eclipse' of class struggle.[3] At the same time, however, the transcendent normative impulse that animates critical theory has not died with the radically dimmed prospects for working-class revolution, and critical theory provides important insights into our contemporary situation. There is still a general need for a critique of domination, and the work of the Frankfurt theorists continues to provide important resources for clarifying the struggles and wishes of the early twenty-first century.

Clearly one important feature of today's 'struggles and wishes of the age' – one that diverges from both the mid-twentieth-century context of the Frankfurt School and Marx's nineteenth-century context – relates to the rise of environmentalism and to heightened concerns (or, at least, rhetoric) about ecological sustainability. Consider the multitude of institutions concerned with ecological sustainability that have arisen and become increasingly normalized over the last half-century: governmental environment ministries, environmental NGOs, corporate sustainability offices, Environmental Studies programs, and even the modern environmental movement itself – all were at best uncommon as recently as the middle of the last century. To be sure, this is at least in part due to the increasingly visible signs of ecological strain and crisis – an oil 'spill' in the Gulf of Mexico spewed a total of 700 *million* litres of oil over the course of almost three months in the summer of 2010, to cite just one prominent recent example.[4] But concern for the environment is being incorporated into our 'structure of feeling' unevenly and (at times) in ways of which we are hardly aware. And as this process unfolds, a number of paradoxes have revealed themselves. As will be made clearer in this volume, the Frankfurt School thinkers, though they barely engaged with the range of issues that have since been constituted as 'environmental,' offer a considerable resource for understanding and perhaps undoing these paradoxes.

Three Paradoxes of Contemporary Environmental Crises

The first and perhaps most obvious paradox is that the human species itself has become increasingly powerful but at the same time increasingly vulnerable. On the one hand, our capacity to transform the natural environment has reached unprecedented heights and continues to soar. Dizzying developments, in everything from nanotechnology and genetic manipulation to geo-engineering on a planetary scale, threaten to overwhelm even the powers of the imagination. There is, it seems, almost nothing that we cannot do to control our non-human environment and place it at the service of human life. Yet at the same time, these transformations of our ecologies are creating feedbacks that are increasingly difficult to control: urbanization and its associated processes – such as deforestation – are destroying the habitats of many non-human beings, producing cataclysmic rates of species extinction; genetic engineering and the 'green revolution' technologies associated with industrialized agriculture are making our food production systems increasingly fragile; and – perhaps the best-known example – our burning of massive amounts of fossil fuels is leading to increased atmospheric concentrations of greenhouse gases, warming the climate on a global scale, and creating more extreme weather, to the point that large parts of the globe may soon be rendered uninhabitable. In other words, at the same time as we have tremendously increased our power over nature, we have been subjecting ourselves more and more to the negative repercussions that arise from our exercise of that power.

A second paradox confronts us when we unpack the 'human species' as a whole and consider the enormous divisions that overlay our common humanity. While some degree of inequality may be as old as human society, inequality today – particularly between the global North and South – has reached unprecedented levels. Never has aggregate human wealth been greater; yet never greater, as well, has been the sheer number of people forced to live without the most basic amenities of 'civilization': over one billion people lack secure access to clean water, two-and-a-half billion lack adequate sanitation, and so on. Moreover, this rising wealth *and* impoverishment has been occurring in tandem with the development of a more or less global civilization, a development that includes the global spread of democratic norms and human rights. In other words, we seem committed more than ever to the proposition of human equality, yet at the same time, we seem powerless to prevent the development of unprecedented and staggering inequalities among human beings. Put another way, our power to manipulate our natural environment has generated incredible wealth, yet the *social* environment resists manipulation, and individuals are finding themselves increasingly at the mercy of the anonymous and impersonal forces of global markets and bureaucratic states.

The third and perhaps most contentious paradox has to do with environmentalism itself as a social movement. Here, on the one hand, we find increasingly broad recognition of the scope and scale of the environmental challenges (even crises) that we face. There is, for example, scientific consensus – and increasingly broad public consensus – on the reality of global warming and its anthropogenic causes. The same can be said of other environmental issues, from biodiversity loss and declining resource stocks to increased pollutant loads in our air, soil, food, and water. But even while environmentalists' assertions are increasingly accepted as fact, environmentalism as a movement seems incapable of mobilizing more than anaemic, and often individualized, responses. The need to change dramatically how we relate to the non-human world has perhaps never been more urgent; yet the political will to make such changes – and especially collective changes – is clearly almost absent.

Critical Ecologies

Of course, all of the above paradoxes have been noted before, and the lens of critical theory – including the critical theory of the first generation of the Frankfurt School – is hardly necessary to bring them to light. Important strands of contemporary environmental thought have grappled with these paradoxes – in particular, the first paradox of increased power and vulnerability, which arguably provided much of the impetus for the birth of modern environmentalism. And indeed, a number of 'critical ecologies' are already offering a wealth of insights when it comes to how we must grapple with the paradoxes of increased power and vulnerability, overconsumption and underdevelopment, and knowledge and collective inaction. A partial list of these critical ecologies would include the following: biocentrism, bioregionalism, deep ecology, eco-feminism, eco-socialism, ecological economics, environmental justice, and social ecology. And each of these has its own divisions and subdivisions. The political-intellectual terrain here is complicated, contested, and constantly evolving, but all of these discourses broadly share – at least in some of their instantiations – a commitment to radical critique, or in other words an understanding that adequately addressing the environmental crises we currently face will require us to rethink some of our fundamental sociopolitical institutions. On this basis we can distinguish '*critical* ecologies' from more reform-minded discourses such as ecological modernization, environmental economics, green liberalism, market environmentalism, and sustainable development. At the same time, while these analyses do not have as their purview an 'external nature' abstracted from human intervention, they can be described as 'critical *ecologies*' because their central focus is the *oikos*, or human dwelling place.[5]

With the appropriate caveats that come with such broad brush-strokes, we can briefly identify how some of these critical ecologies have responded to the three paradoxes outlined above. For example, one response to the paradox of increased power and vulnerability has been to argue that we should attempt to step back from or refuse the power that produces this vulnerability. The essence of the argument is that contemporary social structures and technologies have become unmanageable as a consequence of their scale and complexity. Prescriptive responses to this diagnosis vary quite widely in terms of their specific content and their level of sophistication; that said, cornerstone concepts include rescaling, localization, 'appropriate technology,' and slowness. At their most simplistic, these concepts are expressed as quasi-conservative idealizations of past forms of socioecological interaction. The danger here lies not so much in a misdiagnosis, as in an insufficiently elaborated sense of the Janus-faced nature of how the human capacity to transform the environment has developed – that the capacity to transform the environment is not entirely undesirable and indeed is necessary for survival. However, even where a kind of immersion in nature is rejected in favour of the development of social structures for the more rational governance of human–environment interactions, particularly careful attention must be paid to the dialectical nature of human and environmental change. Arguments for rescaling and appropriate technology cannot be advanced taking a static conception of human nature – that is, without asking: 'How, in remaking nature, do we remake ourselves?'[6]

The second paradox identified above, of overconsumption and underdevelopment, has been increasingly engaged with as critical ecologies have evolved over the past three or four decades. In the 1970s the discourse of 'limits' was arguably the centrepiece of radical environmental criticism; relatively little attention was paid to the unequal ways in which limits were being established as well as breached.[7] The great ideological triumph of the 'sustainable development' discourse of the 1980s was that it appeared to finesse the choice between environmental sustainability on the one hand and development on the other. Critical ecologies of various kinds sought to expose the ways in which the logics of sustainability and development either were independent of each other (meaning that 'sustainable development' necessarily highlighted those areas where the two coincided, and downplayed areas where they conflicted) or were structurally antagonistic (meaning that 'development,' at least as it was generally construed, was more or less inherently unsustainable). Critical ecologies – in particular, Murray Bookchin's social ecology and a variety of eco-feminist discourses – drew attention to a deeply rooted connection between ecological devastation and the deepening and strengthening of inequality among human beings. That is to say, ecologically unsustainable practices drove *and* were driven by both overconsumption and underdevelopment.

Finally, the third paradox – the recognition of crisis coupled with a lack of collective action – is one that has only begun to be recognized now that environmentalists are increasingly being forced to confront the limited successes they have achieved despite decades of struggle.[8] Whether the roots of environmental degradation are conceived as capitalism, social complexity and hierarchization, a loss of connection with 'nature' associated with urbanization and mediatization, or even human 'overpopulation,' those roots have been strengthened since the modern environmental movement first took shape in the 1960s. And predictably, very many environmental indicators have worsened over that time. Environmental thinkers and activists today are forced to confront the fact that this failure has occurred despite compounding scientific evidence and the frequent voicing of passionate jeremiads. One result has been the proliferation of environmental campaigns focusing on the positive outcomes of more ecologically sustainable choices rather than on stern moralizing judgments; the latter are increasingly seen as discouraging rather than encouraging action.[9] Yet even campaigns of 'encouragement' seem to have had limited effectiveness thus far, especially insofar as they risk falling into the same naive optimism that hobbled sustainable development. A second response has been the cultivation of more deliberative, leisurely, or slower-paced modes of living ('slow food,' voluntary simplicity, and so on), as countertempos to the frenetically paced institutions of modernity. But to the extent that these 'lifestyle choices' have been politicized, their content sits somewhat uneasily with the formal urgency of the diagnosis of environmental crisis. Because of the time lag between particular environmental changes and the recognition of their deleterious effects, idealized solutions (such as the precautionary principle) presume that we are temporally ahead of a curve that, in fact, is always already behind us. The result is a recognition of the need for immediate action, and a simultaneous recognition of the need for far deeper attitudinal changes that would embed behavioural changes and ensure they are 'sustainable.' If we recall that Frankfurt School critical theory originated in the context of the rise of fascism and the absence of a political base equipped to respond to it except in an authoritarian fashion (whether in Stalinist Soviet Communism or in the increasingly administered monopoly capitalism), we can see that the problems they dealt with are not so different from our own.

Bringing Critical Theory into Critical Ecology

With only a few exceptions, however, these critical ecologies have not drawn on the critical theory of the Frankfurt School. What Robyn Eckersley in the early 1990s called the 'failed promise of Critical Theory' for environmentalism has remained largely unredeemed.[10] At the same time, the Habermasian turn in particular has meant that the tradition of Frankfurt School critical theory has become increasingly disengaged from ecological issues, notwithstanding the emphasis that Horkheimer, Adorno, and Marcuse placed on the 'domination of nature' as key to understanding human psychological and sociocultural development. This collection of essays seeks to begin the redemption of critical theory's 'failed promise,' using the resources of the Frankfurt School to grapple with the paradoxes which in some sense define our time: increased power over and vulnerability to nature; a social realm resistant to conscious transformation; and increased knowledge of the pernicious ecological impacts of human behaviour without an attendant will to change. Such an engagement clearly will not in and of itself solve environmental crises. But it is necessary if we are to deal with environmental crises with an honest eye and if we are to maintain critical theory's dictum to engage with and understand 'the struggles and wishes of the age.'

What then can the critical theory of the Frankfurt School contribute to our understanding of contemporary environmental issues? Obviously, this introduction can only gesture at some of the themes that will emerge in the rest of the book – which is itself posited as the beginning of a conversation rather than the last word on this question. Both the paradoxes noted above and the themes discussed below can be understood as points in a critical ecology constellation – points that are separated here for purposes of analytic and narrative convenience but that when connected begin to map out a greater whole. Similarly, the sections into which this book is divided (see below) provide a loose narrative framework; but neither the paradoxes above nor the themes below map simply onto particular sections or chapters of the book.

Writing under different historical circumstances, the Frankfurt School critical theorists began to develop a concept of the 'domination of nature' – a concept that helps illuminate the first two paradoxes by showing how increased power over nature can yield increased vulnerability as well as, in turn, an increasingly powerful social apparatus, one that takes the form of a reified 'second nature.' While the particular Freudian framework employed by the first-generation Frankfurt School theorists has fallen more and more into disfavour, a premise underlying their commitment to Freudian theory is still worth preserving: that is, their general commitment – especially visible in Marcuse's work – to developing a dialectical account of human biology and to basing projects of social transformation on a firmer understanding of what *really* motivates human behaviour, without succumbing to biological determinism or essentialism.

As for the third paradox, as was mentioned earlier, the Frankfurt School's theoretical innovations emerged from a commitment to the possibility and even necessity of radical transformation, even if the political will to effect it seemed absent. The Frankfurt School thinkers in the 1930s and 1940s faced a bleak prognosis; and certainly today a sober assessment of multiple and intersecting ecological crises, and of the current balance of political forces, does not lend itself to optimism. Their response was to conceive of their work as a 'message in a bottle,' sent out to future generations, to be uncorked when political conditions had changed.[11] But it is important to be clear about what such a future might look like: if the prospects for replacing a fundamentally irrational and chaotic political-economic system with a rational system grounded in humane values were already clearly on the horizon, then there would be no need for the Frankfurt School's highly theoretical critiques. Instead we can read those 'changed political conditions' as the supercharged development of technological innovation, and as the elevated ecological stakes that our collective capacity to reshape our world brings with it. Today, the rising seas of anthropogenic global warming have delivered to us the Frankfurt School's bottle. The message in it, for us, is that increased technological capacity does not necessarily lead to increased domination *and also* that rational social and ecological relations are indeed possible. The goal, to borrow from Walter Benjamin (as do a number of contributors to this volume), is 'not the mastery of nature but of the relation between nature and man.'[12]

Outline of the Book

The chapters in Part I of this collection in particular thus deal with the 'domination of nature' and its relevance in light of contemporary scientific and sociotechnical developments. *William Leiss*'s opening chapter argues against the fatalism of Horkheimer and Adorno's *Dialectic of Enlightenment*. The 'disease of reason' identified by Horkheimer and Adorno ought not to be associated with the human condition as such, but rather with particular historical developments. Seen in this light, contemporary developments in molecular biology and neuroscience, where the human mind itself becomes the object of scientific investigation and technological manipulation, render the inward turn of the 'domination of nature' – turning the human subject into scientific object – most clearly visible. A more nuanced and historically contingent extension of the insights of first-generation critical theorists who first insisted on clarifying this 'dialectic of enlightenment' is needed at this moment, now that the stakes in 'the mastery over the mastery of nature' (Walter Benjamin) are the survival of the human species as such.

In chapter 2, *Christoph Görg* discusses the disconnect between the contemporary human capacity to transform our environment and our lack of control over those processes. Görg situates this particularly within the development of 'post-Fordist' capitalism, arguing that the insights of the early Frankfurt School, properly updated, provide a valuable resource for understanding contemporary societal relationships with nature. While post-Fordism and associated discourses such as ecological modernization appear to have given up on the earlier goal of total mastery of nature, rendering obsolete critical theory's notion of the 'domination of nature,' Görg argues that the transition to post-Fordism has largely been one in which environmental issues have become sites of risk management (climate change) as well as new avenues for capitalist accumulation (biodiversity, carbon markets). We have moved away from a project of the domination of nature toward one of the 're-flexive mastery of nature.' The alternative, then, is not simply a passive attentiveness to nature's otherness (this otherness is already to some extent accounted for in the *reflexive* mastery of nature); it also involves examining how nature is constructed with a view to seeing which environmental problems are treated and for whom.

In chapter 3, *Katharine N. Farrell* continues the discussion about bringing critical theory into conversation with contemporary science. Leiss concentrated on contemporary developments in scientific understanding; Farrell now shifts our focus to contemporary scientific practice and the role that science plays in environmental governance. For Farrell, contemporary 'postnormal' science can be understood as a concrete elaboration of the 'new modality of science' proposed by Herbert Marcuse in *One-Dimensional Man*. In this regard, Marcuse's theories could be powerful referents in discussions about the democratic legitimation of the 'extended peer review' processes that increasingly characterize environmental governance.

The Frankfurt School's project of developing a dialectical account of human nature is another important component of what its work can contribute to critical ecology. In particular, that project can temper the ways in which radical ecology's critique of anthropocentrism has at times – particularly in deep ecology – veered toward misanthropy. In other words, such an account of human nature can help us cull the humane aspects of modernity and historical 'progress' (or 'enlightenment' to use Horkheimer and Adorno's preferred term) from those aspects that perpetuate domination. Thus in Part II, in chapter 4, **D. Bruce Martin** turns to Adorno's account of the logic of sacrifice as a counterpoint to deep ecologists' calls for sacrifice in the name of saving nature. Martin argues that Adorno and Horkheimer offer the category of 'repressed mimesis,' which allows us to understand oppression and exploitation as based on 'naturalized' categories to which deep ecology seems blind. Whereas deep ecologists propose to sacrifice human interests for the sake of wilderness preservation, following Robert Hullot-Kentor, Martin argues that Adorno's analysis of sacrifice reveals a 'logic of sacrifice' that ultimately leads to self-destruction, and that only an awareness of the futility of sacrifice – a memory of the self as part of nature, and a memory of suffering and oppression throughout human history – can lead to liberation.

A similar dialectical reversal structures chapter 5, in which **Colin Campbell** starts with the work of Hans Jonas, who provides a highly distilled and philosophically rigorous version of the 'deep ecological' or 'biophilic' desire. Jonas (who was a student of Martin Heidegger) can provide a compelling account of the causes of ecological crisis (an instrumental conceptualization of the non-human world as what Heidegger calls 'standing reserve'), and his prescriptive response vividly reflects the dominant – yet inadequate – response of collective guilt and individual effort, or what Michael Maniates has identified as the 'individualization of responsibility.' At the same time, Marcuse's *Eros and Civilization* – in particular, its critical account of Freud – provides an immanent critique of this biophilic desire or impulse, and thus a way 'to move beyond the bad dialectic of collective guilt and isolated effort.'

If the relevance of the Frankfurt School for environmental studies has been largely underappreciated, the same cannot be said for cultural studies – a field where the Frankfurt School is a theoretical touchstone. Yet from the beginning, the early Frankfurt School thinkers insisted on seeing 'nature' and 'culture' as a dialectical totality. In Part II, maintaining this position helps us avoid the polarizations of the pro-/anti-anthropocentrism debates. In Part III, more detailed engagements with 'culture' emerge: a focus on the aesthetic – including images of the future and present – and on sharpening our understanding of reconciliation and its obverse, alienation. Both the focus on alienation and the 'aesthetic turn' are reminders of critical theory's commitment to the possibility and even necessity of radical transformation, even if the political will to effect it appears absent – a point that remains equally relevant in the context of today's struggles for ecological sustainability. *Donald A. Burke* begins by delving into Adorno's aesthetic theory, arguing that Adorno destabilizes the hierarchical arrangement of natural and artistic beauty found in Kant and Hegel; in doing so, he provides a historical materialist aesthetics that is especially useful for contemporary ecological politics. Adorno's account, which seeks to *reclaim* natural beauty (against Hegel) without *privileging* it (against Kant), sees aesthetics as a form of rationality that can be counterposed to instrumental, dominating approaches to nature. The path to a more ecologically responsible mode of living (or reconciliation with nature) thus lies in the capacity of the aesthetic to remind us of the ways in which instrumental human activity involves the repression of nature.

According to Burke, 'nature' for the Frankfurt School is always socially mediated: nature's expression is found in images of the 'cultural landscape,' understood as the memorialization of human suffering. *Steven Vogel*'s contribution similarly tackles what is often taken to be a commonsensical division between nature and culture. Ultimately, he argues that it is alienation from our *built* environment that should be a cause for concern, rather than 'alienation from nature' – a conceptual category that he argues is grounded in circular reasoning. Instead of the Frankfurt School, with its 'tragic' (his term) view of alienation as an inevitable part of the human condition, Vogel turns to the early works of Karl Marx, for whom the social practice of labour constitutes our environment. While other authors in this collection (e.g., Farrell) argue that Habermas made a 'wrong turn' when he shifted his focus to communicative interaction, and consequently neglected environmental questions, Vogel sees Habermas's communicative turn as itself a result of the first-generation Frankfurt School's commitment to the 'tragic' view of alienation. Reaching back to Marx, Vogel argues that the way out of our current environmental plight must lie in a materialist conception of world-constituting activity. Only once the practices that constitute our environment are subjected to democratic deliberation and rational debate can we hope to lead an unalienated existence.

Picking up a theme from Martin's chapter in Part II, *Shane Gunster* begins his chapter by noting potential affinities between Adorno and deep ecology – in particular, their shared critique of instrumentalist approaches to the world. But Gunster further notes that while it may be true that human beings as a species are able to dominate nature (as well as the 'second nature' of social relations and institutions), most individuals experience the world of objects (again, including the second nature of social objects) as overwhelmingly powerful: bureaucracies and markets, like the climate, are things to which we must adapt, not things we can control. Adorno's critique of the domination of nature can be cited as the potential basis for ecological ethics: because nature is more than instrumental reason's conception of it as a stockpile of resources, a certain humility or passivity is required if we are to avoid misrecognizing nature and engaging in what Martin refers to as the 'false projection' of subjective characteristics onto the object. But, Gunster points out, when it comes to the *social* environment – second nature – Adorno seems to turn 180 degrees. Here, instead of lamenting the interference caused by conceptual mediation, he emphasizes the importance of human reason and concepts' roles in mediating the relation between subject and environment. Adorno's thought does not in the end prescribe one extreme or the other; rather, it is best understood as prescribing contextual specificity (particularly the extent to which subjective experience is governed by fear) as well as the dialectical thought that is produced through the tension of holding both that nature is more than human reason can understand *and* that it is the ideological projection of social characteristics.

Gunster's chapter concludes with a brief discussion of how reverence for the 'majesty and beauty of nature' might participate in rather than subvert consumer culture's aestheticization of alienation. This sets the stage for *Andrew Biro*'s chapter, which concludes Part III by examining environmental crisis as a cultural phenomenon and by applying the Frankfurt School's analysis of mass culture to the discourse of environmental crisis. Like Fredric Jameson's theorizations of postmodernity, the Frankfurt School's analysis of the culture industry emphasizes the extent to which the instrumentalization of cultural production forecloses the possibility of imagining what a future radically different from the present might look like and how we might work toward it. Given that environmental crisis narratives are predicated on the *unsustainability* of current patterns of consumption – that the future cannot look like the present – this presents a particular challenge for environmental communication. Ultimately, what Vogel sees in the young Marx, Biro finds in Jameson and the Frankfurt School theorists: the means to recollect that environmental debates ultimately must be (re)connected to the construction of a humane environment in which humans and others can flourish.

Part IV more directly confronts the question of the *contemporary* relevance of Frankfurt School critical theory – it particular, how its analysis of tendencies within second-stage or monopoly capitalism both anticipates and is complicated by the transition to a third stage of capitalism. While the Frankfurt School thinkers clearly did not anticipate anthropogenic global warming, *Jonathan Short*'s chapter argues that Adorno, brought into conversation with Giorgio Agamben, can help us see some of the political pitfalls created by global warming. Occidental rationality (Adorno) and state sovereignty (Agamben) have become obstacles to solving the challenges to human survival posed by anthropogenic climate change, in that they have mobilized nature as a constitutive 'outside' to frame a logic of 'survival or doom.' Global warming, in Short's account, demonstrates the relevance of the Frankfurt School today, in that it provides an especially compelling example of how instrumental rationality and state sovereignty, in the pursuit of survival, are undermining the conditions for human existence.

In chapter 11, *Michael Lipscomb* considers not only the timeliness of Frankfurt School critical theory, but also temporality itself, juxtaposing the urgency of contemporary environmental discourse with the democratic impulse for considered deliberation. Lipscomb brings Adorno's thought to bear to help answer this question: 'How can we become the kind of people who are capable of realizing and sustaining the environmental future that we want to bring into being?' For Lipscomb, an environmental politics informed or inspired by Adorno's thought undertakes the necessary negotiation between the need for timely action, and the need for hesitation and reflection, as a means for interrupting the dominant rhythms and temporalities that constitute us as productivist and consumerist subjects.

Adorno begins *Negative Dialectics* by noting that the moment when philosophy might have been realized has been missed.[13] It seems thus fitting, as a number of chapters in this volume testify, that the contemporary moment is defined by what has been exceeded: postmodernity, post-Fordism, postnormal science, postcoloniality, postfeminism, postenvironmentalism ... the list could be extended almost indefinitely. In chapter 12, *Timothy W. Luke* focuses on the discourse of post-humanism. Critical theory's defence of individual freedom and rationality in the mid-twentieth century serves as a touchstone for those seeking to avoid an administrative–managerial response to environmental crises (which would further entrench class and state power) on the one hand, and an anti-anthropocentrism that not only devalorizes human lives but also – and because of that – fails to gain any political traction. Reaching back to Horkheimer's 1957 essay 'The Concept of Man,' Luke uncovers an anticipatory critique of the enthusiastic post-humanism of Katherine Hayles and the information-based multinational capitalism described in Jean-François Lyotard's *The Postmodern Condition*. While celebrating the unprecedented technological control over both non-human and human nature, Luke argues that post-humanist ideologies (con)fuse instrumental and substantive rationality and are therefore incapable of recognizing the contemporary operation of the dialectic of enlightenment: that the conquest of nature is achieved at the cost of our very humanity, or 'concept of Man.'

Finally, *Andrew Feenberg*'s Afterword considers Marcuse's notion of the 'liberation of nature.' Returning to a theme that marks many of the chapters in this volume, Feenberg reiterates Marcuse's insistence that what is required is a defence of nature that does not return us to premodern essentialism. To this end, Marcuse connects nature's 'flourishing' to normative (i.e., anthropocentric) values that are rooted in the judgments that ground our experience of the world. Aesthetics, biology, and normativity are all intimately connected and provide the platform on which progressive environmental politics – critical ecologies – might be constructed. At the same time, Feenberg – again echoing earlier contributors – notes important limitations to the critical theory project as developed by the first-generation Frankfurt School theorists. He mentions their theories of technology and of media; their concept of experience, which remains rooted in Freudian theory; and their at best only 'buried' engagement with a phenomenology that does not presuppose romantic immediacy.

More generally, Feenberg's conclusion highlights that the first-generation Frankfurt School thinkers cannot provide us with the last word. Critical theory is a living tradition: struggles and wishes do change from one age to the next, and the insights derived from an earlier historical context cannot be rigidly applied today. While this book aims to show that today's environmentalists can learn important lessons from the critical theory of the first-generation Frankfurt School theorists, the contributors also seek to show how today's environmental challenges can shape critical theory as a living tradition and how the insights of the Frankfurt School can be enriched by an engagement with contemporary science, environmentalism, and theory. The 'domination of nature' in much of first-generation critical theory remains a broad and underdeveloped category; except in Marcuse's last works, the Frankfurt School thinkers provide little if any systematic engagement with ecological issues *per se*. Only in the past few years has work begun to more thoroughly integrate Frankfurt School critical theory with environmental concerns[14] and with the increasingly rich literature on environmental political theory. This book seeks to take up that urgent task in the hope of lighting a path out of the paradoxes in which contemporary environmental politics finds itself and, in so doing, undertaking what Horkheimer and Adorno suggest is the task of critical theory – indeed, enlightenment itself: 'the redemption of the hopes of the past.'[15]

NOTES

1 Karl Marx, *Early Writings*, ed. Quentin Hoare, trans. Rodney Livingstone and Gregor Benton (New York: Vintage, 1975), 209.
2 Richard Wolin, 'Critical Theory and the Dialectic of Rationalism,' *New German Critique* 41 (1987): 28, emphasis in original.
3 See, for example, Fredric Jameson, *Late Marxism: Adorno, or, the Persistence of the Dialectic* (London: Verso, 1990).
4 Timothy J. Crone and Maya Tolstoy, 'Magnitude of the 2010 Gulf of Mexico Oil Leak,' *Science*, 23 September 2010, 10.1126/science.1195840.
5 *Oikos* is the Greek root for both ecology and economics, with the latter understood by the Ancient Greeks (most famously Aristotle) as the science of household management.
6 Donald Worster, *Rivers of Empire: Water, Aridity, and the Growth of the American West* (Oxford: Oxford University Press, 1985), 30. Worster cites the work of the Frankfurt School as an important part of the theoretical framework for his book.
7 See, for example, the 'Limits to Growth' report issued by the Club of Rome: Donella H. Meadows, Dennis L. Meadows, Jorgen Randers, and

William W. Behrens III, *Limits to Growth* (New York: Universe, 1972). Nor has this entirely disappeared: note for example the subtitle of Jared Diamond's highly acclaimed and popular *Collapse: How Societies Choose to Fail or Succeed* (New York: Viking Penguin, 2005).

8 See, for example, Michael Shellenberger and Ted Nordhaus, *The Death of Environmentalism: Global Warming Politics in a Post-Environmental World* (Breakthrough Institute, 2004).

9 See, for example, Gil Ereaut and Nat Singer, *Warm Words: How Are We Telling the Climate Story and Can We Tell It Better?* (London: Institute for Public Policy Research, 2006); see also Shellenberger and Nordhaus, *The Death of Environmentalism*.

10 Robyn Eckersley, *Environmentalism and Political Theory: Toward an Ecocentric Approach* (Albany: SUNY Press, 1992), 97–117.

11 Zygmunt Bauman, 'Melting Modernity: Each Time Unique.' Ralph Miliband Public Lecture, 8 November 2005; see also Richard Leppert, introduction to *Essays on Music* by Theodor W. Adorno (Berkeley: University of California Press, 2002), 70n224.

12 Walter Benjamin, *Reflections*, ed. Peter Demetz, trans. Edmund Jephcott (New York: Schocken, 1978), 93.

13 Theodor W. Adorno, *Negative Dialectics*, trans. E.B. Ashton (New York: Continuum, 1992), 3.

14 One important early exception is William Leiss, *The Domination of Nature* (Boston: Beacon, 1974). Along with other works by the authors of this volume, see Andrew Dobson, 'Critical Theory and Green Politics,' in *Politics of Nature*, ed. Andrew Dobson and Paul Lucardie (New York: Routledge, 1995).

15 Max Horkheimer and Theodor W. Adorno, *Dialectic of Enlightenment*, trans. John Cumming (New York: Continuum, 1987), xv.

BIBLIOGRAPHY

Adorno, Theodor W. *Negative Dialectics*. Translated by E.B. Ashton. New York: Continuum, 1992.

Bauman, Zygmunt. 'Melting Modernity: Each Time Unique.' Ralph Miliband Public Lecture, 8 November 2005. http://www.lse.ac.uk/collections/LSE-PublicLecturesAndEvents/pdf/20051108-Bauman3.pdf.

Benjamin, Walter. *Reflections*. Edited by Peter Demetz, translated by Edmund Jephcott. New York: Schocken, 1978.

Crone, Timothy J., and Maya Tolstoy. 'Magnitude of the 2010 Gulf of Mexico Oil Leak.' *Science*, 23 September 2010, 10.1126/science.1195840.

Diamond, Jared. *Collapse: How Societies Choose to Fail or Succeed*. New York: Viking Penguin, 2005.

Dobson, Andrew. 'Critical Theory and Green Politics.' In *Politics of Nature*, edited by Andrew Dobson and Paul Lucardie. New York: Routledge, 1995.

Eckersley, Robyn. *Environmentalism and Political Theory: Toward an Ecocentric Approach*. Albany: SUNY Press, 1992.

Ereaut, Gil, and Nat Singer. *Warm Words: How Are We Telling the Climate Story and Can We Tell It Better?* London: Institute for Public Policy Research, 2006.

Horkheimer, Max, and Theodor W. Adorno. *Dialectic of Enlightenment*. Translated by John Cumming. New York: Continuum, 1987.

Jameson, Fredric. *Late Marxism: Adorno, or, the Persistence of the Dialectic*. London: Verso, 1990.

Leiss, William. *The Domination of Nature*. Boston: Beacon Press, 1974.

Leppert, Richard. Introduction to *Essays on Music*, by Theodor W. Adorno. Berkeley: University of California Press, 2002.

Marx, Karl. *Early Writings*. Edited by Quentin Hoare, translated by Rodney Livingstone and Gregor Benton. New York: Vintage, 1975.

Meadows, Donella H., Dennis L. Meadows, Jorgen Randers, and William W. Behrens III. *Limits to Growth*. New York: Universe, 1972.

Shellenberger, Michael, and Ted Nordhaus. *The Death of Environmentalism: Global Warming Politics in a Post-Environmental World*. Oakland: Breakthrough Institute: 2004.

Wolin, Richard. 'Critical Theory and the Dialectic of Rationalism.' *New German Critique* 41 (Spring–Summer 1987): 23–52.

Worster, Donald. *Rivers of Empire: Water, Aridity, and the Growth of the American West*. Oxford: Oxford University Press, 1985.

PART ONE

Science and the Mastery of Nature

1 Modern Science, Enlightenment, and the Domination of Nature: No Exit?

WILLIAM LEISS

Introduction and Overview

The disease of reason is that reason was born from man's urge to dominate nature.

Max Horkheimer, *Eclipse of Reason* (1947)

In the fuller passage from which this extract is taken, Horkheimer locates the origins of the 'collective madness' of modern times 'in primitive objectification, in the first man's calculating contemplation of the world as prey.'[1] Perhaps all one can say in response is, if this diagnosis is correct, there is certainly no cure, so we might as well get on with our lives.

In the early sections of this chapter I will note briefly the argument that the approach taken in *Dialectic of Enlightenment* and *Eclipse of Reason* ends in a cul-de-sac. Then I will offer a somewhat different interpretation of the historical dialectic of enlightenment, arguing that we are still today in the midst of a real, historical conundrum – one with potentially fateful consequences – that is playing itself out in contemporary society. Returning once again to the main theme – the relation of modern science to enlightenment and the domination of nature – I will then try to show how the 'stakes' in this 'game' are now being raised by molecular biology and the neurosciences. For it was inevitable that 'human nature' and its most precious attribute, the human mind, would one day become 'objects' to be mastered by the methodology of the natural sciences.

Here is where I will end up: domination of nature through the progress of the modern natural sciences is the defining historical dialectic of modernity, one that has a distinctive internal contradiction that must be addressed and resolved if humanity is ever to transcend this stage of historical development. I argue against the 'dialectic of enlightenment' because it presupposes what it ought to prove, namely, that there is no exit. At the same time, this defining historical dialectic is still in the process of development, driven forward by its own internal tensions. Thus it is still 'open' to qualitatively different final outcomes.

Dialectic of Enlightenment Revised

In Horkheimer's two main texts from the 1940s, *Dialectic of Enlightenment* (with Adorno; complete typescript 1944, first published 1947) and *Eclipse of Reason* (1947), three different sets of key concepts appear. One is, of course, 'dialectic of enlightenment,' which may be summed up in the proposition that enlightenment, the enemy of myth, falls victim to its opposite: 'The more completely the machinery of thought subjugates existence, the more blindly is it satisfied with reproducing it. Enlightenment thereby regresses to the mythology it has never been able to escape.'[2] The second is the opposition of objective versus subjective reason: the latter holds that 'reason is a subjective faculty of the mind' and serves the subject's interest in self-preservation; the former holds that 'reason is a principle inherent in reality.'[3] The third is the domination of nature. In seeking to understand how nature works, and thus to control its powers for their benefit, 'human beings distance themselves from nature in order to arrange it in such a way that it can be mastered.' But the enlarged social apparatus that is required to refine, enlarge, and administer control over nature takes its revenge, for 'the power of the system over human beings increases with every step they take away from the power of nature.'[4] Enlarged, collective domination over nature is matched at every stage by a comparably heightened domination by some people over others.

Though there are differences in the modes of expression used for these three sets of concepts, there are enough similarities, even in the brief quotes given above, to suggest that they should be regarded as variations on a single theme.[5] That they may represent a single core idea is affirmed in a passage that Horkheimer wrote toward the end of his life:

The immanent logic of social development points to a totally technicized life as its final stage. Man's domination of nature reaches such proportions that scarcity, and thus the necessity of man's dominion over man, disappears. But at the same time, the end is total disillusionment, the extinction of mind insofar as it differs from the tool that is reason ... All this is part of the dialectic of the Enlightenment, the change from truth into unconditioned conformity with meaninglessness, with reality generally.[6]

These sentences evoke nothing so much as Max Weber's 'iron cage' of rationality. Horkheimer's own heading for this passage is 'On Pessimism.' The idea of a 'final stage' of life that is 'totally technicized' leaves little doubt that this is a path of regressive social development having no exit into a better future (utopia).[7]

This fatalism and explicit pessimism is also summed up well in the sentence quoted at the outset: 'The disease of reason is that reason was born from man's urge to dominate nature.' In locating this dialectic within the 'human condition' as such – in particular, in the very nature of human reason – Horkheimer appeared to pose an insoluble dilemma for social theory. Among other things, this perspective does seem to contradict the underlying basis of critical theory, to the degree that it is a variant of the Marxist theory of social change in general, and of modern society in particular, because it places the key issue in human development entirely outside of history and presents it as a constant and essential feature of the species in all of its manifestations over time.

One of the main difficulties created by this overly expansive concept of instrumental reason is encountered in the indiscriminate use of the word 'domination' in the phrase 'domination of nature.' For those words make no sense when applied to what Horkheimer refers to as the 'primitive' state of *Homo sapiens*, presumably meaning before the time of early agriculture and settled societies (as opposed to purely hunter-gatherer societies). Nor do they make much better sense when applied to premodern civilizations, because in those, there was very little *control* over nature to speak of.[8] In those times nature was fate, especially for women, on account of their role in childbearing: before the age of modern medicine and public health, as many as half of all newborns died in the first year of life, and pregnancy and childbirth represented severe risks of death for women (as is still true today in many places in the world).

Thus there is no sensible way in which 'primitive objectification' can be regarded as the first step on the road to the modern epoch and the form that the domination of nature takes there. This error is compounded in critical theory when the phenomenon of enlightenment is 'generalized' and presented as a historical constant, applicable equally to ancient Greece and eighteenth-century Europe. The result is to misrepresent in a fundamental way the true function of the modern enlightenment.

The French Enlightenment

The opening pages of *Dialectic of Enlightenment* correctly present Francis Bacon as the original Enlightenment thinker of the modern period, for without a doubt it was Bacon who developed the clearest and most straightforward conception of 'domination over nature' and its relation to the new sciences of nature. In a nutshell, he put the concept in the form of this paradox: *Command* over nature can only be achieved by *following* nature.[9] One must patiently observe how nature works, taking careful measurements and confirming their accuracy through systematic experimentation (i.e., replication) – a process that should be driven by the recursive interplay of theory and evidence and not solely by a speculative natural philosophy. We require patience if we are ever to reveal the underlying structure of matter that hides behind the phenomenal appearances of things (Bacon thought the alchemists were too impatient, for example). Patience requires a long-range, integrated perspective developed gradually over time by a community of scientists working in different places and corresponding with one another. Bacon also realized that government resources would be needed to subsidize the venture, but he was ahead of his time in this respect, and when he died, he thought himself a failure.

The first – false, because partial or incomplete – form of the dialectic of modernity was the perceived conflict between the new sciences and the dominant religious world view. Bacon resolved this apparent conflict quickly, and over time his resolution became widely accepted.[10] He acknowledged the dilemma – namely, that an enlarged 'power over nature' placed in humanity's hands would need somehow to be superintended – but he dismissed it with a formulaic response. In *The New Organon* (1620) he wrote: 'Only let the human race recover that right over nature which belongs to it by divine bequest, and let power be given it; the exercise thereof will be guided by sound reason and true religion.'[11] He would not live to see the triumph of his program, however. Toward the end of his life he consoled himself by writing a utopian fantasy, *The New Atlantis* (first published posthumously in 1627), in which he depicted a society where an elite scientific research establishment set its own rules and ran investigations of nature independently of political authority.

Only toward the end of the eighteenth century, after the French Enlightenment and the French Revolution had swept away the ancient dogmas that stood in the way of the new sciences, could it be said that Bacon's view had finally triumphed. (For the Enlightenment thinkers, Bacon was a hero.) And only in the works of these eighteenth-century thinkers did the richness of Bacon's original message became fully evident – for remarkably, Bacon, standing at its point of origin, had already sensed the internal tension at the core of modernity. This tension may be described in terms of the two-sided significance of science and technology for society; and here, I shall apply the labels *inventive science* and *transformative science*.

1. By *inventive science* I mean the promise of 'the conquest of nature,' the vision of an endless stream of new products and technologies to enhance the material conditions of life and human well-being.
2. By *transformative science* I mean the penetration of the 'ethos' of the modern scientific method *throughout all of society and its institutions*. This ethos includes the experimental method, with its emphasis on the objective demonstration of results, confirmed through peer review; a thoroughly sceptical attitude toward all received wisdom and traditional belief; the search for 'laws of nature' existing independently of human thought and interests; and what we would now call an 'evidence-based' approach to analysing the causes of human misery, ignorance, and backwardness.[12]

The second is even more important than the first, in my view, but it has been virtually forgotten, shoved aside in the course of the triumphant march of the great triumvirate of science, technology, and industry. Yet the two forms of science together, and the tensions between them, are what comprise the essential dialectic of modernity. To the extent that the two sides exist in a creative tension, thereby fostering historical progress, they counteract the twin obstacles to human development: first, the lack of adequate material security – security that is a precondition for the full unfolding of human creativity; and second, a subjection to irrational forms of thought. The two do not exist in creative tension when the hyperdevelopment of one side (inventive) is matched by the underdevelopment of the other (transformative). In the latter case – which is the one that has persisted and intensified over the past two centuries (with some exceptions here and there) – there is a growing risk that expanded technological powers will be placed at the service of irrational social forces.

If that last sentence sounds a lot like the core theme of *Dialectic of Enlightenment*, that is no accident. But the analysis of the underlying problematic is fundamentally different, not least in its concrete histori-cal setting (modernity) and in its source – namely, modern science and its social context. It was the work of the eighteenth-century French En-lightenment – the 'real' Enlightenment, not the generic one construct-ed by Horkheimer and Adorno – that completed the development of Bacon's duality.[13]

To be sure, through the end of the 1800s there were not all that many new 'products' emanating from scientific laboratories, though the foun-dations for their invention were being laid down by the new sciences of chemistry and physics. During that period, however, the second part of the bargain, transformative science, triumphed over its opponents in European culture. This triumph is wonderfully summarized in the great posthumous work by the Marquis de Condorcet (1743–1794), *Sketch for a Historical Picture of the Progress of the Human Mind*, a work he wrote while in hiding from the agents of the Terror.[14] This text is the clearest statement of the idea that the new scientific methods are im-portant for reasons other than the clearer understanding of nature they allow. Indeed, their greatest importance is that they can and should be diffused throughout society, by means of universal education. Once they are, social policy and social institutions will be rendered more humane and just.

Condorcet envisioned a future in which 'the dissemination of enlight-enment' would 'include in its scope the whole of the human race.'[15] He maintained that the process called 'enlightenment' had been founded on a way of thinking that instructed us 'to admit only proven truths, to separate these truths from whatever as yet remained doubtful and uncertain, and to ignore whatever is and always will be impossible to know.' The gradual extension of this method into the realm of 'moral science,' politics, and economics had enabled thinkers 'to make almost as sure progress in these sciences as they had in the natural sciences.' He continued:

> This metaphysical method became virtually a universal instrument. Men
> learnt to use it in order to perfect the methods of the physical sciences ...

and it was extended to the examination of facts and to the rules of taste. Thus it was applied to all the various undertakings of the human understanding ... It is this new step in philosophy that has for ever imposed a barrier between mankind and the errors of its infancy, a barrier that should save it from relapsing into its former errors under the influence of new prejudices.

Condorcet has an interesting reason for suggesting that advances in the natural sciences are the original foundations for a broader social enlightenment. He remarks that 'all errors in politics and morals are based on philosophical errors and these in turn are connected with scientific errors.' He is saying that there is a connection between our conceptions of natural processes, on the one hand, and our understanding of society and individual behaviour, on the other. Once the progress of the physical sciences is launched, he contends, this 'inexorable progress cannot be contemplated by men of enlightenment without their wishing to make the other sciences follow the same path. It offers them at every step a model to emulate.' This theme is nicely summarized in the following sentence: 'Just as the mathematical and physical sciences tend to improve the arts that we use to satisfy our simplest needs, is it not also part of the necessary order of nature that the moral and political sciences should exercise a similar influence upon the motives that direct our feelings and our actions?'[16]

If Condorcet has a core idea, it is surely this: The 'progress of the sciences' that defines the enlightenment project is a double-sided phenomenon. It encompasses both the physical and the moral sciences – or, using my terminology, inventive *and* transformative science, or technology *and* ethos. It is a process with a built-in mechanism ensuring its indefinite continuation: 'The progress of the sciences ensures the progress of the art of education which in turn advances that of the sciences.'[17] The inner unity between these two dimensions is something that Condorcet seems to have taken for granted. He saw the two sides as arising in quick succession over the course of the seventeenth century and then flourishing together throughout the eighteenth. In short, a more sophisticated chemistry and physics, on the one hand, and enlightened social behaviour, on the other, were two sides of the same coin. That this is an inner unity and not just a coincidence is shown by Condorcet's emphasis on the great advances made possible by the invention of the calculus: it is not only a methodological pillar of the new natural sciences, but also of such innovations in social welfare as insurance and pension programs, which require the use of probabilistic analysis in order to function well.

Condorcet's *Sketch* is the most incisive, insightful, and comprehensive presentation of the underlying unity of Enlightenment thought ever written by one of the key participants of the era. (In this respect it is a far better guide than Kant's famous work, *What Is Enlightenment?*) Yet as far as I know there is no mention at all of Condorcet in *Dialectic of Enlightenment*. Thus critical theory never came to terms with the *internal dialectic* of the modern enlightenment; nor did it ever closely examine the indispensable role played in it by the 'new sciences of nature.'

Horkheimer wrote in 1946 – but only in an internal memorandum at the Institute for Social Research – that 'the rescue of the Enlightenment is our concern.'[18] If this is so (and it is believable), they chose a very odd way of going about it. For how could one not fully recognize, for example, the force and range in Condorcet's account of the struggle waged by enlightenment thought against regressive and oppressive forms of law and social custom? Critical theory's failure to acknowledge the true significance of what the modern sciences of nature contributed in this regard is one of its greatest failings. Condorcet's profound insight – that 'scientific errors' supply one of the strongest supports for the errors in thinking that prop up oppressive social relations – was entirely overlooked.

Perhaps the greatest of all failures of critical theory is that it does not engage the specific *content* of what has been achieved in the modern sciences of nature – content that has permanent value for our understanding of the world in which we live. How can there be, in what styles itself as a critique, no mention of any actual achievement? How can there be not even a passing acknowledgment of the scope and profundity of the collective intellectual labour over time that is represented, say, in Einstein's equations of special and general relativity, in molecular chemistry, or in the theory of evolution by natural selection? It is hard to excuse this degree of systematic oversight and condescension. How could these insights not be regarded as contributions to 'objective reason' and instead be relegated implicitly to the sphere of subjective reason's 'interest in self-preservation'?

As Vogel has written, 'dialectic of enlightenment' ends in a cul-de-sac. But that is exclusively the *theory*'s problem. One cannot transcribe its radical shortcomings onto the historical reality it so poorly characterizes.

Scientific Mastery over 'Internal Nature'

Before discussing further where the tension between the two forms of science stands at present, I would like to explain the sense in which the project for the domination of nature is nearing completion. The 400-year trajectory of the new sciences was launched with studies on the forces and materials that make up the external environment – metals, minerals, energy, and organic compounds. Chemistry was the lead science; by the late eighteenth century its industrial applications had already been established, and by the mid-nineteenth century, synthetic compounds – dyes, for example – were pouring from the factories. Then it was the turn of physics, which dominated the late nineteenth century and the first half of the twentieth; the signature of its mastery was the discovery and use of atomic energy.

Progress in biology and genetics began slowly, then accelerated during the second half of the twentieth century. Molecular biology discovered that the book of life is written in the simple four-letter chemistry of the DNA molecule, and with that came the astonishing news that all living things that have ever existed on earth, plant and animal alike, share the same protein chemistry. Thus science's long trajectory now circles back and veers inward, exhibiting the human organism as a natural entity whose evolutionary origins and physiological make-up place it within the class of placental mammals. The genetic endowment of *Homo sapiens* – including the genes that direct the construction of its brain – is so closely aligned with that of its nearest natural relatives, the bonobos and chimpanzees, that some molecular biologists regard all three species as members of the genus *Homo*.[19]

Since 2003 we have had in hand the complete readout of the human genome, a sequence (akin to a barcode) of three billion chemical base-pairs. The search is now on for all of the 20,000 to 25,000 genes contained therein. The potential benefits of this knowledge are vast indeed. Just consider genetic disorders, the source of inherited diseases, which are basically mistakes in the sequence. Consider the disease known as Leigh Syndrome French Canadian Variant, a devastating childhood condition that gives rise to multiple and severe physical and mental illnesses before death intervenes at age five or six. It results from a very small set of sequence errors within a single gene located on chromosome 2, and we now know exactly *where* those errors are and *what* they are.[20] We already have the ability to search for some of these kinds of single-gene errors in human embryos, including those that cause cystic fibrosis, Huntington's chorea, and some cancers – the procedure is called preimplantation genetic diagnostics – and parents can choose to discard the embryos that exhibit the defective gene sequences.[21]

But some day we will be able to repair those errors, too. And then it's a short step to gene enhancement – the construction of 'improved' versions of normal, healthy individuals. Many geneticists will tell you that it's 'impossible' or 'very difficult' to do such things and that serious risks are involved. That doesn't stop athletes from trying to get their hands on unproven technologies right now. My advice is, don't bet on the idea that gene enhancement technologies will never be realized. A safer bet would be to start preparing for the time when such technologies are available, and to expect that there will be a strong demand for them.[22] That is the advice given by an American neurologist, Anjan Chatterjee, in 2004. Chatterjee coined the term 'cosmetic neurology' as a deliberate reference to cosmetic surgery; he maintains that scientists and doctors will be unable to resist parents' demands for 'souped-up' brains for their children.[23] Because in the entire range of human technologies, the ability to manipulate the brain will be seen as the greatest prize of all.

Using the working assumption that the brain gives rise to the mind, we are in the process of discovering, through techniques known as neuroimaging, how the mind works – in other words, which brain functions are correlated with which mental outputs: thoughts, images, behaviours, emotions, reasoning, memory, and so forth.[24] All of these outputs are correlated with the 'firing' of specific neurons across synapses, in a process of electrical signalling among various regions of the brain. This neuronal activity is made possible by doses of chemicals known as neurotransmitters (serotonin, dopamine, norepinephrine, and others); and to a great extent, these chemical cascades are controlled by the on/off switching of the genes in our DNA and by levels of various hormones.

Once we know how brains work, we can of course manipulate them. For example, the manipulation of serotonin levels in the brain, designed as a treatment for clinical depression, is achieved by administering a class of drugs known as SSRIs (selective serotonin reuptake inhibitors), the most famous of which is Prozac. But you don't have to wait for a doctor's prescription: university students today, especially around exam time, are taking a wide variety of 'memory booster' drugs that are available over the Internet.[25] And many more such drugs are being developed.

The project of dominating nature can be said to mean the effort to understand how all natural processes function in terms of physical, chemical, and biological interactions, so that we can first replicate those processes and then intervene in them to produce specific outcomes that we desire. This long historical trajectory, which begins with the external world (environment), ends at the neurological tissue inside our heads, where our most intimate thoughts and feelings are generated. Once we have a good handle on all these functions, and how they are ultimately controlled by genes, we will be asked: 'What would you like us to do "in there"? And while we're at it, should we modify your genes as well, so that your children can inherit the nice new features and accessories we'll be adding?'

Critical theory has maintained that along the way to the present, enlightenment destroyed the possibility of 'objective' value frameworks, so what remains today is simply consumer preferences. If your neighbour's children are competing with yours for limited places in the best schools, and the others have been endowed with souped-up brains, how long will you hold out? (Since this is a zero-sum game, it will be necessary for the schools to keep raising the bar, forcing parents to respond by upping the ante when they visit their genetic-engineering counsellors.)

The 'Task' That Is Posited for Historical Actors

In *One-Way Street*, Walter Benjamin remarked that the essential unfulfilled task for modern society is achieving 'mastery over the mastery of nature.' This aphorism – one of Benjamin's finest – remains as true today as when Benjamin penned it in 1928.

The analysis presented here proposes that domination of nature, considered as a key historical feature of the modern period, has a specific meaning – namely, the project of the modern natural sciences to achieve a complete technological mastery over natural processes. That is how this project is usually understood, but it is a radically deficient understanding, because it ignores the original unity of the two opposing but complementary moments within it. By means of a greatly enlarged technological mastery, humans have achieved powers and capacities of staggering proportions – such as the ability to transform the environment at will and to dispose over the future development of all living things. But as originally conceived in Enlightenment thought, this would be matched by another kind of mastery – namely, self-mastery: the capacity to figure out how to control the irrational impulses of human nature by comprehending (through science) the sources of those impulses and by extending the domain of reason into social relations. The most succinct definition for this program was provided by Freud: 'Where id was, there ego shall be.'

To date the program of balanced development has failed. We face a situation is which there is an escalating hyperdevelopment of one side, namely inventive science, matched by a persistent underdevelopment of the other, namely transformative science. The sudden revival of religious militancy, both in the United States and in the Islamic world, is an ominous sign: the ancient dichotomy of good versus evil; the pleas sent to vengeful deities for the unleashing of every kind of horror on the 'other'; the longing for the End Times to commence, during which the entire earth will be bathed in blood and destruction – these deranged visions now swirl around installations where stores of radioactive substances, nerve gases and other chemical weapons, and genetically engineered plague pathogens sit quietly, waiting to be called into active service.[26]

The radical imbalance between inventive and transformative science has placed modern society at increasing risk that its powerful technologies will be thrown into the all-or-nothing 'final battle' named for the northern Israeli town of Armageddon. Ever since the latter half of the nineteenth century, when industrialists learned how to turn the fruits of inventive science into truly revolutionary technologies, the mad pace of endless innovation has afforded no 'breathing space' in which the other side – Condorcet's transformative science – can even begin to flourish. First chemistry, then physics (especially atomic physics), then biology, then genetics and neuroscience: enhanced technologies for controlling natural processes pour from the laboratories and are applied helter-skelter to weaponry and the manipulation of life processes, with the devotees of innovation reassuring us that we can clean up any unfortunate errors after the fact. The overwhelming pressure from the scope and pace of invention defeats any attempts to stop and discuss the desirability of steering a different course. This great wave, it appears, must be ridden until it breaks upon the shore.

Postscript: Philosophy of History and the Need for Utopia

According to Hegel, human history is the development through discrete stages of the idea of freedom. Historical development is driven, within discrete epochs, by a process of internal tension within a system of ideas that becomes dominant over time.

Progress – conceived of as the progressive deepening of the idea of freedom – is a circle: when an epoch of historical development starts nearing 'fulfilment,' the human actors arrive back where they started – though not at the same place, to be sure. Rather, this 'back to the beginning' means that we are forced to confront, squarely and explicitly, tensions or contradictions that have been present in the entire period of development, and to resolve them. Until this is done we cannot move further forward, and unless it is done, we face regressive forces that threaten to undermine the positive achievements of the entire epoch.

Hegel used a famous metaphor – 'the Owl of Minerva takes flight at dusk' – to convey the idea that our insight into the essence of any historical epoch only develops when that epoch is drawing to a close, when the internal tensions at its core present themselves to historical actors clearly and unequivocally as inescapable tasks to be addressed. I believe we have arrived at this point in the epoch called modernity.

It is the responsibility of critique to name correctly the nature of the stage of historical development that must be confronted and transcended (*aufhebt*). It is the calling of the imaginative faculty to suggest how the work of transcendence might actually be carried out. In its classical period, especially in the writings of Horkheimer and Marcuse, critical theory was suffused with the idea of utopia, the imagining of a better place.[27]

Works of utopian fiction try (among other things) to identify some possible agents for the process of historical transformation that, according to the dialectical analysis, must be carried out.[28] *Hera, or Empathy: A Work of Utopian Fiction*, and its sequel, *The Priesthood of Science*, are the first two volumes of a projected trilogy in which I have made my own attempt to go down this road. The presupposition for these works is the Hegelian philosophy of history just mentioned: modern science in its essential duality (inventive and transformative) is the historical development that defines most concretely the epoch in which we live. The internal tension in that duality is reaching a critical point in the contemporary period. While inventive science turns out ever more powerful and dangerous technologies – for example, nuclear weapons and genetic engineering – the transformative moment appears to be stalled: Condorcet's vision has been replaced by apocalyptic fantasies of total destruction and the End Times for humanity. It follows that confronting and overcoming that tension is a task that present and future generations cannot escape.

In earlier centuries during the modern period, especially the nineteenth, critiques of existing society were usually accompanied by some form of utopian vision, indicating in outline what path history might take after the deficiencies in social organization, identified by the critique, had been overcome. That way of thinking had atrophied by the end of the nineteenth century. I believe it must be revived.

Appendix: Further Remarks on Inventive and Transformative Science

Hegel's dialectic cannot be represented by the mere opposition of two terms that are juxtaposed to each other in some form of 'tension' or perhaps 'contradiction.' Rather, each 'side' in this dynamic relationship is itself a unity of oppositional elements. Instead of two terms, there are actually four, which must be specified. This level of complexity is necessary if the full richness of the different possibilities is to emerge during historical development.

The fourfold nature of dialectical opposition can be illustrated with an example from Marx, who was a very good Hegelian. From the familiar starting point,

$$\text{Proletariat (A)} \leftrightarrow \text{Capitalism (B)},$$

which are the primary terms of opposition, the expansion becomes

$$\text{Proletariat (A1} \leftrightarrow \text{A2)} \leftrightarrow \text{Capitalism (B1} \leftrightarrow \text{B2)}$$

A1: the proletariat (working class) as one social class among others;
A2: the proletariat as a unique social class in all of history, the 'class that will end all classes';[29]
B1: capitalism as an arena in which the private appropriation of social wealth occurs, as it does in all forms of exploitative society;
B2: capitalism as a unique form of exploitative economy, one in which there is a massive expansion of productive resources, leading to qualitatively enhanced opportunities for human progress.

As is well known, Marx assigned to the proletariat the decisive role of agent of change. To the extent to which the proletariat was unable to resolve its own set of inner contradictions (due to the weight of reification, or whatever), it would not be able to overcome the inner contradictions besetting the system of capital. The dialectical tension portrayed in this conception did indeed collapse, and in my view it cannot be revived (the moment has passed); thus it can no longer be considered to represent the driving force of historical change in the modern era.

By analogy, to represent the underlying dynamic of the project for the domination of nature in the terms suggested above – that is, as embracing both inventive and transformative science – we must portray its structure in a similar fashion:

Inventive Science (A1 ↔ A2) ↔ Transformative Science (B1 ↔ B2)

A1: the pure understanding (discovery) of matter – energy transformation and the 'laws of nature,' which have a universal character: knowledge for its own sake;
A2: the secular power and immense wealth that ownership and control of the technologies derived from modern science bestow on certain social classes, individuals, nations, and imperial powers;
B1: the diffusion of an enlightened, 'evidence-based' model of analysis into institutions, welfare policies, laws, universal education, moral theory, somatic and psychiatric medical therapies, penal systems, and behavioural control strategies;[30]
B2: the new potentialities for the control of human behaviour, through the scientific description of the brain and, ultimately, an arbitrary disposition over genomes and genetic inheritances.

At least some of the consequences that flow from the development, over time, of these four dimensions are obvious. The project as a whole raises the stakes enormously in the game that humans are now playing, both with external nature (the environment and other living species) and with their own nature. Put in the language of risk, both the 'upside' and the 'downside' prospects have been magnified enormously, compared to all earlier epochs.

NOTES

1 Max Horkheimer, *Eclipse of Reason* (New York: Columbia University Press, 1947), 176.
2 Max Horkheimer and Theodor W. Adorno, *Dialectic of Enlightenment* (1947,

1969), ed. Gunzelin Schmid Noerr, trans. Edmund Jephcott (Stanford: Stanford University Press, 2002), 20.

3 Horkheimer, *Eclipse of Reason*, 5. 'Subjective reason' is also called 'instrumental' and 'formalized' reason. See also his later work, *Critique of Instrumental Reason* (1967). So far as I know, Horkheimer never acknowledged or discussed the apparent similarity between his two forms of reason and Max Weber's earlier distinction between instrumental rationality and value rationality, developed in his *Economy and Society* (1914) – though he cites Weber on many other points.

4 Horkheimer and Adorno, *Dialectic of Enlightenment*, 30–1.

5 Steven Vogel suggests that 'the project of enlightenment aims above all at the *domination of nature*.' See Vogel, *Against Nature: The Concept of Nature in Critical Theory* (Albany: SUNY Press, 1996), 52 (author's italics). Based on the quotations cited in the text, one could just as well reverse this proposition. In my view, one is not the product of the other, but rather another name for the same phenomenon.

6 Max Horkheimer, *Dawn and Decline: Notes 1926–1931 and 1950–1969*, trans. Michael Shaw (New York: Seabury, 1978), 237; the passage dates from the period 1966–9.

7 The argument that Horkheimer and Adorno's project terminates in a cul-de-sac was made some time ago by Vogel, and I think he is right; see Vogel, *Against Nature*, 67–8. The entire discussion in his chapter 3 is a model of clarity and incisiveness.

8 To be sure, the plausibility of this statement depends upon how one defines 'control.' By somewhere between 10,000 and 5,000 BCE, settled communities were becoming common. 'Ötzi the Iceman,' discovered in a melting glacier in southern Austria in 1991, and thought to be 5,300 years old, may be regarded as a typical human of his time. He was found with a beautiful copper axe, a longbow and bone-tipped arrows, leather clothing, a cloak of woven grass, finely crafted footwear of complex design, a knife, pouch, and flint, and a few other items; he was also carrying medicinal herbs, and his stomach contents included *einkorn*, an early species of cultivated wheat. We can assume he had a thatched hut back home. A few thousand years later, there would be technologies involving massed labour, such as shipbuilding, irrigation works, animal domestication, arts and crafts (metalworking, pottery, fine cloth, etc.), and buildings constructed of massive stones. But in my view, right down to the beginnings of the modern era, none of this constituted 'control over nature' in any meaningful sense.

9 This is the element of 'cunning' featured in the famous discussion of Odysseus in *Dialectic of Enlightenment* (see Vogel, *Against Nature*, 54–5). But

Horkheimer and Adorno can link *The Odyssey* with Francis Bacon's *The New Organon* only on the basis of their own purely formalistic conception of instrumental reason – an ironic situation, to be sure, for those theorists who criticize the Enlightenment as an expression of formalized reason. For actually, *nothing at all* links the story of Odysseus and the Sirens with what Bacon and his followers were attempting to do –indeed, with what they actually achieved. Guided and inspired by Bacon, later generations would develop a historical novelty of immense and fateful significance: a methodical investigation of natural processes, an investigation conceived of as the product of an open-ended *social* and *institutional* agenda, spanning entire generations over what is now a period of nearly 400 years. And it is simply absurd to write off what they created thereby – the now immense structure of the modern sciences of nature, a structure that is surely, among other things, an extraordinary product of the creative human imagination – as nothing more than the most recent expression of a radically deficient instrumentalist approach to life (there is further commentary on this point later in the text).

10 The 'reconciliation' of modern science with ancient religion remains an active project to this day, and theologians and many working scientists are engaged in a dialogue about it.

11 See my own *The Domination of Nature* (Montreal and Kingston: McGill-Queen's University Press, 1994,) ch. 3.

12 See the appendix for a formal analysis of the opposition between transformative and inventive science, represented in terms of the Hegelian dialectic.

13 Thus the claim here is that Horkheimer and Adorno's conception of enlightenment is undialectical, whereas Condorcet's is a proper dialectical formulation (as presented more fully later in the Appendix). Horkheimer and Adorno hypostasize enlightenment as an eternal condition of 'rational' (anti-mythical) thought in which 'thought subjugates existence.' But surely this is just a careless metaphor, because enlightened thought, in the form of modern science, also penetrates the surface layer of existence to reveal the *truth* of matter–energy transformations that lie hidden within. To consider one famous example: In what meaningful sense could it be said that Einstein's equations of special and general relativity are an instance of a process wherein 'thought subjugates existence'? I contend that the word 'subjugates' here has no rational meaning (and merely illustrates the problem created by the paucity of actual examples in *Dialectic of Enlightenment*).

14 Condorcet, a member of the aristocracy, supported the French Revolution, but he was arrested during the Terror and committed suicide while awaiting execution. See my own *The Domination of Nature*, 77–9.

15 Marquis de Condorcet, *Sketch for a Historical Picture of the Progress of the Human Mind*, trans. J. Barraclough (New York: Noonday, 1955), 127ff.

16 Ibid., 163–4, 192. It is a fair generalization to say that all major forms of oppressive social relations were underpinned and rationalized by pseudo-scientific reasoning (i.e., scientific errors) – for example, racism, slavery, eugenics, economic privilege, and female oppression.

17 Ibid., 196.

18 Cited in Noerr's afterword to Horkheimer and Adorno, *Dialectic of Enlightenment*, 241.

19 Derek Wildman et al., 'Implications of Natural Selection in Shaping 99.4% Non-Synonymous DNA Identity between Humans and Chimpanzees: Enlarging Genus *Homo*,' *Proceedings of the National Academy of Sciences* 100 (2003): 7181–8.

20 V.K. Mootha et al., 'Identification of a Gene Causing Human Cytochrome *c* Oxidase Deficiency by Integrative Genomics,' *Proceedings of the National Academy of Sciences* 100 (2003): 605–10. The disease affects 1 out of every 2,000 live births in the Sangueney–Lac-St-Jean region of Quebec.

21 See Amy Harmon, 'Couples Cull Embryos to Halt Heritage of Cancer,' *New York Times*, 3 September 2006.

22 My personal view is that using genetic screening (and eventually gene repair) to eliminate the most serious inherited diseases raises no ethical problems, though careful reasoning will be needed to determine where to draw the line in terms of which sorts of conditions are debilitating enough to justify these procedures. I would proscribe gene enhancement completely. Such matters demand consideration at much greater length.

23 A. Chatterjee, 'Cosmetic Neurology: The Controversy over Enhancing Movement, Mentation, and Mood,' *Neurology* 63 (2004): 968–74.

24 Researchers in Montreal are using a group of elderly Carmelite nuns as research subjects in an attempt to pin down the locus of the 'God spot' in the brain – that is, the site where the *unio mystica*, the mystical union of the person with God, is experienced. See M. Beauregard and V. Paquette, 'Neural Correlates of a Mystical Experience in Carmelite Nuns,' *Neuroscience Letters* 405 (2006): 186–90. For a good general discussion, see July Illes and Eric Racine, 'Imaging or Imagined? A Neuroethics Challenge Informed by Genetics,' *American Journal of Bioethics* 5 (2005): 5–18.

25 If you key 'memory enhancing drugs' into your Google search engine, Google will provide you, on the sidebar, with a nice selection of websites offering products to choose from, which can be ordered conveniently with a click of your mouse.

26 D. Rising, 'Terrorist Exhorts Nuclear Experts to Join Jihad,' *Globe and Mail*, 29 September 2006, A9.
27 This theme is emphasized in the Introduction by Feenberg and Leiss to *The Essential Marcuse* (Boston: Beacon, 2007). To be sure, this was, as Russell Jacoby reminds us in *Future Imperfect* (New York: Columbia University Press, 2005), 'negative utopia' – that is, only the abstract idea of a future, better world.
28 An important theme that cannot be developed here is this: What is presupposed is that the *content* of the knowledge bestowed by the modern sciences – in particular, the biological sciences – must be engaged by social theorists. For example, the following propositions – that the species *Homo sapiens*, including its marvellous brain, is entirely a random result of natural evolution; that this species shares much of its genome with other mammals; and that the human mind is entirely the 'product' of highly-evolved neurological structures – these three truly revolutionary, evidence-based propositions must be considered important factors in the range of possibilities for social development that lie in the future.
29 For nostalgic reasons I must mention an article I published on this remarkable concept almost four decades ago: 'Critical Theory and Its Future,' *Political Theory* 2 (1974): 330–49.
30 Blakeslee offers just one example of how the scientific understanding of the brain and mind provides an alternative explanation to what would otherwise be represented as a 'mystical' phenomenon. See S. Blakeslee, 'Out-of-Body Experience? Your Brain Is to Blame,' *New York Times*, 3 October 2006.

BIBLIOGRAPHY

Beauregard, M., and V. Paquette. 'Neural Correlates of a Mystical Experience in Carmelite Nuns.' *Neuroscience Letters* 405 (2006): 186–90.
Chatterjee, A. 'Cosmetic Neurology: The Controversy over Enhancing Movement, Mentation, and Mood.' *Neurology* 63 (2004): 968–74.
Condorcet, Marquis de. *Sketch for a Historical Picture of the Progress of the Human Mind* [1795]. Translated by J. Barraclough. New York: Noonday, 1955.
Horkheimer, Max. *Critique of Instrumental Reason*. New York: Seabury, 1974.
– *Dawn and Decline: Notes 1926–1931 and 1950–1969*. Translated by Michael Shaw. New York: Seabury, 1978.
– *Eclipse of Reason*. New York: Columbia University Press, 1947.
Horkheimer, Max, and Theodor W. Adorno. *Dialectic of Enlightenment* (1947,

1969). Edited by Gunzelin Schmid Noerr, translated by Edmund Jephcott. Stanford: Stanford University Press, 2002.

Illes, July, and Eric Racine. 'Imaging or Imagined? A Neuroethics Challenge Informed by Genetics.' *American Journal of Bioethics* 5 (2005): 5–18.

Jacoby, Russell. *Picture Imperfect.* New York: Columbia University Press, 2005.

Leiss, William. 'Critical Theory and Its Future.' *Political Theory* 2 (1974): 330–49.

– *The Domination of Nature* (1972). Republished with new Preface. Montreal and Kingston: McGill-Queen's University Press, 1994.

– *Hera, or Empathy: A Work of Utopian Fiction.* Ottawa: University of Ottawa Press, 2006.

– *The Priesthood of Science.* Ottawa: University of Ottawa Press, 2008.

Marcuse, Herbert. *The Essential Marcuse.* Edited by Andrew Feenberg and William Leiss. Boston: Beacon, 2007.

Mootha, V.K., et al. 'Identification of a Gene Causing Human Cytochrome *c* Oxidase Deficiency by Integrative Genomics.' *Proceedings of the National Academy of Sciences* 100 (2003): 605–10.

Vogel, Steven. *Against Nature: The Concept of Nature in Critical Theory.* Albany: SUNY Press, 1996.

Weber, Max. *Economy and Society.* Edited by G. Roth and C. Wittich. 2 vols. Berkeley: University of California Press, 1978.

Wildman, Derek, et al. 'Implications of Natural Selection in Shaping 99.4% Non-Synonymous DNA Identity between Humans and Chimpanzees: Enlarging Genus *Homo*.' *Proceedings of the National Academy of Sciences* 100 (2003): 7181–8.

2 Societal Relationships with Nature: A Dialectical Approach to Environmental Politics

CHRISTOPH GÖRG

Introduction

At the beginning of the twenty-first century, nature is perhaps more contested then ever before in human history. And this is far from being trivial. Whereas some observers at the end of the last century proclaimed the end of history, others announced the end of nature.[1] The idea that nature is something different from societal relationships and thus from human history seemed to be outdated; the same with the idea that nature is a force beyond the control of human beings. Yet only a few years later, nature is back again – as history is. The uncontrollable risk of climate change,[2] the incalculable costs of environmental degradation,[3] and also new capitalist markets for natural resources like water[4] and genetic resources,[5] have raised the matter of 'coming to terms with nature.'[6] The more nature is seen as something influenced and produced by human action, the more our experience is that we are far from having real control over nature. Moreover, the gap between the societal capacity to transform the natural environment and the lack of capacity to control our impact on that environment – and the repercussions of that lack for societies – is one of the major contradictions of contemporary societies. Prevailing attempts to resolve this contradiction by addressing environmental concerns through a narrow managerialism have only widened the gap.[7] This kind of technocratic optimism, expressed in most ecological modernization approaches,[8] contends that the ecological crisis can be resolved by existing institutions. Thus it tends to delegitimize all endeavours that seek to address the real challenge induced by the global ecological crisis: the widening contradiction between our capacity to master nature and our inability to control our relationships with nature. In this way, environmental managerialism and ecological modernization, far from solving the arisen problems, have helped deepen the crisis.

What is needed is a critical theory of society that can explain the relationships between societies and nature, but in ways that do not ignore the huge transformations that human beings have made to nature. This project includes asking whether we should even speak about nature anymore (see Vogel in this volume). What is needed, then, is a theory of society which is capable of analysing how societies are constitutively related to nature and which takes into account, simultaneously, that the term 'nature' should not be restricted to something untouched by or independent of human action. Also needed is a critical account of the vigour with which human societies transform the biophysical conditions of their existence – an account that acknowledges that neither these conditions nor the forces driving global environmental change are really under control. The following chapter assumes, basically, that such a task could be carried out by building on the theoretical approaches that were taken by the critical theorists of the Frankfurt School. In its 'older' version, which we link with Max Horkheimer, Walter Benjamin, Theodor W. Adorno, and Herbert Marcuse, the Frankfurt School developed a dialectical approach to the relations between society and nature, one that in our day is capable of informing recent discussions of environmental politics. But because this approach was not designed to address environmental politics in a narrow sense, we must rework it.

I begin this chapter's argument by reflecting on the historic differences that separate us from the work of these scholars. With these differences in mind, it is still possible to build on their writings. To demonstrate this, I will be referring to theoretical and conceptual discussions that have been ongoing in Germany over the past twenty years – discussions whose goal has been to rework the critical theoretical tradition in order to apply it to environmental concerns. These discussions have focused on the term *societal relationships with nature*, in the theoretical tradition of Hegel and Marx as reinterpreted by the Frankfurt School in light of the experiences of the twentieth century. The focus, then, is on how society, even while *producing* nature, is materially *mediated* through its biophysical conditions. Furthermore, this chapter addresses how nature has been symbolically/discursively constructed in culture and science, as well as the links between the material and the symbolic in nature and society. Having built on this complex dialectical approach, we will be able to examine the *limits* to the production of nature as articulated in environmental concerns, and do so without reverting to naive or naturalistic approaches to nature. Dealing with nature in a dialectical way will let us focus on the societal construction of nature without ignoring our lack of 'real control' over nature. I will be introducing Adorno's terms 'second reflection' (*zweite Reflexion*) and 'priority of the object' (*Vorrang des Objekts*) to deal with this issue and to confront some of the challenges that have emerged from current debates over how to reconcile environmentalism with constructivism. At the conclusion of this theoretical reconstruction, I will elaborate a specific understanding of the mastery of nature (*Naturbeherrschung*). Regarding contemporary capitalism, I will show how recent forms of capitalism – what is called 'post-Fordism' – are characterized by a 'reflexive mastery of nature.'

Core Meanings and Lines of Interpretation

Critical theorists[9] in the tradition of the Frankfurt School always placed a strong emphasis on their work's historical 'index' (*Zeitkern der Wahrheit*).[10] So, when trying to learn from their writings, we must pay heed to the history that separates us from their original work. They developed their theory during an era whose central crisis was not an ecological one, but rather the attempted extermination of Europe's Jews – that is, the rupture in history (*Zivilisationsbruch*) denoted by the name 'Auschwitz.' Of all the critical theorists of that time, only Marcuse ever referred directly to ecology or the environment, and only during the protest movements of the 1970s.[11] Direct analogies – for example, an 'ecological holocaust,' or a 'human genetic dialectic of enlightenment'[12] – contradict the methodology of critical thinking, which calls for us to reflect on our place in history and, in particular, to pay careful heed to ruptures in the civilization project. Which is not to say that we live under totally different (democratic) societal conditions that call for a paradigmatic break in theory.[13] The point here is that when referring to critical theory's basic ideas, we have to reconstruct its concepts in light of historical developments and recent theoretical discussions. To recast this as a paradox: to apply critical theory properly in our present day, we must rework its concepts even while using them.

So we must, in other words, historicize critical theory; but that historicization then reveals how important critical theory's approach is, especially in terms of the relations among society, history, and nature. It was Walter Benjamin[14] who first questioned the general understanding of history and society with reference to the role their relations played in societal development. Against a naive belief in historical progress, deeply rooted in the Social Democratic Party in Germany before the Second World War (as well as in most leftist parties all over the world, sometimes even to this day), he contended in 'On the Concept of History' (Über den Begriff der Geschichte) that this belief refers only to progress in mastering nature.[15] What is needed, however, is a new concept of social emancipation, one that addresses the emancipation of human beings but *not* at the cost of nature. In other words, it is not nature we need to master, but rather our societal relationships with nature – that is, we need to control the impact those relationships have on nature, with all the societal repercussions they entail.[16]

This idea became paradigmatic for Horkheimer and Adorno in their *Dialectic of Enlightenment*.[17] In their view, human history was 'enlightenment' that ended in the reversal of enlightenment, symbolized by Auschwitz. Enlightenment in *Dialectic of Enlightenment* is a broad concept that encompasses mythological and philosophical thinking as much as science and technology. The common feature here is that enlightenment's purpose is to remove the fear of nature that humans experience. But this is precisely what leads to a return of mythical fears and real threats. The reason for this involves is a *false alternative* in the concept of enlightenment: 'For the "enlightenment," the choice is always between controlling nature and being controlled by it.'[18] Thus, according to Horkheimer and Adorno, social progress is based on the mastery of nature; but that mastery cannot achieve its aim – real control over nature – and instead remains tied to 'compulsion of nature' (*Naturzwang*).[19] In other words, with enlightenment, in philosophy, science, and technology, humans perpetuate this law of nature (or what they believe the laws of nature are; see below): eat or be eaten.

Note well, however, that the real meaning of *Dialectic of Enlightenment* is contested.[20] The book is neither easy to read nor comprehensively argued. Referred to as 'philosophical fragments' in its subtitle, it requires interpretation. Two controversies are particularly important to this chapter's purpose. First, it has been contested whether *Dialectic of Enlightenment* represents a (negative) philosophy of history or a critique of the very possibility of a philosophy of history. Two opposing arguments can be found in *Dialectic of Enlightenment*. In a chapter from the appendix, 'On the Critique of a Philosophy of History,'[21] the authors declare that a philosophical interpretation of world history must explain an ever more complete mastery of nature. But what is meant by a *critique* or a *negative philosophy* of history?[22] Most readers interpret *Dia-*

lectic of Enlightenment as a negative, pessimistic philosophy of history, one in which progress in history leads not to a positive future but rather to the catastrophes of the twentieth century. The problem with this interpretation, though, is that Adorno and Horkheimer do not want to abandon emancipation, critique, and enlightenment. On the contrary, they want to provide a 'positive concept of enlightenment'[23] that might guide us to another future. In this regard, the authors often maintain that the alternative between controlling nature or being controlled[24] amounts to a metahistoric law that has guided human history from the beginning.[25] But that law is also the object of Horkheimer and Adorno's critique; and in that sense, they deconstruct it as a metahistoric law.[26]

So it seems more appropriate to focus on the second alternative and to take seriously the argument that there is no universal logic of history. Accordingly, no possibility exists to create a philosophy of history as a unique entity or a single law of human activity. Following this argument, we have to deal with social reflexivity, which always changes the way of history and thereby generates historical differences. This reflexivity – that 'men make their own history,' as Marx puts it – is the reason why a critical approach to history is necessary: our interpretation of history is part of history, and 'we' produce as a performative act what we call the laws of history. Historical differences, then, are the reasons for what the authors call the 'historical index of theory': we inevitably reflect the specific historical conditions in which we produce interpretations, and in that way we are involved in making history. So we need no universal, ahistorical interpretation of what society, humans, or nature might be; rather, we need to analyse the specific societal conditions in which the ecological crisis is developing – and currently those conditions express the crisis of Fordism and the transition to post-Fordism (see below).

The second contested topic in interpretations of *Dialectic of Enlightenment* focuses on the disputed relationship between the mastery of nature and societal forms of domination, in particular class rule. What is the precise meaning of 'mastery of nature'? This question is closely related to a second one: In a theory of society, what is the place of societal relationships with nature? Earlier interpretations assumed that in *Dialectic of Enlightenment*, critical theory had replaced the Marxist emphasis on class struggle with the larger conflict between man and nature.[27] More accurately, though, in the first published edition of *Dialectic of Enlightenment* (1947; some copies had been distributed privately in 1944), Horkheimer and Adorno weakened their references to Marx and deleted some references to class struggle.[28] In its overall logic, however, *Dialectic of Enlightenment* gives a prominent place to social domination (especially in its references to the dialectic of master and slave as a metaphor for class domination). So it seems more appropriate to clarify the meaning of the critique of the mastery of nature in relation to other kinds of domination. In this vein, *Dialectic of Enlightenment* deals with three kinds of domination: the *mastery of nature; societal domination* (e.g., class and gender relations, but also racist and anti-Semitic oppression); and *domination within the subject* (which includes the 'identical male concept of self,' which implies mastery over 'natural' desires). Following these lines of interpretation, this question arises: Is the mastery of nature the 'original' mastery, from which other forms of domination are derived? 'Yes' to this question is a basic assumption of the critiques by Jürgen Habermas[29] and Axel Honneth;[30] indeed, that 'yes' is the point of departure for both. But at the same time, it could be argued that no form of domination is independent of the other two; and furthermore, that social domination, in particular, is not simply derived from the mastery of nature. Horkheimer and Adorno argue that abstraction and domination in the sphere of logic – which is the foundation of the mastery of nature – is based on domination in social reality and in the relations between master and slave,[31] whereas social domination and the self-identical male subject are rooted in relations with nature.[32] By this interpretation, *Dialectic of Enlightenment* deals with *changing constellations* among these three kinds of domination – or, as Adorno[33] puts it later, with changing constellations in the relations among *society, nature, and the individual*.

This interpretation leads to some conclusions that are central to our purpose. First of all, the mastery of nature is always mediated through different forms of societal domination, including specific forms of subjectivity. Therefore we cannot talk of replacing class rule with struggles between man and nature. Instead, societal relationships with nature[34] are closely linked to social relationships and the power relations involved in these, including class relations; but also to gender relations and ethnic supremacy. This, indeed, is the basic idea underlying the concept *societal relationships with nature:* the ways in which societies appropriate nature are deeply affected by these kinds of social domination; thus there exist no universal or anthropologically rooted laws such as the struggle between man and nature.

Moreover, mastery of nature does not mean 'to establish true control over nature.' As in social domination – Horkheimer and Adorno refer to Hegel's dialectic between master and slave[35] – the master cannot really achieve control over the mastered. The master is dependent on the slave's work, and a society is similarly always dependent on its material conditions of existence, which are anchored in nature (in the sense of biophysical conditions, not necessarily something untouched by society). Thus the more society ignores that such dependencies exist, the more often it will be reminded of these dependencies through 'natural' disasters and catastrophes.

This brings forth a very specific meaning of the mastery of nature – one that does not focus on the fact of control over nature in a broad sense.[36] Instead, we must distinguish among the *appropriation* of nature for human needs (which is in itself a condition of human existence); the *destruction* of nature (which is basically a transformation of one certain status to another one, from a more favourable kind of nature to a more unfavourable one, more unfavourable mostly for human beings but sometimes also for other species); and the *mastery* of nature. The former two are to some degree 'necessary';[37] whereas the mastery of nature refers to a neglect of the *non-identity of nature*, which means a *total subsumption* of nature under societal aims (i.e., under capitalist forms of appropriation), without respecting that nature has its own meaning. This concept of the non-identity of nature is at the core of what will be developed below as a *critique* of the mastery of nature – and it is one of the basic assumptions of the following arguments that this concept can only be grasped *negatively* in the way of a critique.

Societal Relationships with Nature in Current Debates

The concept of societal relationships with nature emphasizes that society and nature are constitutively interconnected. Put another way, both parts are what they are only through their relationships to each other. Thus, societal development is deeply engraved by the way in which nature is appropriated; human history is nothing independent, following social laws of its own – as other theorists of society such as, in particular, Niklas Luhmann[38] would put it; rather, human history is always *mediated by* or *interconnected with* nature (the German *Vermittlung* as it is used in Hegelian philosophy means constitutive interconnectedness). At the same time, nature is always socially constructed, in two senses: it is *materially produced* by economic and technical practices; and it is *symbolically constructed* through cultural interpretations, including those of science.

But even if society and nature are constitutively interconnected, we must still *distinguish* the two from each other. And it is important to distinguish between this distinction and something like a dualism or a dichotomy of nature and society. To distinguish between nature and society by no means implies that both are entities following logic of their own, as the dualism of nature and societies suggests, where causality in nature and morality in society are seen as governing completely separate realms.[39] In this regard, a dualism tends to justify a mastery of society over nature, whereas a dichotomy deals with the two as entirely separate entities. Instead, we can see society and nature as related to each other in a *dialectical* relationship.[40] This implies that they to some degree are coupled with each other, as current approaches in environmental research assume: societal development is in many regards strongly linked to the state of the natural environment.[41] But at the same time, we cannot describe natural and social processes with exactly the same terms; so we must distinguish between them. Moreover, when we look at the ecological crisis, we see that societal and natural processes are not only in opposition to each other but also in a real *contradiction*: socioeconomic appropriation of nature contradicts the ways in which biophysical processes function – indeed, it *undermines* their ability to function. This does not mean that societies simply transform untouched nature or wilderness: in this era of global environmental change, societies are actually *undermining* the benefits they can derive from nature, by using nature in an unsustainable way. In distinguishing between society and nature, then, it is important to analyse these contradictions so as to contribute to a shaping of this relationship – and even to formulate a utopian reconciliation between society and nature, as we will see later.

The concept of societal relationships with nature – of seeing society and nature as both separable *and* constitutively interconnected – provides a starting point for environmental investigations. To demonstrate this, some brief remarks concerning the application of this concept might be helpful. In Germany the concept of societal relationships with nature was introduced in the mid-1980s to highlight that what we are facing is not just a series of discrete environmental problems, but an overarching crisis of sciences and societies.[42] The introduction of this concept was stimulated by the struggles of new social movements and by the social transformations that brought this crisis to the fore. The crisis, however, is ambiguous in that it includes both material aspects and scientific and cultural representations. It encompasses not only environmental aspects such as polluted water and air – that is, the material dimensions of the metabolism between society and nature – but also the ways in which nature and environmental problems are addressed by scientists, in public discussions, and in cultural representations. Huge expectations relating to the ability of specific natural science concepts such as ecosystems to reorient our behaviour have been accompanied by deepening scepticism regarding the natural sciences in general. Technical risks (e.g., nuclear power) and the role of technical and scientific experts have also been challenged, so as to undercut the credibility of scientific and technical rationality. Here, the concept provides an alternative between both extremes while balancing a critique of science with an alternative approach to science.

Another advantage to this concept is that it provides the starting point for a critical analysis. The starting point is not an unchangeable (ecological or societal) law, but a critique of *how* nature is constructed, as mentioned above: practically (through economic or technical measures) and/or symbolically (in cultural or scientific terms). To deal with the relationships between nature and society in a dialectical way is to imply that there is no return to a precritical approach to nature. Nature is not something given, and there is no privileged way to perceive nature. Furthermore, it is not necessary to say what nature 'is.' If nature is always constructed – as a term and as a real world, that is, as a landscape[43] – critical theory can start with a critical analysis of this process of construction. Therefore, its 'radical' constructivism amounts to a clear advantage and could guide a critique of naturalism in environmental politics.[44] At the same time, however, critical theory inherits from realism the assumption that 'something' outside exists. But that 'something' is not given, nor is it a remainder to be found once all construction has been subtracted. Rather, we can build on Adorno's notion in *Negative Dialectics* that every construction is a construction of 'something' (*etwas*).[45] It is precisely here that we can demonstrate the ways in which critique refers to the non-identity of nature – not as something unchangeable that pre-exists social constructions, but rather as something that *appears within human experience only through a critique of social construction processes*, or through a critique of the various cultural, scientific, economic, and political processes by which nature is constructed. For this purpose Adorno developed the concepts of 'second reflection' and 'priority of the object.'[46]

Second reflection refers to the reflection on the subjective construction of nature (e.g., in philosophy, culture, science, technology, or economy).

Following the theory of cognition of Immanuel Kant,[47] every truth re-flects back to the subject of knowledge – the transcendental subject, behind which we can recognize the society as 'the real subject of cogni-tion.'[48] A second reflection reflects back on this subject of cognition and analyses how this subject is constituted in relationship to its objects. Or as Adorno puts it: 'Thinking breaks in a second reflection the superior-ity [*Suprematie*] of thought over something different, because thought actually represents something different within itself.'[49] Because society is always not only society, but also connected with its natural or mate-rial environment, its supremacy over nature – supremacy in our think-ing, but also in practical terms, in our behaviour – could be overcome in a second reflection. In a similar way, Adorno writes that 'every intel-lectual [impulse] is always a modified somatic impulse.'[50] Thus we can-not simply state that nature is our product and that the mind prescribes natural law;[51] we also have to reflect on these dialectical relationships between subject and object. Neither subject (society, the individual) nor object (nature) is something given; it is always connected with its op-posite. If the concept of second reflection deals with the way nature is constructed in society in general, then this refers to various societal construction processes. In practice, a critical reflection has to deal not only with philosophical or pure scientific issues but also with cultural and socioeconomic processes and the economic interests and power re-lations involved in them (see below).

The second concept, *priority of the object*, refers to two very different aspects of Adorno's theory: to *societal objectivity*, and to the *non-identity of nature*. Societal objectivity is an expression of the priority of the object because society – at least under capitalist conditions – has a priority over the actors and individuals that create society. In capitalist societ-ies, all actors find themselves situated in a society governed by 'laws' or processes not really under their control. Society as a whole is not governed by the actors who in general are supposed to make history, but rather by the law of value (*Wertgesetz*), which works behind the backs of the actors.[52] Somewhat similarly, the non-identity of nature is a version of the priority of the object because society – including all individual actors – finds itself situated in relationships to nature; and these relationships are not really under the control of societal actors, even if these actors produce and construct nature. This non-identity of nature is not something given and is never purely available. It can only be reached by way of *critique*, or by a *self-reflection* of societal construc-tion processes. Only in this way can natural properties neglected in, or not yet represented by, scientific and other cultural representations be experienced, albeit indirectly.[53]

For example, ongoing global climate change suggests that human societies, while transforming nature and causing such global change, lack real control over nature and are thus facing uncontrollable risk. Until now we have had only limited knowledge of how the global climate system actually functions (i.e., what nature really 'is'), and we are learning about that system by transforming it: its 'identity' independent of human action is never fully available. But we have learned in recent years in a highly contested process that we must respect the functioning of this global climate system – that it is shaped by factors that we neglected before.[54] Thus, these factors appear as something non-identical with former scientific and cultural construction processes (e.g., that climate is something unchangeable that evolves over a very long time outside of human influence), through a self-reflection of scientific representations. Moreover, nature in the form of the global climate system is marked through a priority of the object, because global societies find themselves dependent on its functioning, even when this functioning is itself modified by humans.

The concept of the non-identity of nature avoids referring to an unchangeable, untouched nature; it also focuses attention as much on the discursive (scientific, cultural) construction of nature as on the practical appropriation of natural resources. With this specific approach to materialism, Adorno does not refer to an ontological materialism as a specific *Weltanschauung* (which was overcome by Marx),[55] but rather to a kind of materialism constructed as a critique of idealism. This dialectical approach is what makes Adorno's theory so important for ongoing discussions of postconstructivism and of how a constructivist approach can be reconciled with environmentalist concerns. Moreover, it is precisely the tensions and possible contradictions among various scientific and practical construction processes that allow for the experience of some dimensions of nature, which could be labelled an appearance (*Vorschein*) of non-identity.

To give an example: In the mid-twentieth century, traditional crops as much as the knowledge related to them were perceived as something old-fashioned that should be replaced by science and technology, by modern hybrid seeds and industrialized agriculture. By the mid-1960s, costly epidemics in American agriculture and experiences with the 'Green Revolution' in developing countries – which tried to replace traditional varieties with hybrid seeds – revealed that genetic erosion amounted to a dramatic threat.[56] Since then, after a long global struggle, it has been acknowledged that genetic diversity has value, and that so do traditional varieties of crops created by human action over thousands of years, and that so do the traditional knowledges that developed those crops. Clearly, genetic diversity is strongly related to societal relations, both in terms of economic and technical production (i.e., in specific forms of agriculture) and in terms of cultural and symbolic representation (including the values associated to them). But that diversity also presents something that we can call an appearance of the non-identity of nature: we are dependent on something that appears through our experience of transforming nature, which we now call genetic diversity. Adorno's theory opens up the space to acknowledge these properties as something real without mystifying them as something representing a pristine unity of nature and some indigenous cultures.[57] Moreover, this symbolic representation, as much as the praxis connected with it, is highly contested. Even if today the value of genetic diversity is generally acknowledged, it is by no means clear whether or in what ways this acknowledgment will lead to a real protection of both nature and traditional societal relations. Genetic resources have now taken on enormous economic relevance for modern biotechnologies as well as for the life science industries, and the measures undertaken to create global markets that putatively aim to protect genetic diversity (e.g., patents on genetic resources) tend to undermine indigenous and traditional knowledge and social practices.[58]

The world's present experience with global environmental change reveals that the ways in which global societies have come to depend on the benefits of nature – often referred to collectively as 'ecosystem services' – are highly unsustainable: current patterns of use are undermining future benefits.[59] This revelation, however, is very much contested in terms of what the real problem is: 'What,' it can be asked, 'is the scientific "fact"? And how are we to respond?' Both these questions raise various struggles at different political levels involving a variety of actors with different interests and world views. New perspectives on the limits to the appropriation of nature – and thus on nature's non-identity – arise within these struggles in the form of critiques of dominant discursive framings (which include scientific and socioeconomic ones). The self-reflection of a given symbolic construction of nature – which includes a 'second reflection' on its construction processes – addresses scientific representation and socioeconomic practices but is also affected by political struggles and power relations. Nevertheless, scientific representations are important, and it is only through a critique of scientific representations that specific material properties that should be respected (i.e., the non-identity of nature) can be revealed.

This argument reveals a shortcoming of Adorno's theory and represents a point of departure from his version of critical theory. Environmental policy cannot ignore the results offered by the natural sciences those results challenge those policies. That said, environmental research and environmental policy often refer uncritically to those results, making the assumption that natural science results are immune from political struggles and power relations and that they represent 'the truth' about nature. Note as well that without the methods and practices of the natural sciences, issues such as global climate change and biodiversity loss would not 'exist': they exist as social or political facts only after they have been described scientifically (e.g., in studies about the rise of average temperature or the distribution of species). Moreover, especially in environmental research, new kinds of scientific knowledge have emerged that straddle the boundary between the natural and social sciences and between the basic and applied sciences; an example is the new field of 'sustainability science.' Thus a critical theory must critically examine the construction processes *within* sciences. From the perspective of classical critical theory, however, this presents an obstacle. Adorno and Horkheimer refer to natural sciences and technology only as something deeply entangled in the dialectic of enlightenment; they do not take into account even the possibility of a more nuanced view. Their assumption, however, is misleading.[60] If all natural sciences and technologies represented only an element or an aspect of the mastery of nature, this mastery would lack any alternative and the dialectic of enlightenment would not be able to contribute to a 'positive concept of enlightenment.'[61] Horkheimer and Adorno do not refer to this sort of critical approach to modern natural sciences; Herbert Marcuse[62] at least offers some suggestions about a totally different science. But what is needed is not so much a totally different approach to science as a whole; needed, rather, is a critical approach to environmental issues that refers to the natural sciences in an inter- and trans-disciplinary way, while remaining aware that the sciences, both natural and social, are always connected to social struggles and power relations.[63] Needed as well is a critical approach that would allow the sciences to reflect on their part in the mastery of nature.

The terms *second reflection* and *priority of the object* could be taken as a basis for such a self-reflection of sciences and help reveal the societal implications of science and technology.[64] It could be seen as an advantage that such an approach references not only the microlevel of societal construction processes – in particular the laboratory – but also societal transformation processes.[65] Moreover, it could connect investigations of the transformation of societal structures and power relations with those of the fate of non-identical nature. In this way it could contribute to ongoing discussions about how to address environmental concerns while neither referring to a given nature nor ignoring material properties.[66]

Post-Fordist Conditions and the Fate of Nature

Classical critical theory was linked to a particular era of capitalist development, described by critical theorists as late capitalism, now often called Fordism. During this era, for the first time the whole of society was penetrated by the capitalist mode of production and reproduction. During the nineteenth century the labouring classes had remained external to the capitalist reproduction process;[67] under Fordism their individual modes of reproduction were increasingly included in capitalist accumulation processes. Moreover, cultural ways of thinking and feeling were exploited by consumerism and the industrialization of culture became an integral part of capital accumulation. This process was analysed by Adorno, Horkheimer, and Marcuse as a means of creating total capitalism (*Totalisierung*). As Jameson puts it, late capitalism 'can therefore be described as the moment when the last vestiges of nature which survived onto classical capitalism have been eliminated: namely the Third World and the unconscious.'[68] Seeing late capitalism in this way means the end of nature as something outside capitalism, as something 'other.' Jameson's diagnosis follows the dialectic of enlightenment, in which the tendency to eliminate every 'otherness' was seen as the underlying purpose of both enlightenment and capitalism.

But in light of the arguments developed above, we could also see that this totalization of capitalism does not really mean the end of this 'otherness.' To understand this point, it is important to grasp the relations among society, nature, and the individual in a dialectical manner – that is, as a contradiction where the elements, while subsumed under societal conditions, are not really controlled or dismissed. Nature, while being subsumed under capitalist conditions of production, retains a logic of its own, as the unconscious or the Third World does. Moreover, what we call the environmental crisis is an articulation of the ongoing contradictions between society's appropriation and transformation of nature and nature's own internal logic (*Eigenlogik*). Thus, as the Fordist phase of capitalism came into crisis in the late 1970s, the relationships with nature were at the centre of this crisis: access to natural resources, in particular oil and gas, and the crisis of the foundations of this accumulation model – namely, consumerism and the expanded reproduction of capital – became central drivers behind the search for new modes of regulation and for new accumulation strategies.[69]

So when discussing phases of capitalist development we should avoid two shortcomings often associated with Adorno's critical theory. The first is more of a misunderstanding; the second is in my view a real shortcoming. First, Adorno's diagnosis of late capitalism is often associated with a totality that implies the loss of all tensions and contradictions. This interpretation is of course misleading. Adorno used the term *totality* as a critical concept and always emphasized that capitalism never can eliminate all of its own contradictions.[70] Yet even with this in mind, Adorno provides no answer as to how these contradictions influence societal processes – in particular, how they could lead to new phases of capitalist development. The term 'late capitalism' is thus confusing because it rules out these questions terminologically: it seems to be the end version of capitalism. But as in history in general, there is a history of capitalism after its announced end.[71] The main difference between both ways of periodization – late capitalism and post-Fordism – is that post-Fordism does not emphasize the intensification or even hyperrealization of Fordist tendencies so much as a new historical constellation. This new constellation represents as much discontinuities with Fordism as continuities (or intensification processes).[72] It could even be said to represent a new constellation of society, nature, and the individual (see above). But as noted above, this may to some extent be characterized as a misunderstanding, the clarification of which could form the basis for a historicization of critical theory.

Critical theory's real shortcoming lies in the foundations of its theory of society, which refers to basic aspects such as economics[73] and politics, with particular attention to society's political steering mechanisms. This does not mean, as often assumed, that critical theorists totally ignored political interventions in society. As Alex Demirovic[74] has shown, Horkheimer and Adorno, when they returned to Germany after the Second World War, worked hard to change the specific conditions of Germany after fascism. The forms of fascist thinking and behaviour inscribed in German political and social institutions were at the centre of their political interventions. Yet a real shortcoming remains regarding the political steering of the new capitalist mode of regulation. What is needed today is a way for critical theory to deal with the capitalist restructuring often denoted as 'globalization': the transition to a post-Fordist era of capitalism and the emergence of post-Fordist relationships with nature.[75]

For attempts to do this, a clear advantage of beginning with the concept of societal relationships with nature is that it places environmental problems at the *centre* of societal development. In this way, environmental concerns are not mere problems of luxury or abundance, but are connected with basic questions of resource supply and use, and consequently with global economic restructuring and power relations. In this regard, critical theory can help us address the possibility of a greening of capitalism more properly. Discussions of this question are trapped between two poles. One pole explains that capitalism is the main enemy of nature.[76] According to this argument, any environmental reforms within the capitalist mode of production are impossible or irrelevant. The other pole contends (e.g., as in ecological modernization approaches) that a green capitalism will be able to solve the principal threats connected with the global environmental crisis. Both poles have some arguments in their favour. The latter can point to the huge number of measures at different levels that have been introduced in recent years – from international agreements down to local initiatives – all of which are meant to mitigate the impacts of ecological problems. Such measures seem to substantiate the possibility of environmental reforms within the capitalist system; however, it is increasingly clear that such reforms *cannot* resolve these problems: global climate change, for more than fifteen years a major concern in international politics, is far from being under control.[77] The playing out of climate change politics buttresses the argument that capitalism is driven by a compulsion for accumulation (*Akkumulationszwang*) – a compulsion that negates the possibility of a steady-state economy or other ways of adapting to ecological limits. The point of departure that critical theory offers focuses on how nature is subsumed under capitalist means of production and reproduction, but it analyses this subsumption as a contradictory process. It follows that the emerging societal and environmental contradiction should be in the centre of our analysis.

To deal with this process properly we should start by recognizing a *plurality* of societal relationships with nature and ask *how* environmental problems are framed and for which interests. The basic assumption of a critical theory approach is that global environmental change is tightly linked to present-day global conflicts of the sort that revolve around the strengthening of domination and marginalization, but also around the counterstruggles that are occurring at and among various levels or social scales. Strongly connected to these social struggles are new ways in which the mastery of nature is developing in post-Fordism. Such an approach does not dismiss attempts to deal with the environmental problems within capitalism. Generally speaking, there is no reason why environmental problems could not be addressed under capitalist conditions, at least to some degree. Because they represent costs and unquantifiable risks for companies or entire societies, it is quite rational to address them. The recent Stern Report[78] is one example of support for this argument. Taking a market-based governance approach, it offers a specific capitalist way of dealing with environmental problems.

But after more than thirty years of environmental struggles, it is today widely recognized that increased mastery of nature has not brought us closer to real control over nature; it has only improved our 'mastery of secondary effects' (*Herrschaft der Nebenfolgen*).[79] Societies are being confronted more and more with the unintended consequences of the appropriation of nature; the result has been additional costs and a great deal of trouble, with climate change being just one example. As one consequence, the idea of the complete control of nature has been at least partly abandoned and the scarcely controllable risks associated with the appropriation of nature are being taken into account in terms of uncertainty or the precautionary principle. More and more, the appropriation of nature is being accompanied by attempts to mitigate its destructive effects proactively or to eliminate them reactively, for the purpose of protecting nature and the environment. But does this mean that society has *acknowledged* the non-identity of nature? Or does all of this amount simply to a tandem attempt to *mitigate* the mastery of nature because of the uncontrollable consequences it threatens? In other words, has society now acknowledged that nature cannot be subsumed entirely and that we must try to respect nature's own logic? Or are we dealing with a *reflexive form of the mastery of nature*, one that takes into account that we may face negative consequences but that does not affect our goals? Such questions can be answered by considering the fate of strategies that follow different, less destructive forms of the appropriation of nature – forms that attempt to treat nature in ways that respect its non-identity (i.e., that are not guided mainly by capitalism's social logic of accumulation). Biofuels suggest one likely answer to these questions. Such fuels are promoted as a strategy for mitigating climate change. But instead of changing our attitudes, so that we reduce our energy consumption or developing less destructive forms of energy, biofuels are threatening to distort food prices and are exacerbating food insecurity, and in addition are threatening forests, which are being transformed into plantations for biofuel crops.[80]

We thus have to investigate contested terrains in the appropriation of nature. In these terrains, different strategies with different social and environmental consequences clash with one another. Until now, strategies of capitalist valorization (*Inwertsetzung*) have been the dominant ones.[81] Thus, even if the idea of total control over nature has been largely abandoned, the subsumption of nature under capitalist conditions is continuing to an unprecedented degree. In particular, the most recent valorization of natural resources, such as water and biodiversity, indicates that there is no recognition of the non-identity of nature. This tendency toward strategies that emphasize valorization has led to selective treatment of environmental problems, which has had huge social consequences, such as the undermining of non-capitalist ways of living and of using nature. In this sense, approaches such as 'ecological modernization' and the 'greening of capitalism' could be understood as new steps in the 'dialectic of enlightenment.' Having acknowledged uncontrollable risk and uncertainties – thereby abandoning the idea of total control over nature – we can speak about a *reflexive mastery of nature in post-Fordism.*

The most important trends are therefore toward struggles and counterstrategies regarding the capitalist valorization of nature. In particular today, biodiversity and genetic resources[82] but also water supply[83] and ecosystem services[84] are highly contested. Building on the concept of societal relationships with nature, we should not ask primarily *whether* environmental risks are being properly addressed. More important are, first, *how* nature is being constructed in environmental politics and beyond (in science, culture, and the economy); and second, the *selective treatment* of environmental problems that has developed from the play of socioeconomic interests and power relations (including gender-specific ideologies) and, more generally, from societal forms of domination. For example, the valorization of genetic resources is a key element in the new phase of capitalist development and *post-Fordist relationships with nature.*[85] If the novelty of this phase – W.F. Haug calls it 'biocapitalism as a mode of production'[86] – and its central elements were taken into account, then conflicts over the organization of relationships with nature could be grasped more adequately. Moreover, the chances of alternative forms could be estimated more precisely.

What we can observe is an ongoing process of the dialectic of enlightenment, one that does not lead necessarily toward a catastrophe. Indeed, catastrophic rhetoric is *part of* the ongoing 'dialectic of enlightenment,' in that it is contributing to mythological fears instead of helping us analyse the societal roots of ecological crises.[87] Furthermore, environmental reforms are possible under capitalist and even under neo-imperialist conditions, albeit in highly selective ways. Neoliberalism produces it own nature,[88] even if different from what was known as nature before. It is the *subsumption* of nature and the accompanying *neglect* of nature's non-identity that engenders new risks and dangers. Critical theory thus should reconstruct the contradictions and struggles among various kinds of societal relationships with nature and try to estimate their impacts on nature and society – and not contribute to the chorus hailing the end of nature.

NOTES

1 Bill McKibben, *The End of Nature* (New York: Random House, 1989).
2 IPCC, *Fourth Assessment Report* (Cambridge: Cambridge University Press, 2007).
3 Nicholas H. Stern, *The Economics of Climate Change: The Stern Review* (Cambridge: Cambridge University Press, 2007).
4 Erik Swyngedouw, 'Scaled Geographies: Nature, Place, and the Politics of Scale,' in *Scale and Geographic Inquiry: Nature, Society, and Method*, ed. Eric Sheppard and Robert B. McMaster (Oxford: Blackwell, 2004).
5 Ulrich Brand et al., *Conflicts in Environmental Regulation and the Internationalization of the State: Contested Terrains* (London and New York: Routledge, 2008).
6 Leo Panitch and Colin Leys, *Socialist Register 2007: Coming to Terms with Nature* (London: Monthly Review, 2006).
7 See Michael Redclift, 'Development and the Environment: Managing the Contradictions?' in *Capitalism and Development*, ed. Leslie Sklair (London: Routledge, 1994).
8 Maarten A. Hajer, *The Politics of Environmental Discourse: Ecological Modernization and the Policy Process* (Oxford: Oxford Unversity Press, 1997).
9 In the following, the term *critical theory* is used to denote the work of the 'older version' of the Frankfurt School, in particular that of Max

Horkheimer, Walter Benjamin, Theodor W. Adorno, and Herbert Marcuse. There are plenty of other versions of CT, and not just the 'younger version' of Jürgen Habermas or Axel Honneth. There are also approaches that refer to Marxist, feminist, ecological, and various other traditions. For a history of the Frankfurt School, see Rolf Wiggershaus, *The Frankfurt School: Its History, Theories, and Political Significance* (Cambridge: MIT Press, 1994).

10 See Max Horkheimer and Theodor W. Adorno. 'Dialektik der Aufklärung. Philosophische Fragmente,' in *Gesammelte Schriften* vol. 5, ed. Max Horkheimer (Frankfurt am Nain: Fisher, 1987), 13.

11 Herbert Marcuse, 'Konterrevolution und Revolte,' in *Schriften*, vol. 9, ed. Herbert Marcuse (Frankfurt am Main: Suhrkamp, 1972).

12 See Ulrich Beck, *Ecological Politics in an Age of Risk* (Cambridge: Polity, 2002).

13 As Habermas puts it. Jürgen Habermas, *Theorie des kommunikativen Handelns* (Frankfurt am Main: Suhrkamp, 1981).

14 See also Walter Benjamin, 'Über den Begriff der Geschichte,' in *Illuminationen* (Frankfurt am Main: Suhrkamp, 1980).

15 Ibid., 256f.

16 Benjamin demanded a shift from the mastery of nature to 'the mastery of the mastery of nature'; see Peter Wehling, *Die Moderne als Sozialmythos* (Frankfurt and Main: Campus Verlag, 1992); 'Dynamic Constellations of the Individual, Society and Nature. Critical Theory as an Approach to Environmental Problems' (paper presented at the Conference on Sociological Theory and the Environment, Woudschoten Conference Centre (The Netherlands), 20–22 March 1997); and the chapters by Leiss and Gunster in this volume.

17 Horkheimer and Adorno, 'Dialektik der Aufklarung.'

18 Andrew Biro, *Denaturalizing Ecological Politics: Alienation from Nature from Rousseau to the Frankfurt School and Beyond* (Toronto: University of Toronto Press, 2005), 120.

19 See Horkheimer and Adorno, 'Dialektik der Aufklarung,' 35.

20 For an interpretation, see Biro, *Denaturalizing Ecological Politics*, 118–24.

21 Horkheimer and Adorno, 'Dialektik der Aufklarung,' 254.

22 For a more detailed reading, see Christoph Görg, *Regulation der Naturverhältnisse* (Münster: Verlag Westfälisches Dampfboot, 2003) and Christoph Görg, 'Nichtidentität und Kritik,' in *Kritische Theorie der Technik und der Natur*, ed. Gernot Böhme and Alexandra Manzei (Munich: Fink, 2003).

23 Horkheimer and Adorno, 'Dialektik der Aufklarung,' 21.

24 Ibid., 55.

25 See Jürgen Habermas, *Der philosophische Diskurs der Moderne* (Frankfurt am

Main: Suhrkamp, 1985); and Axel Honneth, *Kritik der Macht* (Frankfurt am Main: Suhrkamp, 1989).

26 Görg, *Regulation der Naturverhältnisse* (Münster: Westfälisches Dampfboot, 2003), 37–41.

27 See David Harvey, *Justice, Nature, and the Geography of Difference* (Malden: Wiley Blackwell, 1996); Honneth, *Kritik der Macht*; Martin Jay, *The Dialectical Imagination* (Berkeley: University of California Press, 1973); and Neil Smith, *Uneven Development: Nature, Capital, and the Production of Space* (Macon: University of Georgia Press, 1990).

28 See the editorial remarks in Horkheimer and Adorno, 'Dialektik der Aufklarung'; and Alex Demirovic, *Der nonkonformistische Intellektuelle. Die Entwicklung der kritischen Theorie zur Frankfurter Schule* (Frankfurt am Main: Suhrkamp, 1999).

29 Habermas, *Der philosophische Diskurs der Moderne*.

30 Honneth, *Kritik der Macht*.

31 Horkheimer and Adorno, 'Dialektik der Aufklarung,' 36.

32 Ibid., 56f; for a full interpretation, see Christoph Görg, 'Kritik der Naturbeherrschung,' *Zeitschrift für kritische Theorie* 5 (1999): 73–88; and *Regulation der Naturverhältnisse*.

33 Theodor W. Adorno and Max Horkheimer, *Soziologische Exkurse. Nach Vorträgen und Diskussionen* (Frankfurt am Main: Institut für Sozialforschung, 1956), 43.

34 The societal relationships could not be restricted to a more negative form like a struggle. There remains a fundamental ambiguity in the meaning of the term *nature* in the DoE, as Gunzelin Schmid Noerr has shown; see Schmid Noerr, *Das Eingedenken der Natur im Subjekt* (Darmstadt: Wissenschaftliche Buchgesellschaft, 1990). The term is used neither in a purely negative way, as something we have to fight against, nor in a purely positive way, as something like a paradise. It is both, as nature is symbolically constructed in a contradictory way (see below).

35 See Görg, 'Kritik der Naturbeherrschung'; Georg W.F. Hegel, *Phänomenologie des Geistes* (Frankfurt am Main: Suhrkamp, 1970); and Jürgen Ritsert, *Das Bellen des toten Hundes* (Frankfurt am Main: Campus Verlag, 1988).

36 For another interpretation, see William Leiss, *The Domination of Nature* (Boston: Beacon, 1974); and the chapter by Leiss in this volume.

37 Necessary at least in its basic meaning: we cannot assume that humans avoid appropriating and transforming nature, for this is a 'natural' aspect of human societies. But of course there are plenty of options and alternatives when it comes to *how*. And if nothing else, the *extent* of the appropriation (more crucially, the *destruction*) of nature is always contested in

society. Indeed, most environmental struggles are directed toward what can be called a less destructive societalization of nature. But to determine what could be less destructive, we need the term nature in its basic meaning, as something that is not identical with society (see below).

38 See Niclas Luhmann, *Die Gesellschaft der Gesellschaft*, 2 vols. (Frankfurt am Main: Suhrkamp, 1997).

39 See, for example, Emile Durkheim, 'Der Dualismus der menschlichen Natur und seine sozialen Beziehungen,' in *Geschichte der Soziologie*, vol. 2, ed. Friedrich Jonas (Hamburg: Rohwolt, 1980); for a critique, see Christoph Görg, *Gesellschaftliche Naturverhältnisse* (Münster: Westfälisches Dampfboot, 1999).

40 See Jürgen Ritsert, *Was ist Dialektik? Studientexte zur Sozialwissenschaft*, vol. 9 (Frankfurt am Main: FB Gesellschaftswissenschaften, 1995).

41 Including an approach that also builds on the term *societal relationships with nature:* see Egon Becker and Thomas Jahn, *Soziale Ökologie. Gründzuge einer Wissenschaft von den gesellschaftlichen Naturverhältnissen* (Frankfurt am Main: Campus Verlag, 2006); for the differences, see below.

42 See Egon Becker and Thomas Jahn, *Soziale Ökologie als Krisenwissenschaft* (Frankfurt am Main: Verlag für interkulturelle Kommunikation, 1987). Today in Germany there are several different approaches to dealing with this term. The interpretation offered here is not agreed upon by all of them. The most important approaches are those of Egon Becker and Thomas Jahn, 'Growth or Development,' in *Political Ecology: Global and Local*, ed. David Bell et al. (London and New York: Routledge, 1998); Becker and Jahn, *Soziale Ökologie*; Alex Demirovic, *Demokratie and Herrschaft. Aspekte kritischer Gesellschaftstheorie* (Münster: Westfälisches Dampfboot, 1997); Demirovic, *Der nonkonformistische Intellektuelle*; Görg, *Gesellschaftliche Naturverhältnisse*; Görg, 'Kritik der Naturbeherrschung'; *Regulation der Naturverhältnisse*; 'Nichtidentität und Kritik'; 'Dialektische Konstellationen,' in *Modelle kritischer Gesellschaftstheorie. Traditionen und Perspektiven der Kritischen Theorie*, ed. Alex Demirovic (Stuttgart: Metzler, 2003); 'Postfordistische Transformation der Naturverhältnisse,' in *Kritische Theorie im gesellschaftlichen Strukturwandel*, ed. Joachim Beerhorst, Alex Demirovic, and Michael Guggemos (Frankfurt am Main: Suhrkamp, 2004); Michael Weingarten, *Wissenschaftstheorie als Wissenschaftskritik* (Bonn: Pahl-Rugenstein, 1998); and *Strukturierung von Raum und Landschaft. Konzepte in Ökologie und der Theorie gesellschaftlicher Naturverhältnisse* (Münster: Westfälisches Dampfboot, 2005). Additionally, there is a broad and long feminist tradition that makes use of central elements of CT – in particular, the critique of the domination of nature. See, for example, Elvira Scheich,

'Naturbeherrschung und Weiblichkeit. Feministische Kritik der Naturwissenschaften,' in *Gesellschaft im Übergang*, ed. Christoph Görg (Darmstadt: Wissenschaftliche Buchgesellschaft, 1994). More recently, some volumes have dealt with several aspects of the foundations of CT, or of its actual meaning; see Joachim Beerhorst, Alex Demirovic, and Michael Guggemos. *Kritische Theorie im gesellschaftlichen Strukturwandel* (Frankfurt am Main: Suhrkamp, 2004); Gernot Böhme and Alexandra Manzei, *Kritische Theorie der Technik und der Natur* (Munich: Fink, 2003); and Alex Demirovic, *Modelle kritischer Gesellschaftstheorie. Traditionen und Perspektiven der Kritischen Theorie* (Stuttgart: Metzler, 2003).

43 See Christoph Görg, 'Landscape Governance: The "Politics of Scale" and the "Natural" Conditions of Places,' *Geoforum* 38 (2007): 954–66.

44 Biro, *Denaturalizing Ecological Politics*.

45 Theodor W. Adorno, *Negative Dialektik* (Frankfurt am Main: Suhrkamp, 1982).

46 See Theodor W. Adorno, 'Zu Subjekt und Objekt,' in *Stichworte. Kritische Modelle 2*, ed. Theodor W. Adorno (Frankfurt am Main: Suhrkamp, 1969); and *Negative Dialektik*.

47 Immanuel Kant, *Kritik der reinen Vernunft*, in *Werkausgabe*, vol. 3 (Frankfurt am Main: Suhrkamp, 1982).

48 Karl Marx, *Grundrisse der Kritik der Politischen Ökonomie* (Berlin: Dietz, 1974), 22.

49 'Denken bricht in zweiter Reflexion die Suprematie des Denkens über ein Anderes, weil es Anderes immer in sich schon ist.' Adorno, *Negative Dialektik*, 201; my translation.

50 Adorno, *Negative Dialektik*, 202.

51 As Kant puts it (Kant, *Kritik der reinen Vernunft*).

52 According to Marx, it works 'hinter dem Rücken der Akteure' (behind the backs of the actors). But this does not mean that the law of value is something like an eternal law of history, because it is a historical finding and it could be recognized and changed by societal actors. For this interpretation, developed under the regulation approach, see Christoph Görg, 'Der Institutionenbegriff in der Theorie der Strukturierung,' in *Politik, Institutionen und Staat. Zur Kritik der Regulationstheorie*, ed. Joseph Esser, Christoph Görg, and Joachim Hirsch (Hamburg: VSA, 1994).

53 See Görg, 'Nichtidentität und Kritik.'

54 An important part of this learning process must be the acknowledgment that not all national societies have contributed to global warming in the same way; its societal origins are deeply marked by inequalities between industrialized capitalist countries and 'developing' countries.

55 Alfred Schmidt, *Der Begriff der Natur in der Lehre von Marx* (Hamburg: Europäische Verlagsanstalt, 1993).
56 See Pat R. Mooney, *The Parts of Life: Agricultural Biodiversity, Indigenous Knowledge, and the Role of the Third System. Special Issue of Development Dialogue* (Uppsala: Dag Hammarskjöld Foundation, 1998); and Vandana 'Shiva, *Monocultures of the Mind* (London: Zed, 1993).
57 This mystification takes place very often in statements about indigenous communities; for an overview, see Darrell A. Posey, *Cultural and Spiritual Values of Biodiversity* (London: Practical Action, 1999); for a critique, see Görg, *Regulation der Naturverhältnisse*, 242–62.
58 Brand et al., *Conflicts in Environmental Regulation*.
59 See MA, *Millennium Ecosystem Assessment Synthesis Report* (Washington: Island, 2005).
60 Egon Becker and Thomas Jahn, 'Umrisse einer kritischen Theorie gesellschaftlicher Naturverhältmisse,' in *Kritische Theorie der Technik und der Natur*, ed. Gernot Böhme and Alexandra Manzei (Munich: Fink, 2003).
61 Horkheimer and Adorno, *Dialektik der Aufklarung*, 21.
62 Herbert Marcuse, 'Industrialismus und Kapitalismus im Werk Max Webers,' in *Kultur und Gesellschaft 2*, ed. Herbert Marcuse (Frankfurt am Main: Suhrkamp, 1979); see also Farrell, this volume.
63 Görg, *Regulation der Naturverhältnisse*; Becker and Jahn, *Soziale Ökologie*.
64 For this task, a critical examination of modern studies in science and technology is necessary. See, for example, Bruno Latour, *Politics of Nature: How to Bring the Sciences into Democracy* (Cambridge, MA: Harvard University Press, 2004); and Sheila Jasanoff and Marybeth L. Martello, *Earthly Politics: Global and Local in Environmental Governance* (Cambridge: MIT Press, 2004). The advantage of CT might be seen in the relevance of a theory of society; see below.
65 The 'knowledge society' and knowledge-based economy; see Brand et al., *Conflicts in Environmental Regulation*.
66 For these discussions, see Ted Benton, 'Marxism and Natural Limits,' *New Left Review* 178 (1989): 51–86; Bruce Braun and Noel Castree, *Remaking Reality: Nature at the Millennium* (New York: Routledge Chapman and Hall, 1998); William Cronon, *Uncommon Ground: Toward Reinventing Nature* (New York: Norton, 1995); and Swyngedouw, 'Scaled Geographies.'
67 Theodor W. Adorno, *Soziologische Schriften 1* (Frankfurt am Main: Suhrkamp, 1979), 100.
68 Fredric Jameson, *The Ideologies of Theory*, vol. 2, *The Syntax of History* (Minneapolis: University of Minnesota Press, 1988), 207, cited in Biro, *Denaturalizing Ecological Politics*, 7.

69 Alain Lipietz, *Mirages and Miracles* (London: Verso, 1987).
70 Adorno, *Soziologische Schriften 1*, 237.
71 For discussions concerning the periodization of capitalism, see Robert Albritton et al., *Phases of Capitalist Development: Booms, Crises, and Globalization* (London: Palgrave Macmillan, 2001). Post-Fordism, of course, shares this fate of being something unspecified after Fordism, and there is a discussion in regulation theory, too, regarding whether Post-Fordism is something well established or not; see Sbah Alnasseri et al., 'Space, Regulations, and the Periodisation of Capitalism,' in *Phases of Capitalist Development: Booms, Crises, and Globalization*, ed. Robert Albritton et al. (London: Palgrave Macmillan, 2001).
72 For a discussion of the dialectic of continuity and discontinuity in the regulation approach, see Joseph Esser, Christoph Görg, and Joachim Hirsch, *Politik, Institutionen und Staat. Zur Kritik der Regulationstheorie* (Hamburg: VSA, 1994).
73 Thomas Sablowski, 'Entwicklungstendenzen und Krisen des Kapitalismus,' in *Modelle kritischer Gesellschaftstheorie. Traditionen und Perspektiven der Kritischen Theorie*, ed. Alex Demirovic (Stuttgart: Metzler, 2003).
74 Demirovic, *Der nonkonformistische Intellektuelle*.
75 See Brand et al., *Conflicts in Environmental Regulation*; Demirovic, *Modelle kritischer Gesellschaftstheorie*; and Görg, 'Postfordistische Transformation der Naturverhältnisse.'
76 For example, Joel Kovel, *The Enemy of Nature: The End of Capitalism or the End of the World* (Halifax: Zed, 2002).
77 IPCC, *Fourth Assessment Report*.
78 Stern, *The Economics of Climate Change*.
79 Ulrich Beck, Anthony Giddens, and Scott Lash, *Reflexive Modernization* (Stanford: Stanford University Press, 1994).
80 See GRAIN, 'Stop the Agrofuels Craze,' *Seedling*, July 2007; Third World Network, 'Biofuels: An Illusion and a Threat,' *Resurgence*, April 2007.
81 For the field of biodiversity, see Brand et al., *Conflicts in Environmental Regulation*.
82 Ibid.
83 Swyngedouw, 'Scaled Geographies.'
84 MA, *Millennium Ecosystem Assessment Synthesis Report*.
85 Brand et al., *Conflicts in Environmental Regulation*.
86 Wolfgang F. Haug, 'Fragen einer Kritik der Biokapitalismus,' *Das Argument* 242 (2001): 449–65 at 451.
87 See Biro, this volume.

88 James McCarthy and Scott Prudham, 'Neoliberal Nature and the Nature of
Neoliberalism,' *Geoforum* 35 (2004).

BIBLIOGRAPHY

Adorno, Theodor W. *Negative Dialektik*. Frankfurt am Main: Suhrkamp, 1982.
– *Soziologische Schriften 1*. Frankfurt am Main: Suhrkamp, 1979.
– 'Zu Subjekt und Objekt.' In *Stichworte. Kritische Modelle 2*, edited by Theodor
W. Adorno, 151–68. Frankfurt am Main: Suhrkamp, 1969.
Adorno, Theodor W., and Max Horkheimer. *Soziologische Exkurse. Nach Vorträ-
gen und Diskussionen*. Frankfurt am Main: Institut für Sozialforschung, 1956.
Albritton, Robert, Makatho Itoh, Richard Westra, and Alan Zuege. *Phases of
Capitalist Development: Booms, Crises, and Globalization*. London: Palgrave
Macmillan, 2001.
Alnasseri, Sbah, Ulrich Brand, Thomas Sablowski, and Jens Winter. 'Space,
Regulations, and the Periodisation of Capitalism.' In *Phases of Capitalist
Development: Booms, Crises, and Globalization*, edited by Robert Albritton,
Makatho Itoh, Richard Westra, and Alan Zuege, 163–179. London: Palgrave
Macmillan, 2001.
Beck, Ulrich. *Ecological Politics in an Age of Risk*. Cambridge: Polity, 2002.
Beck, Ulrich, Anthony Giddens, and Scott Lash. *Reflexive Modernization*. Stan-
ford: Stanford University Press, 1994.
Becker, Egon, and Thomas Jahn. 'Growth or Development.' In *Political Ecology:
Global and Local*, edited by David Bell, Leesa Fawcett, Roger Keil, and Peter
Penz, 68-86. London and New York: Routledge, 1998.
– *Soziale Ökologie. Gründzuge einer Wissenschaft von den gesellschaftlichen
Naturverhältnissen*. Frankfurt am Main: Campus Verlag, 2006.
– *Soziale Ökologie als Krisenwissenschaft*. Frankfurt am Main: Verlag für inter-
kulturelle Kommunikation, 1987.
– 'Umrisse einer kritischen Theorie gesellschaftlicher Naturverhältmisse.'
In *Kritische Theorie der Technik und der Natur*, edited by Gernot Böhme and
Alexandra Manzei, 91–112. Munich: Fink, 2003.
Beerhorst, Joachim, Alex Demirovic, and Michael Guggemos. *Kritische Theorie
im gesellschaftlichen Strukturwandel*. Frankfurt am Main: Suhrkamp, 2004.
Benjamin, Walter. 'Über den Begriff der Geschichte.' In *Illuminationen*. Frank-
furt am Main: Suhrkamp, 1980.
Benton, Ted. 'Marxism and Natural Limits.' *New Left Review* 178 (1989):
51–86.
Biro, Andrew. *Denaturalizing Ecological Politics: Alienation from Nature from*

Rousseau to the Frankfurt School and Beyond. Toronto: University of Toronto Press, 2005.

Böhme, Gernot, and Alexandra Manzei. *Kritische Theorie der Technik und der Natur.* Munich: Fink, 2003.

Brand, Ulrich, Christoph Görg, Joachim Hirsch, and Marcus Wissen. *Conflicts in Environmental Regulation and the Internationalization of the State: Contested Terrains.* London and New York: Routledge, 2008.

Braun, Bruce, and Noel Castree. *Remaking Reality: Nature at the Millennium.* New York: Routledge Chapman and Hall, 1998.

Cronon, William. *Uncommon Ground: Toward Reinventing Nature.* New York: Norton, 1995.

Demirovic, Alex. *Demokratie and Herrschaft. Aspekte kritischer Gesellschaftstheorie.* Münster: Westfälisches Dampfboot, 1997.

– *Modelle kritischer Gesellschaftstheorie. Traditionen und Perspektiven der Kritischen Theorie.* Stuttgart: Metzler, 2003.

– *Der nonkonformistische Intellektuelle. Die Entwicklung der kritischen Theorie zur Frankfurter Schule.* Frankfurt am Main: Suhrkamp, 1999.

Durkheim, Emile. 'Der Dualismus der menschlichen Natur und seine sozialen Beziehungen.' In *Geschichte der Soziologie,* vol. 2, edited by Friedrich Jonas. Hamburg: Rohwolt, 1980.

Esser, Joseph, Christoph Görg, and Joachim Hirsch. *Politik, Institutionen und Staat. Zur Kritik der Regulationstheorie.* Hamburg: VSA, 1994.

Görg, Christoph. 'Dialektische Konstellationen.' In *Modelle kritischer Gesellschaftstheorie. Traditionen und Perspektiven der Kritischen Theorie,* edited by Alex Demirovic, 39–62. Stuttgart: Metzler, 2003.

– *Gesellschaftliche Naturverhältnisse.* Münster: Westfälisches Dampfboot, 1999.

– 'Der Institutionenbegriff in der Theorie der Strukturierung.' In *Politik, Institutionen und Staat. Zur Kritik der Regulationstheorie,* edited by Joseph Esser, Christoph Görg, and Joachim Hirsch, 31–84. Hamburg: VSA, 1994.

– 'Kritik der Naturbeherrschung.' *Zeitschrift für kritische Theorie* 5 (1999): 73–88.

– 'Landscape Governance: The "Politics of Scale" and the "Natural" Conditions of Places.' *Geoforum* 38 (2007): 954–66.

– 'Nichtidentität und Kritik.' In *Kritische Theorie der Technik und der Natur,* edited by Gernot Böhme and Alexandra Manzei, 113–33. Munich: Fink, 2003.

– 'Postfordistische Transformation der Naturverhältnisse.' In *Kritische Theorie im gesellschaftlichen Strukturwandel,* edited by Joachim Beerhorst, Alex Demirovic, and Michael Guggemos, 199–226. Frankfurt am Main: Suhrkamp, 2004.

– *Regulation der Naturverhältnisse*. Münster: Westfälisches Dampfboot, 2003.
GRAIN. 'Stop the Agrofuels Craze.' *Seedling*, July 2007. http://www.grain
.org/agrofuels.
Habermas, Jürgen. *Der philosophische Diskurs der Moderne*. Frankfurt am Main:
Suhrkamp, 1985.
– *Theorie des kommunikativen Handelns*. Frankfurt am Main: Suhrkamp,
1981.
Hajer, Maarten A. *The Politics of Environmental Discourse: Ecological Moderniza-
tion and the Policy Process*. Oxford: Oxford University Press, 1997.
Harvey, David. *Justice, Nature, and the Geography of Difference*. Malden: Wiley
Blackwell, 1996.
Haug, Wolfgang F. 'Fragen einer Kritik der Biokapitalismus.' *Das Argument*
242 (2001): 449–65.
Hegel, Georg W.F. *Phänomenologie des Geistes*. Frankfurt am Main: Suhrkamp,
1970.
Honneth, Axel. *Kritik der Macht*. Frankfurt am Main: Suhrkamp, 1989.
Horkheimer, Max, and Theodor W. Adorno. 'Dialektik der Aufklärung.
Philosophische Fragmente.' In *Gesammelte Schriften*, vol. 5, edited by Max
Horkheimer, 364–72. Frankfurt am Main: Fisher, 1987.
IPCC (Intergovernmental Panel on Climate Change). *Fourth Assessment Report.*
Cambridge: Cambridge University Press, 2007.
Jameson, Fredric. *The Ideologies of Theory*, vol. 2, *The Syntax of History*. Minne-
apolis: University of Minnesota Press, 1988.
Jasanoff, Sheila, and Marybeth L. Martello. *Earthly Politics: Global and Local in
Environmental Governance*. Cambridge, MA: MIT Press, 2004.
Jay, Martin. *The Dialectical Imagination*. Berkeley: University of California
Press, 1973.
Kant, Immanuel. *Kritik der reinen Vernunft*. In *Werkausgabe*, vol. 3. Frankfurt am
Main: Suhrkamp, 1982.
Kovel, Joel. *The Enemy of Nature: The End of Capitalism or the End of the World*.
Halifax: Zed, 2002.
Latour, Bruno. *Politics of Nature. How to Bring the Sciences into Democracy*. Cam-
bridge, MA: Harvard University Press, 2004.
Leiss, William. *The Domination of Nature*. Boston: Beacon, 1974.
Lipietz, Alian. *Mirages and Miracles*. London: Verso, 1987.
Luhmann, Niclas. *Die Gesellschaft der Gesellschaft*. 2 vols. Frankfurt am Main:
Suhrkamp, 1997.
MA. *Millennium Ecosystem Assessment Synthesis Report*. Washington: Island,
2005.
Marcuse, Herbert. 'Industrialismus und Kapitalismus im Werk Max Webers.'

In *Kultur und Gesellschaft 2*, edited by Herbert Marcuse. Frankfurt am Main: Suhrkamp, 1979.

– 'Konterrevolution und Revolte.' In *Schriften*, vol 9, edited by Herbert Marcuse. Frankfurt am Main: Suhrkamp, 1972.

Marx, Karl. *Grundrisse der Kritik der politischen Ökonomie*. Berlin: Dietz, 1974.

McCarthy, James, and Scott Prudham. 'Neoliberal Nature and the Nature of Neoliberalism.' *Geoforum* 35 (2004): 275–83.

McKibben, Bill. *The End of Nature*. New York: Random House, 1989.

Mooney, Pat R. *The Parts of Life: Agricultural Biodiversity, Indigenous Knowledge, and the Role of the Third System. Special Issue of Development Dialogue*. Uppsala: Dag Hammarskjöld Foundation, 1998.

Panitch, Leo, and Colin Leys. *Socialist Register 2007: Coming to Terms with Nature*. London: Monthly Review, 2006.

Posey, Darrell A. *Cultural and Spiritual Values of Biodiversity*. London: Practical Action, 1999.

Redclift, Michael. 'Development and the Environment: Managing the Contradictions?' In *Capitalism and Development*, edited by Leslie Sklair, 123–9. London: Routledge, 1994.

Ritsert, Jürgen. *Das Bellen des toten Hundes*. Frankfurt am Main: Campus Verlag, 1988.

– *Was ist Dialektik? Studientexte zur Sozialwissenschaft*, vol. 9. Frankfurt am Main: FB Gesellschaftswissenschaften, 1995.

Sablowski, Thomas. 'Entwicklungstendenzen und Krisen des Kapitalismus.' In *Modelle kritischer Gesellschaftstheorie. Traditionen und Perspektiven der Kritischen Theorie*, edited by Alex Demirovic, 101–30. Stuttgart: Metzler, 2003.

Scheich, Elvira. 'Naturbeherrschung und Weiblichkeit. Feministische Kritik der Naturwissenschaften.' In *Gesellschaft im Übergang*, edited by Christoph Görg, 179–201. Darmstadt: Wissenschaftliche Buchgesellschaft, 1994.

Schmid Noerr, Gunzelin. *Das Eingedenken der Natur im Subjekt*. Darmstadt: Wissenschaftliche Buchgesellschaft, 1990.

Schmidt, Alfred. *Der Begriff der Natur in der Lehre von Marx*. Hamburg: Europäische Verlagsanstalt, 1993.

Shiva, Vanada. *Monocultures of the Mind*. London: Zed, 1993.

Smith, Neil. *Uneven Development: Nature, Capital, and the Production of Space*. Macon: University of Georgia Press, 1990.

Stern, Nicholas H. *The Economics of Climate Change: The Stern Review*. Cambridge: Cambridge University Press, 2007.

Swyngedouw, Erik. 'Scaled Geographies: Nature, Place, and the Politics of Scale.' In *Scale and Geographic Inquiry: Nature, Society, and Method*, edited by Eric Sheppard and Robert B. McMaster, 129–53. Oxford: Blackwell. 2004.

Third World Network. 'Biofuels: An Illusion and a Threat.' *Resurgence*, April 2007. http://www.twnside.org.sg/title2/twr200.htm.

Wehling, Peter. 'Dynamic Constellations of the Individual, Society, and Nature: Critical Theory as an Approach to Environmental Problems.' Paper presented at the Conference on Sociological Theory and the Environment, Woudschoten Conference Centre (The Netherlands), 20–2 March 1997.

– *Die Moderne als Sozialmythos*. Frankfurt am Main: Campus Verlag, 1992.

Weingarten, Michael. *Strukturierung von Raum und Landschaft. Konzepte in Ökologie und der Theorie gesellschaftlicher Naturverhältnisse*. Münster: Westfälisches Dampfboot, 2005.

– *Wissenschaftstheorie als Wissenschaftskritik*. Bonn: Pahl-Rugenstein, 1998.

Wiggershaus, Rolf. *The Frankfurt School: Its History, Theories, and Political Significance*. Cambridge: MIT Press, 1994.

3 The Politics of Science: Has Marcuse's New Science Finally Come of Age?[1]

KATHARINE N. FARRELL

Introduction

In keeping with the theme of this collection, the argument presented here builds on the work of a major critical theorist – Herbert Marcuse – in the course of addressing a central twenty-first century environmental politics issue: the role of science in environmental governance. As with many of the chapters in this volume, the distinction between human and non-human nature plays a central role in the argumentation. Specifically, the focus here is on the *complex interplay* between the domination of human nature, humans, and non-human nature in late-industrial societies.

Whereas most of the other authors in this volume, except for Vogel and perhaps Leiss, argue for renewed attention to the human/non-human nature dialectic, following Marcuse,[2] it is the relationship between this distinction and human purposive action that is considered here. Again following Marcuse,[3] it is proposed that the traditional human/nature dialectic of nineteenth- and early twentieth-century industrial societies (with nature as other and opponent to human) has been historically surpassed in the late-industrial societies of the late twentieth and early twenty-first centuries, in which technology – a product of the human project to subdue nature – has replaced nature as the dominant other. In these societies, technologies (roads, telephones, computers, televisions, washing machines, refrigerators) are the basic references for ordinary daily life. Technological systems have become the reality against which reasonable propositions for human purposive action are to be measured. However, if the project of developing technologies is understood to be basic to human nature, as it is for Marcuse, then this ascent of technology need not automatically correspond with the descent of nature to a subordinate position. Instead, in historically surpassing the comparatively simple self-versus-other, human/nature dialectic of the twentieth century, these late-industrial societies are confronting a complex, self-as-other dialectic comprised of human being and human project.

The inability of freethinking individuals to grasp and engage with this new dialectic occupied Marcuse's attention in most of his later writings, and it will be the main concern of the following pages. In keeping with the central theme of this book, the aim of this chapter is not to advance new political theory proper, but rather to demonstrate the enduring relevance of the Frankfurt School for developing theory that is meaningful to twenty-first century environmental politics. Though there are similarities to arguments presented elsewhere by Haraway[4] and by Leiss in this collection, here it is presumed that the dialectical tension between human and non-human nature remains relevant as a force in the history of late-industrial societies, albeit with its composition changed. In the situation of 'pacified existence'[5] described by Marcuse – achievable in late-industrial societies 'because technological progress has reached a stage in which reality no longer need be defined by the debilitating competition for social survival and advancement'[6] – the physical task of achieving liberation from the vagaries of nature has been replaced by the intellectual task of achieving liberation from a set of human-generated technological and social systems that were designed to subdue nature. However, nature has not left the scene. Because these systems are a response to nature's domination, their structures are determined in large part by the ways in which humans have previously conceptualized and experienced their struggles with both human and non-human nature in industrial societies.

Working from a presumption that the scientific method of reduction and falsification, as practised in the laboratories of the nineteenth and twentieth centuries, was intimately bound up with this project, Marcuse proposed that the reductive, linear logic of this method is reified in the technologies to which it gives rise. Building on arguments originally presented in *Eros and Civilization*, which he followed up and reiterated in *An Essay on Liberation*, Marcuse argues in *One-Dimensional Man* that, due to its historical role as a means for subduing nature and its later ubiquity and operational necessity in the activities of daily life in late-industrial societies, technology achieves an ideological status. Whereas the daily needs of water, shelter, and food are met for almost all members of these societies, the basic human need for intellectual freedom is almost impossible to satisfy because the capacity to think freely about the project of human progress has been lost. Due to the insidious regularity of their presence, these products of humanity's labours have lost their artefact character: the rhythms and routines of technology have become natural, and like nature, they cease to be a matter for debate. In the spirit of critical theory and dialectical reasoning, Marcuse concludes that if critique of this path of human progress is to be advanced under these conditions, then it must be advanced as an immanent critique, arising from within the logic of the project of technological development – that is to say, from within science.

The core thesis proposed in the following pages is that a recently arising scientific methodology discourse and related collection of methods, which have come to be referred to as postnormal science,[7] can be understood as a realization of just such an immanent critique, where 'pacified existence ... the repressed final cause behind the scientific enterprise ... were [it] to materialize and become effective, [is accompanied by a situation where] the Logos of technics would open a universe of qualitatively different relations between man and man, and man and nature.'[8] This is significant for twenty-first-century environmental politics because Marcuse suggested that such a new modality of science might provide a means for escaping the passive oppression of one-dimensional thinking, which he associated with late-industrial societies and identified as a major contributor to human oppression throughout the modern world.[9]

In the following pages it will be argued that Marcuse's treatment of the concept of technology as ideology is both historically and conceptually compatible with the discourse on postnormal science. Where Marcuse envisioned that a new science, concerned specifically with late-industrial problems, might serve as a means for reintroducing critique into a world dominated by one dimensional technological rationality, within the postnormal science discourse the need for new scientific methods is explicitly related to the problem of generating and presenting scientific analysis concerning complex late-industrial problems: '(and here is our crucial distinction) the sciences which are required to *solve* the problem [of technologically induced environmental damage] are systematically different from those that *created* the problem in the first place.'[10]

Marcuse's *One-Dimensional Man* (1964) provides a systematic historical explanation concerning the origin of the set of problems and practices that fall under the heading of postnormal science. It also offers a careful philosophical exploration of the potential contribution that the methods of postnormal science could make toward resolution of twenty-first-century problems of environmental politics. On this basis, it is proposed that careful attention to *connections between* these two concepts can bring at least two things to the academic discourse on environmental politics in the twenty-first century: (1) an improved picture of the historical political context, for use in understanding late-industrial problems within environmental politics, such as large-scale anthropogenic habitat and climate disruption, mega-industrial contaminations, and the creation and use of genetically modified organisms and nanotechnologies; and (2) a concrete elaboration of how and why Marcuse's work remains relevant for theory concerning environmental politics. In addition, this approach has the potential to contribute to the postnormal science discourse by putting a whole new body of theoretical works at the disposal of its methodologists.

Structure of the Argument

This chapter begins with a review of the main protagonists: Marcuse's new science, and the discourse on postnormal science. Two fundamental links between the two concepts are considered, in turn and in detail, in order to present the case that the two concepts are at least very similar if not more or less identical: (1) both concepts have a complex, phenomenological cum epistemological aspect that places them within history and more specifically at the *vanguard* of the human project of progress through scientific and technological development; and (2) both are concerned, in a world full of hard facts, soft values, and reductionist attention to components, with soft facts, hard values, and complex wholes.[11]

The case having been stated for understanding the postnormal science discourse as a manifestation of Marcuse's new modality of science, attention is turned to the question of what this might mean in practice. Here, the focus shifts to the increasingly common postnormal science practice of using ideas drawn from Habermasian discursive ethics to justify the ways in which consultations between scientists and non-scientists are organized. In light of the arguments presented here, this practice is problematic for two reasons: (1) Habermas strongly critiqued and explicitly rejected Marcuse's hypothesis;[12] and (2) Marcuse clearly anticipated that this new science, if it manifested, would take the form – at least initially – of a democratically illegitimate oligarchy: 'But who has the right to set himself up as judge of an established society, who other than the legally constituted agencies or agents and the majority of the people? Other than these, it could only be a self-appointed elite, or leaders who would arrogate to themselves such judgement.'[13] Here two related questions arise, which are addressed in turn below: (1) How and to what extent might Habermas's 1971 critique of Marcuse's 1964 arguments, in which he rejected Marcuse's proposition that a new modality of science was possible, be reconciled with the use of Habermas's arguments concerning deliberative democracy and discursive ethics within the postnormal science discourse?[14] And (2), to what extent do emerging methods of postnormal science have the potential to fulfil Marcuse's hope[15] that such an oligarchy could and would place itself before the judgment of a democratic majority? If it is plausible that Habermas's arguments concerning deliberative democracy and discourse ethics can be invoked to assist with the design of methods for operationalizing Marcuse's new modality of science, then they can be seen both as tools with which the new accountability for which Marcuse hoped might be achieved and as means for providing the democratic control of technological development that Habermas demands.

In a brief review of Habermas's original critique of Marcuse's arguments about a new science, it is contended that the critique entirely eschews a fundamental aspect of Marcuse's position, one that can be traced back to *Eros and Civilization*: that the human project of technological development is historical, with particular shapes and forms (both empirical and epistemological) that are influenced by how the project has developed and that influence its potential paths for future development. In particular, Habermas's critique completely ignores the epistemological and ontological influence that Marcuse attributes to technology as ideology, which, having supplanted nature as the external referent for reality, is presumed to exert influence over not only the material world within which humans live but also the cognitive world within which they develop their understandings of self and of others, including nature and technology. Interestingly, it is Habermas himself who resolves the first set of difficulties, having made more recent arguments concerning the politics of nature[16] – arguments that are more open to the idea that legitimate democratic discourse can remain viable in spite of epistemological diversity. Dealing with the second set of problems – those relating to the potentially undemocratic character of Marcuse's new science – then brings us to the close of this chapter, where it is proposed that much work is still to be done if emerging post-normal science methods, which are often still quite oligarchic, are to be exposed to public judgment, as Marcuse had hoped and Habermas would demand.

Marcuse's New Science and the Discourse on Postnormal Science

Three basic texts from Marcuse (*Eros and Civilization, One-Dimensional Man,* and *An Essay on Liberation*) can be understood as elaborating the basic structure of his arguments concerning the emergence of technology as ideology. It is impossible to summarize here the arguments presented in these texts.[17] However, one of the many threads woven through them can be followed without too much difficulty: his specific arguments concerning the potential liberating role of a new modality of late-industrial science. First, in *Eros and Civilization* and then in *One-Dimensional Man,* he defines the material, psychological, historical, and social conditions that give rise to technology as ideology and its psychological companion, one-dimensional thinking. He then concerns himself, in *One-Dimensional Man,* directly with the passive oppression of one-dimensional thinking, which he treats as an operationalization of technology as ideology. Arguing that even critical scholars, including he himself, are constrained by this one-dimensional thinking, he explicitly shifts his discussion from the level of political theory to that of pure philosophy, in an attempt to escape the 'overwhelming concreteness'[18] of technology as ideology. Once there, he identifies the possibility that a new kind of science, focused on the new kinds of empirically and episte-mologically complex technological problems that arise in late-industrial societies, might advance an immanent critique of the analytical (breaking into pieces) rationality of the project of industrialization, serving, in this way, no longer to oppress but to help liberate human society.

Marcuse's New Science

In the introduction to this chapter I proposed that the discourse on postnormal science can be understood as a manifestation of the kind of basic transformation in scientific thinking that Marcuse imagined might be possible.[19] To support that proposition, we next consider two key points raised by Marcuse, which can then be mapped onto the post-normal science discourse.

The relationship between human and non-human nature (man and nature) is a fundamental topic in philosophy and a constant point of discussion in environmental politics. It is also the first major dialectical relationship explored by Marcuse in both *Eros and Civilization* and *One-Dimensional Man*. In *One-Dimensional Man* he attributes the one-dimensional thinking of late-industrial societies to the historical stage of these societies, which have surpassed an earlier opposition between human and nature based on the human pursuit of freedom from material want, and which are characterised by a new opposition between humanity and technology. A detailed discussion of Marcuse's arguments concerning this initial opposition between 'man and nature,' as elaborated in *Eros and Civilization*, would take us far from the topic at hand. However, we can turn to Albert Camus, a contemporary of Marcuse's, for a concise summary of the theme.

In his text *The Rebel* (*l'Homme révolté*), Camus sets out to understand how the revolutionary moments of twentieth-century Europe ended with the establishment of the Third Reich in Germany and Stalinism in the Soviet Union.[20] To do this, he considers the act of rebellion in terms of the personal confrontation between master and slave, while exploring the series of revolutionary movements that marked (or are presumed to have marked) the march toward human liberation in Europe over the past three centuries. At the risk of oversimplification, his basic proposition can be understood as follows: when I am enslaved, and I reject the presumption that my master has a right to enslave me, I am affirming two propositions: (1) that we are at least equal, and (2) that it is not acceptable for one of two equals to enslave the other. When I act on this affirmation, *because* I am enslaved, I must subdue my master in order to gain my freedom. In so doing, I offend myself. I do precisely that for which I have condemned my master: I enslave him/her, if only temporarily. The contradiction arises in that I must oppress my master in order to gain my freedom.

The human/non-human nature relationship, as conceptualized by Marcuse in *Eros and Civilization* and *One-Dimensional Man*, can be understood within this simple framework developed by Camus. In the first instance, prior to the Industrial Revolution, humans lived at the pleasure of nature; we were slaves, nature our master. The development of culture and norms served mainly to better regulate human behaviour, so as to ensure that we could get along well with our master. Successful industrialization (the condition of late-industrial societies) can be understood as the moment of liberation described by Camus, where the rebel subdues his/her master. In this moment, the project of liberation is realized in the act of oppression and the human/nature dialectic changes its shape. Technology, which had served as liberator, now oppresses. The very material facts of late-industrial life – the washing machine, the television, the computer – that originally served the project of liberating humans from the oppressions of a masterful nature, have, in fulfilling their purpose, replaced her. Inasmuch as technology replaces nature as the context for daily life in these societies, it also takes over nature's place in the human understanding of one's place in the world; it becomes the relevant reality principle[21] through which the appropriateness of behaviours and aspirations is judged: by society as a whole and by the social individual.

Marcuse proposed that successful technological revolution has substantively transformed the world in which members of late-industrial societies live. The automobile, the television, the vending machine, the drive-through restaurant, and the washing machine have become the basic framework through which individuals interact with the world around them. Technology has become the environment; and the one-dimensional, linear, mechanical character of technology has become the reference for understanding reality: as such, an ideology.[22]

For Marcuse, technology as ideology is not a positive choice but a historical consequence arising from the success of a science and technology that have fulfilled their project. They have achieved conditions that make it *possible* to live 'a life without fear.'[23] Such societies can be understood to have historically surpassed humanity's basic struggle to be free from enslavement by nature. However, the means by which this liberation has been achieved determine the context in which life then proceeds.

The intractability of one-dimensional thinking is directly related to the role it has played in liberating humans from material insecurity. In late-industrial societies the material battle between humanity and nature, the daily struggle to secure the basic stuffs required for survival, has been won: 'It's a good way of life – much better than before – and as a good way of life, it militates against qualitative change.'[24] Plentiful production yields a well-fed worker who no longer has any conscious grounds for rebelling against the system of industrial economic production.

This is the first clear cross-reference between Marcuse's arguments and the postnormal science discourse: that there arises, in late-industrial societies, an empirical as opposed to an interpretive shift in the relations among humanity, technology, and nature. The second is related to his postulations about how this new form of 'passive oppression' might be overcome: through a reassertion of the relevance of the substantive universal to the project of improving the human condition.

Marcuse begins the philosophical stage of his argument through reference to the original role of negation and opposition in Western philosophy – the assigning of meaning: where 'dialectical thought understands the critical tension between "is" and "ought" first as an ontological condition, pertaining to the structure of Being itself,'[25] whereas 'under the rule of formal logic [the first step on the long road to scientific thought], the notion of the conflict between essence and appearance [, between ought and is,] is expendable if not meaningless.'[26] He argues that in late-industrial societies, where 'the struggle for existence and the exploitation of man and nature become ever more scientific and rational ... scientific-technical rationality and manipulation are welded together into new forms of social control.'[27]

Having established the relations among scientific thinking, technological rationality, and one-dimensional thinking as constituting a major form of domination in late-industrial societies, he goes on to maintain that one-dimensional thinking has infiltrated even philosophy: a position that he illustrates through a discussion of behavioural linguistics, the details of which need not concern us here. What is relevant here is Marcuse's means of escape: substantive universals, such as the State of England, which have individual representatives (such as the Parliament and the Queen) but no concrete individual manifestations. To reach this position, Marcuse makes an explicit shift in his style of argument: between Part I of *One-Dimensional Man*, which focuses on the social and political conditions of late-industrial societies caught in one-dimensional patterns of thinking and constrained by a style of 'overwhelming *concreteness*';[28] and Part II, where he shifts to the more abstract level of pure philosophy in an effort to escape from the confines of one-dimensional thinking, to imagine how a critique of technology as ideology might be developed.

He proposes that his contemporaries' exclusive focus on recording and reporting discourse, through a sort of positivist linguistics, leads to philosophy 'without any explanation.'[29] Wishing to advance arguments capable of analysis *and* explanation, he asks what is missing from the behavioural linguistics frame. His answer: substantive universals – because 'no particular entities whatsoever correspond to these universals,'[30] they cannot be described or discussed through exclusive reference to behaviours. Using the irrefutable reality of these universals as a wedge, Marcuse achieves a critical position by forcing onto the table complex concepts that reside outside the behaviouralist logic of his colleagues' one-dimensional thinking, such as Beauty, the State, the Good, or Justice.

He then takes up and develops Whitehead's distinction between Reason in art and Reason in society, where 'in Whitehead's definition of the function of Reason, the term "art" connotes the element of determinate negation.'[31] Here he sets out a dialectical relationship between science and art, where science is concerned with pieces and facts and art with values and wholes. This eventually enables him to develop a critical position with respect to the technological rationality that structures his own late-industrial context. Identifying the distinction between facts and values – the great achievement of modern science and the mother of industrialization – as the dialectical schism that eventually leads to one-dimensional thinking in late-industrial societies, he proposes that

> the quantification of nature, which led to its explication in terms of mathematical structures, separated reality from all inherent ends and, consequently, separated the true from the good, science from ethics ... If the Good and the Beautiful, Peace and Justice cannot be derived either from ontological or scientific-rational conditions, they cannot logically claim universal validity and realization ... [In a world where science is the only adjudicator of truth] the ideas [of The Good, Beautiful, Peace, Justice] become mere *ideals*, and their concrete, critical content evaporates into the ethical or metaphysical atmosphere.[32]

The two-dimensional rapport between facts and values is lost, and truth is confined to a one-dimensional world of facts.

Through this process, Marcuse eventually arrives at the assertion that 'at the advanced stage of industrial civilization, scientific rationality, translated into political power, appears to be the decisive factor in the development of historical alternatives.'[33] This, in turn, leads him to pose this question: 'Does this power tend toward its own negation – that is, toward the promotion of the "art of life?"'[34] With the posing of this question, Marcuse is led to suggest that liberation from one-dimensional thinking might come about through basic transformations occurring within pure science.

On this basis, Marcuse identifies one-dimensional, positivist scientific methods and their products as the historical force giving rise to the more general one-dimensional thinking dominating late-industrial societies: 'These central notions of modern science emerge, not as mere by-products of a pure science, but as pertaining to its inner conceptual structure ... In this project, universal quantifiability is a prerequisite for the *domination of nature*.'[35] Accordingly, he looks to science itself in his search for a way to achieve liberation from the oppression of this late-industrial ideology.

The Discourse on Postnormal Science

Having presented Marcuse's ideas concerning the liberating potential that might be found in a new, late-industrial approach to the work of science, we can now turn our attention to the discourse on postnormal science, which is concerned with precisely the kinds of problems that Marcuse associated with technology as ideology. It seems unlikely that Marcuse had an explicit structure in mind for the new science of which he spoke in 1964, since it was his view that it was positioned in his future, and therefore subject to the forces of history as much as he, his objects, and his own works would be. Though it is not precisely what Marcuse seems to have envisioned, postnormal science fits surprisingly well within his arguments.

In postnormal science situations, decision stakes are high and/or the science is uncertain (see Figure 1). The lines between science and politics and between facts and values have become blurred. However, as with technology as ideology, this blurring of facts and values is understood to be phenomenological rather than normative, arising with the arrival of particular types of complex, scientifically entailed, policy-related problems peculiar to late-industrial societies.[36] Examples of postnormal science problems include the development of information about and responses to the origins and impacts of anthropogenic climate change; the management of megacontamination sites; and the regulation of the production and use of nanotechnologies and genetically modified organisms.

In these complex policy situations, sound science is both essential to policy making and irredeemably uncertain in its prognostications. Though they enjoy substantial political influence, scientists have lost their traditional authority to speak truth to power, because they cannot, in good conscience, offer definitive truth statements on these subjects.[37] Funtowicz and Ravetz maintain that to address this empirical problem,

Figure 1: Postnormal Science in Perspective

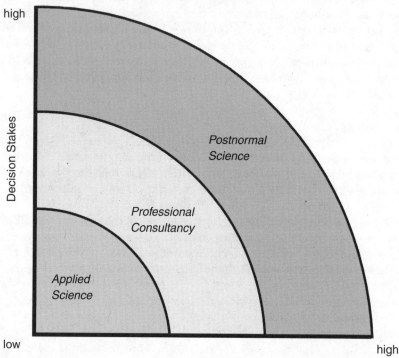

Source: Funtowicz and Ravetz (1991, 1993); included here with the permission
of the authors.

there is a need for a new social contract between science and society,
one that democratizes the work of scientific knowledge production.[38]

    To appreciate the thinking behind the concept of postnormal science,
one must first come to grips with the concept of 'normal science,' which
was introduced by Thomas Kuhn in 1962. Kuhn (1970[1962]) employs
the term 'normal science' in his argument that scientific knowledge
progresses through socially constructed paradigm shifts, from normal
science (the rules are agreed; science solves puzzles), to revolutionary
science (important rules are called into question), to a new normal science (new rules are accepted; science returns to solving puzzles; there
is a new paradigm).[39] A clear illustration of Kuhn's theory in practice is

the Copernican Revolution, where Copernicus' idea of a solar system was largely ignored (not in the rules); then Galileo was deemed a heretic (rules called into question); and today the theory of the solar system is taken as an obvious and foundational part of scientific knowledge (new rules).

In presenting the concept of postnormal science, Funtowicz and Ravetz propose that, when human societies confront politically charged *and/or* profoundly complex, scientifically involved policy questions, the social community of concerned scientific *and* political actors faces a Kuhnian revolution of exceptional character.[40] Under 'normal' conditions, scientific peer review can be understood as a routine assessment of the accuracy of a piece of scientific work; policy debates concerning how to apply scientific information are a separate affair. However, under postnormal conditions, value-oriented social issues intrude into the technical domain of science proper, undermining the presumption that conventional peer review is sufficient for judging the technical quality of a piece of scientific work. Moving from the bottom left to the top right of Figure 1, a progression can be observed: from normal science situations, where technical quality can be judged using conventional peer review methods; to postnormal science situations, where conventional peer review, which is concerned only with criteria of adequacy, is ill equipped to moderate complex debates that mix contentions regarding the technical *and* the social quality of a piece of scientific work.[41]

In these situations we find grounds for interpreting a Kuhnian revolution of a different order, because the revolutionary thesis of postnormal science does not just suggest revision of one or another rule; It advances the heretical assertion that under certain conditions, 'normal' puzzle-solving science (regardless of the rules) is not a scientific approach, because sometimes the puzzle cannot be solved: 'we have seen the man behind the curtain and objectivist realism is now compromised.'[42] The choice to continue relying on puzzle-solving science in such situations is unavoidably, if not consciously, politically inflected,[43] and a new picture of the social role of scientific knowledge production is needed, *in order to correctly understand and effectively engage with the empirical problems at hand.*[44]

The new picture proposed by Funtowicz and Ravetz is one in which scientific quality is judged by an extended peer community, where what is 'extended' is the community of individuals with a role to play in describing and deciding what does or does not constitute a scientific 'fact.'[45] That is to say, the community of individuals with the authority to judge a piece of scientific work based on adequacy criteria (is it right?) is extended to include individuals who are normally responsible for making quality judgments based on value criteria (is it useful?). The quality of scientific insights is no longer determined solely by a scientific peer community but by an extended peer community, including scientists from other disciplines and laypeople from outside scientific society. Under such conditions, descriptions of scientific problems and adjudications regarding the quality of assessments are 'operationalized through plurality of competencies, [plurality of] perspective and [plurality of] commitments.'[46] The higher aim of science is no longer the simple pursuit of truth but rather the complex pursuit of quality knowledge production, where quality is defined as fitness for a specified purpose.[47]

The production of quality scientific knowledge under postnormal science conditions requires systematic and procedural reference to the purpose for which the knowledge is being produced. Since the designation of purpose is the task not of science but of society,[48] this needs to be supported through some kind of structured combination of the activities of scientific knowledge production and those of political discourse. In their foundation text on the topic,[49] Funtowicz and Ravetz refer to this as the democratizing of expertise, and meeting that challenge can be understood as the main task standing before individuals and communities concerned with developing postnormal science methods and methodologies.

Situations of postnormal science can be understood as arising in part because science has reached its own limits[50] and in part because late-industrial societies place new demands on science.[51] In both respects, the emergence of postnormal science can be understood as a historically positioned phenomenon that is relevant for late-industrial human understanding of human/nature relations. From the scientific perspective, physical observation of nature in late-industrial societies has reached to the minutest of details; as a consequence, fundamental questions of fact that remain in debate cannot be definitively resolved. From the social perspective, late-industrial human societies are no longer focused on straightforward survival problems, such as averting hunger and securing shelter, but rather on value-laden, judgment-based quality-of-life problems, such as determining acceptable levels of pollution and judging the safety of processed foods.[52]

Having considered the conditions that give rise to the postnormal science discourse, we can now turn our attention to the strategies that have been developed for responding to them. When problems fall within the frame of postnormal science, where decision stakes and/or epistemological uncertainties are high, there are no longer any merely technical or purely scientific matters: 'The traditional fact/value distinction has not merely been inverted; in post-normal science the two categories cannot be realistically separated.'[53] In practice, a community of scientists and policy makers concerned with developing strategies for achieving sustainable development is confronted with 'the impossibility to define in absolute terms the optimal way to sustainability.'[54] This is for two reasons: first, because the aim of identifying what constitutes optimal sustainability is scientifically problematic; and second, because sustainability is a politically charged problem. Addressing such issues requires some effective combination of these two modes of problem solving – a combination that nonetheless retains the fundamental capacities of both.

Under postnormal science conditions, a new modality of science is operating and new modes of scientific method and standards of quality are required. A wide range of work of varying quality has been presented under the rubric of postnormal science; that said, the core methods – which include NUSAP,[55] GLUE,[56] multiscale and participatory approaches to integrated assessment,[57] and sensitivity analysis[58] – all concern themselves first and foremost with how to address scientific problems. In this respect, postnormal science is precisely the kind of 'pure science' to which Marcuse was referring in 1964. Specifically, he predicted that the gates out of the prison of one-dimensional thinking might open with the emergence of some new form of pure science – a form that rejects universal quantifiability on scientific grounds and that calls for a focus on (1) substantive universals and (2) the dialectical rapport between facts and values. This is precisely what postnormal science does, and it does so specifically with respect to the kinds of issues – cloning, anthropogenic climate change, nanotechnologies – that Marcuse imagined would be the focus of concern for such a new science. Here the fit is better than good; it seems plausible (though further analysis is certainly required) that the concept of postnormal science occupies precisely the historical position that Marcuse anticipated.

Habermas's 1971 Critique of Marcuse's *One-Dimensional Man*

I have argued that the postnormal science method of extended peer review, or the democratizing of expertise, may offer a route out of the situation of passive oppression characterized by one-dimensional thinking. However, it is important to keep in mind that it is not always democratically motivated individuals who create extended peer communities. For certain types of environmental issues, such as managing the sustainable use of ocean fisheries or tracing the pattern of the nuclear fallout from the Chernobyl disaster, the involvement of politics in defining the principles guiding scientific investigation is *de facto* and not at all democratic.[59] This means that *un*democratic extended peer review processes are also possible. Indeed, it would seem that it is these processes, as opposed to the ones typically discussed in the postnormal science discourse, that Marcuse anticipated. If the liberating potential of postnormal science is to be fulfilled, the means by which expertise is democratized cannot be taken for granted.

But this creates an awkward situation, because regardless of whether they are viewed as a *fait accompli* or good scientific method, extended peer review processes are discussed almost entirely with reference to the concept of deliberative democracy. Specifically, Habermasian communicative rationality[60] – mainly as expounded by Dryzek[61] – has been taken up by both scientists and policy makers as a foundation context for the design of extended peer review processes and the practice of participatory science.[62] This is awkward here, because Habermas has aggressively critiqued Marcuse regarding precisely those points in his argument upon which I drew earlier.[63] If an understanding of the historical position of postnormal science in late-industrial societies is to be informed by ideas drawn from Marcuse, while employing tools provided by Habermas to ensure democratic accountability, then it must be demonstrated that Habermas was wrong to reject Marcuse's arguments; otherwise, a new interpretation of Marcuse's position – one that does not fall victim to Habermas's critique – must be developed.

Returning to Habermas's critique, it can be seen that there is at least one fundamental concept in Marcuse's position with which he does not engage – that of the epistemological influence of collective social understanding. Surprisingly, because he would presumably have had access to the text, and more so because he does reference Marcuse's later work concerning Freud, there is no reference in Habermas's 1971 critique to *Eros and Civilization*. When we read Habermas with this in mind, remembering that in a much later work he does address the question of cultural identity,[64] it is possible to find grounds for reconciliation between the two thinkers. However, this requires that we first briefly consider what it means to speak of the epistemological influence of collective social understanding.

In discussions of environmental political philosophy, relations between humans and the naturally occurring worlds we inhabit (including our own relations to our own bodies and to one another) must be
formally engaged not only epistemologically and existentially but also
ontologically. That is to say, how the epistemological and existential
questions of environmental politics are formulated within a society
becomes ontologically important for understanding how relations between human and non-human nature are conceptualized and operationalized in the daily practice of human societies. Under the conditions
that Marcuse described as one-dimensional thinking, where technology has become an ideology, the conquest of nature is no longer just
a project for late-industrial societies; indeed, it has become the main
existential context with which these societies must contend. Ensuring
appropriate responses to an operating context where conquering nature is the main social priority has become the main task of culture in
these societies. Coping with the impacts of this project-turned-phenom-
enon can be understood as the main concern for environmental politics
and for postnormal science; it is also a key issue for both Marcuse and
Habermas. On that basis, we can begin now to consider how their respective contributions, which have been related to postnormal science,
might be reconciled with each other.

First, concerning facts and values and looking to the thinking that
informed his critique of Marcuse, Habermas is clearly against their conflation: 'it seems advisable not to confuse decisions about the choice of
norms [values], that is, about moral or political problems, with problems of the empirical sciences [facts].'[65] However, the possibility that
this conflation is phenomenological, as opposed to normative, is never
addressed. While careful to reject the radical positivist position that
values are not relevant for steering science, he nonetheless proposes
that 'the unity of theoretical and practical reason that does not hold for
scientific theories themselves is preserved [also for philosophy].'[66] For
Habermas, while values and facts each have their place in philosophy
and in science, philosophy remains the rightful home of values and
science the rightful home of facts. Here Habermas clearly contradicts a
fundamental presumption underlying both the postnormal science discourse and Marcuse's arguments concerning one-dimensional thinking: that under certain conditions, the distinction between facts and
values is no longer ontologically plausible.

Though Habermas does systematically discuss the rapport between
social organization and technological development, he maintains
firmly that there is a fundamental distinction between what is techno-

logically feasible and what a society wills or desires to accomplish. In addition, he argues that there is a moral superiority to values, which makes them the right, just, and appropriate driver in this collaboration. For him, ecological problems associated with technological develop-ment, such as those elaborated in Carson's *Silent Spring*,[67] are problems of poorly organized political institutions that have failed to 'elaborate this dialectic [of *potential and will*] with political consciousness,' leav-ing society unable to 'succeed in directing the mediation of technical progress.'[68]

His proposed solution is entirely in keeping with this framing: 'The irrationality of domination, which today has become a collective peril to life, could be mastered only by the development of a political decision-making process tied to the principle of general discussion free from domination.'[69] The argument seems to be that, by enclosing the value-laden issues surrounding technological development within an expanded deliberative democratic political discourse, room can be made for the new (late-industrial) problem of how to direct and medi-ate technical progress. There is, as I pointed out earlier, no room for the prospect that the conflation of facts and values – which concerned Marcuse and which continues to concern postnormal science – could be empirical as opposed to definitional.

In arguing that causal authority *must* rest within the political (values) sphere, Habermas demonstrates his distance from Marcuse. Though sharing a common topic of concern – how late-industrial societies might regain control of the technological systems they have created – Haber-mas opposes Marcuse's fundamental proposition that technological rationality has become the causal authority in these societies. However, the one-dimensional thinking that Marcuse describes is, by definition, a condition outside of which one cannot step. It infiltrates purpose set-ting and will formation, becoming final causal.[70]

In rejecting technological rationality as antithetical to freedom and as largely responsible for environmental destruction, Habermas and Marcuse are in agreement. However, Habermas seeks to prescribe how a society might control and redirect the progression of technological mastery of nature; whereas for Marcuse, in keeping with the dialectical approach of critical theory, the only way around is through. Since the project of mastery over nature is, for him, bound up with the project of social organization of industrial human society, the replacement of nature by technology in late-industrial societies changes the relation-ship of these societies not only to nature and to technology but also to themselves and, more important, to their self-understanding. Since this understanding of the place of humans in the world is presumed to be shaped by technology as ideology, the project of technological development has ostensibly become its own master. Hence Marcuse's suggestion that if there is a way to gain purchase on this new structure of social organization – a structure that perpetuates a generalized one-dimensional thinking – it is likely to come from within pure scientific theory: 'Consequently, what is at stake is the redefinition of values in *technical terms*, as elements in the technological process. The new ends, as technical ends, would then operate in the project and in the construction of the machinery, and not only in its utilisation. Moreover, the new ends might assert themselves even in the construction of scientific hypothesises – in pure scientific theory.'[71]

That Habermas originally rejected the above argument is beyond doubt: 'Our only hope for the rationalization of the power structure lies in conditions that favour political power for thought developing through dialogue. The redeeming power of reflection cannot be supplanted by the extension of technically exploitable knowledge.'[72] But this critique misses the epistemological complexity of the problem that Marcuse is attempting to address. The idea that Marcuse is advocating – as opposed to observing or predicting – this extension is easily dismissed when his position is read with an eye on his preceding arguments concerning the interplay between technology and human self-understanding (both individual and social) – arguments that were first developed in *Eros and Civilization* and reaffirmed in *An Essay on Liberation*.

The extension to which Habermas is referring is, for Marcuse, a *fait accompli* that arose with the completion of the project of industrialization. Marcuse does not entertain the presence of choice in the way that Habermas would seem to demand; nonetheless, it seems clear that for Marcuse, subjecting this extension to democratic accountability is absolutely essential if its embodiment in a new science is to be liberating as opposed to oppressive.[73] In this respect, it can be expected that Marcuse would have been quite in favour of applying democratic theory to help design accountable and extended peer review processes.

While postnormal science is often presented as one among a range of new science/policy interface or participatory science methods, it is not merely a method for conducting policy-oriented science. First and foremost, it is an empirical observation and an attempt to theorize and cope with a technical issue:[74] there are some scientific problems where complexities inherent in the object of investigation (river basin system management) and/or inescapable political sensitivities (megacontaminated sites) render traditional methods of scientific knowledge production, including conventional peer review, insufficient to requirements. If Habermas can accept the empirical character of this extension, then the choice becomes not one of *whether* but of *how* to democratize expertise, and his first clash with Marcuse – at least as it pertains to postnormal science – is resolved.

However, the difficulties do not end there. In critiquing Marcuse, Habermas goes on to argue:

> What Marcuse conceives of as world-historically new [is that] the forces of production appear to enter a new constellation with the relations of production. Now they no longer function as the basis of a critique of prevailing legitimations in the interest of political enlightenment, but become instead the basis of legitimation.[75]

Tightly focused on this point, he continues:

> But if this is the case, must not the rationality embodied in systems of purposive-rational action be understood as specifically limited? Must not the rationality of science and technology, instead of being reducible to unvarying rules of logic and method have absorbed a substantive, historically derived, and therefore transitory a priori structure? Marcuse answers in the affirmative: 'The principles of modern science were *a priori* structured in such a way that they could serve as conceptual instruments for a universe of self-propelling, productive control; theoretical operationalism came to correspond to practical operationalism. The scientific method which led to the ever-more-effective domination of nature thus came to provide the pure concepts as well as the instrumentalities for the ever-more-effective domination of man by man through the domination of nature.'[76]

Habermas' summary of Marcuse's arguments is thorough, and the point of argument that he rejects is clearly the following one:

> Under this aspect [that science itself has rendered it possible to make final causes the proper domain of science], 'neutral' scientific method and technology become the science and technology of a historical phase which is being surpassed by its own achievements – which has reached its determinate negation.[77]

His critique?

> An Alternative Science would have to include the definition of a New
> Technology ... a sobering consideration because technology, if based at all
> on a project, can only be traced back to a 'project' of the human *species as a
> whole*, and not to one that could be historically surpassed.[78]

Arguing that technology is a *projection of human purposive-rational action* onto the plane of technical instruments, involving the extension of motor, sensory, and eventually cognitive apparatuses, Habermas proceeds to put forward the case that, because technological developments derive from human purposive-rational action, technological development cannot be surpassed 'as long as the organisation of human nature does not change and as long therefore as we have to achieve self-preservation through social labour and with the aid of means that substitute for work.'[79] It is difficult to read this as anything less than an outright rejection of Marcuse's starting premise: that in late-industrial societies an earlier human/non-human nature dialectical relationship of master and slave has been rendered obsolete, because in such societies, the task of pacifying nature has been accomplished.

Here again, the absence in Habermas's critique of any reference to *Eros and Civilization* – in which Marcuse lays out his case for this position – helps explain how and why the two thinkers seem to differ so greatly on this point. A central premise underlying all the arguments in *One-Dimensional Man* is that the organized self-understanding of human societies – which for Marcuse is always both a project of humanity and a condition of human existence – is also a force in history. If technological development is understood as a historical project – which is a point upon which the two seem to agree – then for Marcuse, technological rationality is merely the most recent in a series of reality principles, one conceived of by industrial human society in order to structure its understanding of and engagement with its environment.

If one accepts Marcuse's premise, then one must contend with his assertion that 'this development confronts science with the unpleasant task of becoming *politica* – of recognizing scientific consciousness as political consciousness, and the scientific enterprise as political enterprise.'[80] So long as science and politics remain clearly distinguished from each other, then, while the historical status of the laws of science is permissible (e.g., the progression of the Copernican Revolution described above), the historical status of the logic of science is not.[81] Yet it is precisely the logic – as opposed to the laws – that is called into question under postnormal science conditions, and it is precisely a change in the logic of science – as Habermas rightly points out – that Marcuse imagines may give rise to a liberating change of thinking in late-industrial societies.

On the basis of the preceding argument, it seems difficult to justify developing methods for operating in postnormal science situations based upon Habermas's political theories. However, some recent arguments by Habermas, concerning the relationship between technology and politics, seem to open the way for rapprochement on this point as well, precisely where Marcuse's arguments overlap with the postnormal science discourse.[82]

What Habermas originally refused to accept in Marcuse's argument was the idea that the logic of science could be historically embedded, which is precisely the proposition advanced in the postnormal science discourse: under certain conditions – specifically those in which 'facts are uncertain, values in dispute, stakes high and decisions urgent'[83] – the traditional ontological and methodological foundations of normal (puzzle-solving) science are called into question.[84] However, quite recently Habermas has proposed that the relationship between technology and values in the late-industrial society of the twenty-first-century Europe is no longer one of dialectical rapport but of conflation and ambiguity. He presents his case through a discussion of preimplantation genetic diagnosis (PGD): a procedure, made possible by reproductive medical technologies, in which human embryos are tested for lethal and life-devastating genetic diseases before implantation in a woman's womb. Habermas argues that the technological advances that make PGD possible confront 'the ethical self-understanding of *humanity as a whole*'[85] with ethical issues 'of *an altogether different kind*,'[86] where the 'boundary between persons and things' is obliterated:[87] precisely the conflation discussed by Marcuse when he speaks of technology as ideology subordinating humans to the logic of things!

This more recent position from Habermas, posed in the context of a post-9/11 world, can be understood as endorsing a form of communicative rationality that seeks to remain open to cooperation among actors with incommensurable epistemological positions, where what is an obvious fact for one participant may be incomprehensible for another: 'in its willingness to learn … democratic common sense remains osmotically open to *both* sides, science and religion, without relinquishing its independence,'[88] 'not singular; it describes the mental state of a *many-voiced* public.'[89]

Where he is reconciled with Marcuse, acknowledging that the project of the human species as a whole has been historically surpassed as a consequence of technological developments such as PGD,[90] Habermas is also reconciled with postnormal science, acknowledging that a plurality of incommensurable perspectives can nonetheless engage in democratically legitimate debate. This more recent, epistemologically complex position is reconcilable with both Marcuse and postnormal science; it also speaks directly to issues that Dryzek tried to address in his communicative ethics paper of 1990.[91] This is significant for the current discussion, for Dryzek's early work on ecology and democracy tends to provide the theoretical basis for applying communicative rationality within the discourse on postnormal science methodology.[92]

Dryzek's position can be understood as an attempt to provide a theoretical basis for including the interests of the environment in political discourse. He sought to do this by justifying the inclusion of natural phenomena as deliberants in the discursive setting of communicative rationality. This is, of course, highly problematic operationally: direct representation *by* these phenomena is very difficult to imagine, particularly in the context of a discursive ethic. But in the context of democratized extended peer review, it becomes plausible to speak about epistemological representations of the functional requirements of environmental phenomena.[93] Though bringing a river basin into the political forum 'in person,' as an ethically open and discursive communicant, is not possible, bringing best available but uncertain scientific knowledge of river basins to a discursive democratic forum, where it can be collectively modified and revised, *is* possible – at least in the context of extended peer review.

When science is viewed as one of many ways of understanding human/non-human nature relationships, there is scope for meeting Habermas's aspiration to bring technological rationality and human relations with environments under the control and direction of democracy. However, scope is a far way from inevitability, and here it is important to recall both Marcuse's caveats and some accusations of tendencies toward authoritarianism that have been levelled against him.[94]

Under postnormal science conditions, science is simply unable to make the kinds of truth claims that are expected of it in late-industrial societies. The empirical reality of fact/value ambiguity requires a reconceptualizing of the relationship between science and politics. However, there is no guarantee that this reconceptualization will be democratic. Quite to the contrary, there is considerable evidence that, at least in the

first instance, it will not.[95] The question of how such undemocratic development can be avoided is beyond the scope of this chapter. However,
we can at least put to rest the idea that this is something Marcuse would
have advocated. Looking at the 1966 Political Preface to *Eros and Civilization*, it is clear that he envisioned a new science that would serve not
as a political end, but rather as a beginning: 'Today, the organized refusal to cooperate of the scientists, mathematicians, technicians, industrial
psychologists, and public opinion pollsters may well accomplish what
a strike, even a large-scale strike, can no longer accomplish but once
accomplished, namely, the beginning of the reversal, the preparation of
the ground for political action.'[96] His point is not that scientists should
rule as a technocratic elite but that 'the chain of exploitation must break
at its strongest link.'[97] And lest there be lingering doubt as to where
Marcuse ends up on this point, we can turn to his own final word. In the
closing chapter of *An Essay on Liberation* he concerns himself with the
question of how liberation from one-dimensional thinking, and from
the tangible oppression it causes in a world dominated by late-industrial societies, can be achieved. In the closing words of that chapter, he
wonders: If this could indeed happen, what might replace the passive
oppression of late-industrialization? And he poses a question, to which
he provides a response: 'What are the people of a free society going to
do? The answer which, I believe, strikes at the heart of the matter was
given by a young black girl. She said: for the first time in our life, we
shall be free to think about what we are going to do.'[98]

Conclusions

The arguments presented in this chapter have been developed in three
stages: *first*, the character of Marcuse's new science was discussed;
second, the postnormal science discourse was introduced and links
to Marcuse's new science were highlighted. It was argued that the
fundamental, historically embedded politicization of basic scientific
problems, the conflation of facts and values, and the importance of irreducible substantive universals can all be linked with Marcuse's propositions concerning a new modality of science and with the postnormal
science discourse.

On this basis, it has been posited that development of the postnormal science discourse, over the past twenty years, provides empirical
corroboration for Marcuse's predictions. Having established a link between Marcuse's new modality of science and the postnormal science
discourse, the *third* stage of this paper dedicated itself to addressing

what this could mean in practice. Here, a potentially problematic set of contradictions was identified between Habermas's critique of Marcuse's proposition that the logic – as opposed to the instrumental details – of science and technology are historically positioned and appeals made to Habermas's arguments concerning deliberative democracy and a discursive ethic, within the course of designing postnormal science methods. Through critique of Habermas's critique of Marcuse, and through reference to more recent arguments by Habermas,[99] it has been argued that where Habermas is reconciled with Marcuse, he is also reconciled with postnormal science. Indeed, Habermas's original position – that there is and must remain a clear line between facts and norms, even if the task of discourse is to mediate and manage the boundary between them – is no longer one that even he stands fully behind.

Finally, concerns that Marcuse was advocating an undemocratic new science were addressed by returning to his own words on the question, which clearly demonstrate his presumption that no liberation is possible without democratic freedom. With Habermas and Marcuse reconciled on those points where they are brought together within the postnormal science discourse, it has been argued not only that discourse ethics and deliberative democracy are valid political theory frames for developing postnormal science methodology, but also that there is strong consistency between such an approach and an interpretation of postnormal science as a manifestation of Marcuse's new modality of science.

In this chapter we have only touched the surface of this picture. However, it seems fair to surmise that for scholars returning to Marcuse's work, there remains much to be learned for both environmental politics and postnormal science. On the one hand, consideration of Marcuse's arguments and their implications in a twenty-first-century context can strengthen the historical and philosophical bases of the postnormal science discourse. On the other, supporting the work of designing democratically legitimate extended peer review processes provides theorists of environmental politics with a new, concrete, practical problem from which they can, if they wish, work to develop new theory that follows the progress of history.

NOTES

1 The work presented here is part of the EU Research Project ALIVE: Accountability and Legitimacy in Governance Institutions That Support Viable Environments (EIF 024688). The basic argument was developed

under the guidance of John Barry at Queen's University of Belfast and has benefited enormously from discussions with Jerry Ravetz and Silvio Funtowicz and from discussion during the symposium 'Critical Ecologies: The Frankfurt School and Environmental Politics in the 21st Century.' I am indebted to Timothy Luke, Andrew Biro, Ariel Salleh, and Nancy Ratey for extremely helpful written comments and to Christoph Görg for his collaborations on the ALIVE research project, which have lent a great deal to my understanding of the topics addressed here. Errors, omissions and so forth remain, of course, solely my own responsibility.

2   Herbert Marcuse, *Eros and Civilization* (London: Abacus, 1969[1955]).
3   Marcuse, *One-Dimensional Man: Studies in the Ideology of Advanced Industrial Society*, 2nd ed. (London: Routledge, 1991[1964]).
4   Donna J. Haraway, *Simians, Cyborgs, and Women: The Reinvention of Nature* (London: Free Association, 1991).
5   Marcuse, *One-Dimensional Man*, 254.
6   Marcuse, *An Essay on Liberation* (London: Penguin, 1969), 5.
7   The concept of postnormal science is elaborated upon below. It is concerned with the relationship between scientific expertise on the one hand and, on the other, policy concerning complex, generally technology- and environment-related problems arising in late-industrial societies. The term and associated discourse were presented by Funtowicz and Ravetz in the early 1990s; see S.O. Funtowicz and J.R. Ravetz, *Uncertainty and Quality in Science for Policy* (Dordrechts: Kluwer, 1990); and 'A New Scientific Methodology for Global Environmental Issues,' in *Ecological Economics: The Science and Management of Sustainability*, ed. Robert Costanza (New York: Columbia University Press, 1991).
8   Marcuse, *One-Dimensional Man*, 237.
9   Ibid., 236; Marcuse, *Eros and Civilization*, 11–19; *Essay on Liberation*.
10   Funtowicz and Ravetz, *Uncertainty and Quality*, 65–6, emphasis in original.
11   Usage here of the terms 'soft facts' and 'hard values' is drawn from Funtowicz and Ravetz, 'A New Scientific Methodology.'
12   Jürgen Habermas, *Toward a Rational Society: Student Protest, Science, and Politics* (London: Heinemann Educational, 1971).
13   Marcuse, *Essay on Liberation*, 70.
14   Jürgen Habermas, *The Theory of Communicative Action*, vol. 1, *Reason and the Rationalization of Society* (London: Heinemann, 1984); *The Theory of Communicative Action*, vol. 2, *Lifeworld and System* (Cambridge: Polity, 1987); and *Between Facts and Norms: Contributions to a Discourse Theory of Law and Democracy* (Cambridge: Polity, 1996). See, for example, S.U. O'Hara, 'Discursive Ethics in Ecosystem Valuation and Environmental Policy,'

Ecological Economics 16 (1996); B. De Marchi et al., 'Combining Participative and Institutional Approaches with Multicriteria Evaluation: An Empirical Study for Water Issues in Triona, Sicily,' *Ecological Economics* 34 (1996); and Giuseppe Munda, 'Social Multi-Criteria Evaluation: Methodological Foundations and Operational Consequences,' *European Journal of Operational Research* 158 (2004).

15 Marcuse, *Essay on Liberation*, 70.

16 Jürgen Habermas, *The Future of Human Nature* (Oxford: Polity, 2003). I am greatly indebted to Fred Luks for bringing this text to my attention.

17 Readers wishing to read more about Marcuse's overall arguments concerning technology and the role of science in history will find detailed discussion in C. Fred Alford, *Science and the Revenge of Nature: Marcuse and Habermas* (Gainesville: University Presses of Florida, 1985); John Bokina and Timothy J. Lukes, eds., *Marcuse: From the New Left to the Next Left* (Lawrence: University Press of Kansas, 1994); and John Abromeit and W. Mark Cobb, eds., *Herbert Marcuse: A Critical Reader* (London: Routledge, 2004).

18 Marcuse, *One-Dimensional Man*, 98.

19 For additional background arguments relating to this proposition, see Katharine N. Farrell, 'The Politics of Science and Sustainable Development: Marcuse's New Science in the 21st Century,' *Capitalism, Nature, Socialism* 19, no. 4 (2008): 68–83.

20 Albert Camus, *The Rebel* (London: Hamish Hamilton, 1953[1951]). This line of inquiry has, of course, also occupied the attention of many Frankfurt School theorists.

21 Marcuse, *Eros and Civilization*, 35–54; *Essay on Liberation*.

22 Here it is important to distinguish Marcuse's position from Haraway's glorification of cyborgism, which he would probably have classified as a form of technological fetishism.

23 Marcuse, *One-Dimensional Man*, 254.

24 Ibid., 14. It should be noted that one might present problems such as anthropogenic climate change as evidence that the battle against nature has not been won. However, these phenomena are not part of 'daily life': for the individual, if not for the species, the old battle of daily survival is, in late-industrial societies, over.

25 Ibid., 137.

26 Ibid., 141.

27 Ibid., 149.

28 Ibid., 98; emphasis in original.

29 Ibid., 183.

30 Ibid., 209.

31 Ibid., 233; A.N. Whitehead, *The Function of Reason* (Boston: Beacon, 1959).
32 Marcuse, *One-Dimensional Man*, 150–1.
33 Ibid., 235.
34 Ibid.
35 Ibid., 168, emphasis in original.
36 Katharine N. Farrell, *Making Good Decisions Well: A Theory of Collective Ecological Management* (Aachen: Shaker, 2009).
37 The recent chaos in European air travel, associated with an eruption of Iceland's Eyjafjallajökull volcano – where inredeemably uncertain, weather-related computer models served initially to justify grounding most European air traffic but were eventually more or less ignored – illustrates the impotence of conventional scientific assessments when faced with complex late-industrial problems.
38 Funtowicz and Ravetz, *Uncertainty and Quality*; Jerome R. Ravetz, *The Merger of Knowledge with Power: Essays in Critical Science* (London: Mansell, 1990).
39 Thomas S. Kuhn, *The Structure of Scientific Revolutions*, 2nd ed. (London: University of Chicago Press, 1970[1962]).
40 Funtowicz and Ravetz, 'A New Scientific Methodology'; 'The Good, the True, and the Post-Modern,' *Futures* 24, no. 10 (1992); 'Science for the Post-Normal Age,' *Futures* 25, no. 7 (1993).
41 Katharine N. Farrell, 'Snow White and the Wicked Problems of the West: A Look at the Lines between Empirical Description and Normative Prescription,' *Science, Technology, and Human Values* (2010), in press. For an elaboration of the foundational concepts giving rise to this position, see Jerome R. Ravetz, *Scientific Knowledge and Its Social Problems* (Oxford: Clarendon, 1971), 157–62.
42 T.F.H. Allen et al., 'Dragnet Ecology – "Just the Facts, Ma'am": The Privilege of Science in a Postmodern World,' *BioScience* 51, no. 6 (2001): 476.
43 I am indebted to Andrew Biro for suggesting the term 'inflected.'
44 Funtowicz and Ravetz, 'A New Scientific Methodology,' 144; Fred Luks, 'The Rhetorics of Ecological Economics,' *Ecological Economics* 26 (1998); Fred Luks, 'Post-Normal Science and the Rhetoric of Inquiry: Deconstructing Normal Science?' *Futures* 31 (1999).
45 Funtowicz and Ravetz, *Uncertainty and Quality*; Silvio O. Funtowicz and Jerome R. Ravetz, 'The Worth of a Songbird: Ecological Economics as a Post-Normal Science,' *Ecological Economics* 10 (1994).
46 Funtowicz and Ravetz, 'The Worth of a Songbird,' 204–5. The concept of extended peer review can be traced back to Ravetz's 1971 discussion of 'facts and their evolution,' in which he describes 'extended facts' and the

The Politics of Science 101

extended communities of individuals interested in and contributing to the reification of those facts. See 'Snow White and the Wicked Problems of the West' for a detailed presentation of this argument. It can also be related to Latour's recent discussion of the politics of nature, the formulation of facts, and the identification of matters of concern; Bruno Latour, *Politics of Nature: How to Bring Science into Democracy* (Cambridge, MA: Harvard University Press, 2005). For helpful background on the concepts that Latour applies in his 2005 text, see Bruno Latour and Steve Woolgar, *Laboratory Life: The Social Construction of Scientific Facts* (London: Sage, 1979).

47 Funtowicz and Ravetz, *Uncertainty and Quality;* 'The Good, the True, and the Post-Modern'; 'The Worth of a Songbird'; 'Emergent Complex Systems,' *Futures* 26, no. 6 (1994); 'The Poetry of Thermodynamics,' *Futures* 29, no. 9 (1997); Silvio Funtowicz and Martin O'Connor, 'The Passage from Entropy to Thermodynamic Indeterminacy: A Social and Science Epistemology for Sustainability,' in *Bioeconomics and Sustainability: Essays in Honor of Nicholas Georgescu-Roegen*, ed. Kozo Mayumi and John Gowdy (Cheltenham: Edward Elgar, 1999).

48 Ravetz, *Scientific Knowledge*, 157–62; Stephen Jay Gould, *The Hedgehog, the Fox, and the Magister's Pox* (London: Jonathan Cape, 2003), 140, 259.

49 Funtowicz and Ravetz, *Uncertainty and Quality*, 210.

50 T.F.H. Allen et al., 'Dragnet Ecology'; Mario Giampietro, 'Sustainability and Technological Development in Agriculture: A Critical Appraisal of Genetic Engineering,' *Bioscience* 44 (1994); *Multi-Scale Integrated Assessment of Agroecosystems* (London: CRC, 2004).

51 L. Pellizzoni, 'Uncertainty and Participatory Democracy,' *Environmental Values* 12 (2003); Ravetz, *The Merger of Knowledge with Power*.

52 There are, of course, strong similarities between this description of post-normal science conditions and Beck's description of subpolitics: Ulrich Beck, *Risk Society: Towards a New Modernity* (London: Sage, 1992). Indeed, it seems entirely plausible to describe postnormal science as a subpolitical realm. However, whereas Beck is looking from a social theory perspective, the aim here is to focus on how challenges to scientific methods have contributed to the formulation of the postnormal science concept and related practices, since it is in this respect that postnormal science can be directly related to Marcuse's work.

53 Funtowicz and Ravetz, 'Science for the Post-Normal Age,' 751.

54 Giampietro, *Multi-Scale Integrated Assessment of Agroecosystems*, 77.

55 NUSAP stands for *numeral, unit, spread, assessment, pedigree.* It is a sort of scientific analysis disclosure procedure. Funtowicz and Ravetz developed it in *Uncertainty and Quality* as a tool for providing scientific information to

policy makers in a way that highlights not only the results of the scientific assessment but also the imprecisions and limitations inherent in the data and procedures of analysis employed. It can be understood as a tool for disclosing to an audience of non-scientists the value judgments and choices associated with the creation of scientific facts. For more information, see http://www.nusap.net

56 GLUE (Generalized Likelihood Uncertainty Estimation) is a methodology based on Monte Carlo simulation for estimating the predictive uncertainty associated with models. For further information on GLUE, see http://www.es.lancs.ac.uk/hfdg/freeware/hfdg_freeware_gluepapers.htm.

57 De Marchi et al., 'Combining Participative and Institutional Approaches'; Mario Giampietro and Kozo Mayumi, 'Multiple-Scale Integrated Assessment of Societal Metabolism: Introducing the Approach,' *Population and Environment* 22, no. 2 (2000); 'Multiple-Scale Integrated Assessment of Societal Metabolism: Integrating Biophysical and Economic Representations across Scales,' *Population and Environment* 22, no. 2 (2000); Munda, 'Social Multi-Criteria Evaluation.'

58 A. Saltelli, K. Chan, and E.M. Scott, eds., *Sensitivity Analysis* (London: Wiley, 2000); Andrea Saltelli, *Sensitivity Analysis of Scientific Models* (London: Wiley, 2007).

59 See, for example, problems of fisheries management, discussed by T. Dietz, E. Ostrom, and P.C. Stern, 'The Struggle to Govern the Commons,' *Science* 302, no. 52 (2003); and the role of farmers' local knowledge in tracing the Chernobyl fallout in Scotland, as discussed by Brian Wynne, 'May the Sheep Safely Graze? A Reflexive View of the Expert–Lay Knowledge Divide,' in *Risk, Environment, and Modernity*, ed. Scott Lash, Bron Szerszynski, and Brian Wynne (London: Sage, 1996).

60 Habermas, *The Theory of Communicative Action*, vols. 1 and 2; *Between Facts and Norms*.

61 John S. Dryzek, *Rational Ecology: Environment and Political Economy* (London: Basil Blackwell, 1987); *Discursive Democracy: Politics, Policy, and Political Science* (Cambridge: Cambridge University Press, 1990).

62 See, for example, Dryzek, *Rational Ecology; Discursive Democracy*; O'Hara, 'Discursive Ethics'; Sybille van den Hove, 'Participatory Approaches to Environmental Policy-Making: The European Commission Climate Policy Process as a Case Study,' *Ecological Economics* 33, no. 3 (2000); De Marchi et al., 'Combining Participative and Institutional Approaches'; Pellizzoni, 'Uncertainty and Participatory Democracy'; Graham Smith, *Deliberative Democracy and the Environment* (London: Routledge, 2003); and Munda, 'Social Multi-Criteria Evaluation.'

63 Habermas, *Toward a Rational Society.*
64 Habermas, *The Future of Human Nature.*
65 Habermas, *Toward a Rational Society,* 6.
66 Ibid., 8.
67 Rachel Carson, *Silent Spring* (London: Hamish Hamilton, 1963).
68 Habermas, *Toward a Rational Society,* 61.
69 Ibid.
70 Marcuse, *One-Dimensional Man,* 260. For discussion of this point in a twenty-first-century context, made through reference to Horkheimer and Adorno's *Dialectic of Enlightenment* and the works of Niklas Luhmann, see Ingolfur Blühdorn, *Post-Ecologist Politics: Social Theory and the Abdication of the Ecologist Paradigm* (London: Routledge, 2000).
71 Marcuse, *One-Dimensional Man,* 236, emphasis in original.
72 Habermas, *Toward a Rational Society,* 61.
73 Marcuse, *Essay on Liberation,* 70–1.
74 S.O. Funtowicz and J.R. Ravetz, 'Three Types of Risk Assessment,' in *Risk Analysis in the Private Sector,* ed. C. Whipple and V.T. Covello (New York: Plenum, 1985); Funtowicz and Ravetz, *Uncertainty and Quality.*
75 Habermas, *Toward a Rational Society,* 84.
76 Marcuse, *One-Dimensional Man,* as quoted by Habermas, *Toward a Rational Society;* Habermas, *Toward a Rational Society,* 84.
77 Marcuse, *One-Dimensional Man,* 236.
78 Habermas, *Toward a Rational Society,* 87, emphasis in original.
79 Ibid.
80 Marcuse, *One-Dimensional Man,* 237, emphasis in original.
81 Max Horkheimer, 'Notes on Science and the Crisis,' in *Critical Theory and Society: A Reader,* ed. Stephen Eric Bronner and Douglas MacKay Kellner (London: Routledge, 1989[1932]).
82 Habermas, *The Future of Human Nature.*
83 Funtowicz and Ravetz, 'A New Scientific Methodology,' 137.
84 Allen et al., 'Dragnet Ecology'; Giampietro, 'Sustainability and Techno-logical Development in Agriculture'; *Multi–Scale Integrated Assessment of Agroecosystems.*
85 Habermas, *The Future of Human Nature,* 15, emphasis added.
86 Ibid., 14, emphasis in original.
87 Ibid., 13.
88 Ibid., 105.
89 Ibid., 109, emphasis in original.
90 Habermas, *Toward a Rational Society,* 87; *The Future of Human Nature.*
91 John S. Dryzek, 'Green Reason: Communicative Ethics for the Biosphere,'

Environmental Ethics 12, no. 3 (1990); Katharine N. Farrell, 'Inter-Disciplinary Deliberative Democracy,' paper presented at the 6th Open Meeting of
the Human Dimensions of Global Environmental Change Research Community, University of Bonn, 9–13 October 2005).
92 Dryzek, *Rational Ecology*; 'Complexity and Rationality in Public Life,'
Political Studies 35 (1987); *Discursive Democracy*.
93 Farrell, *Making Good Decisions Well*, 184.
94 See Marcuse, *Essay on Liberation*, 69–71. For caveats and for a review of critiques, see W. Mark Cobb, 'Diatribes and Distortions: Marcuse's Academic
Reception,' in *Herbert Marcuse: A Critical Reader*, ed. John Abromeit and W.
Mark Cobb (London: Routledge, 2004).
95 Marcuse, *Essay on Liberation*; Robert L. Heilbroner, *An Inquiry into the
Human Prospect: Looked at Again for the 1990s* (New York: Norton, 1991);
Friedrich Hinterberger, Fred Luks, and Marcus Stewen, *Ökologische
Wirtschaftspolitik. Zwischen Ökodiktatur und Umweltkatastrophe* (Berlin:
Birkhäuser, 1996).
96 Marcuse, *Eros and Civilization*, 19.
97 Marcuse, *Essay on Liberation*, 82.
98 Ibid., 91.
99 Habermas, *The Future of Human Nature*.

BIBLIOGRAPHY

Abromeit, John, and W. Mark Cobb, eds. *Herbert Marcuse: A Critical Reader*.
London: Routledge, 2004.
Alford, C. Fred. *Science and the Revenge of Nature: Marcuse and Habermas*. Gai-
nesville: University Presses of Florida. 1985.
Allen, T.F.H, Joseph A. Tainter, J. Chris Pires, and Thomas W. Hoekstra. 'Drag-
net Ecology – "Just the Facts, Ma'am": The Privilege of Science in a Post-
modern World.' *BioScience* 51, no. 6 (2001): 475–85.
Beck, Ulrich. *Risk Society: Towards a New Modernity*. London: Sage, 1992.
Blühdorn, Ingolfur. *Post-Ecologist Politics: Social Theory and the Abdication of the
Ecologist Paradigm*. London: Routledge, 2000.
Bokina, John, and Timothy J. Lukes, eds. *Marcuse: From the New Left to the Next
Left*. Lawrence: University Press of Kansas, 1994.
Camus, Albert. *The Rebel*. London: Hamish Hamilton, 1953[1951].
Carson, Rachel. *Silent Spring*. London: Hamish Hamilton, 1963.
Cobb, W. Mark. 2004. 'Diatribes and Distortions: Marcuse's Academic Recep-
tion.' In *Herbert Marcuse: A Critical reader*, edited by John Abromeit and W.
Mark Cobb, 163–87. London: Routledge, 2004.

de Marchi, B., S.O. Funtowicz, S. Lo Cascio, and G. Munda. 'Combining Participative and Institutional Approaches with Multicriteria Evaluation: An Empirical Study for Water Issues in Triona, Sicily.' *Ecological Economics* 34 (2000): 267–82.

Dietz, T., E. Ostrom, and P.C. Stern. 'The Struggle to Govern the Commons.' *Science* 302, no. 52 (2003): 1907–12

Dryzek, John S. 'Complexity and Rationality in Public Life.' *Political Studies* 35 (1987): 424–42.

– *Discursive Democracy: Politics, Policy, and Political Science.* Cambridge: Cambridge University Press, 1990.

– 'Green Reason: Communicative Ethics for the Biosphere.' *Environmental Ethics* 12, no. 3 (1990): 195–210.

– *Rational Ecology: Environment and Political Economy.* London: Basil Blackwell, 1987.

Farrell, Katharine N. 'Inter-Disciplinary Deliberative Democracy.' Paper presented at the 6th Open Meeting of the Human Dimensions of Global Environmental Change Research Community, University of Bonn, 9–13 October 2005.

– *Making Good Decisions Well: A Theory of Collective Ecological Management.* Aachen: Shaker, 2010.

– 'The Politics of Science and Sustainable Development: Marcuse's New Science in the 21st Century.' *Capitalism, Nature, Socialism* 19, no. 4 (2008): 68–83.

– 'Snow White and the Wicked Problems of the West: A Look at the Lines between Empirical Description and Normative Prescription.' *Science, Technology and Human Values* (2010), in press.

Funtowicz, Silvio, and Martin O'Connor. 'The Passage from Entropy to Thermodynamic Indeterminacy: A Social and Science Epistemology for Sustainability.' In *Bioeconomics and Sustainability: Essays in Honor of Nicholas Georgescu-Roegen*, edited by Kozo Mayumi and John Gowdy, 257–86. Cheltenham: Edward Elgar, 1999.

Funtowicz, S.O., and J.R. Ravetz. 'Emergent Complex Systems.' *Futures* 26, no. 6 (1994): 568–82.

– 'The Good, the True, and the Post-Modern.' *Futures* 24, no. 10 (1992): 963–76.

– 'A New Scientific Methodology for Global Environmental Issues.' In *Ecological Economics: The Science and Management of Sustainability*, edited by Robert Costanza, 137–52. New York: Columbia University Press, 1991.

– 'The Poetry of Thermodynamics.' *Futures* 29, no. 9 (1997): 791–810.

– 'Science for the Post-Normal Age.' *Futures* 25, no. 7 (1993): 739–55.

– 'Three Types of Risk Assessment.' In *Risk Analysis in the Private Sector*, edited by C. Whipple and V.T. Covello, 217–31. New York: Plenum, 1985

- *Uncertainty and Quality in Science for Policy.* Dordrechts: Kluwer, 1990.
- 'The Worth of a Songbird: Ecological Economics as a Post-Normal Science.' *Ecological Economics* 10 (1994): 197–207.
Giampietro, Mario. *Multi-Scale Integrated Assessment of Agroecosystems.* London: CRC, 2004.
- 'Sustainability and Technological Development in Agriculture: A Critical Appraisal of Genetic Engineering.' *Bioscience* 44 (1994): 677–89.
Giampietro, Mario, and Kozo Mayumi. 'Multiple-Scale Integrated Assessment of Societal Metabolism: Integrating Biophysical and Economic Representations across Scales.' *Population and Environment* 22, no. 2 (2000): 155–10.
- 'Multiple-Scale Integrated Assessment of Societal Metabolism: Introducing the Approach.' *Population and Environment* 22, no. 2 (2000): 109–53.
Gould, Stephen Jay. *The Hedgehog, the Fox, and the Magister's Pox.* London: Jonathan Cape, 2003.
Habermas, Jürgen. *Between Facts and Norms: Contributions to a Discourse Theory of Law and Democracy.* Cambridge: Polity, 1996.
- *The Future of Human Nature.* Oxford: Polity, 2003.
- *The Theory of Communicative Action,* vol. 1, *Reason and the Rationalization of Society.* London: Heinemann, 1984.
- *The Theory of Communicative Action,* vol. 2, *Lifeworld and System.* Cambridge: Polity, 1987.
- *Toward a Rational Society: Student Protest, Science, and Politics.* London: Heinemann Educational, 1971.
Haraway, Donna J. *Simians, Cyborgs, and Women: The Reinvention of Nature.* London: Free Association, 1991.
Heilbroner, Robert L. *An Inquiry into the Human Prospect: Looked at Again for the 1990s.* New York: Norton, 1991.
Hinterberger, Friedrich, Fred Luks, and Marcus Stewen. *Ökologische Wirtschaftspolitik. Zwischen Ökodiktatur und Umweltkatastrophe.* Berlin: Birkhäuser, 1996.
Horkheimer, Max. 'Notes on Science and the Crisis.' In *Critical Theory and Society: A Reader,* edited by Stephen Eric Bronner and Douglas MacKay Kellner, 52–7. London: Routledge, 1989[1932].
Kuhn, Thomas S. *The Structure of Scientific Revolutions,* 2nd ed. Chicago: University of Chicago Press, 1970[1962].
Latour, Bruno. *Politics of Nature: How to Bring Science into Democracy.* Cambridge, MA: Harvard University Press, 2005.
Latour, Bruno, and Steve Woolgar. *Laboratory Life: The Social Construction of Scientific Facts.* London: Sage, 1979.
Luks, Fred. 'Post-Normal Science and the Rhetoric of Inquiry: Deconstructing Normal Science?' *Futures* 31 (1999): 705–19.

- 'The Rhetorics of Ecological Economics.' *Ecological Economics* 26 (1998): 139–49.
Marcuse, Herbert. *Eros and Civilisation*. London: Abacus, 1969[1955].
- *An Essay on Liberation*. London: Penguin, 1969.
- *One-Dimensional Man: Studies in the Ideology of Advanced Industrial Society*, 2nd ed. London: Routledge, 1991[1964].
Munda, Giuseppe. 'Social Multi-Criteria Evaluation: Methodological Foundations and Operational Consequences.' *European Journal of Operational Research* 158 (2004): 662–77.
O'Hara, S.U. 'Discursive Ethics in Ecosystem Valuation and Environmental Policy.' *Ecological Economics* 16 (1996): 95–107.
Pellizzoni, L. 'Uncertainty and Participatory Democracy.' *Environmental Values* 12 (2003): 195–224.
Ravetz, Jerome R. *The Merger of Knowledge with Power: Essays in Critical Science*. London: Mansell, 1990.
- *Scientific Knowledge and Its Social Problems*. Oxford: Clarendon, 1971.
Saltelli, Andrea. *Sensitivity Analysis of Scientific Models*. London: Wiley, 2007.
Saltelli, A., K. Chan, and E.M. Scott, eds. *Sensitivity Analysis*. London: Wiley, 2000.
Smith, Graham. *Deliberative Democracy and the Environment*. London: Routledge, 2003.
van den Hove, Sybille. 'Participatory Approaches to Environmental Policy-Making: The European Commission Climate Policy Process as a Case Study.' *Ecological Economics* 33, no. 3 (2000): 457–72.
Whitehead, A.N. *The Function of Reason*. Boston: Beacon, 1959.
Wynne, Brian. 'May the Sheep Safely Graze? A Reflexive View of the Expert–Lay Knowledge Divide.' In *Risk, Environment, and Modernity*, edited by Scott Lash, Bron Szerszynski, and Brian Wynne, 44–83. London: Sage, 1996.

PART TWO

Critical Theory, Life, and Nature

4 Sacred Identity and the Sacrificial Spirit: Mimesis and Radical Ecology

D. BRUCE MARTIN

What would happiness be that is not measured by the immeasurable grief at what is? For the world is deeply ailing.

Theodor Adorno[1]

Many who identify themselves with the radical ecological stance of 'deep ecology' share a perception with the early Frankfurt School critical theorists: that the planet is rushing toward not progress but catastrophe. Despite sharing that perception, the two groups differ significantly in their respective historical situations and in how they believe the world could be otherwise. Radical ecologists – especially those who identify with 'deep ecology' – focus on species extinction and eco-system collapse and view their activism as largely a salvage process; they hope to save remnants of this planet's biodiversity so that it can eventually recover, albeit with a greatly reduced human population (if any).[2] Also, many radical ecologists align themselves with non-human nature – with wildness and 'big wilderness' – and perceive their actions as a 'sacred' duty.[3] They are willing to sacrifice themselves in the hope of saving the complexity of planetary life, and they believe their actions amount to participation in a sacred being, or in a spirit that transcends the merely human.[4] They view their sacrifices – indeed, their self-sacrifice – as an ecological necessity, one that reflects a far different understanding of sacrifice than that held by the early critical theorists. One commentator-translator has contended that Theodor Adorno's fundamental philosophical innovation was to establish that 'the unity of the self is the work of a sacrificial cunning.'[5] This chapter will explore the relationship between sacrifice and nature; it will suggest that overcoming the logic of sacrifice is necessary for there to be hope of solving the current ecological crisis.

For all the power of its adherents' beliefs, the radical ecology movement remains marginalized and often incoherent. It has been insightfully criticized from many perspectives, including that of 'eco-feminism,' as well as by those who draw from contemporary critical theory. Though critics inspired by eco-feminism and critical theory have highlighted important weaknesses in the core beliefs and philosophies of 'deep' versions of radical ecology, those core beliefs continue to sustain the radical ecologists' political actions.[6] Insights from the early Frankfurt School critical theorists, especially Adorno, can help correct the philosophical shortcomings of deep ecology as well as provide a more coherent basis for activist interventions. Specifically, the early critical theorists' analyses of sacrifice can help us understand the radical ecologists' commitments as well as the fundamental challenges of addressing adequately the growing ecological catastrophe.

Sacrifice is a thread woven through the writings and actions of radical ecologists; indeed, their understanding of their own sacrifice is based in identification with non-human nature – an identification often described in 'sacred' terms. Horkheimer and Adorno's *Dialectic of Enlightenment* links sacrifice with identity as well, but critically. This early work, which examines the links among the sacred, identity, and sacrifice, can help us better understand the unfolding catastrophe; it can also uncover a path that leads from the history of barbarity and the suffering of nature up to the present day. To reverse the headlong rush toward catastrophe will require a fundamentally new understanding of our relationship to nature and self-identity – a relationship characterized, especially in Adorno's work, as an alternative to sacrifice. Reconciliation with nature through a non-dominating mimesis of the Other in nature, or mimetic identification, will allow us to abandon the logic of sacrifice that results in the dominating self and self-domination. Once domination of self and Other is replaced with a transformed mimetic identity, the self-sacrifice that radical ecologists practise as a sacred duty will become unnecessary, and reconciliation with nature a possibility.

Radical Ecological Identities

Arne Naess, a major philosophical influence on many deep ecologists, contends that identification is at the heart of the development of an 'ecological self.' In 'Identification as the Source of Deep Ecological

Attitudes,' he argues that those in the deep ecology movement have in common 'ways of experiencing nature and diversity of cultures.'[7] For Naess, self-realization is the 'mature experience of oneness in diversity.' Furthermore, 'increased maturity involves increase of the wideness of the self.'[8] He distinguishes a deep ecological 'Self' from an 'egoistic,' utilitarian, or instrumental self: 'The minimum is the self-realization by more or less consistent egotism – by the narrowest experience of what constitutes one's self and a maximum of alienation.'[9] In contrast to this narrow egotism, the mature, ecological Self involves 'a process of ever-widening identification and ever-narrowing alienation which widens the self. The self is as comprehensive as the totality of our identifications.'[10]

Naess relies on various 'prophets and teachers' from mystical and meditative traditions to indicate the intended concept of the Self that develops with ecological awareness and 'maturity.' But he recognizes that mystical traditions emphasize experiences that deny or dissolve the individual self into a 'nondiversified supreme whole,' resulting in a vague, confused mystical consciousness that cannot be sustained in normal, everyday activities.[11] As an alternative, he encourages an ecological identification that avoids mystically collapsing all distinctions into an undifferentiated oneness or wholeness. This wider identification would allow for further development of the ecological Self: 'Identification is a spontaneous, non-rational, but not irrational, process through which *the interest or interests of another being are reacted to as our own interest or interests.*'[12] Deep ecological identification leads to 'obliteration of the experience of distinction between ego and alter, between me and the sufferer.' It is this claim, however, that has generated criticisms that deep ecology is simply another form of mysticism.[13] Naess asserts that the wider identification of the Self results in a fundamentally different experience for the individual, where identification with the Other, in joy as well as in suffering, is only momentary or intermittent, thus preserving receptivity to individual difference. In this regard, the danger of losing both the uniqueness of the individual and the individual's potential for spontaneous or free activity was a central concern of the early Frankfurt School theorists, as will be discussed below. Naess's thinking on identification, and on identity itself, needs to be rethought in light of critical theory.

Naess also insists that deep ecological identification must not be confused with an altruism based on the suppression of selfishness – that is, on the sacrifice of one's own interest for the sake of others. He insists that the unecological, psychologistic understanding of altruism requires 'alienation' from one's own interests, which in turn prevents full maturation of the individual; therefore, what is typically understood as altruistic behaviour is better understood as 'immature' behaviour. Alienation and identification, he argues, are opposites because the world or 'reality' consists of original 'wholes' that have become fragmented through human 'development.' Instead of viewing the world as consisting of isolated items or things that human thought lumps together to produce recognizable information, 'reality consists of wholes which we cut down.'[14] Ecological identification reverses alienation from the real world and our true interests: 'In other words: there is not, strictly speaking, a primordial causal process of identification, but one of largely unconscious alienation which is overcome in experiences of identity.'[15] Furthermore, he tells us, this process of identification is 'natural,' a consequence of the individual's maturation. The 'shallow' eco-philosophical necessity of 'altruistic' behaviour is eliminated by this deeper identification, and 'the gradual maturing of a person *inevitably* widens and deepens the self through the process of identification.'[16] In the end, 'altruistic' self-sacrifice loses its meaning: 'The process of identification is sometimes expressed in terms of loss of self and gain of Self through "self-less" action. Each new sort of identification corresponds to a widening of the self, and strengthens the urge to further widening, furthering Self-seeking.'[17]

These are strong claims about maturation, and it is unclear why this development is 'inevitable' or how it results in a process of *ecological* identification. Clearly problematic are Naess's faith in the possibilities of 'Self-realization' and his insistence that deep ecology is not simply another form of mysticism. Yet Naess's deep ecological perspective on contemporary history does share much with critical theory: 'Human conduct still today as a pioneer invading species present [*sic*] a catastrophic cultural lag.'[18] Here Naess is arguing for a shift in the human relationship with nature from one that currently resembles a 'pioneer invading species' to one 'better suited to restablize and mature' ecosystems. This would involve a moderating of material consumption and a turn toward a more sensitive, compassionate culture focused on the 'richness of ends.'[19] The current culture of consumption interferes with the possibilities of identification; if unchecked, it will extend the 'catastrophic' into the future: 'The increasing destruction plus increasing information about the destruction is apt to elicit strong feelings of sorrow, despair, desperate actions and tireless efforts to save what is left ... The most probable course of events is continued devastation of conditions of life on this planet, combined with a powerless upsurge of sorrow and lamentation.'[20]

In response to this vision, any effort to develop a critical ecology based on the work of the early Frankfurt School theorists should be understood not only as an attempt to 'save the planet' but also as an operation to rescue hope.

Identity and Sacrifice

Deep ecologists often appeal to the 'primitive' or to aboriginal peoples' knowledge of nature as a basis for their condemnation of contemporary ways of life, and for examples of ways of relating to non-human nature that would not include its domination and destruction. But this appeal often resembles a romantic longing for a return to an idealized past, a return containing seeds of oppression within the utopian vision. Similarly, radical ecologists of a 'spiritual eco-feminism' often praise a reinvigorated ritualism and eclectic spirituality as a guide to 'women's ways of knowing.' In this regard, some eco-feminists essentially identify with the deep ecology position: 'Ecofeminism represents the union of the radical ecology movement, or what has been called "deep ecology," and feminism.'[21] The early critical theorists had a much different understanding of the consequences of shamanistic ritual magic – and activities linking nature, sacrifice, and identity – than either deep ecologists or eco-feminists. This critical appraisal of ritual and sacrifice is prominent in *Dialectic of Enlightenment*, in which Horkheimer and Adorno link both to anti-Semitism and fascism. A closer look at this early Frankfurt School analysis can help illuminate dangers of an uncritical identification with nature.

Critics of deep ecology have portrayed it as having deeply fascist tendencies because of its philosophical reliance on intuitive knowledge and identification with nature.[22] One of the early difficulties with Earth First! cofounder Dave Foreman's deep ecological position – which led critics to accuse him of racism – is the value system that arises from an uncompromising defence of genetic diversity, the 'refusal to use human beings as the measure by which to value others.'[23] This problem goes beyond deep ecology's critical insistence on civilization's anthropocentrism to its seeming embrace of an underlying misanthropy. The most notorious of these value dilemmas was expressed by Foreman in the context of his evaluation of ecological collapse: 'Human suffering resulting from drought and famine in Ethiopia is tragic, yes, but the de-struction there of other creatures and habitat is even more tragic.'[24] This privileging of the non-human over the human has the characteristics of a simple reversal of the culture/nature duality; it has succumbed to the same conceptual structuring as critical theory revealed in its analysis of instrumental rationality. Contrast this with *Dialectic of Enlightenment*, where the point of the analysis is *not* to abandon 'enlightenment' or human reason, but implicitly to provide hope: 'The accompanying cri-tique of enlightenment is intended to prepare the way for a positive no-tion of enlightenment which will release it from entanglement in blind domination.'[25]

Adorno and Horkheimer's attention to fascism's relationship to 'primitive' experience may help clarify deep ecology's recurring con-tradictions. In the opening essay of their foundational work, the prehis-tory of science and art is linked to the development of fascism. A key to understanding this early critical theory analysis of both instrumental rationality and fascist anti-Semitism is the concept/term *mimesis*, which repeatedly returns in Adorno's later work, always consistent with this initial analysis. In the early work, mimesis appears as an adaptive im-pulse responding to 'Nature,' which appears to early humans as an overwhelming force that must be appeased or fooled:

> Only consciously contrived adaptation to nature brings nature under the control of the physically weaker. The ratio which supplants mimesis is not simply its counterpart. It is itself mimesis: mimesis unto death. The subjec-tive spirit which cancels the animation of nature can master a despiritual-ized nature only by imitating its rigidity and despiritualizing itself in turn. Imitation enters into the service of domination inasmuch as even man is anthropomorphized for man.[26]

Horkheimer and Adorno elaborate on the transformation of mime-sis into instrumental rationality by way of innovative interpretations of both shamanistic magic and Homer's *Odyssey*. In their reading, hu-man reason 'degenerated' as it imitated the nature it came to dominate; in so doing, it created a vicious, lifeless circle of domination perpetu-ated by a 'rational' society that has come to dominate the individual as much as 'nature' ever did. Rational pursuit of freedom and happiness has become instead a system of domination – the 'administration of things.' Enlightened reason, initially the path for overcoming myth and mythlike nature, wielding the power to dissolve nature 'red in tooth and claw,' has become simply a mask for 'anthropomorphizing' this power: 'Enlightenment has always taken the basic principle of myth to be anthropomorphism, the projection onto nature of the subjective. In this view, the supernatural, spirits and demons, are mirror images of men who allow themselves to be frightened by natural phenomena. Consequently the many mythic figures can all be brought to a common denominator, and reduced to the human subject.'[27]

Enlightenment asserts that everything of meaning is available to the reason of 'man' and that formal logic and its mathematicization in science make the world calculable, predictable, and (most important) available for utilization by man. The earliest conversion of myth – from *explanation* of the world to potential *control* and *use* of that world – took the form of magic, that is, the precursor to science. Yet within magic, nature was not organized conceptually as so many examples of a common characteristic; rather, the specificity or uniqueness of the object of magic was constitutive of the priest's or shaman's efforts to influence events. It is not the invisible power of nature as a whole (its 'laws') that the magician seeks to influence; instead, there remains in shamanistic ritual the recognition of specific qualities of the object influenced: 'In magic there is specific representation. What happens to the enemy's spear, hair or name, also happens to the individual; the sacrificial animal is massacred instead of the god. Substitution in the course of sacrifice marks a step toward discursive logic.'[28]

For Horkheimer and Adorno, sacrifice is a prototypical form of exchange: even while honouring the uniqueness of the individual as it attempts an influence that opposes the mythic or fated character of the world (the repetition of nature), shamanistic magic reduces nature to category and example. Science demythologizes or disenchants the world, but at the expense of individual uniqueness. Though a precursor to science, magic retained an affinity for individuality by its use of mimesis: 'Like science, magic pursues aims, but seeks to achieve them by mimesis – not by progressively distancing itself from the object.'[29] The shaman's mimetic magic still recognized affinities or similarities between self and other, between the human and the 'other' in nature. The essence of science, as it is for magic, is the identification and control of nature, and this involves a further transformation of mimetic potential. Science ultimately extends its control of nature to 'human nature' as well, and in so doing acquires the characteristics of the mythic nature it first attempted to control.[30] In a society dominated by the 'exchange principle' broadly understood, science transforms the individual into yet another example of universal processes, merely another specimen available for control and manipulation. Historical 'progress' from magic to science, from myth to enlightenment, is therefore also a story of regression, of return into the mythic, of renewed confrontation with fateful necessity.

Ever increasing domination, beyond that of external nature to the psychological or internal 'human nature,' also comes to characterize philosophical thought, which Adorno critiqued as 'identity thinking.' In identity thinking, spirit itself is sacrificed to the rational calculation of instrumental reason as humans become both *means of* domination and *material for* domination. Breaking the spell of the logic of domination requires awareness that repressed fragments of mimesis hold possibilities for hope – for potential alternative thought: 'The point which thinking aims at its material is not solely a spiritualized control of nature. While doing violence to the object of its syntheses, our thinking heeds a potential that waits in the object, and it unconsciously obeys the idea of making amends to the pieces for what it has done. In philosophy, this unconscious tendency becomes conscious. Accompanying irreconcilable thoughts is the hope for reconcilement.'[31]

Philosophy must make conscious the potentials of the objects it responds to, potentials suppressed by the activities of identifying thought, including various forms of substitution or exchange. For Adorno, the critique of identity thinking requires that the form of presentation of philosophy be consistent with its content: 'Its integral, nonconceptually mimetic moment of expression is objectified only by presentation in language. The freedom of philosophy is nothing but the capacity to lend a voice to its unfreedom.'[32] Borrowing from Hegel, Adorno asserts that 'yielding' to the object is the only way for its possibilities to be expressed. However, if the Hegelian system is followed to its conclusion, thought merely returns on itself as a reflection of the subject, not the revelation of the object. Adorno does not simply reject Hegelian dialectics; he radicalizes them and their already radicalized forms as found in Marx. At the same time, he attempts to rescue Marx's insights from the Marxists who captured his critical philosophy, exemplified by those who used 'dialectical materialism' to perpetuate totalitarian socialisms.[33] Adorno dedicates this rescue mission to non-identity or particularity in nature: 'If the thought really yielded to the object, if its attention were on the object, not on its category, the very objects would start talking under the lingering eye.'[34]

The relationship between identity and non-identity also is at the heart of the analysis of 'anti-Semitism' in *Dialectic of Enlightenment*, specifically as it clarifies the difference between projection and false projection. 'Projection' is tracked to its animal origins and the organism's attempt to survive: 'In a certain sense all perception is projection. The projection of sensory impressions is a legacy of our animal prehistory, a mechanism for self-preservation and obtaining food.'[35] Projection, like mimesis (which is not entirely different), is refined or extended with civilization's development, at both the social and individual levels: individuals refine and inhibit projections through science, which extends the abstract ordering of nature. But this 'refinement' of projection can go awry: 'By learning to distinguish between his own and extraneous thoughts and feelings under the force of economic necessity, a distinction is made between without and within, the possibility of distancing and identifying, self-awareness and the conscience. Further consideration is necessary to understand the controlled projection, and the way in which it is deformed into false projection – which is part of the essence of anti-Semitism.'[36]

The abstracting, identifying self internalizes its impressions of the world as the human organism struggles for survival; this eventually results in the formation of the 'individual.' However, this formation of the individual self is unstable; the process of 'projecting' the outside world into the individual psyche requires sustained effort. 'False projection' in a sense reverses the process of individual identity formation: what is perceived as external is actually a representation of the subject. According to Adorno, this can easily be seen in the practice of astrology, where the movement of the stars is interpreted as relations of the self. This process becomes extreme or 'morbid' in the thinking of the paranoiac: 'As an astrologer he endows the stars with powers which lead to the ruin of the unheeding – either in the preclinical stage of eternal relations or in the clinical stage of his own ego.'[37]

Clearly, unlike for Naess, identity formation for the critical theorists is not a simple process of maturation with an 'inevitable' outcome (as it is for Naess). Any attempt to overcome the domination of nature and create a world in which true freedom and happiness are possible must recognize the necessary role that critical interpretation plays in that effort. Rescue of nature will also be rescue of reason from its reduction to instrumental rationality, accomplished by attending to what is not identical to reason. For the critical theorists, interpretation is 'conscious projection,' in which the subject is aware of the process that results in the 'synthetic unity' of the object (nature). Yet always present is the potential for false projection – that is, projection that does not make the necessary distinctions between self and the independent objects of the external world:

> Anti-Semitism is based on a false projection. It is the counterpart of true mimesis, and fundamentally related to the repressed form; in fact, it is probably the morbid expression of repressed mimesis. Mimesis imitates the environment, but false projection makes the environment like itself. For mimesis the outside world is a model which the inner world must try to conform to: the alien must become familiar; but false projection confuses the inner and outer world and defines the most intimate experiences as hostile. Impulses which the subject will not admit as his own even though they are most assuredly so, are attributed to the object – the prospective victim.[38]

False projection is a repressed mimesis, where the self or subject is projected onto the external world. The result is often fear of the other and subsequent attempts to master or dominate it. The concept of 're-pressed mimesis' can become a key for critical ecology's understanding of various forms of oppression and exploitation, including those based on race, gender, class, and other 'natural' categories. In contrast, reversal of domination requires 'mimetic identification' – that is, internalization of the external that honours the particularity or individuality of the other.[39]

A non-dominating identification with nature has been a focus of other radical ecologists besides Arne Naess.[40] But these descriptions lack the conceptual distinctions necessary for a critical ecological awareness capable of sufficiently analysing existing social, economic, and political structures to enable a coherent radical ecological practice. Needed here is not reliance on mystical religious traditions or positivist science, but rather an interpretation of the full richness of relationships between humans and non-human nature – an interpretation that does not sacrifice the human subject to a fateful nature, or nature to the aggrandizement of the human ego.

Critical Spirit

Critical theory also resembles deep ecology in the way critics have charged both with reversion to mysticism. In the post-Adorno critical theory of Jürgen Habermas, Adorno is read as calling for reconciliation with nature by means of a mystical-metaphysical regression. Habermas chided Adorno for not developing a theory of mimesis, for circling around such a theory with the use of 'images from Judaeo-Christian mysticism.'[41] Adorno and Horkheimer had called for being 'mindful' or 'remembering' nature in the subject – a process that might result in recognition that the 'truth' of culture and enlightenment is their opposition to domination.[42] Habermas dismisses the usefulness of much of his predecessors' work because of their unwillingness to relate the idea of reconciliation to 'mimetic impulses' in a way that is 'not merely intuitive.'[43] Early critical theory's dilemma is that reducing 'mimetic impulse' – which is also a foundation of the concept of reconciliation – to a specifiable meaning reproduces the activity of identifying thought itself. To define mimesis is to run the danger of reducing this 'impulse' to a controllable concept, yet again returning the (potential) subject to the bonds of instrumental reason. However, by embracing this paradox of the mimetic, Habermas contends, Adorno can only 'gesticulate' toward expressions of the truth, including those in autonomous art, since truth cannot be represented directly in philosophical discourse.[44] The truth of the mimetic relationship is non-conceptual, and this forces Adorno's negative dialectics to become an exercise in 'models' that gesture toward what lies outside themselves.[45]

But rather than viewing 'mimesis' as the opposite of reason and therefore as irrational, which is what Habermas does (thereby repeating the subject–object dualism at the level of the description of reason itself, as mind or spirit opposed to nature),[46] we could more adequately view this term as representing the 'pre-rational.'[47] In this regard, a consistent analysis of early critical theory's use of mimesis circulates among the multiple meanings of the term as developed in *Dialectic of Enlightenment*.[48] There it is placeholder for nature dominated by instrumental rationality, but *also* stand-in for a non-dominating relationship between humans and nature, a relationship not reducible to a 'communicative rationality.' Adorno argued against reducing a non-dominating subject–object relationship to any model based on 'intersubjectivity.' His work is more plausibly understood as an attempt to represent philosophically the conceptually unrepresentable experience of non-domination, with *Negative Dialectics* and *Aesthetic Theory* serving as explications of this receptivity to nature and 'otherness.' Adorno specifically rejects attempts to link his discussion of receptive experience to metaphysical understandings of the subject and subjectivity. Quite explicitly, he rejects a metaphysical understanding of concepts such as reconciliation:

> Authentic philosophic interpretation does not meet up with a fixed mean-
> ing which already lies behind the question, but lights it up suddenly and
> momentarily, and consumes it at the same time ... Interpretation of the un-
> intentional through a juxtaposition of the real by the power of such inter-
> pretation is the programme of every authentically materialist knowledge,
> a programme to which the materialist procedure does all the more justice,
> the more it distances itself from every 'meaning' of its objects and the less
> it relates itself to an implicit, quasi-religious meaning.[49]

The operations of mimesis in any possible humans-to-nature reconciliation are not reducible to the conceptual structure of discourse,
even that of a 'communicative rationality.' Neither are the complex
relationships between interpretation and the sensuous experiences of
the subject – even those found in experiences of autonomous art – reducible to traditional terms of modern aesthetic rationality – especially
not to harmonious reconciliation of subject and object. The possibility
of experiencing a non-dominating relationship with 'nature' must be
represented very differently: 'Every act of making in art is an endless
endeavour to articulate what is not makeable, namely spirit. This is
where the function of art as a restorer of historically repressed nature
becomes important. Nature does not yet exist. To the degree to which
art pines after an image of nature, it represents the truth of non-being.
Art becomes conscious of it in a non-identical other.'[50]

Adorno's late works touched on many of the same issues as now
preoccupy the radical ecologists. One of the major difficulties in comprehending negative dialectics is Adorno's necessary insistence on the
impossibility of reducing philosophical interpretation to a single fundamental principle. Accordingly, negative dialectics' analysis of the
'object' attempts to include full recognition of its uniqueness, difference, or otherness, while also acknowledging the history of the object
and the history *in* the object – those impacts and elements of society
that penetrate the object as well as the interpreting subject. Interpretation, both negatively and dialectically, results in a layered complex of
mediations. Compounding the difficulty of interpretation is Adorno's
assertion (contra Hegel) that the whole is not rational – that the whole is
the false. The world is not tending to a synthetic resolution of its contradictions in a positive absolute; instead it continues to 'radiate disaster
triumphant.'[51]

Deep ecologists' representation of identification as a return to full-
ness-of-experience, or as an original, immediate relation to nature, is

an idealistic and romantic delusion with inescapable reactionary consequences. Instead of viewing ecological identification as a potential avenue to immediate access to truth, 'right living,' or primordial 'dwelling,' we would better understand it as an anticipation of the 'not yet.' This is Adorno's term for the anticipation of a 'utopia' still to come, an existence currently unavailable in the world, a nature that has yet to exist, not even in the mythic past. This 'not yet' can only come into being through the adequate interpretation of the existing situation, an interpretation that indicates how the other of nature is repressed – how suffering manifests itself. Bringing this suffering to consciousness requires that we mediate between the present fragmented ecological existence and a future world in which contradiction and the ideology of domination will no longer exist: 'Utopia would be above identity and above contradiction; it would be a togetherness of diversity.'[52]

For Adorno, the reconciled future takes the form of 'exact imagination,' an image of a future possibility. In this 'not yet' future, 'reconciliation' of humans with nature will have taken place. This future is not simply an extension of the present, but its mimetic transformation or metamorphosis, a translation of existing elements into an image that anticipates a situation of reconciliation, when possibilities and potentials have developed that exist only latently in the present damaged life.[53] Adorno agrees that identification may lead to the desired relationship with nature, but he rejects assertions that reconciliation with nature is possible in its full sense in a world of suffering and catastrophe. He acknowledges the awareness generated in identification with others, but he also returns to the observation that identification has the tendency to posit the self in the other. The danger consists in projecting characteristics of the self onto the other, subjecting the other to the needs of the self as yet another extension of the domination of nature. Mimesis is a mode of cognition that makes knowledge possible without domination or mysticism and without sacrificing the uniqueness of the particular, a uniqueness in which every entity is an object of ethical consideration for its own sake.

Immanent criticism or negative dialectics begins with the object of interpretation and then attempts to weave a conceptual net that suspends the object 'momentarily' to reveal the process it contains, including that which it is potentially becoming. In the historical situation that culminates in destruction, where neither the 'individual' nor 'nature' yet exist, identification in the here and now does not lead to the truth of the ecological situation, but rather to an indication of its negative existence – to the *absence* of reconciliation between subject and object, history and nature. What is possible is not immediate access to original nature, or ecological truth, but awareness that reconciled nature would be radically otherwise than it is at present. What is needed is not a mystical identification with nature and subsequent defence of its 'essential' characteristics as established by personal assertion or scientific fiat, but an interpretive strategy that is capable of grasping the contradictory, antagonistic world in its complexity.[54]

In *Negative Dialectics*, Adorno proposes a theory of philosophy that attempts to do justice to the non-identical, to that which is not the subject. The challenge for radical ecology is to translate this theory into a fully ecological understanding and interpretive strategy. If ecological awareness is to go beyond mere affirmation of the existing ideology of domination, be it as liberal reformism or in more brutally authoritarian forms, then radical ecologists must move beyond a naive belief in immediate access to the truth of nature. A critical, radical ecology must develop an interpretive 'method' aimed at obtaining an ecological understanding of the relationship between society and nature that gives full credit to the non-identical and that fully acknowledges the contradictions of existing society.

Among the many thinkers Adorno critiques and draws from is Karl Marx. He utilizes Marx's concept of the 'laws' of capitalism to reveal the workings of domination, a process that has become so extensive that what is in fact historical appears to have the status of the 'natural.' Adorno also shows that it is in Marx's predecessor that philosophical fulfilment of domination is best exemplified. In Hegel, spirit comes to dominate all existence, finally rising to the status of a 'second nature.' Against Hegel, Adorno claims that this represents not the unfolding of necessity, but rather the formulation of the 'bourgeois consciousness,' a consciousness that views its power to rule as an expression of natural necessity, thus veiling its program of self-interested domination: 'Spirit as a second nature is the negation of the spirit, however, and that the more thoroughly the blinder its self-consciousness is to its natural growth. This is what happens to Hegel. His world spirit is the ideology of natural history. He calls it world spirit because of its power. Domination is absolutized and projected on Being itself, which is said to be the spirit.'[55]

Adorno's critical theory reveals that domination has extended to the totality of society, leaving only fragments and marginal existences to mark the possibility of its overcoming; whereas when the 'bourgeois consciousness' represents this to itself, it reverses the human and the natural and mystifies history as fate.

Adorno asserts that Reason, as the expression of the antithesis of nature and history, is both true and false. The truth of the opposition of nature and history is a result of humans' treatment of nature, of their domination of it so as to make it the 'other' to be dominated – and feared, because it can potentially overwhelm the subject. The opposition is false to the extent that philosophy constructs its categories in such a way as to conceal the truth – which is, that history is used to conceal the historical nature of existing domination and exploitation. Unveiling these philosophical mystifications requires a critical interpretive approach: 'History can be considered from two sides, divided into the history of nature and the history of mankind. Yet there is no separating the two sides; as long as men exist, natural and human history will qualify each other.'[56] (That quote is from Marx; Adorno is using it to 'irritate dogmatic materialists.') Adorno extends Marx's early insights into the relationship of nature and society, going so far as to indicate how capitalism has permeated the very psychology and biology of its inhabitants: 'The inner constitution of the individual, not merely his social role, could be deduced from this ... Only when the process that begins with the metamorphosis of labour-power into a commodity has permeated men through and through and objectified each of their impulses as formally commensurable variations of the exchange relationship, is it possible for life to reproduce itself under the prevailing relations of production.'[57]

Sacrifice and Self-Denial

Various authors have challenged deep ecologists' understanding of identification, questioning the type of self or subjectivity they assume. Deep ecological identification has been shown to be both class based and masculinist or androcentric.[58] The early deep ecologists' understanding of identification does not produce merely another 'citizen' in the biosphere of equality, or even of equality in the sphere of social relations; rather, it produces an identity complicit with a mode of production, consumption, and reproduction that replicates systematic domination and exploitation of nature. And the knowledge this identity makes possible is not of immediate truth; rather, it is knowledge mediated through both history and nature's entwinement with history. The deep ecological understanding of identification lacks sufficient distinctions among different types of selves; it also pays insufficient attention to the historical situation of the identification process itself. Intuitive identification with nature combined with minimal social analysis results in a philosophy of radical ecology that threatens to remain abstract and contradictory and to further intensify domination and exploitation, all in the name of 'defending external nature' and 'liberating internal nature.'[59]

At the heart of the deep ecology wing of the radical ecology movement is its 'no compromise' stand on wilderness preservation and restoration. The primary reason for the emphasis on preserving and extending wilderness is to keep intact the processes of evolution expressed through the genetic material and behaviours of individual species, which represent life's various evolutionary journeys. Radical ecologists view wilderness as necessary to preserve biological diversity, and this prompts them to take actions aimed at allowing existing species to continue even if (or, as some radical ecologists believe, *when*) this reduces human beings to a post-exuberant minimum, perhaps even extinction.[60] As the radical ecologists have observed, the rate of species extinction is greater now than at any other time in natural history, even greater than the fabled die-off of the dinosaurs.[61] Some have even speculated that vertebrate evolution 'may be at an end' as an ultimate consequence of 'industrial humans.'[62] Even if humans do not bring about their own extinction in the short term – so argue these radical ecologists – human population still should be greatly reduced and 'wilderness' gradually expanded, not for the sake of human habitation, but for the sake of non-human nature and the continued evolution of all species. They argue for large preserves of land that would allow for the 'free-flow of natural processes,' a preservation that is 'entirely apart from any human value placed upon it.'[63] Thus their 'sacred' self-sacrifices aim not to grandly establish a sustainable society, but simply to make possible the continuation of the evolution of complex life based on the genetic material and intact ecosystems that remain. These actions raise a crucial question: Is radical ecological sacrifice truly a manifestation of the sacred, or is it an unwitting accomplice of the forces of domination it opposes?

Besides examining how sacrifice of the other results in both (self-) identity and domination, Horkheimer and Adorno reveal how the further intensification of sacrifice in the form of self-denial strengthens the domination of nature. They develop this in their interpretation of the journeys of Odysseus, specifically his acts of sacrificial *self-denial*. Odysseus' adventures in Homer's poem are interpreted from a unique perspective: the hero becomes the prototypical example of the 'bourgeois individual,' and his adventures the story of the creation and preservation of the bourgeois self.[64] More broadly, the hero's adventures represent the various developmental stages of self-identity, recounting both the development of subjectivity generally, and particularly its bourgeois or individualistic form. Odysseus confronts various challenges to both his survival and his individual autonomy when nature or fate, in the form of impulse or instinct, tempt him to abandon his self in exchange for pleasure or happiness. He overcomes these temptations and challenges through often clever or 'cunning' means that result in the denial of his desires in the service of self-preservation: 'The very spirit that dominates nature repeatedly vindicates the superiority of nature in competition ... The pattern of Odyssean cunning is the mastery of nature through such adaptation. Renunciation, the principle of bourgeois disillusionment, the outward schema for the intensification of sacrifice.'[65]

Mastery of nature is achieved through clever calculation, what the authors will call 'instrumental rationality,' an extension of the logic of sacrifice. This 'rational' domination of nature, again understood as the control of fate or mythic forces, preserves the self of instrumental rationality. Domination of external nature is accomplished by way of the internal domination of the self – that is, through sacrificial self-denial:

> The deception in sacrifice is the prototype of Odyssean cunning; many of Odysseus' stratagems are, so to speak, inset in a contest of sacrifice to natural deities. All human sacrifices, when systematically executed, deceive the god to whom they are made: they subject him to the primacy of human ends, and dissolve his power ... By calculating his own sacrifice, he effectively negates the power to whom the sacrifice is made. In this way he redeems the life he had forfeited.[66]

In this interpretation, sacrifice is another early form of 'rational exchange,' enabling humans to gain control over the actions of the gods and the mythic forces of fate, nature, and men. Specific episodes of Odysseus' journey become for the critical theorists a narrative of the history of Western civilization; as archaic prototype of the bourgeois individual, Odysseus anticipates what later will be the general structure of society. This same interpretation returns to sacrifice as the location of catastrophe: 'The institution of sacrifice itself is the occasion of an historic catastrophe, an act of force that befalls men and nature alike.'[67]

Robert Hullot-Kentor has elaborated on critical theory's focus on sacrifice, beginning with the observation that what is accomplished in sacrifice is the 'exchange as equivalents something less valuable for what is more valuable.'[68] He asserts that Adorno's writings should be understood as an attempt to reverse the process of domination that is typical of Western civilization. The negation of domination requires the recognition of the futility of sacrificial substitution: '[These] are only instances of the basic issue of the possible reversal of mediation with which *Dialectic of Enlightenment* is concerned: the reversal of subjectivity from the domination to the liberation of nature.'[69] Adorno makes clear the relation of sacrifice to the future possibility of a society beyond the present one: 'Odysseus is at the same time a sacrifice for the abrogation of sacrifice. His masterful renunciation, as a struggle against myth, stands in for a society that no longer demands renunciation and domination: one that masters itself, not in order to coerce itself and others, but for reconciliation.'[70]

The thrust of Hullot-Kentor's argument is that all of Adorno's works are dedicated to revealing the internal tendency for sacrifice to serve cunning or reason, a tendency culminating in self-destruction. But this reason eventually becomes aware of the futility of its own sacrifice, which creates the possibility of its reversal from domination to liberation. Internalization of sacrifice first establishes the self, then preserves the self: 'The internalization of sacrifice is the establishment of the principle of identity as the principle of the self.'[71] However, this 'self-identical self' cannot be sacrificed because there is no substitute for it, as Adorno explains: 'The self is precisely the human being to whom the magical power of substitution is no longer attributed. The establishment of the self severs that fluctuating unity with nature that the sacrifice of the self claimed to achieve.'[72]

In other words, continuation of the logic of sacrifice contradicts the purpose of self-preservation. The basis for the *critique* of sacrifice – that sacrifice carried out by an instrumental reason cunningly offers the unequal exchange as if equivalent – itself develops out of the process of sacrifice. The non-substitutable self (the self-identical self, the inimitable self) is essentially different from or other than nature; yet when this self forgets that it is nature, it also forgets the purposes for which it was formed. Adorno explains: 'As soon as man discards his awareness that he himself is nature, all the aims for which he keeps himself alive – social progress, the intensification of all his material and spiritual powers, even consciousness itself – are nullified and the enthronement of the means as an end, which under late capitalism is tantamount to open insanity, is already perceptible in the prehistory of subjectivity.'[73]

Only through the memory of itself as always and still part of nature can the self obtain freedom from its self-built prison of second nature: 'Precisely reason that no longer takes itself to be absolute, that recognizes itself as nature and no longer as something absolutely opposed to nature, precisely this reason that is conscious of itself as nature, ceases to be mere nature.'[74] Freedom from a fateful, mythic nature is lost when the nature of the unique individual is forgotten. Without awareness of self as nature, even in acts of self-sacrifice the individual reinforces the structures of domination: 'The irrationalism of totalitarian capitalism, whose way of satisfying needs has an objectified form determined [sic] by domination which makes the satisfaction of needs impossible and tends toward the extermination of mankind, has its prototype in the hero who escapes from sacrifice by sacrificing himself.'[75] Like the eco-warriors sacrificing themselves for the preservation of non-human nature, Odysseus with his heroic acts reinforces the structures of domination. The basic challenge to critical theory and a critical ecology is to answer the question of how the self can remember its nature, thereby replacing domination with liberation.

If the logics of sacrifice and identity result ultimately in the 'totally administered society,' from where will the models for an alternative future come? Nature, perhaps? No, at least not the nature 'red in tooth and claw' that is beyond good and evil: 'Nature herself is neither good, as the ancients believed, nor noble, as the latter day Romantics would have it. As a model and goal it implies the spirit of opposition, deceit, and bestiality.'[76] However – in a negative or negating moment always hovering near the critical theorists' most pessimistic claims   nature may be able to serve as a model to the extent that it is remembered: 'Only when seen for what it is, does nature become existence's craving for peace, that consciousness which from the very beginning has inspired an unshakable resistance to Fuhrer and collective alike. Dominant practice and its inescapable alternatives are not threatened by nature, which tends rather to coincide with them, but by the fact that nature is remembered.'[77]

Remembering nature includes remembering those who have suffered from oppression throughout history. The exact image of the 'reconciled' future will be negatively permeated by past suffering; the not-yet of nature is always indebted to past domination.

Conclusion

Deep ecology offers profound insights into the possibilities of a non-dominating relationship to nature; but it has also generated a disturbing tendency toward misanthropy. Critical theory may help deep ecologists escape the unfortunate tendencies in their philosophy. A more fully adequate critical ecology will require that the concept of identification be rearticulated to distinguish 'projective' identification – which (against the intentions of radical ecologists) simply maps the prevailing categories of nature onto the world – from 'mimetic identification.' (Of course, Adorno would reject the use of this term as self-contradictory.) Mimetic identification attempts to overcome the present conceptual system – a system that results in the domination of nature – and thereby to overturn the simplifications and reductions that consign nature to human production and consumption as its sole purposes.[78]

Deep ecologists' overriding practical goal is ecosystem preservation, but their 'actionist' approach repeats the patterns of domination that are at the heart of the ecological crisis. In their analysis of ecosystems, deep ecologists have a complex, advanced, empirical understanding of the intimate interdependence of human and non-human nature; yet their social analyses tend to simply project the categories of first nature onto society. In this way they dishonour what should be their fundamental insight: the irreducible uniqueness of each species and each individual within the species, including the human species. Deep ecologists have often failed to honour the unique otherness of the individual human being, instead lumping individuals into mere examples of the species. Recognition of individual human value should be compatible with concern for individual members of other species and for nature as a whole. Deep ecology must develop analyses that generate social insights at the same advanced level as its insights into appropriate ecological relationships with 'non-human nature.' To that end, deep ecology must more self-consciously and self-reflexively learn from the critical theorists.

Adorno's view of history would be slightly modified if cast in radical ecological terms: Modern ecological history is the history of catastrophe. Against claims about the end of evolution or of history,[79] a more accurate understanding sets aside premature announcements of utopia, recognizing instead that we simply are experiencing new forms of the dialectic of history and nature.[80] Evolution is being transformed into devolution with the destruction of species and entire ecosystems. We face the increasing possibility of an irrevocable disintegration of planetary ecology and a rush toward the deep ecologists' nightmare prophecy – destruction of human 'civilization' (if not the human species) in a final catastrophic global ecological collapse.[81]

Difficult as it is to excavate the concepts contained in the work of the early critical theorists – especially those of Adorno – those concepts offer more fertile ground for developing radical ecological thought than do existing philosophies of deep ecology. Early critical theorists imagined a retreat from the abyss of domination by way of a non-repressive mimesis. If radical ecologists and others are even close to being right about the approaching ecological catastrophe, then a critical ecology that can provide an adequate basis for addressing the situation is urgently needed. Only when human beings become capable of interpreting their everyday activities from their individual ecological self-perspectives will there be hope of developing non-destructive modes of interaction with nature. A new (mimetic) self-identity must inform both everyday activities and the politics of ecological citizens. In this time of catastrophe, truly ecological self-identity remains utopian, but utopian in Adorno's sense of a 'not yet' nature requiring 'exact imagination.'

Now needed is a translation of radical ecology's understanding of nature into social and cultural images of a future possibility, one in which the 'reconciliation' of humans with nature will have taken place. This radical ecological future can emerge through a mimetic transformation, not to be understood as a mere copying of the given, but as its metamorphosis – as a translation of existing elements into an image of nature that 'does not yet exist.' When this spirit of nature is fully remembered, the sacrificial spirit will vanish.

NOTES

1 Theodor W. Adorno, *Minima Moralia* (London: NLB, 1974), 200.
2 An early text informing the deep ecological perspective (especially the American version closely associated with Earth First! and its progeny) on the relationship of ecological science to possible social and political futures is William Catton's neo-Malthusian *Overshoot*. Catton analyses various population ecology models, the most pessimistic of which ends with an

unsustainable 'exuberance' of consumption, followed by a future with severely limited resources that 'could preclude a later cycle of regrowth.' William R. Catton, *Overshoot: The Ecological Basis of Revolutionary Change* (Urbana: University of Illinois Press, 1982), 253.

3 A useful analysis of the relationship of the sacred to the defence of wilderness – one that is characteristic of deep ecologists – can be found in William Cronon's 'The Trouble with Wilderness; or, Getting Back to the Wrong Nature,' in William Cronon, ed., *Uncommon Ground* (New York: Norton, 1996).

4 There are some besides deep ecologists who consider themselves 'radical ecologists' – social ecologists, eco-marxists, eco-feminists, eco-socialists, and so on. The focus here is on the deep ecology version of radical ecology, for two reasons. First, many of those who were attracted early on to the anarchist philosophy of the American version of deep ecology were later at the forefront of 'actionist' practices, such as the 'monkey wrenching' and similar activities carried out by (for example) the Animal Liberation Front and the Earth Liberation Front. To the extent that other radical ecologists 'identify' with nature in ways similar to those of deep ecologists, the same critique holds.

5 Robert Hullot-Kentor, 'Back to Adorno,' *Telos* 81 (Fall 1989): 20.

6 Critiques come from a variety of perspectives, including those inspired by eco-feminism/feminism, social ecology, and critical theory. Tim Luke, 'The Dreams of Deep Ecology,' *Telos* 76 (Summer 1988): 65; Andrew Biro, *Denaturalizing Ecological Politics: Alienation from Nature from Rousseau to the Frankfurt School and Beyond* (Toronto: University of Toronto Press, 2005); Val Plumwood, 'The Ecopolitics Debate and the Politics of Nature,' in *Ecological Feminism*, ed. Karen J. Warren (London and New York: Routledge, 1994), 64.

7 Arne Naess, 'Identification as the Source of Deep Ecological Attitudes,' in *Deep Ecology*, ed. Michael Tobias (San Diego: Avant, 1985), 258.

8 Ibid., 261.

9 Ibid.

10 Ibid.

11 Ibid.

12 Ibid., emphasis in original.

13 Ibid.

14 Ibid., 262.

15 Ibid.

16 Ibid., 263, emphasis in original.

17 Ibid.

18 Arne Naess, *Ecology, Community, and Lifestyle*, ed. and trans. David Rothen-
    berg (Cambridge: Cambridge University Press, 1989), 183.
19 Ibid.
20 Naess, *Identification*, 269.
21 Rosemary Radford Reuther, 'Ecofeminism: Symbolic and Social Con-
    nections of the Oppression of Women and the Domination of Nature,' in
    Ecofeminism and the Sacred, ed. Carol J. Adams (New York: Continuum,
    1994), 13.
22 Critiques of deep ecology's fascist tendencies are to be found in various
    places, including George Bradford, *How Deep Is Deep Ecology?* (Hadley:
    Times Change, 1989); and Anna Bramwell, *Ecology in the 20th Century: A
    History* (New Haven: Yale University Press, 1989). Also, William Cronon in
    'The Trouble with Wilderness' connects the radical ecologists' associations
    between wilderness and the sacred to deeply reactionary politics.
23 Dave Foreman, *Confessions of an Eco-Warrior* (New York: Harmony, 1991),
    26.
24 Ibid., 8.
25 Max Horkheimer and Theodor W. Adorno, *Dialectic of Enlightenment* (New
    York: Continuum, 1987), xvi.
26 Ibid., 57.
27 Ibid., 6–7.
28 Ibid., 10. For an examination of many of these issues in relation to anthro-
    pology, see Michael Taussig, *Mimesis and Alterity* (New York: Routledge,
    1993).
29 Horkheimer and Adorno, *Dialectic of Enlightenment*, 11.
30 Herbert Marcuse would later call for a 'new science' and a 'new technol-
    ogy' based on an alternative relationship to nature. Marcuse, *One-Dimen-
    sional Man* (Boston: Beacon, 1964), 225 ff. Feminists, too, have provided a
    powerful critique of science and suggested ways to overcome its patriar-
    chal limitations. I have discussed these alternatives in D. Bruce Martin,
    'Mimetic Moments,' in *Feminist Interpretations of Theodor Adorno*, ed. Renee
    Heberle (University Park: Penn State University Press, 2006), 141–71.
31 Theodor W. Adorno, *Negative Dialectics* (New York: Continuum, 1966), 19.
32 Ibid., 18.
33 Ibid., 355.
34 Ibid., 27–8.
35 Horkheimer and Adorno, *Dialectic of Enlightenment*, 187.
36 Ibid., 188.
37 Ibid., 191.
38 Ibid., 187.

39 Something similar to what is here called 'mimetic identification' is addressed by Shierry Weber Nicholsen in terms of 'recognition.' Nicholsen, *The Love of Nature and the End of the World: The Unspoken Dimensions of Environmental Concern* (Cambridge, MA: MIT Press, 2003).
40 Warwick Fox, *Toward a Transpersonal Ecology* (Boston: Shambala, 1990).
41 Jürgen Habermas, *Theory of Communicative Action*, vol. 1, trans. Thomas McCarthy (Boston: Beacon, 1981), 383.
42 Horkheimer and Adorno, *Dialectic of Enlightenment*, 40; Habermas, *Theory of Communicative Action*, vol. 1, 384.
43 Ibid., 384.
44 Ibid., 385.
45 Ibid., 385.
46 Ibid., 390.
47 Martin Jay, *Adorno* (Cambridge, MA: Harvard University Press, 1984), 156.
48 The term may or may not have been appropriated from Walter Benjamin; or more accurately, Benjamin's use of the term was only one (perhaps primary) source for Adorno and Horkheimer. See Benjamin, 'The Mimetic Faculty,' in *Illuminations*, ed. Hannah Arendt, trans. Harry Zohn (New York: Schocken, 1968). See also Susan Buck-Morss, *Origins of Negative Dialectics* (New York: Free Press, 1977), 85 ff; Fredric Jameson, *Late Marxism: Adorno, or, the Persistence of the Dialectic* (London: Verso, 1990); and Shierry Weber Nicholsen, *Exact Imagination, Late Work: On Adorno's Aesthetics* (Cambridge, MA: MIT Press: 1997), especially chapter 4, '*Aesthetic Theory*'s Mimesis of Walter Benjamin.'
49 Quoted in Jay, *Adorno*, 77–8. Originally from Theodor W. Adorno, 'The Actuality of Philosophy,' *Telos* 31 (Spring 1977): 120–33.
50 Theodor W. Adorno, *Aesthetic Theory*, ed. Gretel Adorno and Rolf Tiedemann, trans. C. Lenhardt (London: Routledge, 1984), 191.
51 Horkheimer and Adorno, *Dialectic of Enlightenment*, 3.
52 Adorno, *Negative Dialectics*, 150.
53 Nicholsen, *Exact Imagination*, 4–5; Buck-Morss, *Origins of Negative Dialectics*, 85–8.
54 This claim is similar to the aim of establishing a 'positive notion of enlightenment' referenced in Horkheimer and Adorno, *Dialectic of Enlightenment*, xvi (see n25 above). This, of course, does not imply that science – even current ecological science – can serve as the basis for a sufficient interpretive strategy. Discussion of this point can be found in Martin, 'Mimetic Moments,' esp. 145. See also the brief discussion of Marcuse's proposal for a 'new' science in *One-Dimensional Man*, n30 above.
55 Adorno, *Negative Dialectics*, 356.

56 Ibid., 358; Karl Marx and Frederick Engels, 'The German Ideology,' in Karl Marx and Frederick Engels, *Collected Works*, vol. 5 (New York: International, 1976).

57 Adorno, *Minima Moralia*, 229.

58 Marti Kheel, 'Ecofeminism and Deep Ecology: Reflections on Identity and Difference,' in *Reweaving the World*, ed. Irene Diamond and Gloria Feman Orenstein (San Francisco: Sierra Club, 1990); Luke, 'The Dreams of Deep Ecology,' 65–92; *Ecocritique* (Minneapolis: University of Minnesota Press, 1997); and Luke's essay in this volume. Critical theory, too, has suffered from an androcentric blindness – or, at least, an inadequate examination of the differences between masculine and feminine relationships with respect to the issues it considers central, including the domination of nature. See Josephine Donovan, 'Animal Rights and Feminist Theory,' *Ecofeminism: Women, Animals, Nature*, ed. Greta Gaard (Philadelphia: Temple University Press, 1993); Patricia J. Mills, *Woman, Nature, and Psyche* (New Haven: Yale University Press, 1987); and Renee Heberle, ed., *Feminist Interpretations of Theodor Adorno* (University Park: Penn State University Press, 2006).

59 Foreman, *Confessions*.

60 Catton, *Overshoot*, 53. Catton's section on 'Pasts and Their Futures' discusses the increasingly likely scenario that the current 'exuberant' period of the human species will be followed by the absence of a regrowth or recovery of the species. See also UNDP, *Global Environment Outlook 4: Environment for Development*, (Malta: Progress, 2007).

61 Foreman, *Confessions*, 1.

62 Ibid. (quoting Michael Soulé), 2.

63 Rik Scarce, *Eco-Warriors: Understanding the Radical Environmental Movement* (Chicago: Noble, 1990), 66.

64 Horkheimer and Adorno, *Dialectic of Enlightenment*, first two essays.

65 Ibid., 57.

66 Ibid., 50.

67 Ibid., 51.

68 Hullot-Kentor, 'Back to Adorno,' 20.

69 Ibid., 22.

70 Quoted and retranslated by Robert Hullot-Kentor, 23. Originally, Horkheimer and Adorno, *Dialectic of Enlightenment*, 56. In the article, Hullot-Kentor has retranslated certain passages of *Dialectic of Enlightenment* to re-establish the meaning that he argues has been lost or reversed in the standard translation.

71 Hullot-Kentor, 'Back to Adorno,' 23.

72 Quoted and retranslated by Hullot-Kentor, 'Back to Adorno,' 23. Origi-nally, Horkheimer and Adorno, *Dialectic of Enlightenment*, 51.
73 Ibid., 54.
74 Quoted and retranslated by Hullot-Kentor, 'Back to Adorno,' 23. Origi-nally from Adorno's lecture series 'Einleitung in die Moralphilosophie,' 193; more recently translated as *Problems of Moral Philosophy*, ed. Thomas Shroeder, trans. Rodney Livingstone (Stanford: Stanford University Press, 2000).
75 Horkheimer and Adorno, *Dialectic of Enlightenment*, 55.
76 Ibid., 254.
77 Ibid., 254–5.
78 For additional considerations of 'mimetic identification,' see Martin, 'Mimetic Moments,' 141–71. Further treatments of mimesis and sacrifice can be found in other essays in Heberle, *Feminist Interpretations of Theodor Adorno*; see especially those by Eva Geulen and Lisa Yun Lee.
79 Francis Fukuyama, *The End of History and the Last Man* (New York: Simon and Schuster, 2006). Michael Soulé in Foreman, *Confessions*, 2.
80 Theodor W. Adorno, 'The Idea of Natural History,' *Telos* 60 (Summer 1984): 111–24.
81 There has recently developed an entire literature on 'catastrophe' that could itself be examined in light of these considerations of the logic of sacrifice, including James Lovelock's *Gaia*-inspired writings. Beyond the more strictly radical ecologically inspired treatment of catastrophe are more American mainstream works such as Jared Diamond, *Collapse: How Societies Choose to Fail or Succeed* (New York: Penguin, 2005); and Thomas Homer-Dixon, *The Upside of Down* (Washington: Island, 2006).

BIBLIOGRAPHY

Adorno, Theodor W. *Aesthetic Theory*. Edited by Gretel Adorno and Rolf Tiede-mann, translated by C. Lenhardt. London: Routledge, 1984.
– 'The Idea of Natural History,' *Telos* 60 (Summer 1984): 111–24.
– *Minima Moralia*. London: NLB, 1974.
– *Negative Dialectics*. New York: Continuum, 1966.
Benjamin, Walter. 'The Mimetic Faculty.' In *Illuminations*, edited by Hannah Arendt, translated by Harry Zohn. New York: Schocken, 1968.
Biro, Andrew. *Denaturalizing Ecological Politics: Alienation from Nature from Rousseau to the Frankfurt School and Beyond*. Toronto: University of Toronto Press, 2005.
Bradford, George. *How Deep Is Deep Ecology?* Hadley: Times Change, 1989.

Bramwell, Anna. *Ecology in the 20th Century: A History*. New Haven: Yale University Press, 1989.

Buck-Morss, Susan. *Origins of Negative Dialectics*. New York: Free Press, 1977.

Catton, William R. *Overshoot: The Ecological Basis of Revolutionary Change*. Urbana: University of Illinois Press, 1982.

Cronon, William. 'The Trouble with Wilderness; or, Getting Back to the Wrong Nature.' In *Uncommon Ground*, edited by William Cronon. New York: Norton, 1996.

Diamond, Jared. *Collapse: How Societies Choose to Fail or Succeed*. New York: Penguin, 2005.

Donovan, Josephine. 'Animal Rights and Feminist Theory.' In *Ecofeminism: Women, Animals, Nature*, edited by Greta Gaard. Philadelphia: Temple University Press, 1993.

Foreman, Dave. *Confessions of an Eco-Warrior*. New York: Harmony, 1991.

Fox, Warwick. *Toward a Transpersonal Ecology*. Boston: Shambala, 1990.

Fukuyama, Francis. *The End of History and the Last Man*. New York: Simon and Schuster, 2006.

Habermas, Jürgen. *Theory of Communicative Action*, vol. 1. Translated by Thomas McCarthy. Boston: Beacon, 1981.

Heberle, Renee, ed. *Feminist Interpretations of Theodor Adorno*. University Park: Penn State University Press, 2006.

Homer-Dixon, Thomas. *The Upside of Down*. Washington: Island, 2006.

Horkheimer, Max, and Theodor W. Adorno. *Dialectic of Enlightenment*. New York: Continuum, 1987.

Hullot-Kentor, Robert. 'Back to Adorno.' *Telos* 81 (Fall 1989): 5–29.

Jameson, Fredric. *Late Marxism: Adorno, or, the Persistence of the Dialectic*. London: Verso, 1990.

Jay, Martin. *Adorno*. Cambridge, MA: Harvard University Press, 1984.

Kheel, Marti. 'Ecofeminism and Deep Ecology: Reflections on Identity and Difference.' In *Reweaving the World*, edited by Irene Diamond and Gloria Feman Orenstein. San Francisco: Sierra Club, 1990.

Luke, Tim. 'The Dreams of Deep Ecology.' *Telos* 76 (Summer 1988): 65–92.

– *Ecocritique*. Minneapolis: University of Minnesota Press, 1997.

Marcuse, Herbert. *One-Dimensional Man*. Boston: Beacon, 1964.

Martin, D. Bruce. 'Mimetic Moments.' In *Feminist Interpretations of Theodor Adorno*, edited by Renee Heberle, 141–71. University Park: Penn State University Press, 2006.

Marx, Karl, and Frederick Engels. 'The German Ideology.' In *Karl Marx and Frederick Engels, Collected Works*, vol. 5. New York: International, 1976.

Mills, Patricia J. *Woman, Nature, and Psyche*. New Haven: Yale University Press, 1987.

Naess, Arne. *Ecology, Community, and Lifestyle*. Edited and translated by David Rothenberg. Cambridge: Cambridge University Press, 1989.

– 'Identification as the Source of Deep Ecological Attitudes.' In *Deep Ecology*, edited by Michael Tobias. San Diego: Avant, 1985.

Nicholsen, Shierry Weber. *Exact Imagination, Late Work: On Adorno's Aesthetics*. Cambridge, MA: MIT Press, 1997.

– *The Love of Nature and the End of the World: The Unspoken Dimensions of Environmental Concern*. Cambridge, MA: MIT Press, 2003.

Plumwood, Val. 'The Ecopolitics Debate and the Politics of Nature.' In *Ecological Feminism*, edited by Karen J. Warren. London and New York: Routledge, 1994.

Reuther, Rosemary Radford. 'Ecofeminism: Symbolic and Social Connections of the Oppression of Women and the Domination of Nature.' In *Ecofeminism and the Sacred*, edited by Carol J. Adams. New York: Continuum, 1994.

Scarce, Rik. *Eco-Warriors: Understanding the Radical Environmental Movement*. Chicago: Noble, 1990.

Taussig, Michael. *Mimesis and Alterity*. New York: Routledge, 1993.

UNDP (United Nations Environmental Program). *Global Environment Outlook 4: Environment for Development*. Malta: Progress, 2007.

5 From 'Unity of Life' to the Critique of Domination: Jonas, Freud, and Marcuse

COLIN CAMPBELL

In 'Individualization: Plant a Tree, Buy a Bike, Save the World?' Michael Maniates demonstrates with admirable clarity the ecological predicament that late capitalism has induced. In its attempt to promote a less destructive relationship between human and non-human nature, the modern environmental movement (considered broadly as an ensemble of activists, government actors, corporate managers, and so on) invariably tends to promote the individualization of responsibility. What this means in practice is that environmental initiatives devolve into the production of alternative 'green' commodities for individual consumers: 'The individually responsible consumer is encouraged to purchase a vast array of "green" or "ecofriendly" products on the premise that the more such products are purchased and consumed, the healthier the planet's ecological processes will become. "Living lightly on the planet" and "reducing your environmental impact" becomes, paradoxically, a consumer-product growth industry.'[1]

Maniates reports that students in his university classes tend overwhelmingly to believe that environmental redemption will only emerge from a 'sea change in the choices individual consumers are making' (Maniates 2002, 50). He observes that 'Americans seem capable of understanding themselves almost solely as consumers who must buy "environmentally sound" products (and then recycle them)' (ibid., 51).

At the root of the current ecological impasse – that is, collective political inaction in the face of ongoing ecological degradation, with the prospect of global disaster – Maniates finds a one-dimensional sense of political citizenship and agency. All one can and need do to contribute to saving our planet is alter one's consumption choices, opting for the 'vast range of environmentally friendly, economically attractive technologies, from compact fluorescent lights to ultra fuel-efficient automobiles' (ibid., 53). The global citizenry 'increasingly understands environmentalism as an individual, rational, cleanly apolitical process that can deliver a future that works without raising voices or mobilizing constituencies' (ibid., 55).

Maniates sees the dialectical forces at work behind this 'everyone do their part' environmental voluntarism. The narrowness of the individualistic attitude is a direct and precise result of the *global* nature of the ecological threat and the *collective* responsibility we bear for it. As 'our collective perception of environmental problems has become more global, our prevailing way of framing environmental problem solving has become more individualized' (ibid., 59). Faced with global phenomena such as climate change and ozone depletion, and guided by the global application of biomanagerial formulae such as IPAT ('[ecological] impact = population x affluence x technology'), the environmental movement tends to privilege an 'everything is connected to everything else' attitude toward managing ecosystems, and then drops the responsibility for altering the pattern of that management into the hands of individual consumers. The problem, in effect, is framed as being so enormous that there is no point in trying to address it directly as a collective problem.

Maniates insists that what is required in the first place is a discussion in the fullest political sense about 'power, privilege and larger possibilities' (ibid., 62). Briefly, his argument is that we cannot expect to alter our ecologically destructive way of life without practically and collectively addressing much broader economic questions about profit, the imperative of growth, and the inequities of wealth distribution in free markets. He brings us back – quite possibly with some discomfort – from the land of high-efficiency light bulbs and hybrid automobiles to the question of the viability of capitalism itself, and the possibility of a radically different way of living politically on this planet.

Meanwhile, as conservation and management efforts under the status quo continue to fail to effect significant improvement, faced with an ever growing mountain of individualized and commodified ecological 'solutions,' ecological thinkers and activists understandably want to 'go deeper.' Against individualism, they assert more stridently, more insistently – and at times more angrily – that 'we are all connected.' In this context, the 'unity of life,' the image of humanity's total embeddedness in the larger ecosystem, is the perennial 'new big idea' that will supplant the traditional sense of human separateness that, it seems, is what really explains the inadequacy of contemporary responses to ecological problems. It is not anything specific to our social organization, the theory goes, but the chauvinism of a humanity that insists 'we are different' that explains why we continue to eradicate biodiversity and threaten our own survival. This 'biophilic' urge to identify with nature is not at all necessarily related to the kind of critique of capitalism that Maniates is advancing. Rather, it is a 'grand unified theory' of human and non-human nature in general – as opposed to a critique of contemporary forms of human social relations in particular.[2] 'Deep' ecologist Arne Naess celebrates the realization of a 'large comprehensive Self (with a capital "S") [that] embraces all the life forms on the planet';[3] and James Lovelock says that 'Gaia theory looks at the whole Earth from the outside and sees it as a live entity.'[4] Morality is redefined in terms of our responsibility to the Earth rather than to particular individual humans or a particular community of humans: 'Gaia can punish us if we transgress, for the theory stresses that any species that adversely affects the environment of its progeny will perish' (Primavesi 2000, xi).

In this chapter I follow Maniates's insight into how capitalism individualizes collective ecological problems, but my focus will be on the other side of the ideological dialectic – the collective, global, and perhaps even totalitarian side – rather than on the individualist consumerism that masks it in 'developed' liberal democracies. I will take up Hans Jonas's philosophy of the 'unity of life' in order to show that the impulse toward unity is not really an effective counter to individualization, but is actually only its dialectical counterpart. Individualization and consumerization, in other words, go hand in hand with grand ideologies of 'unity,' and this will become evident in an immanent citique of Jonas.

I suggest reading Jonas as an exemplary figure, because his work expresses the deep ecological desire for the 'unity of life' in a highly distilled and deeply compelling philosophical form. With a rigour reflecting that of his teacher, Martin Heidegger, Jonas proposes an epistemological direction for harmonizing humanity with life on earth as a whole. Central to his philosophy is the insight that modern science since Descartes has taken a deeply unfortunate wrong turn. Modern science pursues a clinical analysis of the lifeworld, viewing it in terms of mere matter, as a set of isolated parts, as a 'standing reserve' of resources to be *used*, rather than in terms of phenomena to be *lived with*. Considered as a set of isolated, fragmented objects, the phenomenon of life remains mysterious to the scientific outlook. For Jonas, what is needed is for us to come to terms with the phenomenon of life in its most basic sense, with what modern science in its current form can and cannot understand about how life works. For Jonas, this means ultimately that we need to recapture (in a new form, of course) the *panvitalistic* sense that seems evident in the earliest known human experiences and knowledge, to 'once again' experience the world as an organic unity of which humans are both part and reflection.

Certainly this attitude would appear to be as opposed as possible to the ongoing instrumentalization of life, to the subjugation of nature to destructive industrial processes, and to the capture of the ecological movement by the collective sales pitch of individualized responsibility. What could be more appropriate for a 'deeper' ecological philosophy? To frame a critical answer to this question I will be turning to another of Heidegger's students, Herbert Marcuse. Marcusean theory, like that of other thinkers of the 'first generation' Frankfurt School (including Adorno, Horkheimer, and Benjamin), shares much with Jonas's panvitalism and with the broader Heideggerian confrontation with modernity, of which Jonas's theory can be considered one expression.[5] Heidegger and the thinkers of the Frankfurt School are as one in emphasizing the enormously destructive impact of modern technology, of what they call 'instrumental reason.' All seem to agree here that we are faced with the imperative to completely rethink our relationship with nature.[6]

I will argue that an immanent and incisive critique of Jonas's Heideggerian, 'unitarian' attitude is implicit in Marcuse's *Eros and Civilization*, and furthermore, that this is the particular critique that needs desperately to be heard by the ecological movement if we are to move beyond the bad dialectic of collective guilt and isolated efforts. Marcuse's investigation of Eros, of the instinctual drive that also appears as the instinct of life in general in Freud's later psychology, illustrates a deep, unresolved problem in the 'biophilic' outlook. The ecological critique implicit in *Eros and Civilization* is this: forms of ecological thinking that elude or mystify *human social* relations – and most of all, the *guilt* engendered by the ongoing exploitation by some human beings of their fellows – will find that their celebrations of 'Being' or the 'unity of life' will fall again and again on the deaf ears of atomized, apolitical consumers.

Hans Jonas vividly demonstrates the contours of this dialectical impasse, but Marcuse goes further: he expresses its meaning. Marcuse suggests that without a deep and open confrontation with the biological and instinctual roots of guilt and fear in their social and historical context, the panvitalist ecological urge will at best remain a demonstration: that is, an example or a symptom of the crisis. Even worse, it may be conscripted into the service of some part of the prevailing global state of war, into actively promoting and perpetuating the generalized war against humanity and the rest of nature alike that is one of the primary characteristics of what he calls a 'one-dimensional society.'[7] This does not mean that Heideggerian and biophilic philosophies and other, less professional ideas about humanity living in much deeper harmony with other living things are simply wrong, morally evil, or totally incompatible with the ideals of a deeply pluralist democracy that would truly respect individuality. They do, as Adorno says of Heidegger, approach 'the borderline of dialectical insight,'[8] and to the extent that they reach this borderline, the Marcusean critique of them is an *immanent* one, aiming to draw out repressed inner potentials. Marcusean theory ultimately aims not at rejecting but at *consummating* the deep ecological desire for harmony with life, and it does so precisely by recognizing the internal contradictions and paradoxes that must define such a project.

'We, the Living'

Following Marcuse's method of immanent critique, I will begin where Hans Jonas begins, at the origin of human consciousness, the hypothetical moment when human awareness evolved from the animal. In the earliest human cultures, Jonas speculates, the cosmos would have been experienced as a great living entity, or an aggregation of living entities. The incipient self-awareness of the earliest people was extended in a kind of organic unity that included the entire cosmos. What Rousseau, in his essay on the origins of human inequality, called the *'amour de soi'* of the 'natural man'[9] is a kind of 'sentiment' or 'love' of existence that does not recognize clear boundaries between past and future, self and world, self and other.

Incidentally but not accidentally, Jonas's recognition of this stage of consciousness can be related by analogy with Freud's discovery of the 'limitless narcissism' of the human infant. In *Civilization and Its Discontents*, Freud suggests that this experience of a relative absence of boundaries accounts for the 'oceanic feeling' – wrongly imagined by some to be merely blissful – that lies at the root of religious and moral prohibitions. What characterizes the earliest stages of our development both as a species and as individuals is the absence of a capacity to create the boundaries that enable analytic thinking. Jonas suggests – in many ways echoing Rousseau – that the earliest forms of human consciousness would have been analogous in some respects to infancy: as in infancy, the boundary between self and other, the very sense of self created by that boundary, is confused and indistinct.

Heidegger's concept of 'Being' as the *ur*-ground of existence – as an existential fact that he found was more and more poorly recognized by Western thinkers caught up in the historical development of 'productionist metaphysics' – could be understood as another way of approaching this preindividual condition. In a different vein, the French writer Georges Bataille, often (and understandably) labelled as an irrationalist, has coined a wonderful and evocative phrase to explain this phase of human development: 'the animal is in the world like water in water.'[10] The discovery running through all of these philosophies could be summarized as follows: relative to subsequent stages of phylogenetic (species-level) or ontogenetic (individual-level) development, our earlier evolutionary stages always appear to us as characterized by a relative absence of separation and distinction.

It is Jonas's recognition of this 'oceanic feeling' that sets him apart from conventional scientific thinking, which, no matter how technically sophisticated its instruments and techniques, seems hopelessly anachronistic when it attempts to explain the deeper historical roots of human existence. For Jonas, to perceive the meaning of the initial glimmerings of human self-awareness as they are preserved in myth and folktale we must understand that at this stage, to be described or thought of, a 'thing' *must be experienced as alive:* 'being was only intelligible as living.'[11] If distinction between self and other, between self and world, is still only nascent, it follows that this sense of life 'here' in me, the thinker, is not separate from that object over 'there.' There can in fact be no sense of a clear, distinct object, lifelessly separate, over there. The sense of life within me is relatively extended, relatively continuous with the entire universe. This earliest human self-awareness would for Jonas be an animistic or panvitalistic orientation. The oldest evidence for human religious activity (vibrantly exemplified for Bataille in the cave paintings at places like Lascaux in France[12]) suggests precisely such an orientation: one in which humans and animals are cousin-spirits, intimate partners in a cosmic whole. Animals, trees, places, and stars, as well as people, are filled with spirit, are equally expressions of mind or spirit, and mind or spirit permeates all of these living realities.

Even to call such things 'things' would be to fall into a world view that is alien to the panvitalist one.[13]

Of course, in a world of pure and extended aliveness, death, the end of any thing, 'looms as the disturbing mystery' (Jonas 1966, 8). The reality of death would be intimately experienced within panvitalist human communities, but it would be the limit and end of any explanation, the limit of consciousness, the mystery of mysteries. Death does not form *part* of the panvitalist system of explanation; it is, rather, the mystery that the myth attempts and always fails to unveil. So it is not surprising that funerals appear, in the anthropological record, to be among the earliest religious rites. The function of these earliest religious rites, Jonas surmises, was to try to absorb and forestall the mysterious power of death, 'to negate it by making it a transmutation of life itself' (ibid., 9).

Jonas suggests – and in this suggestion expresses the entirety of his argument in a nutshell – that for us moderns it is not death but life that has become the great mystery. For us, it only seems possible to imagine a panvitalist orientation toward the world. This, after all, would be an orientation devoid of well-defined subjects and objects, of any firm separation between matter and spirit, a kind of experience that our language can express only poetically.[14] The very ability to say 'something is,' to use the verb 'to be' in such a fashion, assumes the ability to identify some *thing*; whereas for the panvitalistic position, there are no things, only a confusing aggregate of living spirits and beings. Our very language precludes us from perceiving the world in such a way. Our language has been marked, at an unconscious level, by the sense that inertness and death is the essential reality, rather than life.

Jonas argues that the closest we can come within the Western tradition to the lost panvitalist world is through a way of thinking that had already decisively broken from panvitalism: that of classical Greece and its philosophers. For Plato, as for the panvitalist, any intelligible pattern indicates intelligence *in the pattern*. Jonas finds that the Platonic definitions of 'life' and 'intelligence' are so closely intertwined as to be almost indistinguishable. As in panvitalism, Plato's cosmos is suffused with spirit – anything that exhibits a pattern appearing rational must have a soul to give it that form. Animals, trees, planets, and people can therefore all equally have 'souls'; they can all be inhabited by the divine spark; they can all be self-motivated and purposive.

But in the post-Homeric world of classical Greece there is a decided break from the world of poetic involvement and vital ritual.[15] Jonas is not alone in this discovery, any more than he is alone in his discovery of the 'oceanic' origins of human consciousness. Adorno and Hork-heimer's *Dialectic of Enlightenment* suggests that Platonism and philo-sophical rationalism take a sense of separation that is only *implied* in the patriarchal Homeric myth and make it a fixed principle, setting rela-tively passive matter on one side, and that spirit which imbues matter with form and purpose on the other.[16] Hans Jonas describes how Plato envisions a world of pure spirit, the quintessential world of forms, gods, and stars, as being separate from and higher than the fallen mate-rial world below, in which spirit is mixed with mere matter. Soul, for Plato, is not simply more noble and more just, as it is already implicitly in Homer. Spirit or intelligence is the very *cause* of material motion and order. As for the panvitalist, spirit pervades the cosmos, but now it does so only *by degrees*: 'the more consistently rational a motion, the higher must be the intelligence of the moving soul' (ibid., 70). According to the Platonic view, it can now be argued – where it would not have been in animistic religions – that on the scale of spiritual greatness, animals are *lower* than humans, women *lower* than men, barbarians *lower* than Greeks.

To explain how Plato and the rest of the classical Greeks could have come to desire to elevate themselves above their natural environment in this way, Jonas relegates Platonism and Western culture in general to the side of death. The *instinctual roots* of Plato's rationalistic disdain for 'lower things' are never interpreted as being related to an impulse toward life; they are, according to him, unambiguously situated over 'there,' on the side of death. The separation enjoined by reason and by Western civilization can only appear to Jonas as a kind of inexplicable fall, as a contamination from the outside of life's unity by a radical ele-ment of evil, the work of a terrible and mysterious fate beyond our control. Of course, this is precisely the way death has always appeared to the panvitalist mind: as an inexplicable, terrible mystery that cannot be confronted rationally, only ritualistically absorbed and neutralized, or opposed. 'We are all connected,' then, indeed, except for those who deny this all-one-connection, who are thereby 'by their fault' separated from us, 'over there,' in the land of death. Throughout his philosophi-cal biology, Jonas speaks in the voice of 'we, the living,' and of death as some monstrous *thing*, over there.

Of course, if Plato introduces a fateful separation between humanity and nature, for Jonas, it is monotheistic religion that lays the crucial foundational elements of the much more destructive modern scientific viewpoint. It is in monotheism, in the Hebrew scriptures, that the material world is for the first time conceived as a *product*, entirely subordinated to the will of an almighty creator of everything: 'Jewish monotheism has abolished the deities of nature and all intermediary powers, leaving God and world in clean-cut division' (ibid., 71). For the Christian thinkers who assimilate the Jewish tradition, the human soul is the only element in the world of nature connected with God's creative power. The human mind thus becomes, to an unprecedented degree, separated from and set above nature, in a 'metaphysics of the will.' The whole of nature, having been created according to the divine plan, can be seen as rational in design, as having order and symmetry, yet as possessing no rationality in itself: 'Thus the idea of a mindless or "blind" nature, which yet behaves lawfully – that is, which keeps an intelligible order without being intelligent – had become metaphysically possible ... There could arise the conception of a nature not only mindless but also inanimate, that is, of a nature not only intelligible without being intelligent, but also moving without being alive' (ibid., 71–2).

Jonas describes this new and monumental shift in human self-understanding in much the same way as he describes the shift from panvitalism to Platonism – as a contamination by the power of death. But in monotheism, Jonas argues, death has achieved a new status and a new role: 'The theoretical shock that once issued from the corpse has turned into a constitutive principle, and in a universe formed after the image of the corpse, the single, actual corpse has lost its mystery' (ibid., 15).

With monotheism, death – or the empty void, or the inert and isolated object – is finally considered the very norm, the 'default position' of the material world. We no longer experience the cosmos as an extension of the life within ourselves, either directly or as mediated through the stars above us. In monotheistic theology, according to Jonas, human life, expressed in our reflection of divine willing, becomes nothing more and nothing less than an exception to the rule of death 'here below.' Descartes's rationalistic reduction of the material world and nature to mere matter in mechanistic motion only draws the logical conclusions of the Judeo-Christian ontology of death. Monotheistic religion, as it appears in Jonas's *Phenomenon of Life*, is death-religion, a religion of the dead, and the only course of action with regard to 'we, the living' might well seem to be to purge it, like a parasite, from our culture. As we will see, Jonas is not at all insensitive to the enormous repercussions that the attitude of cleansing or purging an otherwise healthy social body of perceived parasites has entailed in the twentieth century – indeed, throughout the history of Western civilization.

The great strength of Jonas's argument in *The Phenomenon of Life* is found in the rigour with which he insists that, according to scientific reason itself, life cannot be reduced to mechanistic interactions of analysable parts. The wonderful controlling power we have acquired in separating ourselves from life – in coming to see life as a limited and defined group of individual phenomena 'over there' rather than as an all-encompassing totality – has not actually helped us understand, scientifically or otherwise, how life works. Too often we assume that technological science, with its highly compartmentalized view, comprehends and reflects all of reality. In fact, it cannot even begin to explain the essential metabolic functions of living beings; it can only explain parts of them, isolated from the whole. Furthermore, it cannot produce living phenomena itself; at best, it can only manipulate parts of them to put them in service of non-living machines. And too often it does so in total ignorance of the profoundly negative effects it is having on the larger organism and on the aggregate of organisms as a whole.

It seems undeniable that Jonas's panvitalistic feeling of the grand unity of life constitutes a total philosophical (as well as, presumably, psychological) reversal of mainstream Western psycho-ontology, at least since Homer. For him, this panvitalism would be more than just a feeling; it would be an entirely alternate form of cognition and perceptual experience. He insists that this real and ineradicable life experience is a crucial insight that has been lost by modern analytic science, which now desperately needs to recover it. The explicit ethical recognition of desires, wants, and emotions in 'lower' forms of life reflects the more general recognition of 'aliveness' – one that Jonas insists is crucial not only to life itself but also to the further development of human reason.

Jonas brilliantly illuminates the fact that the creative and purposive self-ordering of the metabolizing organism is something that Cartesian materialism simply cannot comprehend, not least because living matter is governed by more than quantifiable rules of motion. With life, there is a *qualitative* difference from dead matter. This difference cannot be explained in terms of otherwise non-living chains of action and reaction. In its first appearance, life *maintains a whole form* that transcends any reduction to the quantifiable motions of its otherwise non-living parts. This whole metabolic form has remained opaque to Cartesian materialism and to analytical science in general and has therefore been largely ignored. Jonas shows that just as death remains inexplicable and mythic in the panvitalist mindset, life has remained essentially inexplicable according to the modern scientific one.

It is the uniquely intimate relation that living things, including us humans, have with the world – the simultaneity of our separateness and unity with an external environment – that is missed by quantitative science, which would reduce all phenomena to the interactions of isolated particles. Jonas shows clearly and forcefully how the phenomenon of life remains an insoluble problem for any science whose sole project is to analyse and take apart. Forms of activity too often seen as separate must be seen in light of the unity to which analytic thought is blind. Jonas insists that *life as a whole* must from now on take a certain conceptual and also ethical priority if we wish to understand it and if we wish to embrace a scientific or technological orientation that does not entail the dissection and thereby destruction of the lifeworld.

The explicit ethical recognition of recognizable desires, wants, and emotions in 'lower' forms of life reflects the more general recognition of 'aliveness' that Jonas insists is crucial to the further development of human reason. In a pure materialism, without this qualitative and absolute sense of the difference between the living and the dead, the world of matter is reduced to sequences of events that are essentially external and indifferent to one another, that are 'dead.' For Jonas, *qualitative distinctions* referring to lived needs and wants remain necessary to make sense of anything at all, let alone living things. And for Jonas, the distinction that recognizes the quality of *aliveness* shared by all organic forms, including the animal *Homo sapiens*, is of pre-eminent importance. The feeling that 'we the living' are clearly distinct from 'they, the dead' forms the developmental template (in both the phylogenetic-historical and ontogenetic-psychological sense) upon which all more advanced scientific and cultural distinctions can be drawn.

The Ambiguity of the 'Unity of Life'

For Jonas, who is by no means cynical or 'anti-human,' human consciousness itself is not the root problem and is not problematic at its root. On the contrary, the faculty of human consciousness, far from being radically separate from the other organic phenomena, ought to be the consummation of the unity of life. It is only with humans that 'perception by itself becomes imbued with pleasure and assumes the status of an experience sought for its own sake' (Jonas 1966, 184). Of course, perception in general assumes the significance of beholding, of an attitude of separation. Beyond the interposition of metabolism between self and world that characterizes organic beings, and of the perception that characterizes animals, there is a new interposition, a 'mediacy of the third degree' (ibid., 185). This is the mediacy of the *eidos* – the ability to imagine, to form concepts, to speak. Just as the animal is no longer directly metabolically rooted in its environment, but has perception and motility, in the *eidos* speaking and thinking man no longer *perceives* directly. Instead, 'he sees ... through the screen of representations of which he has become possessed by his own previous dealings with objects ... impregnating [present perceptual contents] with their *symbolic charge*' (ibid.).

The greatest significance of human consciousness is that the subject of perception can become aware of itself, can become its own perceptual object by means of thought. And becoming truly aware of itself implies its becoming aware that it is a kind of cosmic pseudopod, an extension of generalized life process. This self-reflection is therefore the most extreme form of simultaneous disconnection from, *and fusion with*, the environment ever developed by an organic being. Animals may feel and satisfy desires, or be unable to do so and feel hunger; but only people can be happy, and only people can despair. Jonas describes enigmatically how a person can be 'absorbed in conformity with [their] society,' or 'withdraw in solitude'; but how they can also 'set up a new image of man and impose it on his society.' The distance opened up between humans and their world by the symbolic order is spanned and reunified by such 'acts of eidetic intentionality' (ibid.).

So – and here a fully dialectical critique of Jonas can begin in earnest – we need to note that what is really striking about Jonas's rigorous reconceptualization of human uniqueness and about the context of the larger unity of life is its *ambiguity*. Human awareness is, from the beginning, a separation, but this separation is made only in order to deepen the sense of dependency and relationship. The separation exists only to create a greater unity. Jonas emphasizes the reality of formal, living, organic *boundaries*, which must be accounted for as the very possibility of thinking even while those boundaries – between the thinking mind of a human being and every other organic process – are being emphatically *eradicated*. For Jonas, every assertion of separation is in the end a drive toward the greater unity of life. But the drive toward the unity of life requires, dialectically speaking, a force of death from which to separate itself. Life must first expel death in order to live, must separate itself from separation, must connect with what is connected with itself and expel that which resists connection.

In his other work, Jonas more clearly expresses the human social dimensions of this problem, which is only hinted at in his work on philosophical biology. In spite of their vital limitations, it turns out that Jewish and Christian monotheisms have played a crucial role in the historical self-assertion of the individual against the classical view of the world and divinity as some eternal, self-identical essence: 'The world had to be diminished in status so as to be brought into that relation with a divine origin which the doctrine of creation demanded ... Traditional philosophy had clearly overvalued the world.'[17] A space for an alternative to the divinely ordered and rational cosmos of the Platonic imagination was opened up by the negativity of biblical contingency, that it was the will of God and not fateful necessity that made the world. This space corresponds to one made for the individual will, which turns toward God and thereby transcends the fatalistic classical universe. The utter negativity of the idea of creation out of nothing – the sense that the natural world is without any creative, ordering principle of its own – had a dialectical counterpoint: it made room for the idea of a radically individual providence, a real concern for and investment of God in this body, this person: 'Against the background of nothingness from which it is called forth, individual being assumes a rank of primacy which all ancient philosophy had denied it' (Jonas 1974, 37).

The value that Jonas ascribes to monotheistic religion here shows the degree to which he has comprehended 'the stand we moderns have reached' (ibid., 35). The devaluation of nature, its treatment as nothing but an aggregate of inert parts subject to analysis, the development in Western civilization of this 'metaphysics of the will,' has a flip side: the freedom of individuals in relation to a totality of society and nature. It turns out that the way back to the unity of life is not so easy, at least not as long as we are not ready to sacrifice individuals to the 'glorious improvement of the race' (ibid., 80). When the holistic vision of unified life confronts the ethical reality of human individuals, Jonas is forced to moderate the claim to a new image of humanity in nature. Instead of a radical return to panvitalism, here Jonas makes a more modest proposal: 'some backswing of the pendulum might be in order' (ibid., 35).

But the question of what such a 'backswing' could mean, given the ambiguities that beset the idea of the unity of life, is a difficult one indeed. Philosophy, he says, remains at an impasse as it attempts to find some 'third way' between rupture and fusion, between individualism and a 'monistic naturalism' that would abolish the individual:

> The illogicality of the rupture, that is, of a dualism without metaphysics, makes its fact no less real, nor its seeming alternative any more acceptable: the state of isolated selfhood, to which it condemns man, may wish to exchange for itself a monistic naturalism which, along with the rupture, would abolish also the idea of man as man. Between that Scylla and her twin Charybdis, the modern mind hovers. Whether a third road is open to it – one by which the dualistic rift can be avoided and yet enough of the dualistic insight saved to uphold the humanity of man – philosophy must find out.[18]

Beginning from the real, practical problem of our destructive relation with the ecological whole, for Jonas, we are left in the end with ambiguity. At the level of practice, we are perpetually looking for norms that philosophy can no longer provide: 'And here is where I get stuck, and where we all get stuck. For the same movement which puts us in possession of the power that have now to be regulated by norms – the movement of modern knowledge called science – has by a necessary complementarity eroded the foundation from which norms could be derived; it has destroyed the very idea of the norm itself' (ibid., 19).

It would be easy enough to set Jonas aside as a philosophical failure, to simply ignore the impasse and return to the panvitalist thesis that says simply that we humans are animals like all the others. We might minimize the enormity of such a claim in a world in which not only animals but also human beings have been subject to programmed mass extermination. We might not distinguish in any practical way between Auschwitz and the factory farm. Indeed, with Jonas's philosophical biology in mind we might see striking and disturbing parallels between the way we treat animals and the way the executioners treat their victims in human extermination programs. But given a world in which animals are farmed industrially – and until we live in a world in which the last factory farm has been closed – is there not, in the meantime, a pressing ethical obligation to distinguish human from animal?

Whatever stance we end up taking on such deep ethical quandaries, I suggest that Jonas demonstrates in an exemplary way the ambiguity at the core of the drive to recognize and to 'be with' the 'unity of life.' This ambiguity, furthermore, is not only between Jonas's religious and ethical writing and his philosophical biology; it is contained *in nuce* in the biology itself, precisely in the idea of the ambiguity of life as something both radically separated from and fused with its environment. To the extent that we take the side of life in general, we ecologists are indeed collectively 'stuck' and it is most difficult to imagine how we could actually get free of the trap, except by denying that it exists in the first place. Does Jonas's trap not explain precisely how it is possible for more people than ever to have an honestly global, holistic ecological sense, while in practice chasing a plethora of piecemeal 'green solutions' that they quite likely know can never substantively address the global problem?[19]

Eros, Thanatos, and Civilization

Marcuse goes beyond Jonas and can help us get 'unstuck' precisely to the extent that Marcuse takes into account the dialectic that Jonas comes so close to revealing, but that remains an insoluble philosophical and ethical paradox. To move beyond Jonas's paradox, we need first to shift focus explicitly from the 'unity of life' to the *dialectics* of life and death as factors that are mutually part of the human experience. The problem is that for Jonas, acknowledgment of the immanent reality of death – of the fact that it might be intertwined with life – brings us to an impasse. Many, including Sigmund Freud, have responded to a similar impasse with pessimism and resignation. Marcuse suggests that what is required, beyond a sense of the duality of life and death (or, as they are referred to in Freudian psychoanalytic theory, Eros and Thanatos), is awareness of the social and historical specificity of that intertwinement *in the context of societies structured by domination*. Marcuse says that if there is a way out of the dialectic of individual bad conscience and collective destruction, it will be found only in a *social* and *historical* transformation of that dialectic beyond its current impasse.

The word 'Eros' is curiously absent from the philosophy that Jonas develops in *The Phenomenon of Life*. This absence is striking, for there is a deeply erotic subtext to his ecological theory, even if only in the sense that he could be called a biophile, a lover of the great unity of life. It was, incidentally but not accidentally, Sigmund Freud who in *Civilization and Its Discontents* defined Eros as the instinct that aims at building 'ever larger unities.' In Freudian psychology, Eros is the dynamic, expansive force of life, in its more familiar dimension of directly sexual existence but also in the rest of instinctual life, in the whole range of more sublimated human cultural forms. Freud argues that 'civilization is a process in the service of Eros, whose purpose is to combine single human individuals, and after that families, then races, peoples and nations, into one great unity, the unity of mankind.'[20]

But much like in Jonas, Freud's treatment of the life-instinct comes (albeit much more quickly and decisively than in Jonas) to its own impasse. It turns out, taking into account the whole development of Freudian theory, that all is not well with Eros. For one thing, Eros cannot involve an unlimited extension of love to the cosmic whole, as Jonas imagines panvitalism would entail. Freud is deeply suspicious of such an 'oceanic feeling': 'The "oneness with the universe" that constitutes its ideational content sounds like a first attempt at a religious consolation, as though it were another way of disclaiming the danger which the ego recognizes as threatening it from the external world' (Freud 1961, 21). The external world in fact threatens the survival of the ego, and the ego must respond in kind to preserve itself. Eros is necessarily confronted from the very beginning by its dark twin, Thanatos, the death instinct, the aggressive and destructive powers of nature, within and without: 'The instinct of destruction, moderated and tamed, and, as it were, inhibited in its aim, must, when it is directed towards objects, provide the ego with the satisfaction of its vital needs and with control over nature' (ibid., 81).

According to Freud, Eros is fraught with the vicissitudes introduced by civilization. The paradox is as follows: civilization is an erotic enterprise, aimed at the preservation of life in 'ever larger unities.' But erotic desire, it turns out, is not always prosocial according to civilized standards. Civilization has been achieved only by means of the *renunciation* and *repression* of a substantial part of the erotic instincts:

> We are saying much the same thing when we derive the antithesis between civilization and sexuality from the circumstances that sexual love is a relationship between two individuals in which a third can only be superfluous or disturbing, whereas civilization depends on relationships between a considerable number of individuals. When a love-relationship is at its height there is no room left for any interest in the environment; a pair of lovers are sufficient to themselves, and do not even need the child they have in common to make them happy. (ibid., 64–5)

Eros has too often appeared as a force subversive of the demands of family, toil, and sacrifice entailed by civilized development. Love builds family and community, but it is also what induces Romeo and Juliet to choose death over family and community. Civilization as a whole, like the individual ego, has needed to conscript the powers of Eros' opposite, Thanatos, partly in order to reign in that part of Eros that would threaten civilization. For Freud, this conscription corresponds to the one made on the individual level that is necessary to preserve the separateness and integrity of the ego. Together they constitute Freud's own vision of the 'human dilemma.'

The upshot of this dilemma is nowhere more evident, according to Freud, than in the development of the psychology of the modern neurotic, in whom aggression – internalized in the form of a repressive superego – forces the ego to renounce antisocial erotic desires, then rebounds and actually *produces* new forms of antisocial behaviour. In the neurotic personality, the overwhelming guilt induced by civilized standards of behaviour can undermine the rational aims of self-preservation that civilization was created to satisfy in the first place. Freud finds again and again, and not without anxiety, that Eros, the fundamental urge of self-preservation, appears to be hopelessly intertwined with Thanatos, the death instinct. Given psychological and social experience, Freud would say that the idea of an undifferentiated and purely positive 'life force' is the worst kind of myth, a kind of wilful blindness. There can be no question of finding some proper 'backswing of the pendulum' toward 'it'; and even if it swung all the way back, it would only be confronted with the deeper destructiveness of the repetition compulsion and the return of the repressed.

Freud envisions the 'life force' in its developed psychological form, the full dimensions of which must remain blinkered for a theory proposing the 'unity of life.' At a general biological level, the 'equilibrium tendencies' of the instincts (the organism's general drive toward preserving itself in its present form) ultimately point back *behind* genesis of the organism, *before* the beginning of life, and thus actually represent the instinct toward stillness and lack of change. An otherwise 'pure' erotic desire for conservation of the life of the organism turns out to have a deathly aspect at its heart: it is the desire for cessation of the tension that life itself has introduced.

The spectre of life's fusion with death – that life might be no more than a detour to death – is counterbalanced in Freud's broader theory and experience of human sexuality. As Marcuse summarizes: 'No matter how universal the regressive inertia of organic life, the instincts strive to attain their objective in fundamentally different modes ... Fresh tensions are introduced by the claims of Eros, of the sexual instincts, as expressed in instinctual needs.'[21] Marcuse finds that in Freudian theory, taken as a whole, 'the ultimate relation between Eros and Thanatos remains obscure' (1966, 27). Sexuality and desire, according to the thesis of the common origin of the life and death instincts, 'would obey the same principle as the death instinct' (ibid., 26). In *Eros and Civilization* he draws out the implicitly dialectical and deeply ambiguous nature of Freud's late theory: 'Never before has death been so consistently taken into the essence of life; but never before also has death come so close to Eros ... The death principle is destructiveness not for its own sake, but for the relief of tension. The descent toward death is an unconscious flight from pain and want. It is an expression of the eternal struggle against suffering and repression' (ibid., 29).

'Basic' Repression, 'Surplus' Repression, and Domination

The impasse faced by civilization, Freud, Marcuse, and Jonas might all agree, is that humanity projects death onto human and non-human nature by the very analytical and technological activity that aims at guaranteeing its preservation. With his idea of the unity of life, and his 'new image of man,' Jonas would like to set himself up in opposition to this instrumental reason, which converts all of nature into a 'standing reserve.' Jonas would like to finally extirpate this intertwinement of life and death, to attain in its place a state of living unity: essentially to experience the cosmos as one giant organism. But to the extent that he does so, Freud and Marcuse would point out, Jonas must simply ignore the problem of dialectical intertwinement.

For both Freud and Marcuse, the meaning of the historical intertwinement of life and death is given in *guilt*. The attainment of the security of advanced civilization, built on the channelling of aggressive energy pursuant to the domination of nature, has exacted a price in terms of renunciation of the erotic instincts, not only on the non-human nature we have dominated, but also on the human organism itself. Ironically, the origin of the aggressive desire to separate humanity from nature is an instinctual response to that very separation. But the response given to the necessity of instinctual renunciation has been, again and again throughout Western history, to intensify rather than mitigate instinctual renunciation: 'Civilization plunges into a destructive dialectic: the perpetual restrictions on Eros ultimately weaken the life instincts and thus strengthen and release the very forces against which they were called up – those of destruction' (ibid., 44).

To the extent that Jonas celebrates the unity of life, he must blind himself to dialectics and recognize that the roots of the current ecological crisis lie in erotic desire for self-preservation, however distorted and perverted it has become. In Freudian psychology the aggressive instinct, which can be disguised as dispassionate objectivity, ultimately aims at serving an erotic desire for self-preservation. Humanity's objectification and exploitation of nature is not rooted in some mythically pure evil, in an aggressiveness epitomized by Judaic or Christian monotheism, or in the modern deification of technological reason. It is rooted in the striving of confused, guilt-ridden human beings to preserve their lives in the face of death. Analytic reason, then, is not the culprit, but the tool: the urge to conceptually kill by separation and analysis issues from fear and guilt about what underlies that process of separation and analysis.

Marcuse acknowledges that a basic degree of repression, a basic sense of separation and renunciation of total unity, is concomitant with human life itself. But he disagrees with Freud's view that the repression which helps constitute the ego is identical with the level of repression demanded by a civilization structured by domination. In *Eros and Civilization*, Marcuse in fact aims at the *liberation of Eros* from the deathly duality that Freud excavates in the 'normal' neurosis of the civilized psyche. In this, Marcuse comes very close to Jonas: he, too, wants to take the side of life, and not only human life but life in general. He aims to convey a vision of an erotic civilization, or an erotic vision of civilization: that is to say, a civilization not marked by the forces of death – by war and unending toil – but rather by an effervescence of life – of work as play, of a life without fear, in harmony with the other inhabitants of the earth. But how is this possible, if he accepts the basic Freudian duality of the life and death instincts?

The answer is that for Marcuse the relation between life and death is not ultimately a duality but a dialectic. The intertwinement of the two, that is, does not make them concomitant, or identical with each other. So in fact it is possible to 'take the side of life,' but this task is considerably more difficult than simply identifying 'we, the living.' According to Marcuse, the dualistic intertwinement of the life and death instincts that we perceive as psychologically and existentially necessary, and the guilt that we necessarily feel about this intertwinement, are the results of a specific set of historical circumstances. They are not basic to the human condition. What we presently experience as 'human nature' arises in a social and historical context where the drives indeed *are* almost fused. This fusion has grown from a social structure in which ruling elites dominate and exploit – often *must* exploit – people lower than themselves in the social hierarchy. What is lacking in both Jonas and Freud is any sense of how domination has created a particularly bad fusion of the life and death instincts.

Marcuse distinguishes between what Freud calls the 'reality principle' – the limits and structures that confront the developing imagination of any conceivable human infant – and the 'performance principle' – the limit that every person experiences at every age under current social conditions. The deep guilt created in a context of structural inequality, the constraints on life and work imposed by the requirement of serving elites or a profit imperative rather than immediate sensual pleasure, have forced us to undergo 'surplus repression.' Some degree of unfulfilling work – for example, work that fails to come to fruition, or that would be necessary due to the ultimate unpredictability of both human and non-human nature – would surely seem to be a fundamental aspect of human existence. But our sacrifices need not serve the irrational, dynamic, and globally destructive hierarchy of capitalism.

What Marcuse is saying to an ecological movement that wants to 'go deeper' is that while most human beings struggle for mere self-preservation, and where the condition of all survival is unending toil and repression of instinctual needs (including, too often, the need to eat), any celebration of the 'unity of life' is *premature*. It remains a utopian exercise in the worst sense, the 'unwanted, built-in automatic utopianism' that Jonas so perceptively identifies as part of the current technological fixation (1966, 18). As long as our instinctual needs are either denied or else recruited to further 'development' in the form of the destructive-productive military-industrial complex, it is not possible to conceive of a relationship of equality between humanity and nature that does not actually imply the degradation of human nature *below* the level of animals. To do so is to put the cart disastrously before the horse. The problem of 'merely human' suffering and guilt is too rarely even mentioned in the popular discourse of the 'Green' movement and 'sustainability.'[22] Obviating this 'merely human' suffering, making a firm political commitment to the emancipation of human beings from this inequality that produces want and fear, is a primary requirement for providing the context for a more harmonious, intimate, and multidimensional relationship with non-human nature.

NOTES

1 Michael Maniates, 'Individualization: Plant a Tree, Buy a Bike, Save the World?' in *Confronting Consumption*, ed. T. Princen, M. Maniates, and K. Conca (Cambridge, MA: MIT Press, 2002). Hereafter 'Maniates.'

2 Since as early as 1984 the highly influential biologist and philosopher Edward O. Wilson has structured his environmental philosophy almost entirely around the concept of 'biophilia,' a generalized love of the shared nature of all living things. If we are no different from the other animals, says Wilson, it follows logically and ethically that we must extend our love equally to all of them. See Edward O. Wilson, *Biophilia* (Cambridge, MA: Harvard University Press, 1984).

3 Michael Zimmerman, ed., *Environmental Philosophy: From Animal Rights to Radical Ecology* (Upper Saddle River: Prentice Hall, 1996), 208.

4 From his foreword to Anne Primavesi, *Sacred Gaia* (London: Routledge, 2000), xii. Hereafter 'Lovelock.'

5 I lack the space in this chapter to fully draw out the unbroken harmony between Jonas and his teacher, notwithstanding that Jonas emphasizes 'Life' whereas Heidegger emphasizes 'Being.' I am arguing in this chapter that the function of the term – an abstract philosophical-existential category that displaces the centrality of analytic-objective thinking – is crucially similar in that it occludes the problem of guilt as it is addressed in *Eros and Civilization*. In *Negative Dialectics*, Adorno argues that 'Heidegger gets as far as the borderline of dialectical insight into the nonidentity in identity. But he does not carry through the contradiction in the concept of Being. He suppresses it'; Theodor W. Adorno, *Negative Dialectics* (New York: Continuum, 1966), 104. The thesis of this chapter is that the pursuit of the concept of 'Life' brings Hans Jonas to the 'borderline of dialectical insight' and then leads him to suppress that same insight. Marcuse's treatment of the life-instincts is more like Adorno's philosophy: more negative, more dialectical.

6 This agreement I think quite clearly extends to all of the authors whose work is collected in this volume. Furthermore, I think that a sense of the limitations of Heidegger and those like him is shared equally by those who come from a Habermasian position (see the contributions of Steven Vogel and Bill Leiss) as well as by those who take a more Adornian view (Don Burke). Note that in this chapter I do not make any significant operative distinction between the Marcusean critique and the Adornian critique, and that furthermore I might ask whether (to paraphrase Walter Benjamin) Habermasian communicative rationality settles the deeply *erotic* and *aes-*

thetic claims (repressed, yet preserved, in the language of 'unity of life') of the Heideggerians 'too cheaply.'

7 On the problem of the relation of the ecological movement to a totalitarian war state, it is worth quoting from a deeply disappointing interview with James Lovelock: 'We need a more authoritative world. We've become a sort of cheeky, egalitarian world where everyone can have their say. It's all very well, but there are certain circumstances – a war is a typical example – where you can't do that. You've got to have a few people with authority who you trust who are running it. And they should be very accountable too, of course. But it can't happen in a modern democracy. This is one of the problems. What's the alternative to democracy? There isn't one. But even the best democracies agree that when a major war approaches, democracy must be put on hold for the time being. I have a feeling that climate change may be an issue as severe as a war. It may be necessary to put democracy on hold for a while.' From Leo Hickman, 'James Lovelock on the Value of Sceptics and Why Copenhagen Was Doomed,' *The Guardian*, 29 March 2010. http://www.guardian.co.uk/environment/blog/2010/mar/29/james-lovelock.

8 Theodor W. Adorno, *Negative Dialectics* (New York: Continuum, 1966), 104.

9 'His soul, agitated by nothing, is given over to the sole sentiment of its present existence without any idea of the future, however near it may be, and his projects, as limited as his views, barely extend to the end of the day.' Jean-Jacques Rousseau, *The First and Second Discourses*, ed. Roger D. Masters and Judith R. Masters (New York: St Martin's, 1964), 117.

10 Georges Bataille, *Theory of Religion* (New York: Zone, 2001).

11 Hans Jonas, *The Phenomenon of Life: Toward a Philosophical Biology* (New York: Harper and Row, 1966), 9. Hereafter 'PoL.'

12 See Georges Bataille, *Prehistoric Painting: Lascaux, or The Birth of Art* (Geneva: Skira, 1955).

13 That the theory of panvitalism is more than empty speculation is supported by ample evidence in the anthropological record. Dorothy Lee's *Freedom and Culture* (Englewood Cliffs: Prentice Hall, 1955), for example, explores with wonderful vividness the perceptions of peoples like the Trobriand Islanders, whose language does not contain adjectives or the verb 'to be.'

14 The deep nostalgia for the Homeric world expressed by Eric Havelock, among many others, could be summarized as nostalgia for a world in which our modern sense of the separateness of things did not yet exist. See Havelock, *Preface to Plato* (Cambridge, MA: Harvard University Press, 1963).

15 See again Havelock's *Preface to Plato* for a deep reading of Homer as the poet-educator of the pre-classical Greek mind.

16 In their excursus on Homer in *Dialectic of Enlightenment* (New York: Continuum, 1982), Theodor W. Adorno and Max Horkheimer examine the character of Odysseus, for whom the renunciation of immediate instinct is a dialectical extension of the instinct for self-preservation. Odyssean cunning consists in the renunciation of the body's immediate urges in favour of the long-term project of the self. Adorno and Horkheimer find that in general, Odysseus expresses his manhood by separating himself from his environment in order to control it.

17 Hans Jonas, *Philosophical Essays: From Ancient Creed to Technological Man* (Englewood Cliffs: Prentice Hall, 1974), 35. Hereafter 'Essays.'

18 Hans Jonas, *The Gnostic Religion: The Message of the Alien God and the Beginnings of Christianity* (Boston: Beacon, 1963), 340.

19 This problem has been posed from another angle, and with remarkable clarity, by Stefan Dolgert in his essay on the animal liberation movement, in which he begins by juxtaposing the enormous amount of money spent on pet care (veterinary care, food, grooming, etc.) in 2006 with the enormous number of unwanted pets abandoned and killed in animal shelters the same year. See Stefan Dolgert, 'Ghosts of Prometheus: The Sacrifice of the Animal in Liberal Animal Rights Theory,' paper presented at the annual meeting of the Midwest Political Science Association, Chicago, 12 April 2007), 3.

20 Sigmund Freud, *Civilization and Its Discontents* (New York: Norton, 1961), 81. Hereafter 'Freud.'

21 Herbert Marcuse, *Eros and Civilization* (Boston: Beacon, 1966), 26-7. Hereafter 'Marcuse.' Marcuse is referring here to Freud's *Ego and the Id* (London: Hogarth, 1950).

22 There are, of course, exceptions to this rule – for example, Vandana Shiva and others, who come from the 'global South,' where the links between inequality and ecological devastation are much more obvious. But Shiva's work has remained a token and an exception in larger discussions of sustainability. The question that Marcusean analysis poses is how any serious discussion of ecological sustainability can afford to ignore the problem of inequality as it is raised by Shiva – *as the primary problem*, and not merely one issue on a list that also includes new designs for packaging.

BIBLIOGRAPHY

Adorno, Theodor W. *Negative Dialectics*. New York: Continuum, 1966.
Bataille, Georges. *Prehistoric Painting: Lascaux, or The Birth of Art*. Geneva: Skira, 1955.

– *Theory of Religion*. New York: Zone, 2001.
Dolgert, Stefan, 'Ghosts of Prometheus: The Sacrifice of the Animal in Liberal Animal Rights Theory.' Paper presented at the annual meeting of the Midwest Political Science Association, Chicago, 12 April 2007.
Freud, Sigmund. *Civilization and Its Discontents*. New York: Norton, 1961.
– *Ego and the Id*. London: Hogarth, 1950.
Havelock, Eric. *Preface to Plato*. Cambridge, MA: Harvard University Press, 1963.
Horkheimer, Max, and Theodor W. Adorno. *Dialectic of Enlightenment*. New York: Continuum, 1982.
Jonas, Hans. *The Gnostic Religion: The Message of the Alien God and the Beginnings of Christianity*. Boston: Beacon, 1963.
– *The Phenomenon of Life: Toward a Philosophical Biology*. New York: Harper and Row, 1966.
– *Philosophical Essays: From Ancient Creed to Technological Man*. Englewood Cliffs: Prentice Hall, 1974.
Lee, Dorothy. *Freedom and Culture*. Englewood Cliffs: Prentice Hall, 1955.
Lovelock, James. Foreword to *Sacred Gaia*, by Anne Primavesi. London: Routledge, 2000.
Maniates, Michael. 'Individualization: Plant a Tree, Buy a Bike, Save the World?' In *Confronting Consumption*, edited by T. Princen, M. Maniates, and K. Conca. Cambridge, MA: MIT Press, 2002.
Marcuse, Herbert. *Eros and Civilization*. Boston: Beacon, 1966.
Primavesi, Anne. Foreword to *Sacred Gaia*, by James Lovelock. London: Routledge, 2000.
Rousseau, Jean-Jacques. *The First and Second Discourses*. Edited by Roger D. Masters, translated by Roger D. Masters and Judith R. Masters. New York: St Martin's, 1964.
Wilson, Edward O. *Biophilia*. Cambridge, MA: Harvard University Press, 1984.
Zimmerman, Michael, ed. *Environmental Philosophy: From Animal Rights to Radical Ecology*. Upper Saddle River: Prentice Hall, 1996.

PART THREE

Alienation and the Aesthetic

6 Adorno's Aesthetic Rationality: On the Dialectic of Natural and Artistic Beauty

DONALD A. BURKE

Though philosophical reflection on the relationship between art and nature – or, more specifically, the relation between artistic and natural beauty – goes back to the time of Kant's *Critique of Judgment*, post-Kantian German idealists such as Schelling and Hegel decisively shifted philosophical aesthetics in the direction of a philosophy of fine art. Hegel's exclusion of natural beauty from deserving a scientific treatment is a result of the spiritualization of content in his system, or 'the essential inner progress of [art's] content and means of expression.'[1] What is common to Kant and Hegel is to conceive of the relation between natural beauty and artistic beauty in a hierarchical arrangement: the former regards natural beauty as superior to artificial beauty; the latter regards the beauty of art to be higher than the beauty of nature. Theodor W. Adorno destabilizes these hierarchies.[2] In his *Aesthetic Theory*, natural beauty is neither superior nor subordinate to artistic beauty, though natural beauty is the precondition for an appreciation of artistic beauty. What is unique to *Aesthetic Theory* in this regard is the way in which Adorno conceptualizes the aesthetic experience of nature, as well as the aesthetic experience of works of art, as the perception of images of a beyond – that is, of that which is beyond exchange society. In this chapter I will demonstrate how Adorno's use of the concepts of natural and artistic beauty – both of which he appropriates from classical German aesthetic theory – transcends the one-sidedness of Kant's and Hegel's positions. Furthermore, only an aesthetic theory that recuperates the concept of natural beauty that Hegel repressed, and that goes beyond a mere philosophy of art, is of value to an ecologically informed politics. In the first two sections of this chapter, I will discuss the relation between the beauty of art and natural beauty in Kant's *Critique of Judgment* and in Hegel's *Aesthetics: Lectures on Fine Art*. Then I will examine Adorno's redemption of natural beauty and the non-dominating nature of aesthetic rationality. Adorno's theory of aesthetic rationality proves to be a way out of the cul-de-sac of totalizing critique of the sort that has been levelled against Adorno by Jürgen Habermas, Steven Vogel, and William Leiss.[3] These critics tend to interpret the dialectic of enlightenment as a historical constant in Horkheimer and Adorno's theory, extending from ancient Greece to the eighteenth-century Enlightenment. Greater attention needs to be paid to the differentiation of types of rationality within Adorno's version of critical theory, particularly between instrumental and aesthetic rationality. Finally, I will address Hans Robert Jauss's criticisms of Adorno's conception of natural beauty by defending the utopian strain in Adorno's thinking.

Kant

In *Critique of Judgment* Kant contends that natural beauty is superior to artistic beauty in that the immediate interest the lover of nature takes in contemplating nature is indicative of a good soul and of one who has cultivated his moral feeling:

> Now I admit at once that the interest in the *beautiful of art* ... furnishes no proof whatever of a disposition attached to the morally good or even inclined thereto. But on the other hand, I maintain that to take an *immediate interest* in the beauty of nature ... is always a mark of a good soul; and that, when this interest is habitual, it at least indicates a frame of mind favorable to the moral feeling if it is voluntarily bound up with the *contemplation of nature*.[4]
>
> This superiority of natural to artificial beauty in that it alone arouses an immediate interest, although as regards form the former may be surpassed by the latter, harmonizes with the refined and thorough mental attitude of all men who have cultivated their moral feeling. (*CJ* §42, 142)

It is important to keep in mind that for Kant, aesthetical judgment leads the subject to recognize the moral law within. In this sense, the concern with nature and art is subordinate to the cultivation of morality. In the analytic of the sublime, for instance, Kant claims that the imagination's effort to attain the ideas of reason is indicative of our supersensible destination.[5]

For Kant, moral beings are oriented to conform to the moral law, that is, the categorical imperative. To ensure that the highest good be accomplished, Kant preserves the ideas of God, freedom, and the immortality of the soul and puts these ideas to a supersensible use. That is to say, a sense of morality is for Kant something that must be cultivated, and as no sensuous intuition is adequate to the ideas of reason, there is a sense of perpetual striving on the part of the imagination to attain these supersensible ideas. The imagination's effort to attain the ideas of reason indicates a supersensible (that which is beyond or above the sensuous) faculty within the subject. It is our moral destination to conform to the categorical imperative; and as the ideas of reason are supersensible, but nonetheless necessary to ensure that the highest good be accomplished, the realization of our moral destination is perpetually deferred and is to that extent supersensible. Now, in the analytic of the sublime, Kant puts nature to a supersensible use in that the contemplation of nature leads the subject to cultivate a sense of morality, which elevates the subject above nature. In this sense, in the pursuit of our moral destination, the subject is in complicity with the domination of nature. In the section 'On the Dynamically Sublime in Nature,' nature, initially viewed as an object of fear, allows the subject to cultivate a sense of morality; and in the infinite striving of the imagination to present an image that would conform to the ideas that Kant preserves for a practical purpose, the subject recognizes a supersensible faculty within, thus viewing herself to be superior to nature.

Kant divides the 'Analytic of the Sublime' into two sections: 'On the Mathematically Sublime' and 'On the Dynamically Sublime in Nature.' The second of these sections opens with the following declaration: '*Might* is that which is superior to great hindrances. It is called *dominion* if it is superior to the resistance of that which itself possesses might. Nature, considered in an aesthetical judgment as might that has no dominion over us, is *dynamically* sublime' (*CJ* §28, 99).

For Kant, in the experience of the sublime, the subject confronts the grandeur of nature, in comparison with which the human being's ability to resist is insignificant. As examples of natural phenomena that possess might yet have no dominion over us, Kant lists the following: 'Bold, overhanging, and as it were threatening rocks; clouds piled up in the sky, moving with lightning flashes and thunder peals; volcanoes in all their violence of destruction; hurricanes with their track of devastation; the boundless ocean in a state of tumult; the lofty waterfall of a mighty river, and such like' (*CJ* §28, 100).

Now, the human subject is powerless to resist the might of such natural phenomena, yet as aesthetical judgments must be pure, the subject cannot be in actual danger. Such phenomena have no dominion over us if they are considered aesthetically. Rather, 'we merely *think* a case in which we would wish to resist [such an object] and yet in which all resistance would be altogether vain' (*CJ* §28, 100). In this case nature elevates the imagination 'to a presentation of those cases in which the mind can make felt the proper sublimity of its destination, in comparison with nature itself' (*CJ* §28, 101). It is important to keep in mind, here, that nature is not in itself sublime; rather, the sublime is a feeling within the subject, who recognizes her superiority over nature: 'the feeling of the sublime in nature is respect for our own destination, which, by a certain subreption, we attribute to an object of nature (conversion of respect for the idea of humanity in our own subject into respect for the object)' (*CJ* §27, 96). That is to say, the feeling of the sublime is ultimately respect for the moral law and a recognition of the boundlessness of the imagination as it strives to attain to the ideas of reason.

The feeling of fear in confronting natural grandeur gives way to a feeling of pleasure in our supersensible faculty, a feeling that leads the subject to repress internal nature. Nature, considered as an object of fear, has no dominion over us if we contemplate her aesthetically – that is, if, in a position of safety, we think of the danger in which we would find ourselves should we encounter natural phenomena that would overwhelm us. Edmund Burke and Immanuel Kant both construe an affinity between the sublime in nature and the feeling of astonishment. In *A Philosophical Enquiry into the Origins of our Ideas of the Sublime and Beautiful*, Burke writes:

> The passion caused by the great and sublime in *nature*, when those causes operate most powerfully, is Astonishment; and astonishment is that state of the soul, in which all its motions are suspended, with some degree of horror. In this case the mind is so entirely filled with its object, that it cannot entertain any other, nor by consequence reason on that object which employs it. Hence arises the great power of the sublime, that far from being produced by them, it anticipates our reasonings, and hurries us on by an irresistible force. Astonishment, as I have said, is the effect of the sublime in its highest degree; the inferior effects are admiration, reverence and respect.[6]

Similarly, in the *Critique of Judgment* Kant evokes the language of astonishment, but Kant directly relates this feeling to the human domination of nature:

> *Astonishment* that borders upon terror, the dread and the holy awe which seizes the observer at the sight of mountain peaks rearing themselves to heaven, deep chasms and streams raging therein, deep-shadowed solitudes that dispose one to melancholy meditations – this, in the safety in which we know ourselves to be, is not actual fear but only an attempt to feel fear by the aid of the imagination, that we may feel the might of this faculty in combining with the mind's repose the mental movement thereby excited, and being thus superior to internal nature – and therefore to external – so far as this can have any influence on our feeling of well-being. (*CJ* §29, 109)

Here Kant uses nature to demonstrate humanity's superiority to internal and external nature; or as Kant puts it, 'the representation of nature is judged available for a possible supersensible use' (*CJ* §29, 107). In judging of the sublime, the subject feels itself superior to the grandeur of nature; and in recognizing the supersensible destination of humanity (that is, the morally good), the subject also represses internal nature – that is, the fact that humans are animals in a natural environment.

According to Adorno, the Kantian sublime conceals human beings' naturalness; and he transforms the concept of the sublime, seeing it as constituent of modern art, whereas Kant for the most part restricts the sublime to a feeling for nature. For Adorno, the Kantian subject becomes hubristic in puffing itself up into an absolute; for while in experiencing the sublime when confronted with the grandeur of nature – an experience that indicates the nothingness of the human – the subject nonetheless recognizes that 'the eternity of his universal destiny – his spirit – was to unfold.'[7] According to Adorno, 'natural grandeur reveals another aspect to its beholder: that aspect in which human domination has its limit and that calls to mind the powerlessness of human bustle' (*AT* 70). Whereas Kant evokes natural grandeur as a means of bringing the subject to recognize a supersensible faculty within, and to feel superior to internal and external nature, Adorno refers to the grandeur of nature as a space liberated from human domination (see also *AT* 199). Viewing external nature as free from human domination and remembering the nature that is internal to the human subject points in the direction of a reconciliation between culture and nature.

According to Adorno, Kant's theory of the sublime is in complicity with the domination of nature. For even in thinking of resisting the might of nature – a thought that leads the Kantian subject to recognize the infinity of its own destiny – the subject elevates itself above nature. Adorno writes that 'by situating the sublime in overpowering grandeur and setting up the antithesis of power and powerlessness, Kant directly affirmed his unquestioning complicity with domination' (*AT* 199). In the infinite striving of the imagination, the Kantian subject recognizes the infinite within in the form of the moral law, which elevates the subject above nature, above mere animality, thus repressing internal nature – that is, that humans are nevertheless part of a natural environment. Yet Kant is not simply in complicity with domination, for as Adorno notes a few lines further on: 'With profound justification [Kant] defined the concept of the sublime by the resistance of spirit to the overpowering' (*AT* 199). The subject recognizes the infinity of the human destiny, which entails both domination and resistance to power.

Adorno considers the sublime to be a dynamic category that can be uplifted from the Kantian context of the domination of nature and that can, in fact, reveal the naturalness of the human being:

> The sublime was supposedly the grandeur of human beings who are spiritual and dominate nature. If, however, the experience of the sublime reveals itself as the self-consciousness of human beings' naturalness, then the composition of the concept changes. Even in Kant's formulation it was tinged with the nothingness of man; in this nothingness, the fragility of the empirical individual, the eternity of his universal destiny – his spirit – was to unfold. If, however, spirit itself is reduced to its natural dimension, then the annihilation of the individual taking place within it is no longer transcended positively. Through the triumph of the intelligible essence in the individual who stands firm spiritually against death, man puffs himself up as if in spite of everything, as the bearer of spirit, he were absolute. He thus becomes comical. (*AT* 198)

Adorno's concept of the sublime deflates the Kantian subject by revealing the human being's naturalness. By transplanting the sublime into advanced modernist art, Adorno recuperates the concept of the sublime, but removes it from the Kantian context of the domination of internal and external nature.

In *Dialectic of Enlightenment*, Horkheimer and Adorno write that 'the control of internal and external nature has been made the absolute purpose of life.'[8] We have already seen how in the perpetual striving of the imagination the Kantian transcendental subject dominates both internal and external nature. In recognizing her destiny as a moral being, the subject's imagination reveals a supersensible faculty within, thus rendering as naught the naturalness of the human being. In *Dialectic of Enlightenment* Horkheimer and Adorno claim that the denial of internal nature is the price that is paid for the domination of external nature and that this tendency has a history that reaches far beyond Kant. Indeed, the denial of internal nature, the domination of external nature, and the dominance of instrumental rationality form a triad that is detectable in the earliest history of subjectivity:

> In class society, the self's hostility to sacrifice included a sacrifice of the self, since it was paid for by a denial of nature in the human being for the sake of mastery over extrahuman nature and over other human beings. This very denial, the core of all civilizing rationality, is the germ cell of proliferating mythical irrationality: with the denial of nature in human beings, not only the *telos* of the external mastery of nature but also the *telos* of one's own life becomes confused and opaque. At the moment when human beings cut themselves off from the consciousness of themselves as nature, all the purposes for which they keep themselves alive – social progress, the heightening of material and intellectual forces, indeed, consciousness itself – becomes void, and the enthronement of the means as the end, which in late capitalism is taking on the character of overt madness, is already detectable in the earliest history of subjectivity. (*DE* 42–3)

If culture has been a process of forgetting internal nature, then the 'remembrance of nature within the subject' (*DE* 32) can bring about a reconciliation of culture and nature. The relevance of Adorno's thinking for contemporary ecological thought is not in applying his theory to a particular environmental issue, but rather in bringing about a change in consciousness; for it is when 'human beings cut themselves off from the consciousness of themselves as nature' that instrumental rationality comes to dominate; which 'is already detectable in the earliest history of subjectivity,' but which in late capitalism, with production for the sake of production, 'is taking on the character of overt madness.' Notwithstanding the denial of internal nature and the domination of external nature that is the occasion for the feeling of the sublime in *Critique of Judgment*, in *Aesthetic Theory* Adorno concedes that natural beauty 'was still the occasion of the most penetrating insights in the *Critique of Judgment*' (*AT* 61). Rather than using natural beauty to bring the subject to an awareness of her supersensible destination, Adorno rescues natural beauty as a means of bringing about the 'remembrance of nature within the subject' (*DE* 32). This act of remembrance is in direct contrast to Kant's use of nature, which leads the subject to a feeling of superiority over internal and external nature. In other words, Adorno strips the concept of natural beauty from the ideology of domination in which it is enmeshed in Kant's *Critique of Judgment*.

Hegel

Whereas Kant privileges natural beauty over artificial beauty because the former leads the subject to an awareness of her supersensible destination, Hegel erects a hierarchy between natural beauty and artistic beauty that works in the opposite direction. In the Introduction to his *Aesthetics*, Hegel writes: 'The beauty of art is *higher* than nature. The beauty of art is beauty *born of the spirit and born again*, and the higher the spirit and its productions stand above nature and its phenomena, the higher too is the beauty of art above that of nature' (*HA1* 2).

Hegel delimits his lectures on aesthetics to a philosophy of fine art (*Philosophie der schönen Kunst*): 'By adopting this expression we at once exclude the beauty of nature' (*HA1* 1). For Hegel, the beauty of art is higher than the beauty of nature taken in its immediacy, for the work of art is a spiritual product that is first conceived in the mind, which refashions natural material that is born again as a work of art imbued with spirit:

> Now art and works of art, by springing from and being created by the spirit, are themselves of a spiritual kind, even if their presentation assumes an appearance of sensuousness and pervades the sensuous with the spirit. In this respect art already lies nearer to the spirit and its thinking than purely external spiritless nature does. In the products of art, the spirit has to do solely with its own. (*HA1* 12)

For Hegel, the fact that in works of art 'the spirit has to do solely with its own' implies that the work of art is 'higher' than nature, that artistic beauty is 'higher' than the beauty of nature, and that the latter must be repressed in philosophical aesthetics.

Adorno, too, uses the term spirit (*Geist*) to refer to that element in a work of art that elevates it above its status as a mere thing: 'That through which artworks, by becoming appearance, are more than they are: This is their spirit ... What appears in artworks and is neither to be separated from their appearance nor to be held simply identical with it ... is their spirit. It makes artworks, things among things, something other than thing' (*AT* 86). This is not to say, however, that Adorno's use of the term spirit is identical with that of Hegel. Hegel's usage of the term spirit in relation to the work of art is of a piece with his philosophical idealism, as art is the first shape of absolute spirit, followed by religion and philosophy. For Adorno, on the other hand, art's spirit is the process that transpires within the work of art through the 'tension between the elements of the artwork' (*AT* 88).

The aesthetics of Schelling and Hegel repressed natural beauty and incorporated into artistic beauty what Kant had earlier attributed to nature. In *Aesthetic Theory*, Adorno writes: 'In the sphere of natural beauty, Kant's theory of the sublime anticipates the spiritualization that art alone is able to achieve' (*AT* 92). While Adorno wishes to reclaim the concept of natural beauty for contemporary aesthetics, he notes that the spiritualization of art in post-Kantian aesthetic theory realizes the elevation above nature that comes with the Kantian sublime. According to Heinz Paetzold, in Adorno's theory of natural beauty 'the historical and theoretical process of dethroning natural beauty is deciphered as an increasing idealization of the spirit.'[9] Just as Adorno deflates the Kantian subject by revealing its comic pretension to be absolute, so does he deflate Hegel's conception of absolute spirit by reducing spirit to the process that transpires within the work of art.

For Hegel, any notion that enters the mind is higher than nature because spirituality and freedom are present: 'Now the highest content which the subject can comprise in himself is what we can point-blank call *freedom*. Freedom is the highest destiny of the spirit' (*HA1* 97). For Adorno, on the other hand, freedom and dignity are what we have yet to achieve. Adorno transfers the concept of human dignity to a utopian perspective on the dignity of nature: 'The dignity of nature is that of the not-yet-existing; by its expression it repels intentional humanization' (*AT* 74). The discourse of the dignity and freedom of the human spirit that one finds in the writings of Kant, Schiller, and Hegel elevates humanity above nature and represses internal nature by attributing a supersensual destiny to the human spirit. The disappearance of theoretical reflection on natural beauty happened conterminously with the rise of the concept of freedom and human dignity, according to which 'nothing in the world is worthy of attention except that for which the autonomous subject has itself to thank' (*AT* 62). The dominance of the concept of human dignity led to the separation of the human and the animal; or in other words, freedom and dignity set humans above the natural world of which they are nevertheless a part. In *Dialectic of Enlightenment*, Horkheimer and Adorno claim that the denial of nature that is internal to the human subject is the price that is paid for the mastery of external nature. And beginning with Schelling, whose *Philosophy of Art* brings aesthetics to focus on works of art rather than the beauty of nature, the concept of natural beauty is repressed.

The discourse of freedom and dignity in German idealist aesthetics has at least three consequences that Adorno seeks to undo: the denial of internal nature; the mastery of external nature; and the repression of the concept of natural beauty. A result of the denial of internal nature is the elevation of humanity over external nature, including the animal world. 'If the case of natural beauty were pending, dignity would be found culpable for having raised the human animal above the animal' (*AT* 62). Indeed, Friedrich Schiller explicitly elevates the human above the animal with his concept of dignity:

> On the wings of fancy, man leaves the narrow confines of the present in which mere animality stays bound, in order to strive towards an unlimited future ... And what are the outward and visible signs of the savage's entry upon humanity? If we inquire of history, however far back, we find that they are the same in all races which have emerged from the slavery of the animal condition: delight in semblance, and a propensity to ornamentation and play.[10]

Schiller considers humanity's 'delight in semblance' to be that which raises the human above the animal; Hegel considers knowledge to be the faculty that separates humans from the world of animals: 'But this elevation of the implicit into self-conscious knowledge introduces a tremendous difference. It is the infinite difference which, for example, separates man from animals ... precisely because he *knows* that he is an animal, he ceases to be an animal and attains knowledge of himself as spirit' (*HA1* 80).

It is not, however, only idealists such as Schiller and Hegel who elevate humanity above nature. In *Economic and Philosophical Manuscripts*, Marx writes:

> Admittedly animals also produce. They build themselves nests, dwellings, like the bees, beavers, ants, etc. ... An animal forms things in accord-

ance with the standard and the need of the species to which it belongs, whilst man knows how to produce in accordance with the standard of every species, and knows how to apply everywhere the inherent standard to the object. Man therefore also forms things in accordance with the laws of beauty.[11]

So while Schiller claims that humans elevate themselves above the slavery of the animal condition through a propensity to ornamentation; and while Hegel asserts that it is self-consciousness that raises humanity above mere animality; Marx's production paradigm also lifts humans above the animal world.

Whereas German idealist aesthetics views humanity to be superior to nature, Adorno's conception of natural beauty brings the idealist subject down from its lofty perch. In 'Adorno's Notion of Natural Beauty,' Heinz Paetzold writes: 'Human beings must learn that we ourselves are, and always will be, of nature.'[12] Adorno introduces a utopian perspective on the dignity of nature as that which is yet to be achieved. Were dignity to be found in nature, humans would no longer view themselves as separate from the animal world. Adorno rescues the concept of natural beauty from the oblivion to which it had been consigned in the aesthetics of Schiller, Schelling, and Hegel, which emphasize human dignity over the dignity of nature. When we reclaim the concept of natural beauty for contemporary aesthetics, we are presented with an image of reconciliation – that of a possible reintegration of humans with their natural environment.

Adorno's Redemption of Natural Beauty

Whereas Kant holds natural beauty to be superior to artificial beauty because the immediate interest the subject takes in contemplating nature is indicative of a 'morally good disposition'; and whereas Hegel regards artistic beauty to be higher than the beauty of nature because 'the beauty of art is beauty *born of the spirit and born again*'; Adorno destabilizes these hierarchies. Adorno rescues the concept of natural beauty from the repression it has undergone since Schelling and Hegel, contending that 'reflection on natural beauty is irrevocably requisite to the theory of art' (*AT* 62). According to Adorno, Hegel's repression of natural beauty is of a piece with his philosophy of subjective spirit: 'Hegel's objective idealism becomes crass, virtually unreflected partisanship for subjective spirit in the *Aesthetics*' (*AT* 75). Adorno's unwavering criticism of all forms of idealism occupies a central place in his aesthetics: 'Perhaps nowhere else is the desiccation of everything not totally ruled by the subject more apparent, nowhere else is the dark shadow of idealism more obvious, than in aesthetics' (*AT* 62). Adorno's historical materialist approach to aesthetics differs from the idealist aesthetics of both Kant and Hegel.

Adorno's materialism is apparent both in his attempt to rescue the concept of natural beauty and in his analyses of (a) artistic means of production and (b) the relation between the technological development of the means of production in a society more generally, and the way in which these means are used in artistic production. This sort of materialist approach lends itself to a concern with contemporary ecological crises. However, rather than attempt to apply Adorno's theory of natural beauty to a specific environmental issue like global warming – an approach that would turn thinking into an instrument – it would be more useful to tap the strength of his theory, which is, that it is capable of rescuing that which has been repressed, namely, the naturalness of human beings and the concept of natural beauty itself. Such a posture might seem impotent when confronting the imminent environmental catastrophe; but the relation between theory and praxis in Adorno is an issue that lies beyond the scope of this chapter. It is, rather, the need in thinking – or what Rodolphe Gasché calls the *honour* of thinking – that is at issue in the present context. Adorno's theory of natural beauty lends itself to ecological concerns because a reorientation of our thinking in relation to our environment is the necessary first step in bringing about any substantial change. It is my argument that Adorno's emphasis on viewing natural beauty as an image can lead us out of simply viewing nature as an object to be dominated for the purposes of self-preservation. By reclaiming the concept of natural beauty and neither subordinating it to artistic beauty *à la* Hegel, nor privileging natural beauty as Kant does, Adorno moves beyond the one-sidedness of Kant's and Hegel's positions.

Adorno's conception of artistic beauty is fundamentally opposed to that of Hegel. Whereas Hegel maintains that artistic beauty is higher than nature, Adorno considers an appreciation for natural beauty to be the prerequisite for an appreciation of artistic beauty:

> Hegel obviously lacked the sensibility needed to recognize that genuine experience of art is not possible without the experience of that elusive dimension whose name – natural beauty – had faded[13] ... What Hegel chalks

up as the deficiency of natural beauty – the characteristic of escaping from fixed concept – is however the substance of beauty itself ... Because natural beauty is not thoroughly ruled and defined by spirit, Hegel considers it preaesthetic. (*AT* 63, 76, 76)

Adorno's criticism of post-Kantian idealist aesthetics is a dialectical, redemptive approach, in that he seeks to give a voice to nature that Hegel repressed. However, it must be kept in mind that Adorno's usage of the term 'natural beauty' is not identical with that of Hegel. Nor, for that matter, is Adorno's conception of 'spirit' the same as Hegel's. By viewing nature aesthetically and by historicizing the concept of nature, Adorno construes an affinity between artistic and natural beauty in that he deems both to be evanescent. Another key term that Adorno uses in this connection is *apparition* (*AT* 88), though Adorno uses this French word in relation to the spirit of artworks and not in conjunction with natural beauty: 'By rejecting the fleetingness of natural beauty, as well as virtually everything nonconceptual, Hegel obtusely makes himself indifferent to the central motif of art, which probes after truth in the evanescent and fragile' (*AT* 76). By making an appreciation for natural beauty the precondition for an appreciation of artistic beauty, and by viewing both nature and art aesthetically – that is, as fleeting, ephemeral apparitions – Adorno recuperates the concept of natural beauty and introduces a non-dominating approach to nature based on a type of rationality that is aesthetic rather than instrumental and that recollects the way in which the natural environment is mediated by human productive activity.

Aesthetic Rationality

For Adorno, the aesthetic experience of natural beauty entails a relation between subject and object that is not that of domination or mastery. Here it is important to note the distinction between instrumental and aesthetic rationality. According to Adorno, aesthetic rationality is that form of rationality which governs the coherence and unity of a work of art: 'Art is not something prerational or irrational ... Rationality in the artwork is the unity-founding, organizing element, not unrelated to the rationality that governs externally, but it does not reflect its categorizing order' (*AT* 55). Technology in the artwork does not adhere to instrumental rationality; rather, aesthetic rationality is independent of the fetishization of means as ends that is the hallmark of instrumental rationality: 'Yet art mobilizes technique in an opposite direction than does domination' (*AT* 54); 'within art, technology is geared towards purposes outside or beyond the domination of nature.'[14] Though artistic techniques may indeed be parasitic on techniques that developed extra-aesthetically, and that might initially have been used for the domination of nature, the same techniques used in the construction of art objects do not serve to dominate nature along the lines of instrumental rationality. For example, electronics, which originated in quite a different context, was being used in music already by Adorno's time. 'In electronics it is already possible to produce artistically by manipulating means that originated extra-aesthetically' (*AT* 33); 'Stockhausen's concept of electronic works – which, since they are not notated in the traditional sense but immediately "realized" in their material, could be extinguished along with this material – is a splendid one of an art that makes emphatic claim yet is prepared to throw itself away' (*AT* 177–8).[15] Let us recall the French word that Adorno used to designate the ephemeral nature of the work of art, namely, *apparition*.

Adorno's emphasis on aesthetic rationality and artistic techniques that initially developed in the broader context of the development of the forces of production of society as a whole, is part of his historical materialist framework. Adorno's aesthetics is an aesthetics of production, as opposed to the reception aesthetics inspired by hermeneutics that has dominated philosophical aesthetics in Germany since the writings of Hans Robert Jauss. Adorno analyses the relation of artistic forces of production to the forces of production in a society as a whole and the relation between viewing nature aesthetically as opposed to viewing it as an object to be mastered. Technique used in the construction of art objects is a historical possibility that is dependent on the development of techniques that emerged extra-aesthetically. Furthermore, taking up an aesthetic attitude toward nature is a historical possibility that only arises when our orientation toward nature is no longer merely that of self-preservation: 'Times in which nature confronts man overpoweringly allow no room for natural beauty; as is well known, agricultural occupations, in which nature as it appears is an immediate object of action, allow little appreciation for landscape' (*AT* 65). The labouring body in agricultural occupations confronts nature as an object to be mastered. The aesthetic experience of natural beauty, on the other hand, is not based on self-preservation.

As opposed to the mastery of nature, the aesthetic experience of nature allows nature to express itself through its evanescent appearance:

Just how bound up natural beauty is with art beauty is confirmed by the experience of the former. For it, nature is exclusively appearance, never the stuff of labor and the reproduction of life, let alone the substratum of science. Like the experience of art, the aesthetic experience of nature is that of images. Nature, as appearing beauty, is not perceived as an object of action. The sloughing off of the aims of self-preservation – which is emphatic in art – is carried out to the same degree in aesthetic experience of nature. (*AT* 65)

An aesthetic experience is a sensuous experience of a beautiful appearance (*schöne Schein*) in an image, and not the experience of an object to be mastered by a subject. Adorno's conception of aesthetic experience is a form of aesthetic negativity: 'Negativity characterizes the literary work and the productions of the fine arts as irreal objects which for the purpose of aesthetic perception – must negate the real as an anterior reality if they are to turn it into image.'[16] For Adorno, the aesthetic experience of both natural beauty and artistic beauty 'is that of images' (*AT* 65). In this regard, Adorno notes that the difference between these two forms of aesthetic experience is scarcely discernible. The image-character of artistic and natural beauty implies that the former is an imitation of the latter. Natural beauty is the prerequisite for artistic beauty, because art is an imitation of natural beauty as an image, and not of nature itself:

Art is not the imitation of nature but the imitation of natural beauty ... Art does not imitate nature, not even individual instances of natural beauty, but natural beauty as such. This denominates not only the aporia of natural beauty but the aporia of aesthetics as a whole. Its object is determined negatively, as indeterminable. It is for this reason that art requires philosophy, which interprets it in order to say what it is unable to say, whereas art is only able to say it by not saying it. (*AT* 71, 72)

Here Adorno claims that 'art is not the imitation of nature,' because even natural beauty appears as an image. When he refers to natural beauty 'as such,' it must be kept in mind that for Adorno, the object of aesthetics, be it of natural beauty or artistic beauty, is indeterminable. An image is not a concept, and the images of natural beauty and artistic beauty need to be deciphered. Because art does not communicate meanings for Adorno, art requires philosophy to decipher its images. Adorno's aesthetics of negativity implies that the object of aesthetics as a whole – including both natural beauty and artistic beauty – is indeterminable, for the 'object' is an image that is non-discursive and hence requires philosophy for its decipherment.

Through his concept of the cultural landscape, Adorno reconciles natural and artistic beauty. This concept brings into play one of Adorno's most fundamental categories, namely, the remembrance of suffering:

> After the abolition of scarcity, the liberation of the forces of production could extend into other dimensions than exclusively that of the quantitative growth of production. There are intimations of this when functional buildings are adapted to the forms and contours of the landscape, as well as when building materials have originated from and been integrated into the surrounding landscape, as for instance with châteaux and castles. What is called a 'cultural landscape' [*Kulturlandschaft*] is a beautiful model of this possibility. A rationality that embraced these motifs would be able to help heal the wounds that rationality inflicted. (*AT* 46–7)

The abolition of scarcity allows for the possibility of viewing nature aesthetically, that is, as an image. With the concept of the cultural landscape, Adorno effaces the difference between the aesthetic experience of nature and the aesthetic experience of works of art. Châteaux and castles that are constructed from local building materials are both works of art and objects of nature. Viewed aesthetically, such structures do not merely serve the purposes of self-preservation, but are aesthetically related to their surroundings:

> Historical works are often considered beautiful that have some relation to their geographical setting, as for instance hillside towns that are related to their setting by the use of its stone[17] ... But perhaps the most profound force of resistance stored in the cultural landscape is the expression of history that is compelling, aesthetically, because it is etched by the real suffering of the past. The figure of the constrained gives happiness because the force of constraint must not be forgotten; its images are a memento. (*AT* 64)

The images of the cultural landscape, which is at once natural and artificial, are mementos of past suffering. The cultural landscape is not nature in its immediacy; rather, it is thoroughly mediated by human suffering, in this case by the labouring body. The expression of suffering in the cultural landscape destabilizes the hierarchy of natural and artistic beauty and serves simultaneously as the remembrance of past suffering and as a utopian image of the possibility of a form of rationality that would not dominate or control nature, but rather could bring about a reconciliation of culture and nature.

As I noted at the beginning of this chapter, Adorno destabilizes the hierarchies between natural beauty and artistic beauty that Kant and Hegel erected and tries to redeem natural beauty as an image (rather than an object) of theoretical reflection. To conceive of natural beauty as an image grants expression to nature: 'Once it no longer serves as an object of action, appearing nature itself imparts expression, whether that of melancholy, peace, or something else' (*AT* 66). Since humanity's relation to nature has always been that of mastery, the orientation to nature that allows for nature to express itself is necessarily utopian in perspective. For Adorno's critics, this utopian perspective precludes intersubjective communication.

Communication versus Expression

Adorno adheres to a philosophy of reconciliation, though unlike in Hegel, reconciliation achieved in the work of art becomes ideology in the midst of an antagonistic society. This is not to say, however, that Adorno privileges the work of art for its symbolic reconciliation. Adorno projects the state of reconciliation of culture and nature, subject and object, into the distant future: 'the beauty of nature is an other; what is reconciled would resemble it' (*AT* 74). This utopian strain in Adorno's thinking came under sharp criticism by German commentators, including the reception aesthetics of Hans Robert Jauss. Jauss claims that Adorno's 'aesthetics of negativity has clearly abolished the concept of nature by *simply* [my emphasis] making it historical and by thus promoting being that cannot be made, that cannot be disposed of, and that has always existed, to being that may be hoped for, that may someday be reconciled, but that is not as yet.'[18] Jauss finds problematic Adorno's futuristic, utopian perspective on natural beauty. By projecting the reconciliation of culture and nature into the future, Jauss contends, Adorno denies a communicative function to the work of art. There is no question whether Adorno denies a communicative function to the work of art: 'For communication is the adaptation of spirit to utility, with the result that spirit is made one commodity among the rest; and what today is called meaning participates in this disaster' (*AT* 74). What Jauss objects to most in Adorno's *Aesthetic Theory* is the denial of the possibility of communication in the aesthetic sphere: 'Adorno must ignore the dialogic process between work, public, and author.'[19] Jauss is much more optimistic than Adorno that works of art can have a transformative impact on everyday processes of communication. For Adorno, however, attributing meaning to natural beauty is part of the 'intentional humanization' that the expression of nature repels. In this sense, the expression of nature rather than intersubjective communication takes priority, for the former is free of human intent. Adorno denies a communicative function to the work of art because he grants expression to nature, and to attribute human meaning or a communicative function to natural beauty would violate the dignity of nature that Adorno projects as a future possibility: 'A qualitative distinction in natural beauty can be sought, if at all, in the degree to which something not made by human beings is eloquent: in its expression. What is beautiful in nature is what appears to be more than what is literally there' (*AT* 70–1).

For Adorno, just as the spirit of the work of art is that which makes it more than a mere thing, so his conception of natural beauty cannot be reduced to nature itself. Rather, the beautiful in nature is nature as it appears as an image. For nature in-itself to correspond with this image of its beauty, Adorno introduces a utopian perspective: 'nature, as it stirs mortally and tenderly in its beauty, does not yet exist' (*AT* 74). Jauss, on the other hand, insists on a non-utopian view of nature: 'Behind this, there lies the intent to restore the "dignity of nature" as authority against the misused rule of "what is of the autonomous subject's own making" (p. 114). But Adorno succeeds here only by according a futuristic meaning to the beautiful in nature, a meaning which no longer has any connection with previous definitions and metaphors of the concept of nature.'[20]

Jauss is correct to point out that Adorno's conception of the beauty of nature 'no longer has any connection with previous definitions and metaphors of the concept of nature.'[21] However, rather than abandon the aesthetics of negativity on this score, I wish to rescue Adorno's theory from Jauss's criticisms. Adorno introduces a utopian perspective, for 'previous definitions and metaphors of the concept of nature' are enmeshed in the domination of nature. Adorno does not call for a return to nature in Rousseau's sense of a state that is at once at 'equal distances from the stupidity of brutes and the fatal enlightenment of civil man ... a golden mean between the indolence of the primitive state and the petulant activity of our vanity,'[22] for humankind's relation to nature has since prehistory been that of domination. 'Natural beauty, such as it is perceived unmediated in appearing nature, is compromised by the Rousseauian *retournon'* (*AT* 68). The experience of natural beauty is not that of a pristine, undefiled, uncontaminated nature. At times Adorno appears to endorse such a view: 'So long as progress, deformed by utilitarianism, does violence to the surface of the earth, it will be impossible – in spite of all proof to the contrary – completely to counter the perception that what antedates the trend is in its backwardness better and more humane' (*AT* 64). However, according to Adorno, nature is and has always been mediated by society. 'For in every particular aesthetic experience of nature the social whole is lodged ... Natural beauty is ideology where it serves to disguise mediatedness as immediacy' (*AT* 68). Our experience of nature is mediated through the world of conventions, of what Lukács called second nature: 'the subject's powerlessness in a society petrified into a second nature becomes the motor of the flight into a purportedly first nature' (*AT* 65). To presume that one can get away from it all by returning to nature is ideologically a false sense that one can grasp or contemplate that which is mediated as immediacy. Rather than return to a mythical golden age free from domination, one that never existed, Adorno projects the site of reconciliation as a future possibility: 'The image of what is oldest in nature reverses dialectically into the cipher of the not-yet-existing, the possible: As its appearance this cipher is more than the existing' (*AT* 73). It is in deciphering the expression of nature and allowing for the possibility of the dignity of nature that Adorno's *Aesthetic Theory* can instruct us in developing an ecological politics.

Conclusion

Rather than using natural beauty to elevate the human, Adorno speaks of a reconciliation of culture and nature. 'For the body to be revived, culture must be reconciled with nature. To be reconciled, culture must reflect on its own tendency to repress nature, particularly that which is internal to the human subject.'[23] For Kant, the feeling of the sublime entails domination of internal nature through the recognition of humanity's eternal destiny. Hegel's spiritualization of art further repressed natural beauty and external nature. Adorno's aesthetics of negativity, on the other hand, grants expression to nature by giving it a voice and by allowing for the remembrance of suffering that is etched in the cultural landscape. The concept of natural beauty in

Adorno's sense offers an image of reconciliation, of nature reconciled with culture. Through the remembrance of internal nature and granting expression to nature, Adorno's theory of natural beauty reorients our relation to external nature, allowing it to appear as an image rather than an object to be mastered. In spite of the criticism of the utopian strain in Adorno's thinking on the part of Jauss, Adorno's concept of natural beauty remains one largely untapped source of inspiration for radical ecological thought.

NOTES

I wish to thank Professors Gisela Argyle and Andrew Biro, and the two anonymous reviewers for the University of Toronto Press, for reading earlier versions of this chapter and for providing me with valuable feedback.

1 Georg W.F. Hegel, *Hegel's Aesthetics: Lectures on Fine Art*, 2 vols., trans. T.M. Knox (Oxford: Clarendon, 1975), 12. Hereafter HA.
2 I became aware of Rodolphe Gasché's 'The Theory of Natural Beauty and Its Evil Star: Kant, Hegel, Adorno' (in *Research in Phenomenology* 32 [2002]) in the final stages of writing this chapter. Gasché argues that 'any difference between [natural beauty and the beauty of art] implies some sort of hierarchy' (104). 'If Adorno plays off Kant against Hegel, it is not to put the latter's valorization of man-made art into question. Indeed, in spite of his scathing criticism of idealist aesthetics' destructive bent, Adorno does not wish to overturn the hierarchy that the latter established between the two kinds of beauty' (116). Though Adorno claims that an appreciation for natural beauty is the precondition for an appreciation of artistic beauty, he plays these two types of beauty off each other in a way that implies, *pace* Gasché, that there is no hierarchy between the two.
3 See Jürgen Habermas, *The Theory of Communicative Action*, vol. 1, *Reason and the Rationalization of Society*, trans. Thomas McCarthy (Boston: Beacon, 1984), 366–99; 'The Entwinement of Myth and Enlightenment: Max Horkheimer and Theodor Adorno,' in *The Philosophical Discourse of Modernity*, trans. Frederick G. Lawrence (Cambridge, MA: MIT Press, 1987), 106–30; Steven Vogel, *Against Nature: The Concept of Nature in Critical Theory* (Albany: SUNY Press, 1996), 67–8; and Leiss in this volume.
4 Immanuel Kant, *Critique of Judgment*, trans. J.H. Bernard (New York: Hafner, 1951), §42, 141. Hereafter CJ.
5 See CJ, §27, 96.

6   Edmund Burke, *A Philosophical Enquiry into the Origin of our Ideas of the Sublime and Beautiful* (Oxford: Oxford University Press, 1990), 53.

7   Theodor W. Adorno, *Aesthetic Theory*, trans. Robert Hullot-Kentor (Minneapolis: University of Minnesota Press, 1997), 198. Hereafter AT.

8   Max Horkheimer and Theodor W. Adorno, *Dialectic of Enlightenment: Philosophical Fragments*, ed. Gunzelin Schmid Noerr and trans. Edmund Jephcott (Stanford: Stanford University Press, 2002), 24. Hereafter DE.

9   Heinz Paetzold, 'Adorno's Notion of Natural Beauty: A Reconsideration,' in *The Semblance of Subjectivity: Essays in Adorno's Aesthetic Theory*, ed. Tom Huhn and Lambert Zuidervaart (Cambridge, MA: MIT Press, 1997), 216.

10 Friedrich Schiller, *On the Aesthetic Education of Man*, trans. Elizabeth M. Wilkinson and L.A. Willoughby (Oxford: Clarendon, 1967), 175, 191–3.

11 Karl Marx, 'Economic and Philosophical Manuscripts of 1844,' in *The Marx–Engels Reader*, ed. Robert C. Tucker (New York: Norton, 1978), 76.

12 Paetzold, 'Adorno's Notion of Natural Beauty,' 222.

13 Here Gasché's observation that any articulation of a relation between natural and artistic beauty implies some sort of hierarchy seems on the mark.

14 Paetzold, 'Adorno's Notion of Natural Beauty,' 227.

15 Karlheinz Stockhausen, who passed away in December 2007, sparked controversy following the terrorist attacks of 9/11, when he claimed that the spectacle was the greatest work of art of all time, with the terrorists prepared to throw away their lives – and the lives of those on board and in the World Trade Center – in a spectacular apparition that the whole world was watching.

16 Hans Robert Jauss, *Aesthetic Experience and Literary Hermeneutics*, trans. Michael Shaw (Minneapolis: University of Minnesota Press, 1982), 13–14.

17 As, for example, the Chalet and Dining Hall at Camp Easter Seal near the author's hometown in Saskatchewan, which was constructed from local fieldstone and wood as a make-work project during the 1930s. Such structures bear the traces of history, for they are 'etched by the real suffering of the past' (AT 64).

18 Jauss, *Aesthetic Experience and Literary Hermeneutics*, 21.

19 Ibid., 19.

20 Ibid., 20.

21 Ibid.

22 Jean-Jacques Rousseau, *The First and Second Discourses*, trans. R. Masters and J. Masters (St Martin's, 1964), 150–1.

23 Lambert Zuidervaart, *Adorno's Aesthetic Theory: The Redemption of Illusion* (Cambridge, MA: MIT Press, 1991), 162–3.

186   Critical Ecologies

BIBLIOGRAPHY

Adorno, Theodor W. *Aesthetic Theory*. Translated by Robert Hullot-Kentor.
    Minneapolis: University of Minnesota Press, 1997.
Burke, Edmund. *A Philosophical Enquiry into the Origin of Our Ideas of the Sub-
    lime and Beautiful*. Oxford: Oxford University Press, 1990.
Gasché, Rodolphe. 'The Theory of Natural Beauty and Its Evil Star: Kant,
    Hegel, Adorno.' *Research in Phenomenology* 32 (2002): 103–22.
Habermas, Jürgen. 'The Entwinement of Myth and Enlightenment: Max Hork-
    heimer and Theodor Adorno.' In *The Philosophical Discourse of Modernity*,
    translated by Frederick G. Lawrence, 106–30. Cambridge, MA: MIT Press,
    1987.
– *The Theory of Communicative Action*, vol. 1, *Reason and the Rationalization of
    Society*. Translated by Thomas McCarthy. Boston: Beacon, 1984.
Hegel, Georg W.F. *Hegel's Aesthetics: Lectures on Fine Art*, 2 vols. Translated by
    T.M. Knox. Oxford: Clarendon, 1975.
Horkheimer, Max, and Theodor W. Adorno. *Dialectic of Enlightenment: Philo-
    sophical Fragments*. Edited by Gunzelin Schmid Noerr, translated by Ed-
    mund Jephcott. Stanford: Stanford University Press, 2002.
Jauss, Hans Robert. *Aesthetic Experience and Literary Hermeneutics*. Translated
    by Michael Shaw. Minneapolis: University of Minnesota Press, 1982.
Kant, Immanuel. *Critique of Judgment*. Translated by J.H. Bernard. New York:
    Hafner, 1951.
Marx, Karl. 'Economic and Philosophical Manuscripts of 1844.' In *The Marx–
    Engels Reader*, edited by Robert C. Tucker, 66–125. New York: Norton, 1978.
Paetzold, Heinz. 'Adorno's Notion of Natural Beauty: A Reconsideration.' In
    The Semblance of Subjectivity: Essays in Adorno's Aesthetic Theory, edited by
    Tom Huhn and Lambert Zuidervaart, 213–35. Cambridge, MA: MIT Press,
    1997.
Rousseau, Jean-Jacques. *The First and Second Discourses*. Translated by R. Mas-
    ters and J. Masters. St Martin's, 1964.
Schiller, Friedrich. *On the Aesthetic Education of Man*. Translated by Elizabeth
    M. Wilkinson and L.A. Willoughby. Oxford: Clarendon, 1967.
Vogel, Steven. *Against Nature: The Concept of Nature in Critical Theory*. Albany:
    SUNY Press, 1996.
Zuidervaart, Lambert. *Adorno's Aesthetic Theory: The Redemption of Illusion*.
    Cambridge, MA: MIT Press, 1991.

7 On Nature and Alienation

STEVEN VOGEL

I

What does it mean to be alienated from nature? It's a familiar claim in contemporary environmental discussions that today we *are* so alienated, but it isn't always clear what such a claim actually comes to. The terms 'nature' and 'alienation' are both famously difficult, first of all; and second, as I'll try to show, under certain standard interpretations of those terms nature is exactly the sort of thing from which one *cannot* be alienated. In its most common form, it seems to me, the claim that we're alienated from nature doesn't actually make much sense. Yet I do think that we are alienated from something *like* nature and that we need to understand and overcome that alienation. What we're alienated from, I'll argue, is the *environment*, meaning by that word something different from what people normally mean when they talk of 'nature.'

Frequently it's claimed that we are alienated from nature because we fail to recognize ourselves as *part* of nature. We are natural beings, dependent on natural forces for our existence, yet we treat nature as if it were something distinct from us and as something we could (and should) master. We view nature anthropocentrically, this claim continues, seeing it merely as a sort of raw material at our disposal, and the upshot is that we destroy it with technologies that attempt to reshape the natural world into an artificial one structured and reorganized for human purposes. Yet such attempts never succeed, because in fact we depend on nature, so it takes its revenge on us, as our technologies produce increasingly dire consequences. To overcome our alienation we would need to give up anthropocentrism and reintegrate ourselves within the natural order, abandoning the impossible dream of replacing the natural world with one created by humans and learning instead to live in harmony with nature.

Familiar as it is, such an account suffers from significant conceptual difficulties, not least regarding what exactly is meant by 'nature.' First of all, if human beings are really part of nature, it isn't at all clear how their actions could possibly destroy it, or why an artificial or human-made world wouldn't still be a natural one. The dams that beavers build are natural: why not the coal-burning power plants that humans build? What exactly does 'natural' mean? If it refers to that which developed in accordance with ordinary physical processes, then – since human beings and their abilities evolved in accordance with the same biological processes as did other species – all human products would seem to be natural, in which case it would be hard to see how our technologies could be said to be *un*natural or how developing them could be said to alienate us from nature. If everything we do is *part* of nature, how could some things we do *alienate* us from it? On the other hand, if the word 'nature' instead refers specifically to that part of the world that has not been affected by human action, then the unnatural character of our technology – and, indeed, our alienation from nature – turn out to be merely a matter of definition. But does it make sense to say that one is alienated from something from which one is excluded *by definition*? How could *that* kind of alienation be overcome? And in any case, how could this definition be justified, given the claim that we are *part* of nature?[1] Furthermore, in what sense has anthropocentrism been avoided in this definition that grants to one species, alone among all the others, the special ability to change an object from being natural to being artificial, and so to destroy nature? When spiders spin a web or beavers build a dam, no one suggests that nature is thereby destroyed; yet our species, apparently, is different, more ontologically potent than these others.

Thus this familiar idea of what it means to be alienated from nature, despite its insistence that we are part of nature, actually seems to require the assumption that we are *outside* of it – in which case it isn't at all obvious how our asserted alienation from it could possibly ever be eliminated. Or might there be a third definition of 'natural' at work here, according to which our actions are neither all natural (as the first definition would suggest) nor all unnatural (as the second definition would), but instead *some* of our actions are natural and some not? This would seem to allow the possibility that we could overcome our alienation from nature by limiting ourselves to the first kind, resolving to act only in 'accordance with nature.' But what would *this* definition of 'natural' be, and how would it distinguish our 'natural' actions from those that are unnatural? And how did we turn out to be (naturally evolved) creatures who are somehow capable of natural *and* unnatural acts? Again, weren't we supposed to be *part* of nature?

Note in particular that while it might seem attractive to say that though humans themselves are part of nature, their *products* aren't (they're 'artificial'), a little thought will show that this won't work either. For it turns out that no one thinks that *all* the objects human beings produce through their actions are artificial: we produce babies, for example, and urine, and carbon dioxide when we exhale, and nobody calls these unnatural. Why not? It won't do to say that only those objects we produce using 'natural biological processes' are natural, because that requires previously deciding what is to count as a biological process or not, which is precisely the question under discussion here. To say that spiders weaving webs is a biological process while humans building nuclear power plants is not is already to have decided that certain human actions (but no spider ones!) aren't natural. And it won't do, either, to say that only those objects we produce intentionally are unnatural, because after all, sometimes people intentionally produce babies (and even, under certain conditions, urine and exhaled CO_2).

The real intuition behind the idea that (some of) our products aren't natural (and therefore could be expressions of an alienation from nature) is the familiar Cartesian one: it's that we are *not* fully part of nature, but rather are some sort of strange, inwardly divided creatures who are partly natural and partly unnatural. But how did *that* happen, in the course of (natural) evolution? And again, why shouldn't this view, with its obvious debt to the sort of metaphysical dualism that nowadays hardly any serious philosopher would dare to defend, be called anthropocentric? We certainly are an amazing species, absolutely unlike any other: rooted in nature but also somehow possessing 'unnatural' or 'supernatural' parts, and also remarkably blessed with the ability to employ those parts to transform ordinary natural objects into things that are *outside nature*. What has happened here to the insight that we become alienated from nature because we forget that we are part of it?

II

It may be useful at this point to distinguish between two versions of the thesis that humans are alienated from nature. One version – what might be called the romantic one – sees contemporary human techno-logical practices as outside of nature but still imagines the possibility of some other sort of practices (in the future, or perhaps also in some preindustrial past) that would be in harmony with it, and so believes alienation to be something that could in principle be overcome. An-other version – what might be called the tragic one – instead views an irreducible distance between humans and nature to be an unavoid-able element of the human condition, and therefore rejects the idea that any final elimination of alienation is really possible. The latter view seems more consistent, in the sense that it is more explicitly willing to assert the kind of sharp distinction between humans and nature that I have been suggesting the notion of alienation from nature seems to require – a distinction that the former view actually also presupposes but about which it is at the same time ambivalent. Alienation, for the tragic view, is simply our ontological condition. Nature is *beyond* us and *other than* us; and it is our failure to acknowledge the inescapable other-ness of nature that leads to the anthropocentric arrogance that views it as something we can entirely domesticate and control. For the trag-ic conception, alienation cannot be overcome, though it can perhaps be minimized or mitigated. Nature always escapes us, so rather than vainly pretending to be its master we ought to find a way to live that acknowledges and respects its essential independence. Whereas for the romantic view, living in harmony with nature takes the form of a return to nature from out of the alienated darkness of technology, for what I am calling the tragic or pessimistic view, an existence *less* (but not un-) alienated from nature would, rather, involve a respectful and humble appreciation of nature, a commitment as much as possible to 'let it be,' along with a chastened recognition that the impossibility of fully doing so is simply part of what it is to be a human at all.

Andrew Biro has argued recently that something like this latter view of alienation from nature is characteristic of the Frankfurt School, and I think he is right about this.[2] Marcuse's distinction between basic and surplus repression – which Biro interestingly broadens into a distinc-tion between basic and surplus alienation from nature – can be under-stood as a version of this view. Marcuse in *Eros and Civilization* agrees with Freud that human civilization is impossible without the 'repres-sive' application of something like the reality principle, and to this ex-tent a certain alienation from nature (internal nature, in the first place, but external nature as well, because of the need for labour to satisfy human needs) is a necessary condition for human history itself. Where

Marcuse breaks with Freud is in rejecting the latter's implicit under-standing of the reality principle as identical to the capitalist 'perfor-mance principle' that comprehends labour only as 'toil.'[3] The challenge for a critical theory of society is not to find a way to abolish labour, or to give up the reality principle entirely, but rather to imagine a new sort of reality in which labour would itself be a source of instinctual grati-fication. Biro writes in this context of drawing 'a distinction between alienation from nature that is biologically necessary for human life and alienation from nature that is only made necessary by particular forms of social organization.'[4] It is only the latter sort of alienation that can be overcome; the former is an inescapable part of the human condition.

At a deeper level, Adorno's notion of negative dialectics can also be seen as an expression of what I have called the tragic or pessimistic view. In works such as *Negative Dialectics* and the unfinished *Aesthetic Theory*, 'nature' repeatedly stands for the moment of non-identity that according to Adorno characterizes all our thoughts and actions.[5] No concept ever fully comprehends its object, he argues, and no act ever fully achieves its goal; it is in that gap between thought and object, be-tween intention and effect, that something like nature can be glimpsed. But only glimpsed: if nature stands for the non-identical, for that which always escapes our thought and action, then of necessity it cannot itself be fully grasped by us either theoretically or in practice. There can be no *concept* of non-identity, and certainly no *theory* of it, only a negative dialectics that humbly calls us to notice, in each attempt to grasp some-thing in the world, the ways in which we inevitably also fail to grasp it. Here again, alienation from nature is built into who we are and what we do. Indeed, to try to 'overcome' this alienation, for Adorno, would simply be again to see identity as capable of mastering the non-identi-cal, and so to repeat the error of identity thinking; instead he calls for a 'thinking against thought' that acknowledges the non-identical and abjures the desire to abolish it.

As I have suggested, this approach to the question of alienation from nature represents an improvement over the romantic one, in that it avoids the contradictions involved in calling on humans to act more naturally while simultaneously defining nature in such a way that hu-man action is excluded from it. But it only does so by insisting on the exclusion of humans from nature more rigorously, so that our alien-ation from nature becomes more clearly just a matter of definition. For Marcuse (and Freud), nature is precisely that which *must* be transcend-ed in order for human history or civilization to be possible; for Adorno, it comes to stand for precisely that which all human action and thought *must* fail to grasp. In both cases the alienation of humans from nature looks like a matter of conceptual necessity, built into the definition of what it is to be human. Furthermore, in both cases it turns out be associated with human *activity in the world*. Biro defines alienation from nature as meaning 'human beings' self-conscious transformation of their natural environment,'[6] and though this is an unusual definition in some ways (and much too strong for those who hold the romantic conception, which still holds out hope for the possibility of *unalienated* self-conscious transformative acts), it does seem to capture what Adorno and Marcuse have in mind. But it raises immediately the question of why self-conscious transformations (or any transformations, for that matter) aren't natural. All organisms transform their environments, after all; some do it with self-consciousness, others do it with their snouts. To say the former method alienates them from nature while the latter does not requires presupposing a definition of nature from which self-consciousness (and thus, the human) has been excluded from the start. Another word for the 'self-conscious transformation of the natural environment' is *labour* – so the real question is: Why is human labour here understood as *against (or outside of) nature*?

The trouble with both views – the romantic and the tragic – is that each begins by assuming an essentially ontological distinction between humans and nature and then calls that distinction 'alienation.' But to be alienated from something isn't only to be separated from it – it is to be *illegitimately* separated from it. And if the distinction between humans and nature is an ontological one, then the separation isn't illegitimate but rather ontologically necessary, which renders it unclear why it deserves the name *alienation* at all, or why it should be a subject of critique or even of regret. The concept 'alienation' threatens to lose its essentially normative character.

Could we imagine a conception of alienation from nature (or something like it) that did *not* presuppose a distinction between humans and nature and that in particular did *not* view the 'self-conscious transformation of nature' by humans as inherently alienating? I believe that such a conception can be found in the work of the young Marx and that this conception would in fact be considerably more helpful in thinking about environmental questions, and their relations to political and social ones, than the views just outlined. This is so, it seems to me, even though of course Marx's views influenced those of the Frankfurt School thinkers; nonetheless, I think the account of alienation one finds in Marx himself is actually more useful for answering these questions than that provided by Adorno or Marcuse.[7]

III

Marx's account, as I reconstruct it, has its philosophical roots in Kant's Copernican Revolution, and most particularly in Kant's radical suggestion that the problem of knowledge can only be solved if the knower is understood not (as empiricism does) as passively receiving information about the world but rather as *actively* imposing structuring categories on the material of sensation. The world we perceive (which is to say, the world we *inhabit*) is a world that we knowers have actively pre-structured; in that sense it is not something external to us or other than us, but rather something in whose production we are ourselves implicated. The post-Kantians radicalized this idea further, Hegel in particular employing it as the paradigm for his mythic retelling of the history of the universe as the story of *Geist* actively overcoming the apparent otherness of the world and coming to recognize that world as its own creation. It is in Hegel's dialectic of master and slave that the crucial move occurs, though, for there the slave's *work* – his concrete shaping of the material of the world into objects for the master's consumption – is shown to be structurally analogous to the active constitution of the world of knowledge by a knowing subject. Labour and knowledge now both appear as active processes in which a worker/subject overcomes the apparent externality of the world and comes to recognize itself in that world. Yet Hegel's account is also an account of *slavery:* though transforming the world through one's work is implicitly a form of self-realization – in the literal sense of putting oneself into the world and thereby making oneself *real* – for the slave, paradoxically, it produces an object that functions as the condition of his oppression. He himself builds the chains that bind him. The object he shapes is his object, an expression of his self, but it appears to him as something *alien,* external, belonging to another: he is alienated from it.

Marx's materialist turn can be understood as replacing the obscure Kantian notion of a disembodied knower magically 'constituting' the world (or the even more obscure Hegelian notion of *Geist* doing so, and coming to know itself in so doing) with the idea of concrete human beings as fundamentally active and transformative creatures: where Kantians speak of constitution, Marx talks of *labour*. We come to know the world by *acting in it*, and to act in it is to transform it. Marx takes the Kantian idea of the phenomenal world of experience as something the knower constitutes, and reinterprets it as meaning that the practical world humans inhabit is something they actively *build*. And alienation occurs when we fail to recognize the objects we have built as such, so that they come to appear as external to us, as alien powers over and against us.

In this way Marx reformulates a series of epistemological categories in terms of *practical human activity*. Knowledge is understood as practice, and more specifically as labour. Accordingly, alienation is reinterpreted as an economic phenomenon in which it is the *worker* who is alienated. Marx takes the master/slave myth not as an allegory but as pointing to a socioeconomic fact: the worker's labour builds an object, but instead of it serving as a means of his self-expression it becomes the property of someone else, the capitalist, and indeed becomes the basis of the capitalist's wealth – and so it turns into the very condition that creates the worker's own poverty. In fact it becomes capital itself, as becomes clear in Marx's later economic works, where capital turns out literally to *be* labour – 'congealed' or 'objectified' or 'dead' labour, the surplus-labour of previous workers that takes the physical form of the factory and machines to which current workers are yoked. Dynamic human activity turns into an object, or rather into a world of objects – the world of capitalist technology, and of capitalist wealth, from which the worker is estranged. 'The worker becomes all the poorer,' Marx writes, 'the more wealth he produces, the more his production increases in power and size ... The *devaluation* of the world of men is in direct proportion to the *increasing value* of the world of things';[8] elsewhere he writes that under capitalism, 'man's own deed becomes an alien power opposed to him, which enslaves him instead of being controlled by him.'[9]

Yet to say the worker is alienated in the sense that he has lost his product and that it has become the property of another is misleading – too beholden to Hegel's master–slave myth in which alienation appears as a relation between two individuals. The Hegelian story assumes a kind of individualized craft production; the utopian ideal it projects is the romantic one of the self-sufficient artisan who recognizes himself in everything he produces. But under modern conditions, production is never so individualized – and a little consideration suggests that premodern craft production was never so individualized either. *All* production is *social* production: factory production surely, but craft production too, since the artisan needs to learn his trade from others and often uses tools made by others. It might be better to say: *every practice is a social practice.* Human practices are linguistically and normatively mediated, and language and norms are essentially social. The artisan who looks on his product with merely personal pride is alienated, too, if he fails to recognize the labour of others that was required for it to come into existence.

The subject who fails to recognize itself in its product and is therefore alienated, that is, is a *social* subject. Under alienation it is not simply the humanly produced character of the object but its social character that is concealed. Marx criticizes the capitalist division of labour on precisely this point: all labour is implicitly social and cooperative, but it appears under capitalism as private and particular. Our social relations with one another appear as external to us, as a set of relations (Marx famously says) between things. This is the point of the account of value in *Capital*: the 'value' of a commodity is in fact an expression of its *social* character as having been produced through cooperative labour for use by community members, but it appears in the form of what seems like a quasi-*natural* fact about the commodity, which is to say its price. Prices are determined by social relations (both in the factory and in the market), but they appear instead as the things that themselves determine those relations. The unemployment rate, the trade surplus, the performance of the Dow Jones Industrial Average: all these things are in truth expressions of the ways in which we relate to one another, the ways in which we cooperatively act so as to satisfy one another's needs, but they appear as things external to each of us that form the given and unchangeable context in which we act. They appear, that is, like *facts of nature*, not as the results of our own doings. 'The social power, i.e., the multiplied productive force that arises through the co-operation of different individuals caused by the division of labor,' Marx writes in *German Ideology*, 'appears to those individuals, since their co-operation is not voluntary but has come about naturally [*naturwüchsig*], not as their own united power, but as an alien force existing outside them, of the origin and goal of which they are ignorant, which they thus are no longer able to control.'[10] What Adam Smith called the invisible hand, Marx sees as alienation: when we are only able to act as private individuals, the social effects of our actions appear to us as external facts of nature that we cannot control but to which we must simply adjust ourselves. The invisible hand, the 'market' itself, is precisely what arises when social action is not recognized and determined as such and so turns into the form of a *thing* – which is to say, turns into something like nature. Overcoming this alienation would take the form of a recognition and reappropriation of these social processes *as social:* which to Marx means something like putting them under the control of democratically organized planning processes.

IV

The implications of Marx's account of alienation for the question of what alienation from nature might mean, and for environmental thought in general, are striking. The moral of his account is that alienation arises when we fail to see the *constructed* character of the objects and institutions that surround us, a constructed character that is inseparable from their *social* character. We are alienated from objects that we have produced through our own actions, and alienation arises when we fail to recognize them as such. And when such a failure of recognition occurs, the result is that objects and institutions look like natural ones. For Marx, then, *the appearance of nature is itself a symptom of alienation.* Alienation occurs when something that is really social, and socially constructed, appears to be natural.

Now at first, this doesn't seem to help much if we're trying to understand alienation from *nature* – after all, nature *is* natural (isn't it?), and it *isn't* socially constructed. Yet there is more to say. For Marx's account, and especially its view of labour, helps us notice how much of the world we actually inhabit – the world that surrounds us, the *Umwelt*, the *environment* – is in fact a world consisting almost entirely of objects that have been built by human beings. (And here I ask the reader to look around himself or herself right now, at the objects by which he or she is 'environed.') Is it possible that we are alienated from *that* world, precisely in that we fail to see it as a human and more specifically a social product? And that a symptom of our alienation is that we think that that which environs us, our 'environment,' should be identified with 'nature' – which is to say, with something which we did *not* help to build, and thus for which we are *not* responsible?

We're back to the question of what 'nature' means. It's true, no doubt, that if it means that part of the world which is separate from humans, then by definition nature cannot be a human product, so in Marx's sense we cannot be alienated from it. Yet as we have seen, construing nature in this way causes some serious conceptual difficulties, not least because it seems to mean that humans aren't natural. And in any case, such a nature turns out to be remarkably hard to find: as Bill McKibben argued two decades ago, in the context of phenomena like global warming every spot on earth has *already* been changed by human action, so 'nature' can be said already to have ended.[11] Yet if nature has ended, still surely the *environment* has not, again if by that word we mean the actual world that surrounds us; and it does not seem so strange to say that *that* world is the product of human action. And isn't it the environment, after all, that is supposed to be the object of environmental philosophy, and of environmental concern?[12]

The environment (if not nature) in this sense *is* something that humans have produced. The world that surrounds us has the shape it has, and consists of the objects it does, because of our activities, our desires, our institutions, our social and economic structures. One might object here that we haven't *produced* it, we have only *affected* it. (There would be weather without us, one might say; we have only changed the weather, not created it.) But all production is like this: one cannot produce anything at all except by affecting something else. No production is *ex ni hilo*. A wooden bookcase is a tree that has been affected by our actions, yet it is surely a *product* of those actions. And the sawdust left behind as it is built is a product of those actions too. The world that surrounds us – the environment – in this sense is our product, both those aspects of it that we deliberately aimed to build and those (like global warming) that we didn't: it takes the form it does because of our acts.

Yet if the environment has come to be what it is through our acts, it is surely also the case that what it has come to be is something pretty bad: ugly, toxic, dangerously warming, harmful to many of the creatures who inhabit it. It is our actions that have led to those results, yet of course no one ever really *intended* such results. They are the consequences of our actions, but they seem to us like – well, like facts of nature. But this is just where Marx's account might be helpful, precisely because it focuses on the question of how our 'own deed' can come to seem like an independent and threatening power opposed to us. We are alienated from our environment when we fail to recognize it as the consequence of our own actions and so fail to acknowledge our own responsibility for it, and so instead it starts to look like a natural fact about which there is nothing we can do: global warming simply part of a natural cycle, pollution an inevitable by-product of technology, urban sprawl the inexorable consequence of market forces, and so on. It's when the environment comes to look like 'nature,' that is, that our alienation from it occurs.

But if this is right, then the very views of alienation I began by describing – views that take for granted that nature is something distinct from human beings and that make this distinction the basis of their account of alienation – *are themselves alienated ones*. The dualism between nature and the human that they presuppose makes no sense, not merely because we humans are natural organisms but, more important, because *as* natural organisms, and like *all* natural organisms, our position in the world is fundamentally active and transformative, so the 'nature' we inhabit (which is to say, our 'environment') is one we have always already helped form. These other views take nature as something external to us which we are either trying to overcome or with which we have to harmonize ourselves; they worry that our actions are ending nature, rather than seeing that all our actions (like those of all other organisms) help *produce* it. And in their talk of nature's revenge, in their worry about the consequences of our failure to acknowledge nature's power over us and our dependence on it, in their warnings against the hubris involved in the attempt to 'dominate' nature, they once again are treating something we have helped produce as if it were a power over and against us.

V

Marx's account can be understood as suggesting that the environment we inhabit is 'socially constructed.' But social construction here doesn't mean, as it frequently does in debates in environmental theory, that our *ideas* or *experiences* of 'nature' are socially variable (a point easily countered by the objection that though 'nature' the idea might be variable, surely *nature* the thing is not).[13] Rather, social construction here is meant *literally*: the environment we inhabit is formed through the socially organized labour of human beings. To say this is in no way to deny the reality or materiality of the world, or to see us as its masters. Construction – in the physical, literal sense – takes place in a real material world; it's hard work, takes effort, sometimes fails, and always turns out differently from what those who engage in it expect. To say that the environment is socially constructed is not to say that humans can make the environment any way they want, or to confuse what a society believes about the environment with what it really is. The environment we inhabit is indeed the product of our practices, but this does not mean it is the product of our desires or our beliefs. What we want or intend to build isn't the same thing as what we *actually* build: every architect and engineer knows that.

That what we build always differs from what we thought we were building is the phenomenon that Adorno tries to comprehend under the term 'non-identity' and that Biro associates with an inevitable alienation between humans and nature. But to put the matter this way is to identify humans with thought and not with building. Adorno writes as though 'nature' stands for a moment of absolute otherness that always eludes our grasp. Yet if one understands our fundamental relation to the world as an active one – as a relation of practice and not of thought – then one soon realizes that this moment of 'non-identity' is not a moment of otherness at all, but rather is simply *part of what it is to be a practice* (and in fact is precisely what distinguishes practice from 'theory.') What Adorno calls non-identity is not other than practice but rather is a condition of the very possibility of practice itself: I could not engage in a practice – I could not act – without the operation of 'natural' forces that are beyond my understanding and control. So it makes no sense to identify this moment with some inevitable alienation built into the human condition: 'alienation' suggests separation, and there's no separation here at all. Practice – 'building,' 'construction,' 'labour' – isn't to be understood as a process whereby a Cartesian mind engages in cogitations and then somehow imposes its thought upon a (recalcitrant) pure matter; rather, for us real, embodied physical organisms it is simply *what we do* – or more precisely, what we are always already doing *before* 'thought' takes place, *before* 'matter' is identified. *Of course* thought or concepts are not identical to matter or nature, but to say this is not to say that the 'human condition' – the condition of actual practical humans acting in the world – is 'marked' by the 'trace' of non-identity, or to see human labour as inevitably involving a moment of alienation. Such language would only make sense if the human condition were a condition of *thought* that unfortunately must 'alienate' itself by mucking around in the world of matter.

Adorno's difficulty here, it seems to me, is symptomatic of a deeper problem characteristic of the early Frankfurt School tradition as a whole (and one that is only exacerbated, I would add, in Habermas's later extension of that tradition). Elsewhere I have argued that that tradition, despite its theoretical affinity for the kind of activist and praxis-oriented epistemology found in the early Marx, nonetheless remains too stubbornly committed to the kind of (late Marxian) 'materialism' that insistently asserts the importance of recognizing a 'natural' 'material' 'substrate' that both grounds and exceeds praxis.[14] Such a view cannot help but issue in ambiguities and even paradoxes, which it tries to cover up by distinguishing between 'first' and 'second' nature (i.e., between the one that precedes practice and the one that practices produce), or between 'basic' and 'surplus' repression (or alienation), or between 'work' and 'interaction.' It fails to grasp that an activist epistemology can itself be a thoroughly materialist one, needing no supplementation by appeal to a 'matter' prior to practice, once that epistemology realizes that the practices it talks about – the ones through which we come to know the world – are themselves material, which is to say are *real* practices and not just a matter of a 'social meaning' attached to a set of physical behaviours. The trouble with the sort of materialism that takes 'matter' to be a substrate beyond or before practice is that if knowledge is truly active, then this putative substrate cannot itself be *known* – which makes it quite uncertain what status the repeated claim that it exists could possibly have, or what relevance its existence might possess for a critical theory of human life given that such a life is of course a *practical* one. And furthermore, as I have argued above, such a substrate – which really turns out to be that 'nature' that I have suggested needs to be distinguished from the 'environment' we actually inhabit – is certainly not anything from which we could be meaningfully said to be 'alienated,' except in the trivial sense that we are alienated *by definition* from it since it is understood precisely as a world prior to and separate from us and our practices.

The views of the classical Frankfurt School thinkers are marked, I would suggest, by a palpable nostalgia for this 'nature,' which their materialism assures them is there but which their epistemology guarantees is unattainable. It is this conflict that accounts for the tone of sadness and bitter paradox that is so characteristic of, especially, Adorno's thought. (Marcuse's too, often, though especially in his later years he moved closer to what I've called the 'romantic' view, allowing himself some hope in the utopian possibilities of a 'new sensibility' that might make possible a kind of reconciliation between humans and nature that Adorno could never really imagine.) Familiar, understandable, and even seductive as this nostalgia is, it ends up, I believe, leaving the Frankfurt School tradition in a cul-de-sac that renders it unable to provide a philosophically adequate basis for anything like a 'critical theory of nature' capable of helping contemporary theorists grasp current environmental problems (and that thus, quite predictably, leads to Habermas's almost complete withdrawal from consideration of environmental issues). A better route toward finding such a basis, I am arguing, would begin by returning to the early Marx and attempting to reconstruct the activist epistemology that he only began to sketch out before he turned instead toward a more direct concern with the economic analysis of capitalism and the political struggles of the proletariat.

VI

For both the 'romantic' and the 'tragic' versions of the alienation thesis, as I have described them, alienation is the inevitable result of human action: any time we transform the world we alienate ourselves from it.[15] But all organisms transform the world: to be an organism is to be active, and to be active is to change something. Alienation, I am suggesting, does not arise from our transformation of the world, but rather from our failure to recognize ourselves in the world we have transformed – a failure, that is, to acknowledge responsibility for what we have done and built. That means, first of all, not recognizing that the environment surrounding us is indeed something that results from human practic- es – our economy and social institutions, our cities and suburbs, our polluted and rapidly warming atmosphere, the 'wilderness' areas we sentimentally preserve as instances of pure nature without recognizing the history of human habitation such areas always evince. And second, it means not recognizing that the practices we each engage in are *so-cial* practices, with social preconditions and social consequences, and that therefore the responsibility for the environment we have is a social one. Marx's account of the contradiction between individual action and social consequences remains valid: we live in a society where each of us can act only as a private individual, with the result that the overall social consequences of our actions appear like 'facts of nature' about which there is nothing any individual one of us can do.

If alienation from nature occurs whenever we act at all, then alien- ation is inevitable. But if alienation from the environment results rather from a failure to recognize the socially constructed character of the world we inhabit, then an overcoming of alienation can be imagined. For Marx, alienation is overcome by a social order where decisions about production are not left to the anarchic workings of the market, but rather are made explicitly and socially, which is to say, democrati- cally. The views of alienation I began by describing employ nature as a normative standard to distinguish environmentally appropriate human acts to transform the world from environmentally harmful ones; yet as we have seen, it isn't at all clear how that standard could possibly work, given that for such a view 'nature' by definition refers to something *outside* of human action. On the view I am proposing, on the other hand, the normative standard is not found in nature, but rather is immanent within human practices themselves. The standard is a familiar and old-fashioned – and Hegelian – one: self-knowledge. We cannot help but transform the world through our practices, but those practices that *know themselves as such* – that recognize their impact on the world and take responsibility for that impact – are better than those that do not.

The environment we inhabit today is a built environment. By this I do not mean that it is entirely made of concrete, but rather that it has always already been affected by human action. Our environmental problems arise *there*, in that environment: they are problems of pollution and global warming and overpopulation and (not least) ugliness and cruelty. They don't arise in a pure 'nature' independent of human action. Our alienation isn't from nature, it's from *that environment*. We are alienated from it not because we don't acknowledge its 'otherness' but rather because we see it *too much* as other, because we fail to acknowledge our responsibility for it, in the causal *and* moral senses of that word. And the responsibility we fail to acknowledge is above all a social responsibility. The problem we have with our environment is not a problem with nature, it's a problem with society.

Our social structure is such that each of us can act within it only as an individual, and we have no way to think collectively about the consequences of our actions, or to decide collectively what we wish to do. The decisions we make and the transactions we engage in are all private, yet as a sum they have public consequences that no individual ever consciously chooses. We are each subject to the problem of the commons: my individual decision whether to use my automobile has no measurable effect on global CO_2 levels, so despite my strong desire to reduce those levels it's perfectly rational for me to drive any time it brings me even a modicum of utility – and this is so despite my knowledge that the same is true for everyone else as well. So the CO_2 level continues to rise. The atmospheric CO_2 that is warming the world is an object that we have socially produced but that to each one of us appears like a fact of nature we cannot control. This *is* alienation, as Marx described it.

Overcoming such alienation would require a social order in which decisions about the social practices we engage in were made communally and consciously, through processes of democratic discourse, and not left to the nature-like workings of a free market. In such a social order, the environment we inhabit would be one we communally *knew* to be our communal responsibility. The view of alienation from nature with which I began wants the standard for deciding what practices to engage in to reside in nature – which is to say, it wants us to give up the responsibility for that decision and to allow nature to decide. This does not seem to me to overcome our alienation so much as to perpetuate it: the practices we engage in, and the environment those practices help produce, remain on such an account subject to something outside of them, and outside of us, just as they are today. The answer is not to abdicate responsibility for our practices and their consequences – we already have done that! Rather, it's to *take back* that responsibility, take it back from things that are external to us, and in that way end our alienation from an environment that we only mistakenly think is beyond us.

NOTES

1 John Stuart Mill's essay 'Nature,' in *Collected Works*, vol. 10 (Toronto: University of Toronto Press, 1963), remains one of the clearest accounts of these two quite distinct meanings that the word 'nature' can have, and of the difficulties they each produce. See also Holmes Rolston, III, 'Can and Ought We to Follow Nature?' in *Philosophy Gone Wild* (Buffalo: Prometheus, 1986), 30–52.

2 Andrew Biro, *Denaturalizing Ecological Politics: Alienation from Nature from Rousseau to the Frankfurt School and Beyond* (Toronto: University of Toronto Press, 2005). 'Tragic' of course is my own term for it.

3 See Herbert Marcuse, *Eros and Civilization* (New York: Vintage, 1962), 32–44; cf. Biro, *Denaturalizing Ecological Politics*, chapter 6.

4 Biro, *Denaturalizing Ecological Politics*, 168.

5 See the section on *das Naturschöne* in his *Ästhetische Theorie* (Frankfurt: Suhrkamp, 1973), 97–122, where for instance he defines natural beauty as 'the trace of non-identity in things under the spell of universal identity' ('die Spur des Nichtidentischen an den Dingen im Bann universaler Identität,' 114).

6 Biro, *Denaturalizing Ecological Politics*, 30.

7 Biro's account of Marx, I should say, is a helpful and interesting one. But in reinterpreting the distinction between objectification and alienation as one between 'alienation from nature' on the one hand and 'alienation from social processes' on the other, he seems to me to miss the key point that for

Marx the former is *not a form of alienation at all*. This is what allows Biro to assimilate Marx's view to that of the Frankfurt School, which again I think fails to grasp some important differences. See Biro, *Denaturalizing Ecological Politics*, 116.

8 Karl Marx, *The Economic and Philosophic Manuscripts*, in Karl Marx and Frederick Engels, *Collected Works*, vol. 3 (New York: International Publishers, 1975), 271–2.

9 Karl Marx and Frederick Engels, *The German Ideology*, in Marx and Engels, *Collected Works*, vol. 5 (New York: International, 1976), 47.

10 Marx and Engels, *The German Ideology*, 48; translation slightly altered. See Karl Marx, *Die Frühschriften* (Stuttgart: Alfred Kröner, 1953), 361–2.

11 Bill McKibben, *The End of Nature* (New York: Anchor, 1989).

12 William Cronon (among others) has pointed to the way an environmentalism focused on the defence of 'nature' (or 'wilderness') defined as independent of human action ends up finding it quite difficult to conceptualize the pressing environmental problems that arise *here*, in the non-natural, non-wild world in which we actually live. See Cronon, 'The Trouble With Wilderness,' in *Uncommon Ground: Rethinking the Human Place in Nature*, ed. William Cronon (New York: Norton, 1996), 84–5.

13 See Kate Soper, *What Is Nature?* (Oxford: Blackwell, 1995), chapter 5.

14 See Steven Vogel, *Against Nature* (Albany: SUNY Press, 1996).

15 The romantic version, it's true, tries to avoid this conclusion, but only by imagining the possibility of a human *action* that does not involve *transformation*. And it isn't at all clear what that could mean.

BIBLIOGRAPHY

Adorno, Theodor W. *Ästhetische Theorie*. Frankfurt: Suhrkamp, 1973.

Biro, Andrew. *Denaturalizing Ecological Politics: Alienation from Nature from Rousseau to the Frankfurt School and Beyond*. Toronto: University of Toronto Press, 2005.

Cronon, William. 'The Trouble with Wilderness.' In *Uncommon Ground: Rethinking the Human Place in Nature*, edited by William Cronon. New York: Norton, 1996.

Marcuse, Herbert. *Eros and Civilization*. New York: Vintage, 1962.

Marx, Karl. 'The Economic and Philosophic Manuscripts.' In Karl Marx and Frederick Engels, *Collected Works*, vol. 3. New York: International, 1975.

Marx, Karl, and Frederick Engels. 'The German Ideology.' In Karl Marx and Frederick Engels, *Collected Works*, vol. 5. New York: International, 1976.

McKibben, Bill. *The End of Nature*. New York: Anchor, 1989.

Mill, John Stuart. 'Nature.' In John Stuart Mill, *Collected Works*, vol. 10, 373–402. Toronto: University of Toronto Press, 1963.

Rolston, Holmes. 'Can and Ought We to Follow Nature?' In *Philosophy Gone Wild*, 30–52. Buffalo: Prometheus, 1986.

Soper, Kate. *What Is Nature?* Oxford: Blackwell, 1995.

Vogel, Steven. *Against Nature*. Albany: SUNY Press, 1996.

8 Fear and the Unknown: Nature, Culture, and the Limits of Reason

SHANE GUNSTER

> The movements of the stars have become clearer; but to the mass of the people the movements of their masters are still incalculable.[1]
>
> Bertolt Brecht, *The Life of Galileo*

> As its final result, civilization leads back to the terrors of nature.[2]
>
> Theodor Adorno and Max Horkheimer,
> *Dialectic of Enlightenment*

> Capitalism was a natural phenomenon with which a new dream-filled sleep came over Europe, and, through it, a reactivition of mythic forces.[3]
>
> Walter Benjamin, *The Arcades Project*

Enchaining Reason: Nature as Other

Obsessed with laying bare the epistemological violence that constitutes the secret foundation of human reason, the work of Theodor Adorno easily lends itself to the argument that human beings must cultivate a fundamentally *passive* relationship with nature as a domain of 'otherness' that eludes or defies human comprehension. Reining in the imperial ambitions of thought appears a promising antidote to the hubris of a species that, for the most part, now treats the natural world as little more than a supply of raw materials to be exploited without end in the satisfaction of human needs. Firm limits must be placed upon the voracious appetite of human reason – 'belly turned mind'[4] as Adorno once put it – to devour any and all empirical phenomena, digesting the infinite, sensuous particularities of the world and turning them into mere conceptual data. A similar perspective often echoes through the work of those calling for a fundamental renovation in how human beings engage with the natural world. For Neil Evernden in *The Social Creation of Nature*, for example, the emancipation of nature from the domination of man requires placing it well beyond the reach of human knowledge:

> In the face of any phenomenon, we have a choice between explaining it or accepting it … If it is accepted *in its full individuality*, as a unique and astonishing *event*, our encounter is entirely different, and is perhaps fundamentally religious in the nonecclesiastical sense. In such instances, we experience what Rudolf Otto called the 'wholly other': 'that which is quite beyond the sphere of the usual, the intelligible, and the familiar, which therefore falls quite outside the limits of the "canny," and is contrasted with it, filling the mind with blank wonder and astonishment.'[5]

Christopher Hitt likewise calls for an 'ecological sublime' to serve as a visceral reminder that 'there will always be limits to our knowledge, and nature will always be, finally, impenetrable … We need, at least occasionally, to be confronted with the wild otherness of nature and to be astonished, enchanted, humbled by it.'[6] The deliberate cultivation of a meek, deferential, even worshipful posture before nature is often offered as an essential first step in constructing a more balanced, ecologically sensitive relationship with the environment that sustains us.

The speculative anthropology in Adorno and Horkheimer's *Dialectic of Enlightenment* offers a bleak confirmation of this line of argument by sketching out the disastrous consequences that have accompanied the historic failure of human beings to grant nature an adequate degree of epistemological respect. Instead, lashed on by the instinctual drive for self-preservation, systems of thought have grown progressively instrumentalized as part of the evolution of the species. The effects have been disastrous: an enlightenment project that 'has always aimed at liberating human beings from fear and installing them as masters' has instead produced a 'wholly enlightened earth … radiant with triumphant calamity.'[7] Autonomy, the classic Enlightenment goal of emancipating the subject from the rule of heteronomous, irrational forces, has been secretly sacrificed in favour of increasing our domination over nature. Both myth and enlightenment, explain Horkheimer and Adorno, are equally implicated in the perpetual struggle to maximize the power of subject over object, the *telos* of all human civilizations unable to shrug off or at least temper their primordial fear of the unknown. The exponential growth in human technological capabilities has brought in its wake new forms of political, economic, and cultural domination. Under the shadow of fear, the subject forgets, *represses*, the presence of 'nature' within itself, and thus is blind and indifferent to whether its objects are human or non-human. The power of instrumental reason to analyse, manipulate, and control the natural environment is then applied with terrifying success to the social world. The one becomes constitutive of the other: humankind's domination over nature simultaneously enables, requires, and intensifies the domination of some human beings over others.

In later works such as *Negative Dialectics* and *Aesthetic Theory*, Adorno speculates that certain forms of philosophical and aesthetic practice might enable a non-instrumental relationship between human beings and the world, thereby suspending the fateful dialectic by which enlightenment fuses with myth. The core principle of such a relationship is the negative affirmation of non-identity by way of a relentless, vigorous, and systematic assault on the narcissistic omnipotence of instrumental reason and an uncompromising exposure of the limitations that attend all forms of conceptual thinking. 'We can think against our own thought,'[8] he counsels, and in so doing we will recognize the sanctity of that which lies forever beyond our power of comprehension. As we come to understand and openly accept the profound limitations of thought, the impulse to control and dominate will itself be broken in favour of an intensified receptivity to otherness. Dialectics, he explains, 'says no more, to begin with, than that objects do not go into their concepts without leaving a remainder ... It indicates the untruth of identity, the fact that the concept does not exhaust the thing conceived.'[9] Keeping faith with the inviolable distance of this remainder is the sacred obligation of the philosophy of non-identity. 'The reconciled condition would not be the philosophical imperialism of annexing the alien. Instead, its happiness would lie in the fact that the alien, in the proximity it is granted, remains what is distant and different, beyond the heterogeneous and beyond that which is one's own.'[10] For the most part, Adorno is careful to avoid simply equating non-identity with nature, in part to avoid any simplistic equation of his work with that of Heidegger, whose project of philosophically subjecting humanity to a 'repristinized' nature he criticized as both impossible and dangerous. Yet there is also clearly a powerful affinity between nature and the non-identical, one that emerges with greatest force in his late work on philosophy and aesthetics. Serious art, for instance, is praised because

its non-conceptual expressive qualities both preserve and spark awareness of an '"indissoluble" something'[11] that exists beyond all efforts to
subsume it beneath the concept. Art enables mimetic forms of rationality in which the subject reverses the polarity of its relationship with the
outside world, bending human praxis in the direction of accommodat-
ing and expressing the sensuous particularity of the object.

Building upon these dimensions of Adorno's thought, Morton
Schoolman develops the idea of 'aesthetic individuality' as a form
of self-development in which an awareness of the limits of cognition
sparks a re-enchantment of the world. 'To be receptive to the world
aesthetically,' he writes, 'is to take the world to be unknown and unknowable and the darkness of the world to be an absolute barrier to the
discovery of truth, so that the world always is recognized as different
from thought's every representation of it.'[12] Under the influence of aesthetic rationality, the world as unknown begins to inspire delight and
creativity instead of fear and violence. We must not only come to accept
the limits of reason, but also actively embrace those limits as constitutive of new forms of subjectivity in which our desire to control the
world is displaced by a fascination with its unfathomable complexity.
Constantly invoking the philosophical vocabulary of essence and appearance, Schoolman argues that while we ought to marvel with poetic
wonder at the surfaces of nature, we must forever renounce the goal of
penetrating its mysterious depths, even in the interests of developing
an expressly non-instrumental, scientific knowledge of the natural
world. 'We can live with nature on its own terms, coexist with nature, if
we leave nature be ... Reason must abandon any practice, such as that
of technological mastery, that presupposes the transparency of nature.
Nature would be left alone to flourish as it would in a world before we
as a species were born.'[13] Celebrating the poetry of Walt Whitman as
exemplary of such an aesthetic disposition, Schoolman explains that
'mystery and wonder urge us to relate to the world receptively *just as
it appears before us.*'[14] At one level, this is a rather extraordinary injunction to pin on Adorno – a man whose sorrow, horror, and contempt for
the world that appeared before him was truly unparalleled, seeping
into virtually everything he wrote about it. Yet a compelling argument
can be made that an epistemological politics grounded in the deliberate renunciation of reason's power to penetrate and conceptualize the
external world ultimately affirms an intellectual posture of acceptance
and submission before that which appears to lie beyond human understanding and control.

Demystification: (Second) Nature as Social

In *Against Nature*, Steven Vogel mounts a persuasive case that Adorno's insistence on the otherness of nature is precisely where he takes a wrong turn. Drawing from Marx and especially Georg Lukács, Vogel argues that what is needed instead is a radical deconstruction of 'nature' as the product of human activity. Enforcing a conception of the outside world as fundamentally unknowable simply compounds the social logic of alienation that Marx identified in the commodification of labour over one-and-a-half centuries ago. 'The *alienation* of the worker in his product means not only that his labour becomes an object, an *external* existence, but that it exists *outside him*, independently, as something alien to him, and that it becomes a power of its own confronting him; it means that the life he has conferred on the object confronts him as something hostile and alien.'[15] In *History and Class Consciousness*, Lukács had broadened the application of this insight to the totality of bourgeois society: as the commodity form spreads beyond the labour process, subsuming more and more use-values (and the human activities that produce them) under the principle of exchange, the experience of alienation becomes generalized throughout capitalist society. Reification – the systematic petrification of social relations and historical processes into things – robs people of the capacity (and the will) to understand and engage with their world as the product of collective human activity. As capitalism shatters the 'natural' bonds of kinship, community, and tradition, human beings 'erect around themselves in the reality they have created and "made," a kind of *second nature* which evolves with exactly the same inexorable necessity as was the case earlier on with irrational forces of nature (more exactly: the social relations which appear in this form).'[16] While this 'second nature,' like the first, is amenable to some measure of analysis, predictability, and quantification, the structural mystification of its social origins ideologically insulates it from the prospect of democratic regulation. 'Man in capitalist society confronts a reality "made" by himself (as a class) which appears to him to be a *natural* phenomenon alien to himself; he is wholly at the mercy of its "laws," his activity is confined to the exploitation of the inexorable fulfilment of certain individual laws for his own (egoistic) interests.'[17] In much the same way that human beings have grown proficient at predicting, adapting to, and exploiting climactic processes and patterns to serve their own interests, the reified structures of bourgeois society have been harnessed to the production of great wealth to the benefit of certain individuals and classes. But just as the weather ultimately remains beyond human control – occasionally acting in an unpredictable manner with often catastrophic consequences – the market logic that mercilessly rules capitalist societies, imposing economic privation and terror upon those who fail to adapt themselves to its inexorable demands, appears (and is systematically portrayed as) equally impervious to social regulation.

Where Adorno decries the aggressive, insatiable qualities of a rapacious technological rationality, Lukács identifies the fundamentally passive or contemplative character of bourgeois knowledge, especially in those disciplines devoted to the study of man and society. 'For the contemplative attitude,' Vogel notes, 'the world that surrounds us is something independent of us, given, and immutable; we observe it but cannot change it.'[18] The world appears 'natural' insofar as it is understood and, more important, *experienced* as a collection of spaces and objects in which all tangible presence of human labour has been eliminated. Conceiving of our environment as natural in this sense, Vogel argues, is both symptomatic and constitutive of a profound alienation from our social world: it reinforces and magnifies experiences of helplessness and disempowerment that have become commonplace under capitalism. Challenging such reified conceptions, unmasking them as obfuscatory of the social practice through which the world – *including* nature – is actually produced, becomes the principal task of critical theory: 'the role of liberatory critique ... is to dereify or "uncongeal" – to dissolve false immediacies, to reveal to human subjects that what they think of as "natural" is actually the product of their own socially organized activity.'[19] For Vogel, Adorno's commitment to the nonidentical is simply incompatible with the use of reification as a critical conceptual tool: such a concept 'must appear [to him] as dangerously infected with idealism and the hubris of identity thinking; much more important for him is to point out cases where objects that *really are* external are mistakenly viewed as merely *for humans.*'[20] Horkheimer and Adorno note in *Dialectic of Enlightenment* that 'all reification is a forgetting.' But for them, unlike Lukács, that which is forgotten is not labour or social relations or, in fact, any human practice at all: instead, what is forgotten is that which negative dialectics compels us to remember, namely, the repressed 'remainder' of the object that always evades conceptual recognition.[21]

Set against the contemporary backdrop of a capitalist system that has become truly globalized and that appears frighteningly impervious to even minimal forms of democratic regulation, Vogel's basic argument that critical theory must enlist the power of reason to *expand* (not diminish) our understanding and control over the environments in which we live is compelling. When we add into the mix the increasingly desperate need to confront patterns of resource use, economic development, and consumer culture that threaten the planet with ecological catastrophe – patterns that not only are championed by powerful economic and political interests but also are so deeply embedded in everyday life that they have become thoroughly 'naturalized' – the injunction to limit reason's capacity to conceptualize the world appears naive, wrong-headed, even spectacularly irresponsible.

Once the unit of analysis shifts from the species as a whole (or contemporary economic, social, and political structures) to real, concrete individuals, the idea that human beings exercise dominion over their world appears rather different. As C.S. Lewis once noted, 'what we call Man's power over Nature turns out to be a power exercised by some men over other men with Nature as its instrument.'[22] Assessing the broader social and normative significance of the epistemological relation between subject and object depends a great deal upon how one defines to both terms. The *collective* power of human beings to dominate the social *and* natural world has never been greater, and this raises fundamental questions about the need to limit the destructive, unsustainable exploitation of natural *and* human resources. Yet the relation of most individuals to this world remains one of dependence and helplessness. For most of us, the fabled power of the subject to use instrumental reason to dominate the object, in a physical *and* cognitive sense, is one that is experienced indirectly, if at all; far more common is an experience of the world of objects – for example, the workplace, the marketplace, the political system, even the commodities that surround us in everyday life – as overwhelming and often unintelligible, as imposing severe and often arbitrary limits on how we think and act. Attacking the 'fetishism' of the concept seems like an irrelevant and counterproductive exercise when reason's power to penetrate, classify, analyse, and control the world of objects has grown so anaemic at the level of the individual. We are confronted with a world whose seemingly fathomless *thing*ness leaves us with little choice but to submit and adapt as best we can. Surely, as Vogel suggests, the task of critical reason today is to shatter and dispel the mysterious opacity of *this* object world, using conceptual thought to strip away the veneer of 'otherness' that is symptomatic, not of the irrepressible remainder that escapes the concept, but rather of the social amnesia of reification – *Verdinglichung*: literally, 'thing-ification' – that makes us forget we are the collective producers of the world that surrounds us.

Yet is such an argument all that different from what Adorno himself recommends? Writing to Walter Benjamin in the late 1930s, Adorno offered much the same advice, taking issue with his friend's commitment to the 'dialectical image' as a means of critical expression, a method of literary montage in which cultural, economic, and political phenomena are meticulously arranged, presented, and juxtaposed with very little theoretical explanation. In particular, he criticizes Benjamin for his naive belief that the objects and spaces of the world, once gathered together in suitably shocking, provocative, and defamiliarizing constellations, could simply speak for themselves. Instead, Adorno argued, it is only through the power of abstract, conceptual thought that those objects and spaces could be fully experienced, that the explosive social energies which lay coiled within them could be released. 'Your dialectic,' he explains, 'is lacking in one thing: mediation … The theological motif of calling things by their names tends to switch into the wide-eyed presentation of mere facts. If one wanted to put it rather drastically, one could say that your study is located at the crossroads of magic and positivism. This spot is bewitched. Only theory could break this spell.'[23] Indeed, Adorno criticizes Benjamin for attributing to certain objects a 'spontaneity, tangibility and density which they have lost under capitalism': instead of waxing romantically for an immediacy that most likely never existed, he insists that 'the materialist determination of cultural traits is only possible if it is mediated through the *total social process*.'[24] In a later exchange, Adorno similarly wonders whether Benjamin's claim that objects with an aura can return the gaze of human subjects is better attributed to the human labour congealed within them. 'Is not the aura,' he asks, 'invariably a trace of a forgotten *human moment* in the thing?'[25] At the very least, such observations disturb the monochromatic vision of his thought that has emerged thus far in this chapter and that often dominates discussions of his relevance for theorizing nature. Without question, Adorno's philosophical and aesthetic writings tend to privilege a (negative) conception of nature as that which eludes (or should elude) conceptualization. Yet when our attention shifts to the relation between human beings and their *social* and *cultural* environment – in particular, the 'naturalized' images of the world one finds in the commodities of the culture industry – all traces of hesitation, caution, and timidity vanish. Instead, Adorno champions a bold, ruthless, and systematic criticism of prevailing forms of thought, language, culture, and communication for their *weakness* (not their strength) in relation to the object: he decries the fact that the power of thought to install some *conceptual* distance between humanity and its environment – to *mediate* that environment – has been abandoned in favour of a servile reproduction of the real.

Reason and Fear: Nature as Terror

As Andrew Biro argues persuasively in *Denaturalizing Ecological Politics*, the idea of nature plays multiple, ambiguous, and occasionally contradictory roles in Adorno's thought, taking on different meanings depending on its placement within specific constellations of concepts and ideas.[26] While as we have seen, a largely positive, benign, and sympathetic account emerges when nature is explored in the context of non-identity, instrumental reason, negative dialectics, and aesthetic practice, it takes on a more sinister dimension when plotted against *Dialectic of Enlightenment*'s thesis that humanity has been enslaved to the rule of a 'second nature' that we find just as inscrutable, unpredictable, and dangerous as the 'first' that terrified our ancestors so many generations ago.

Much of the force of this world-historical narrative depends on a speculative invocation of the overwhelming fear that a fledgling humanity experienced in the face of natural forces that could be neither understood nor controlled. One might even argue that the principal target of critique in *Dialectic of Enlightenment* is not instrumental reason *per se*, but the persistence (and deliberate reproduction) of a condition of primordial fear that necessarily forces all forms of thought into an identitarian mould. Accenting the failure of the concept to fully represent the object is often taken, first and foremost, as expressive of the deficiencies of conceptual thought. Yet the distance between concept and object is *precisely* what Horkheimer and Adorno celebrate as the essence of dialectical thinking – that is, thought's potential to express the object's potential to be something other than what it is:

> If the tree is addressed no longer as simply a tree but as evidence of something else, a location of *mana*, language expresses the contradiction that it is at the same time itself and something other than itself, identical and not identical. Through the deity speech is transformed from tautology into language. The concept, usually defined as the unity of the features of what

it subsumes, was rather, from the first, a product of dialectical thinking, in which each thing is what it is only by becoming what it is not.[27]

Non-identity, in other words, is best conceived *not* as some secret, mystical property of the object but instead as a characteristic of the *relation* between the subject and the object. It is not a thing or a characteristic of a thing but a particular type of theoretically informed and mediated practice: indeed, the very idea of a 'remainder' only makes sense from the perspective of a thinking and labouring subject. Concepts, in other words, do not simply repress and destroy the non-identical; they are also a crucial aspect of its recognition and affirmation.

The underlying condition that binds myth and enlightenment together in such a disastrous union, then, is not conceptual thought – embryonic in myth through sacrifice, ubiquitous in enlightenment through technological rationality and the commodity form – but the pervasive experience of fear that shapes the formation, exercise, and use of such thought in such narrow ways. Crudely put, it is fear – not reason – that inaugurates and sustains the fateful dialectic of enlightenment. Certainly the relentless crusade against difference sponsored by identitarian thought (which culminates in the horrors of the Holocaust) compounds, intensifies, and exploits fear, but one cannot say that fear is immanent to such thought. Immediately following the passage cited above, Horkheimer and Adorno observe that

> this dialectic [of non-identitarian thought] remains powerless as long as it *emerges from* the cry of terror, which is the doubling, the mere tautology of terror itself. The gods cannot take away fear from human beings, the petrified cries of whom they bear as their names. Humans believe themselves free of fear when there is no longer anything unknown … Nothing is allowed to remain outside, since the mere idea of the 'outside' is the real source of fear.[28]

It is not merely the 'idea' of the outside – an epistemological condition – that causes fear. Instead, Horkheimer and Adorno remain sufficiently Marxist (and materialist) to assert that fear is a product of the social, cultural, and material environment in which people live. It would be the worst sort of idealism (not to mention, a self-help cliché) to argue that individuals simply need new ways of thinking (or not thinking) about the 'outside' in order to temper, suspend, or even eliminate their fear. Instead, fear – or, more precisely, the social, material, and cultural conditions that produce fear – must be addressed (and minimized) if the utopian critical and aesthetic dimensions of rationality are ever to achieve their potential. Emancipating that potential is fundamentally a social, material, and political project, not an epistemological or philosophical one. As long as the conditions that produce fear endure, reason cannot evolve into anything other than what it has become: first, a tool for increasing (collective) human power to control and manipulate its environment; and second, a defensive attempt to excise conceptually all forms of difference that threaten to expose the illusory, partial, and ultimately self-destructive character of this power.

As the 'prototype' of the bourgeois subject, Odysseus narratively prefigures the acquiescent logic of positivism in which the instrumental power of thought to understand and control the natural world grows in proportion to its mimetic subordination to nature. 'Only deliberate adaptation to it brings nature under the power of the physically weaker.'[29] Just as the Greek adventurer trumps mythic power by inflicting on himself the punishments that had hitherto been the purview of the gods, reason tears itself free of myth only by binding itself ever tighter to a slavish reproduction of the real, sacrificing the potential for difference between concept and object (and thus non-identitarian dialectics) in favour of a cognitive prostration before the rule of 'brute facts.' True knowledge, Horkheimer and Adorno write, 'does not consist in mere perception, classification, and calculation but precisely in the determining negation of whatever is directly at hand. Instead of such negation, mathematical formalism, whose medium, number, is the most abstract form of the immediate, *arrests thought at mere immediacy*.'[30] There is no reason to believe that thinking about nature is exempt from this injunction: instead of simply accepting the purity, difference, and 'otherness' of the nature as it appears before us, we are enjoined to actively negate the 'immediacy' of nature and especially our historical relationship with it. While some might justifiably object that there is a latent Hegelianism at play here that sits uneasily with the self-reflexive thrust of Adorno's later writings on negative dialectics, the principal objective of such 'determinate negation' is not the (idealist) deconstruction of *all* nature into history but rather the emancipation of thought from the tyranny of the existent so often justified, in *both* the age of myth and that of enlightenment, by recourse to the trope of nature.[31] 'Existence, thoroughly cleansed of demons and their conceptual descendants, takes on, *in its gleaming naturalness*, the numinous character that former ages attributed to demons. Justified in the guise of brutal facts as something eternally immune to intervention, the social injustice from which those facts arise is as sacrosanct today as the medicine man once was under the protection of his gods.'[32]

More directly put, 'it is as if the final result of civilization were a return to the terrors of nature.'[33] And in both cases, a fearful humanity responds by way of desperate and submissive adaptation to forces that are perceived as beyond its control. Under the reign of myth, such submission was governed by primitive rituals of mimesis: humans imitated a wild, unpredictable, and all-powerful nature in the hope of assimilating themselves to it. As science and reason strip the world of its enchantment, these primitive mimetic practices of literally making oneself like something else – becoming the predator or the storm, or the spirits associated with them – are seemingly left behind. Yet mimetic submission to one's environment is not so much abandoned as perfected. 'The reason that represses mimesis is not merely its opposite. It is itself mimesis: of death. The subjective mind which disintegrates the spiritualization of nature masters spiritless nature only by imitating its rigidity.'[34] Where humans once sought power by making themselves resemble a natural world populated by spirits, demons, and gods, today cognitive processes mimic an environment composed of inert matter that is thoroughly subjected to the rule of technology, instrumental reason, and the commodity form.

Reason in Chains: Nature and the Culture Industry

This logic of mimetic adaptation to mythic, natural(ized) powers is at its most insidious in the culture industry. As a form of knowledge, commodified mass culture is to society what positivist science and technology is to nature: both strive to reduce and even eliminate the difference between concept and object, between the representation of a thing and the thing itself. 'The actual is validated, knowledge confines itself to repeating it, thought makes itself mere tautology.'[35] Thinking hardens into a petrified, one-dimensional reproduction of the world outside, leaving us deprived of the cognitive resources to imagine that our environment – and in particular, our *relations* with that environment – might be anything other than it is today. The quest for profits motivates the culture industry to produce commodities that can be quickly and easily consumed in a variety of contexts to maximize their circulation. There is, in other words, a demand for 'predigested' culture: objects and practices that harmonize with existing conceptual frameworks and belief systems minimize the cognitive and affective demands placed upon the audience, thereby accelerating the ease with which they can be promoted and consumed. 'The active contribution which Kantian schematism still expected of subjects – that they should, from the first, relate sensuous multiplicity to fundamental concepts – is denied to the subject by [the culture] industry. It purveys schematism as its first service to the customer.'[36] The content of mass culture is extensively organized, sorted, and classified at the point of production, leaving little that does not mimic pre-existing conceptual schematics. Demographic and psychographic research has become so extensive and efficient that the marketing industry's claim to know its customers better than they know themselves is not an idle boast. Thus the cognitive dimension of cultural experience is limited to the simple recognition of how particular objects (character types, plot lines, harmonies, etc.) are exemplary of fixed universal categories. 'The composition hears for the listener.'[37] To disguise this arbitrary restriction of the cognitive process and to cultivate the illusion of novelty, the entertainment industry develops increasingly sophisticated media technology to multiply the force and types of sensual stimuli with which it can bombard the consumer. The profusion of such stimuli requires the consumer's constant attentiveness in order to process the visual, aural, and tactile sensations that are produced at any given moment: sustained thought on any particular aspect or moment is impossible because of the sheer volume of details to be rapidly absorbed and sorted.

Use of simplistic conceptual patterns to organize an environment of totalizing sensual stimulation produces a relation of immediacy between culture and consumer. The apparent facticity and concreteness of cultural commodities is accentuated: they appear self-contained and autonomous, enabling discrete moments of 'complete experience' in which the subject perceives itself to be directly engaged with the object in an unmediated fashion. Popular music's unrestrained stimulation of affect, for instance, 'leaves no room for conceptual reflection between itself and the subject and so it creates an illusion of immediacy in the totally mediated world.'[38] Furthermore, the developmental logic of media technology strives to eliminate the distance between consumer and culture, delivering ever more totalizing forms of cultural experience in which we are invited to lose ourselves in the moment. Yet for Adorno the elision of the distance between subject and object is entirely ideological: 'thought may only hold true to the idea of immediacy by way of the mediated, but it becomes the prey of the mediated the instant it grasps directly for the unmediated.'[39] As discussed earlier, critical thinking depends upon a subject that is able and willing to recognize the difference between thought and the real, sustaining a tension between them to energize reflection upon their mutual unrealized potential: their non-identity. 'The value of a thought,' observes Adorno, 'is measured by its distance from the continuity of the familiar. It is objectively devalued as this distance is reduced; the more it approximates to the pre-existing standard, the further its antithetical function is diminished.'[40] As the illusion grows that culture and reality come to mirror each other, this speculative dimension of semiotic expression is lost. Tempted by the culture industry's seductive promises to proceed directly to existence, nature, self, or pure being, we lose the reflexive distance afforded by thought in favour of the pseudo-immediacy of the cultural moment.

As such, the capacity of culture to mediate, critique, and defamiliarize fades before the relentless reproduction of the world as fixed and unchanging. In opposition to simplistic accounts of capitalist culture as false consciousness, Adorno maintains that 'there are no more ideologies in the authentic sense of false consciousness, only advertisements for the world through its duplication and the provocative lie which does not seek belief but commands silence.'[41] In other words, the problem with the culture industry is not that it distracts people from reality, but that it does not provide a sufficiently powerful distraction to stimulate the imagination to dream about new forms of thought and being. 'It is not because they turn their back on washed-out existence that escape films are so repugnant, but because they do not do so energetically enough, because they are themselves just as washed-out, because the satisfactions they fake coincide with the ignominy of reality, of denial. The dreams have no dream.'[42] Modelled upon a positivist epistemology that obsessively replicates pre-existing categories of experience as accurately as possible, mass culture offers images of a natural, 'thing-like' world that is static and unchanging. From the perspective of dialectical thought, this iconic fidelity to reality – or, more accurately, to the prevailing patterns of cognition and affect through which reality is experienced – blinds humanity to the possibility that the world – the institutions, practices, and environments in which we live – might ever be any different from what it is today. 'The arid wisdom which acknowledges nothing new under the sun, because all the pieces in the meaningless game have been played out, all the great thoughts have been thought, all possible discoveries can be construed in advance, and human beings are defined by self-preservation through adaptation – this barren wisdom merely reproduces the fantastic doctrine it rejects: the sanction of fate, which through retribution incessantly reinstates what always was.'[43]

'Self-preservation through adaptation' to the forces of nature blends seamlessly into 'self-preservation through adaptation' to the forces of society. While the ontologies of these forces differ in significant ways, they are experienced (and represented) in virtually identical ways; and thus, enlightenment blends seamlessly into myth. Writing about the astrology columns of the *Los Angeles Times*, for instance, Adorno explains how they attribute a 'metaphysical dignity' to the necessity of adapting oneself to irrational, incomprehensible powers. 'In as much as the social system is the "fate" of most individuals independent of their will and interest, it is projected upon the stars in order thus to obtain a higher degree of dignity and justification in which the individuals hope to participate themselves.'[44] The advice administered by these columns is harmless enough, but the fact that it depends on 'the stars' for its authority both indicates and reinforces a conception of the world as composed of forces beyond human understanding that simply must be obeyed. Astrology teaches anew the lessons of mythology: 'Only those who subject themselves utterly pass muster with the gods.'[45] Most disturbing is how modern ideals that once bespoke a critique of human subjection to heteronomy have been restructured in aid of its valorization: 'Freedom [now] consists of the individual's taking upon himself voluntarily what is inevitable anyway.'[46] Placed in this larger context, sublime conceptions of nature as a divine, spectacular refuge of unfathomable otherness that properly inspires awe and wonder (and thereby impresses upon the subject an awareness of its own fragility and insignificance) secretly fulfil – with an almost uncanny precision – the ideological needs of capitalism to represent itself as timeless and inviolable.

History, Mimesis, and Spectacle: Nature and the Task of Critique

But this is not to say that we are forced to choose, once and for all, between *either* the rational deconstruction (and disenchantment) of all that appears to be natural as nothing more than the petrified remains of sensuous human practice *or* the humbling suspension of reason and the narcissistic subject before the unfathomable otherness of phenomena that deserve acceptance, respect, and autonomy. One cannot say with absolute certainty that our relations with nature (or that which appears to be natural) must always be governed by either of these two patterns. Rather than conceive these competing epistemological priorities as mutually exclusive or even contradictory, we should instead understand the tension between them as productive of the truly dialectical thought that Adorno consistently champions. In a 1932 essay, 'The Idea of Natural History,' he explains that 'if the question of the relation of nature and history is to be seriously posed, then it only offers any chance of solution if it is possible *to comprehend historical being in its most extreme historical determinacy, where it is most historical, as natural being, or if it were possible to comprehend nature as an historical being where it seems to rest most deeply in itself as nature* [italics in original].'[47] In calling for the perennial constellation of nature and history together, Adorno is unequivocal that neither term should ever gain the upper hand: or, better stated perhaps, each must be mobilized against the other where it appears at its most powerful, autochthonous, and self-contained. It is precisely those spaces, phenomena, and experiences which seem most 'natural' to us that are most deserving of critical deconstruction as historically constituted. Similarly, recalling the limits of human power, knowledge, and control over the environments in which we live is most important in those institutions, practices, and belief systems in which those limits have been systematically repressed and forgotten. Critical theory must be conjunctural, attentive to the particular social, cultural, and intellectual conditions that shape how any given phenomena will be understood and experienced: developing a critique of the use of nature in fascist cinema will necessarily involve a different set of conceptual tools and normative priorities than understanding the exploitation of natural resources by capitalist industrial practices and different again from comprehending the role that nature plays in Cartesian or Kantian philosophy. A vigorous criticism of nature worship in one context may be justifiably displaced by arguments defending the need to preserve natural beauty in another.

The starkly divergent accounts of mimesis that appear throughout Adorno's work are exemplary in this regard. A mimetic relationship with nature mediated through serious aesthetic practice is often identified as the utopian endpoint of Adorno's negative dialectics of subject and object. Deliberately suspending its egocentric narcissism, the subject 'snuggles' up to (*sich anschmiegen*) the object, assimilating itself to it, thereby temporarily suspending the aggressive, instrumental, and exploitative dimensions of instrumental reason. Rather than changing (dominating) the object to serve our needs, we change ourselves to accommodate the object: our creativity becomes a medium for the (always partial) expression of the object's specificity.[48] When compulsively exercised under the rule of terror, however, mass culture turns the mimetic faculty in the far more sinister direction of imitation. Individuality and autonomy are sacrificed in favour of the transformation of bodies and lives into copies of the images, ideals, and commodities furnished by the culture industry. As Miriam Hansen observes:

> simulating immediacy, individuality, and intimacy, the 'characters' of mass culture spell out norms of social behaviour – ways of being, smiling and mating. Regardless of the explicit messages touted via dialogue and plot, the viewer is ceaselessly asked to translate image into script, to read the individual appearance of a star as an imperative of identity – 'to be like her' – and to articulate the most subtle nuances in terms of the binary logic of 'do and don't.'[49]

In a secret doubling of the commodification of labour, people empathize with commodities in the hopes of partaking of some of the independence, autonomy, and 'life' that they seem to possess. 'As far as mass culture is concerned,' Horkheimer and Adorno argue, '*reification is no metaphor*: it makes the human beings that it reproduces resemble things ... They assimilate themselves to what is dead.'[50] The illusory but no less compelling pursuit of pleasure, happiness, and fulfilment depend upon reducing the distance between the 'talking masks' of the culture industry and our own lives, upon one's success in literally refashioning oneself into a thing. Under the wrong conditions, then – and the unholy trinity of fear, narcissism, and heteronomy are what *Dialectic of Enlightenment* bring to mind – mimetic practices do not mark the mutual emancipation of subject and object; rather, they inscribe the object's tyranny over the subject. The normative valence of mimesis depends upon the broader context in which it occurs (and especially its uncoupling from terror); and given the ravages of capitalist globalization, it is far more likely to reinforce rather than challenge relations of social and natural domination.

Expanding Marx's thesis about alienation to our cultural environment, Guy Debord famously defined the society of the spectacle as one in which the atomized individual is powerless to do anything other than bear witness to the reality that unfolds around her. 'The spectacle,' he argues, 'presents itself as something enormously positive, indisputable and inaccessible. It says nothing more than "that which appears is good, that which is good appears." The attitude which it demands in principle is passive acceptance which in fact it already obtained by its matter of appearing without reply, by its monopoly of appearance.'[51] Nature and our relations with it are hardly immune to this logic: one might even say that the resurrection of nature *in spectacular form* proceeds in lockstep with the speed and intensity with which humanity continues to annex the natural environment to its own ends. Scarcity breeds value, and the more difficult it becomes to 'experience' nature (or places that are sanctified as relatively untouched by human activity), the more appealing a simulacrum of pristine nature becomes as a sign of distinction. Those who call for a posture of reverence before the majesty and beauty of nature would do well to remember that this objective is also shared by those pursuing the transformation of nature into a commodity, yet another species of consumer pleasure. Far more important than this relatively simple point, however, is how cultivating an experience of nature as sublime – that is, as a phenomenon that exceeds or overflows our capacity to give it meaning – can serve to aestheticize the experience of living in a reified world. Taking pleasure from the environment becomes inversely proportional to its lucidity: the less we subject our environment (and our relations with it) to the cold, unfeeling grasp of reason, the more we can revel and delight in the many sensual splendours it has to offer. The familiar breeds boredom and indifference; the novel and the unknown, precisely by virtue of their inscrutable and unpredictable qualities (as well as our wilful forgetting of the historical and social conditions that allow us, and not others, to experience those qualities in very particular ways), promise excitement and stimulation. Among the most remarkable ideological achievements of consumer culture, as Benjamin prophesied in his analysis of fascist aesthetics, has been the transformation of alienation into a cultural spectacle and thus an aesthetic pleasure of the first order.[52] Championing a passive relationship with nature as other inescapably partakes of this logic even as it may also serve to momentarily restrain the rapacious practices of capitalism.

In his conclusion to *One Way Street*, Benjamin offers a more promising avenue through which to explore the relation between humanity and nature:

The mastery of nature, so the imperialists teach, is the purpose of all technology. But who would trust a cane wielder who proclaimed the mastery of children by adults to be the purpose of education? Is not education above all the indispensable ordering of the *relationship* between generations and therefore mastery, if we are to use this term, of that relationship and not of children? And likewise technology is not the mastery of nature but of the *relation* between nature and man.[53]

The technology that Benjamin alludes to here is not, of course, the factories and machines of capitalist industry but the 'second order' technologies of culture and communication. It is well known that Adorno disagreed with Benjamin's (later) optimism about the emancipatory effects of those technologies, but I believe he would have shared this sentiment. Challenging the domination of nature by simply defining it as off limits to human reason is irresponsibly premature in the cultural, economic, and political environment of today; indeed, it is far more likely to bring nature all the more completely under the dominion of instrumental reason and the commodity form. Imposing sustainable and ethical limits on human exploitation of nature will only occur after we use the cultural and communicative resources we have in order to understand, experience, and master the enormous power that we collectively possess but do not yet control to shape and construct our social as well as our natural environment.

NOTES

1 Cited in William Leiss, *The Domination of Nature* (New York: George Braziller, 1972), 3.
2 Max Horkheimer and Theodor Adorno, *Dialectic of Enlightenment*, ed. Gunzelin Schmid Noerr, trans. Edmund Jephcott (Stanford: Stanford University Press, 2002), 89.
3 Walter Benjamin, 'K (Dream City and Dream House, Dreams of the Future, Anthropological Nihilism, Jung) [1a, 9],' in *The Arcades Project*, trans. Howard Eiland and Kevin McLaughlin (Cambridge: Belknap, 1986), 391.
4 Theodor Adorno, *Negative Dialectics*, trans. E.B. Ashton (New York: Continuum, 1995), 22.
5 Neil Evernden, *The Social Creation of Nature* (Baltimore: Johns Hopkins University Press, 1992), 117.
6 Christopher Hitt, 'Toward an Ecological Sublime,' *New Literary History* 30, no. 3 (1999): 619.

7 Horkheimer and Adorno, *Dialectic of Enlightenment*, 1.

8 Adorno, *Negative Dialectics*, 141.

9 Ibid., 5.

10 Ibid., 191.

11 Ibid., 135.

12 Morton Schoolman, *Reason and Horror: Critical Theory, Democracy, and Aesthetic Individuality* (New York: Routledge, 2001), 14.

13 Ibid., 123 and 133.

14 Ibid., 177, emphasis in original.

15 Karl Marx, 'Economic and Philosophical Manuscripts of 1844,' in *The Marx–Engels Reader*, 2nd ed., ed. Robert C. Tucker (New York: Norton, 1978), 82.

16 Georg Lukacs, *History and Class Consciousness*, trans. Rodney Livingstone (Cambridge, MA: MIT Press, 1990), 128, emphasis added.

17 Ibid., 135, emphasis added.

18 Steven Vogel, *Against Nature: The Concept of Nature in Critical Theory* (Albany: SUNY Press, 1996), 21.

19 Ibid., 5.

20 Ibid., 76, emphasis in original.

21 Horkheimer and Adorno, *Dialectic of Enlightenment*, 191. See the discussion in Vogel, *Against Nature*, 78–9.

22 Cited in Leiss, *The Domination of Nature*, 195.

23 Theodor Adorno and Walter Benjamin, *The Complete Correspondence, 1928–1940*, ed. Henry Lonitz, trans. Nicholas Walker (Cambridge, MA: Harvard University Press, 1999), 282, 283.

24 Adorno and Benjamin, *The Complete Correspondence*, 283, emphasis in original.

25 Ibid., 320–1, emphasis added.

26 Andrew Biro, *Denaturalizing Ecological Politics: Alienation from Nature from Rousseau to the Frankfurt School and Beyond* (Toronto: University of Toronto Press, 2005), 124–30.

27 Horkheimer and Adorno, *Dialectic of Enlightenment*, 11.

28 Ibid., 11, emphasis added.

29 Ibid., 44.

30 Ibid., 20, emphasis added.

31 For a contemporary example of how this logic works, see Shane Gunster, '"You Belong Outside": Nature, Advertising, and the SUV,' *Ethics and the Environment* 9, no. 2 (Fall–Winter 2004).

32 Horkheimer and Adorno, *Dialectic of Enlightenment*, 21, emphasis added.

33 Ibid., 113.
34 Ibid., 44.
35 Ibid., 20.
36 Ibid., 98.
37 Theodor Adorno (with the assistance of George Simpson), 'On Popular Music,' *Studies in Philosophy and Social Science* 9 (1941): 22.
38 Theodor Adorno, *Introduction to the Sociology of Music*, trans. E.B. Ashton (New York: Seabury, 1976), 46.
39 Theodor Adorno, 'The Essay as Form,' trans. Robert Hullot-Kentor and Frederic Will, *New German Critique* 32 (Spring–Summer 1984): 167.
40 Theodor Adorno, *Minima Moralia: Reflections from a Damaged Life*, trans. E.F.N. Jephcott (New York: Verso, 1996), 80.
41 Theodor Adorno, 'Cultural Criticism and Society,' in *Prisms*, trans. Samuel Weber and Shierry Weber (Cambridge, MA: MIT Press, 1981), 34.
42 Adorno, *Minima Moralia*, 202.
43 Horkheimer and Adorno, *Dialectic of Enlightenment*, 8.
44 Theodor Adorno, 'The Stars Down to Earth: The *Los Angeles Times* Astrology Column,' in *The Stars Down to Earth and Other Essays on the Irrational in Culture*, ed. Stephen Crook (New York: Routledge, 1994), 42.
45 Horkheimer and Adorno, *Dialectic of Enlightenment*, 5.
46 Adorno, 'The Stars Down To Earth,' 44.
47 Theodor Adorno, 'The Idea of Natural History,' trans. Robert Hullot-Kentor, *Telos* 60 (1984): 117.
48 See the discussion in Martin Jay, 'Mimesis and Mimetology: Adorno and Lacoue-Labarthe,' in *The Semblance of Subjectivity: Essays in Adorno's Aesthetic Theory*, ed. Tom Huhn and Lambert Zuidervaart (Cambridge, MA: MIT Press, 1997), 29–37.
49 Miriam Hansen, 'Mass Culture as Hieroglyphic Writing: Adorno, Derrida, Kracauer,' *New German Critique* 56 (Spring–Summer 1992): 50.
50 Max Horkheimer and Theodor Adorno, 'The Schema of Mass Culture,' in *The Culture Industry: Selected Essays on Mass Culture*, ed. J.M. Bernstein (New York: Routledge, 1991), 82, emphasis added.
51 Guy Debord, *Society of the Spectacle* (Detroit: Black and Red, 1983), §12.
52 Using the representation of space in contemporary television advertising as a case study, I develop these arguments at greater length in '"Second Nature": Advertising, Metaphor, and the Production of Space,' *Fast Capitalism* 2, no. 1 (2006), http://www.fastcapitalism.com.
53 Walter Benjamin, *Reflections*, ed. Peter Demetz, trans. Edmund Jephcott (New York: Schocken, 1978), 93, emphasis added.

BIBLIOGRAPHY

Adorno, Theodor W. 'Cultural Criticism and Society.' In *Prisms*, translated by Samuel Weber and Shierry Weber. Cambridge: MIT Press, 1981.
- 'The Essay as Form.' Translated by Robert Hullot-Kentor and Frederic Will. *New German Critique* 32 (1984): 151–71.
- 'The Idea of Natural History.' Translated by Robert Hullot-Kentor. *Telos* 60 (1984): 111–24.
- *Introduction to the Sociology of Music*. Translated by E.B. Ashton. New York: Seabury, 1976.
- *Minima Moralia: Reflections from a Damaged Life*. Translated by E.F.N. Jephcott. New York: Verso, 1996.
- *Negative Dialectics*. Translated by E.B. Ashton. New York: Continuum, 1995.
- 'The Stars Down to Earth: The *Los Angeles Times* Astrology Column.' In *The Stars Down to Earth and Other Essays on the Irrational in Culture*, edited by Stephen Crook. New York: Routledge, 1994.
Adorno, Theodor W., and Walter Benjamin. *The Complete Correspondence, 1928–1940*. Edited by Henry Lonitz, translated by Nicholas Walker. Cambridge, MA: Harvard University Press, 1999.
Adorno, Theodor (with the assistance of George Simpson). 'On Popular Music.' *Studies in Philosophy and Social Science* 9 (1941): 17–48.
Benjamin, Walter. 'K (Dream City and Dream House, Dreams of the Future, Anthropological Nihilism, Jung) [1a, 9].' In *The Arcades Project*, translated by Howard Eiland and Kevin McLaughlin. Cambridge: Belknap, 1986.
- *Reflections*. Edited by Peter Demetz, translated by Edmund Jephcott. New York: Schocken, 1978.
Biro, Andrew. *Denaturalizing Ecological Politics: Alienation from Nature from Rousseau to the Frankfurt School and Beyond*. Toronto: University of Toronto Press, 2005.
Debord, Guy. *Society of the Spectacle*. Detroit: Black and Red, 1983.
Evernden, Neil. *The Social Creation of Nature*. Baltimore: Johns Hopkins University Press, 1992.
Gunster, Shane. '"Second Nature": Advertising, Metaphor, and the Production of Space.' *Fast Capitalism* 2, no.1 (2006).
- '"You Belong Outside": Nature, Advertising, and the SUV.' *Ethics and the Environment* 9, no. 2 (Fall–Winter 2004).
Hansen, Miriam. 'Mass Culture as Hieroglyphic Writing: Adorno, Derrida, Kracauer.' *New German Critique* 56 (Spring–Summer 1992): 43–75.

Hitt, Christopher. 'Toward an Ecological Sublime.' *New Literary History* 30, no. 3 (1999): 603–23.

Horkheimer, Max, and Theodor W. Adorno. *Dialectic of Enlightenment*. Edited by Gunzelin Schmid Noerr, translated by Edmund Jephcott. Stanford: Stanford University Press, 2002.

– 'The Schema of Mass Culture.' In *The Culture Industry: Selected Essays on Mass Culture*, edited by J.M. Bernstein. New York: Routledge, 1991.

Jay, Martin. 'Mimesis and Mimetology: Adorno and Lacoue-Labarthe.' In *The Semblance of Subjectivity: Essays in Adorno's Aesthetic Theory*, edited by Tom Huhn and Lambert Zuidervaart. Cambridge: MIT Press, 1997.

Leiss, William. *The Domination of Nature*. New York: George Braziller, 1972.

Lukács, Georg. *History and Class Consciousness*. Translated by Rodney Livingstone. Cambridge: MIT Press, 1990.

Marx, Karl. 'Economic and Philosophical Manuscripts of 1844.' In *The Marx–Engels Reader*, 2nd ed., edited by Robert C. Tucker. New York: Norton, 1978.

Schoolman, Morton. *Reason and Horror: Critical Theory, Democracy, and Aesthetic Individuality*. New York: Routledge, 2001.

Vogel, Steven. *Against Nature: The Concept of Nature in Critical Theory*. Albany: SUNY Press, 1996.

9 Ecological Crisis and the Culture Industry Thesis

ANDREW BIRO

[Humankind's] self-alienation has reached such a degree that it can experience its own destruction as an aesthetic pleasure of the first order.

Walter Benjamin[1]

The total mobilization of all media for the defense of the established reality has coordinated the means of expression to the point where communication of transcending contents becomes technically impossible.

Herbert Marcuse[2]

The visual is *essentially* pornographic, which is to say that it has as its end rapt, mindless fascination ... [Films] ask us to stare at the world as though it were a naked body.

Fredric Jameson[3]

Reading Adorno in an Era of Ecological Crisis

In the introduction to their edited collection, *Adorno: A Critical Reader*, Nigel Gibson and Andrew Rubin note that Adorno studies has boomed since the end of the Cold War – that Adorno's 'work has become, as Slavoj Žižek argues, part of an industry.'[4] This judgment is confirmed by a number of other leading left intellectuals cited by Gibson and Rubin, including Edward Said, Judith Butler, and Fredric Jameson.[5] In particular, Adorno's analysis of mass culture (and the Frankfurt School's more generally) is currently enjoying a revival, after having been often dismissed – especially in the emergent field of cultural studies – as an (if not *the*) extreme version of a theory of audience manipulation.[6]

It is perhaps not surprising that Frankfurt School theorizations of the culture industry would regain prominence at the turn of the millennium, now that the global triumph of capitalism has facilitated the spread of American mass culture[7] to every corner of the globe. As Fredric Jameson noted in 1990, it was not until the 1980s, after Adorno's death, that 'Adorno's prophecies of the "total system" finally came true [as] late capitalism has all but succeeded in eliminating the final loopholes of nature and the Unconscious, of subversion and the aesthetic, of individual and collective praxis alike, and, with a final fillip, in eliminating any memory trace of what thereby no longer existed in the henceforth postmodern landscape.'[8]

What is perhaps more surprising is the lack of connection between this resurgence of interest in the Frankfurt School's analysis of mass culture – or to use their now widely and often uncritically reproduced term, the 'culture industry' – and discussions of contemporary environmental crises. Jameson's observation that Adorno diagnosed late capitalism's 'eliminating the final loophole of nature' has generally taken 'nature' as a signifier for elements of human society that remain uncommodified (Jameson elsewhere identifies the nature that is colonized by late capitalism with 'the Third World and the Unconscious'[9]). The evidence of ecological crisis is far more pervasive than it was in Adorno's time, as is evident from recent comprehensive scientific studies such as Millennium Ecosystem Assessment[10] and the reports of the Intergovernmental Panel on Climate Change.[11] And what is more, a *sense* of ecological crisis has become culturally far more pervasive, as demonstrated by the popularity of more serious fare on the subject (Bill McKibben's highly successful 1989 book, *The End of Nature*, or more recently, Al Gore's climate change documentary *An Inconvenient Truth*) as well as by its representations in mass culture, which range from the stark eco-dystopianism of cyberpunk literature; to films like *Blade Runner*, *The Matrix*, and climate change disaster films such as *The Day After Tomorrow*; to moralizations about the wastefulness of consumer society in animated family films such as *Over the Hedge* and *Wall-E*; and, of course, to the phenomenal success of James Cameron's Manichean *Avatar* (industrialized resource extraction: bad; communion with non-human nature: good). At the same time, this culturally pervasive awareness of impending environmental crisis sits largely, and not entirely uncomfortably, within a culture of (and economy devoted to) consumerist individualism (four months after its release, *Avatar* had a worldwide box office gross in excess of $2.7 billion[12]). In an era in which 'environmental crisis' arguably needs to be understood as a *cultural* phenomenon as much as an ecological one, an understanding of the culture industry – its limitations as well as the strategic uses that may be made of it – may be crucial for resolving environmental crises in a humane manner. But as several other contributors to this volume note, to take the work of the first-generation Frankfurt School in general, and Adorno in particular, and apply it rigidly to today's context, would likely be only of limited use and would violate the spirit of the original work. This essay is written in the spirit of Adorno's injunction in 'The Idea of Natural History': '*to comprehend historical being in its most extreme historical determinacy, where it is most historical, as natural being, [and] to comprehend nature as an historical being where it seems to rest most deeply in itself as nature.*'[13]

The Domination of Nature

The link between 'culture' and 'nature,' it is worth emphasizing at the outset, is central to the work of the first-generation Frankfurt School. Adorno in particular – as the quotation from the early essay just cited indicates – insisted from the beginning on seeing the two as a dialectical totality rather than as separate spheres. And indeed, as he later made clear, the connection is at the heart of his theorization of the culture industry itself. In 'Culture Industry Reconsidered,' Adorno explains the subtitle of *Dialectic of Enlightenment*'s chapter on the culture industry – 'enlightenment as mass deception': 'The total effect of the culture industry is one of anti-enlightenment, in which, as Horkheimer and I have noted, enlightenment, that is the progressive technical domination of nature, becomes mass deception and is turned into a means for fettering consciousness.'[14]

This claim about the dialectical nature of enlightenment and domination provides a key to understanding what Frankfurt School critical theory has to offer our understanding of the contemporary environmental crisis, and why this offer has only been taken up to a limited extent.

As is made clear in the passage cited from 'Culture Industry Reconsidered,' the 'domination of nature' does not have an entirely negative connotation. Indeed, 'the progressive technical domination of nature' is here identified with 'enlightenment' itself. And early on in *Dialectic of Enlightenment*, Horkheimer and Adorno state that despite what might appear to be a ruthless critique of enlightenment, 'we are wholly convinced ... that social freedom is inseparable from enlightened thought.'[15] The point that the domination of nature is not entirely negative is considerably elaborated by William Leiss, who argues that 'mastery of nature' is an ideological concept – which is to say it holds an element of truth, but at the same time contains an element of falsity, in that it conceals contradictory or unequal social relations.[16] In this particular case, 'a grand enterprise of the species' that sought 'to break the tyrannical hold of despair over the consciousness of human technical possibilities and to encourage the conviction that men could fundamentally alter the material conditions of existence' has been conflated with the ways in which scientific and technological achievements have been used to reinforce social hierarchy and inequality.[17]

Far from being simply an error at the level of abstract categories, this conflation of the domination of nature as a project of human emancipation with the domination of nature as a tool for reinforcing societal domination has important political consequences. One of the dangers of this ideological conflation, Leiss points out, is that if the two elements remain unseparated, and dissatisfaction with entrenched societal inequality becomes sufficiently pervasive or intense, then the proverbial baby risks being thrown out with the bathwater: 'genuinely progressive aspects may be engulfed in the hatred aroused by the negative conditions with which it [the domination of nature] becomes associated.'[18] In other words, growing awareness of the existence of a technocratic elite that functions as a ruling class can provide the justification for the populist rejection of science more broadly, and for the reduction of the scientific enterprise to more narrowly political concerns. One implication of this is that countering the success that right-wing populist administrations have had in obfuscating the reality of climate warming requires engagement on the materialist terrain of class politics, rather than just the piling on of more scientific evidence.

But for the most part, environmentalists have tended to offer one of two contrasting 'counter-ideologies' (Leiss's term) to the ideology of the domination of nature. One such counter-ideology, especially evident in deep ecology, but more broadly visible in the enormous popular success of cultural narratives like *Avatar*, involves precisely the rejection of the fruits of enlightenment that Leiss cautions against: a return to a primitive 'Earth wisdom' instead of modern science.[19] At the other extreme, evident in technocratic 'eco-managerialist' or 'geo-greening' projects, lies the counter-ideology that exalts the scientific understanding of nature without accounting for the social domination to which the domination of nature has historically been attached. If deep ecologists want to throw out the baby with the bathwater, then those who advocate greater scientific literacy (on the part of either the media or the public more broadly) as the path to save 'us' from ecological crisis, without inquiring too deeply into how 'we' are constituted, are trying to save the baby without dispensing of the dirty bathwater. As Andrew Dobson warns: 'I think it is essential, for example, that Greens take seriously the material and ideological circumstances within which the "call to education" is made, and which are surely in danger of appropriating and disfiguring the project before it gets off the ground.'[20]

The Culture Industry and Subjective Mediation

One way of understanding the project of first-generation Frankfurt School critical theory is as an attempt to negotiate a way between these two poles, which are being drawn ever more closely together in a society characterized by 'rationalized irrationality.' The Enlightenment promised human freedom through a greater understanding of nature, but historically that scientific understanding has been placed in the service of societal domination. Human liberation is thus possible neither through a return to pre-Enlightenment modes of existence (where human beings were largely helpless before the forces of nature), nor through a simple increase in technical understanding of nature (which would only serve to reproduce social domination). The culture industry, for Horkheimer and Adorno in particular, reveals the depth at which societal domination is reproduced through increasing technological mastery of the natural world.

For Immanuel Kant, who is in some sense the paradigmatic philosopher of enlightenment, it was the role of the individual 'to relate the varied experiences of the senses to fundamental concepts.'[21] The mind works to impose structure or meaning on sensory experience. As Horkheimer and Adorno understand it, the culture 'industry robs the individual of his function. Its prime service to the customer is to do his schematizing for him.'[22] If the individual subject no longer undertakes this work, because the mediating is already done for her, then there is no capacity for critical engagement: 'the sound film ... leaves no room for imagination or reflection on the part of the audience.'[23] The resultant atrophying of the schematizing or critical faculties then makes it more difficult to envision a way in which the world of sensory input might be understood and ordered differently. The development of communication technologies, which as Shane Gunster notes (in this volume) takes place in an industrial context whereby technologies are structurally geared to be deployed in particular ways, in fact stultifies the capacity for progressive social development.

Moreover, it is not just the consumers of the culture industry's products whose consciousness is stunted. The culture industry equally performs the schematizing work for *producers* as well. The industrialization of culture necessitates a flattening of the contradiction between a specific work and the social totality from which it emerges, such that 'the work no longer has to test itself against any refractory material.'[24] The term culture *industry*, as Adorno emphasizes, refers to processes of standardization and 'the incorporation of industrial forms of organization,' undertaken to make cultural products more easily digestible as commodities.[25]

In the nineteenth century, Marx identified the commodification of labour as a process whereby human beings' power to self-consciously transform the world around them was alienated from the direct producers. Rather than being (as Leiss terms it) 'a grand enterprise of the species,' the transformation of nature is fundamentally individualized rather than socialized, competitive rather than cooperative, anarchic rather than rationally planned, and governed by considerations of efficiency and profit rather than beauty. In the twentieth century, Horkheimer and Adorno see this process of alienation being extended beyond the space of the factory gates and the time of the workday. Because the production of culture is not obviously governed by the law of value, previous stages of capitalism had left it to function as a relatively autonomous sphere, and culture remained a sphere where the production of social meaning could be achieved through collective practices. The development of a culture industry marks the end of culture as a shared realm constituted by living labour, and hence also as an Archimedean point outside the world of alienated labour: 'mechanization has such power over a man's leisure and happiness, and so profoundly determines the manufacture of amusement goods, that his experiences are inevitably after-images of the work process itself.'[26] Horkheimer and Adorno emphasize that this occurs not so much because of the imposition of mechanization or industrialization (or the 'technical mastery of nature') *per se*, but because it is done in the service of the capitalist drive for accumulation.[27] As culture is industrialized – or in other words more fully incorporated into the capitalist economy – it ceases to become a vehicle for the expression and transformation of lived social forms and increasingly becomes a vehicle for the accumulation of economic value. And as this occurs, the subjects inhabiting a particular cultural environment experience that environment – their culture – as an externally given object rather that a humanly produced social form. In other words, culture itself is encountered as a reified 'second nature.'

This attention to the impacts of instrumental rationality, and its attendant runaway technological development, on *human* culture and consciousness rather than on the non-human world is a point often lamented by environmentalist critics of the Frankfurt School. Notwithstanding the centrality of the category of 'the domination of nature,' Frankfurt School critical theory remains rooted in an anthropocentric vision: the 'domination of nature' is only really a problem to the extent that it 'becomes mass deception and is turned into a means for fettering consciousness.' The Frankfurt School theorists see the truth moment of enlightenment as, in Leiss's words, 'a grand enterprise of *the species*' (my emphasis). Some take this anthropocentric perspective to mean that the work of the Frankfurt School is only of limited use – or even part of the problem rather than the solution – for solving contemporary environmental crises. Below we shall see how this focus on the fate of human consciousness provides a crucial precondition for determining whether or how environmental crises are resolved. Before turning to this point, however, we can see how – most clearly in the work of Herbert Marcuse – the Frankfurt School's critique of instrumental reason works to soften this anthropocentrism considerably, making it much more amenable to ecological concerns.[28]

Non-Instrumental Anthropocentrism

This point is perhaps clearest in Marcuse's arguments that advanced capitalism's technological development had laid the groundwork for the abolition of toil.[29] In *Counterrevolution and Revolt*, where the human relationship to the natural world is perhaps most fully explored, he argues that '"liberation of nature" cannot mean returning to a pre-technological stage, but advancing to the use of the achievements of technological civilization for freeing man and nature from the destructive abuse of science and technology in the service of exploitation.'[30]

For Andrew Dobson, the recognition of nature as a subject (or something that can indeed be 'freed' by the achievements of technological civilization) for Marcuse is to be found in his idea that we have the potential to see 'the natural world as an arena for the practice and ful-

fillment of distinctively human faculties: the "creative, aesthetic faculties."'[31] In other words, the subjective trace in the object is to be found
by understanding the object as part of a world that is always already
shaped by human labour. Here Marcuse prefigures the insights of more
recent environmental philosophy, which has emphasized the extent to
which 'nature' as a putatively 'unworked object' (i.e., wilderness) is itself a cultural construction.[32]

This is similar to the argument developed by Steven Vogel in this
volume and elsewhere.[33] Vogel argues that our environment is necessarily shaped by human practices – in other words, that 'nature' in the
sense of something radically other from the human has always already
ended. Given this, humans ought to take a greater responsibility for
the world we create. For Vogel, then, the task for environmentalism
is to 'find a set of human practices that will make the world a better,
more sustainable, and more beautiful place.'[34] Notwithstanding his critique of the idea of nature as radical otherness, however, Vogel retains
an emphasis on the *resistance* that the material world offers to human
practice – that construction is 'hard work, takes effort, sometimes fails,
and always turns out differently than those who engage in it expect.'[35]

This emphasis on the resistance of the object world and human fallibility might help us deal with some of the confusion created by Marcuse's attempts both to maintain anthropocentrist presuppositions and
to claim that a human revolution is capable of 'liberating nature.' These
arise perhaps most starkly in *Eros and Civilization*[36] but receive somewhat more balanced consideration in *Counterrevolution and Revolt*. In
the latter text, Marcuse notes that 'to treat nature "for its own sake"
sounds good, but it is probably not for the sake of the animal to be
eaten, nor probably for the sake of the plant. The end of this war, the
perfect peace in the animal world – this idea belongs to the Orphic
myth, not to any conceivable historical reality.' He then strikes (somewhat uncharacteristically) a more pragmatic note: 'as the world is, priority must be on human solidarity among human beings. And yet, no
free society is imaginable which does not, under its "regulative idea of
reason," make the concerted effort to reduce consistently the suffering
which man imposes on the animal world.'[37] After going back and forth
on the question of whether human beings can indeed coexist peaceably with other beings in our environment, he concludes that while the
struggle for existence is a necessary feature of life, at least a temporary
suspension of the anthropocentric imperative may be possible: at times
'the struggle may also subside and make room for peace, tranquility,

fulfillment. In this case, not appropriation but rather its negation would be the nonexploitative relation: surrender, "letting-be," acceptance.'[38]

A Show about Nothing?

Marcuse's emphasis on 'surrender' and the suspension of the struggle for survival here echoes Adorno's insistence that the rule of instrumental reason is tied to the hegemony of the self-preservation instinct, and that this is what must be transcended in order to achieve a genuinely human existence. For Adorno in *Negative Dialectics*, even Kantian philosophy fails to see the animalistic drive for self-preservation as historical and therefore capable of being transcended:

> The imprisonment in immanence to which [Kant] honestly and brutally condemns the mind is the imprisonment in self-preservation, as it is imposed on men by a society that conserves nothing but the denials that would not be necessary any more. Once the natural historic cares that we share with beetles were broken through, a change would occur in the attitude which human consciousness takes toward truth. Its present attitude is dictated by the objectivity that keeps men in the state they are in.[39]

But what lies beyond the 'natural historic cares that we share with beetles' is not just a negation of the survival instinct that implies complete passivity. Adorno does appear to gesture occasionally in this direction, suggesting in *Minima Moralia*, for example, the possibility of 'Rien faire comme une bête, lying on the water and looking at the sky, being, nothing else without any further definition and fulfillment.'[40] While this passage explicitly begins by valorizing 'doing nothing like a beast,' the transposition of the phrase into a foreign language both points to the foreignness of the utopian and forces the reader into a more active cognitive engagement with the text, emphasizing the mediation necessary to achieve what otherwise appears to be an immediacy in nature.[41] To be resisted, Adorno asserts earlier in the same section, is 'the conception of unfettered activity, of uninterrupted procreation, of chubby insatiability, of freedom as frantic bustle, [which] feeds on the bourgeois concept of nature that has always served solely to proclaim social violence as unchangeable, as a piece of healthy eternity.'[42] What in contemporary society passes for radical passivity, to the point of a metaphorically vegetative state – the 'couch potato' – is in fact this 'chubby insatiability,' which is actualized through a process of frenetic image consumption that links the subject ever more tightly to, rather than delinking her from, social relations of domination.

Similarly, in *Negative Dialectics*, the transcendence of the survival instinct is seen to require a positive act of human will, or something akin to the ego asserting restraints on the instinctual drives of the id:

> 'What does it really matter?' is a line we like to associate with bourgeois callousness, but it is the line most likely to make the individual aware, without dread, of the insignificance of his existence. The inhuman part of it, the ability to keep one's distance as a spectator and to rise above things, is in the final analysis the human part, the very part resisted by its ideologists.[43]

The feeling of becoming a 'spectator' is associated earlier in the same paragraph with 'thinking men and artists' and in the subsequent paragraph with the expression of 'doubt that this could be all – when the individual, so relevant to himself in his delusion, still has nothing but that poor and emotionally animal-like ephemerality.'[44]

Thus for Adorno, the capacity to *transcend* our 'animal-like' condition appears to involve a passive registering of – or becoming a spectator over – the unfolding of nature. But this must be understood in the context: first, of a rejection of the possibility of returning to immanence in nature; and second – to return again to the terms of 'The Idea of Natural History' – an understanding of 'nature' as historical. What we are spectators to must at the same time be seen as (at least in part) our own creation. Such moments may still involve our active intervention in the natural environment, but in ways that are not immediately instrumental to survival. These non-instrumental approaches are most often characterized by Adorno (and by Marcuse as well) in aesthetic terms – as purposiveness without purpose. Beyond the frenzied struggle for survival that we share with all other animals, in other words, is the realm of culture, or interactions with the natural environment that are (at least to some extent) conscious and aesthetically rather than instrumentally motivated.

But as noted earlier, the more culture has become industrialized and subjected to the rule of instrumental reason or the logic of the commodity form, the less it has retained this character. Kant was criticized for failing to break the subject out of the prison of the survival instinct; but classical Enlightenment thought had at least formally preserved a space within the individual where mediation – necessarily including critical reflection on the world as it exists – can take place, thus allowing for purposive human actions that are guided by the possibility of creating a better world. It is this subjective mediation itself that the culture industry removes, thereby 'stunting ... the mass-media consumer's powers of imagination'[45] and reshaping our very senses. The mediation of sensory input and the possibility of critical reflection on this mediation – seeing the natural (the senses themselves) as historical – are what ground Horkheimer and Adorno's hope, or their ultimate faith in enlightenment. Their pessimism stems from the fact that this is precisely what is tendentially abolished in a 'society of the spectacle'[46] or one with an industrialized culture.

Postmodernity and Consumer Culture

As early as the mid-1970s, Anders Huyssen observed:

> Today, when political and social reforms are being curtailed ... when large-scale mergers in the news media and in publishing are commonplace, when political manipulation of the largely independent TV and radio stations is growing, it is legitimate to ask whether Adorno's theses about culture industry should not command more attention than all those theories that rely on culture, especially mass culture, as a vehicle for revolutionary change.[47]

Global corporate consolidation in the communication industry began in earnest in the 1980s, with a further acceleration beginning in the mid-1990s.[48] Each successive wave of corporate consolidation seems only to confirm the diagnosis that 'cultural products' are to be understood as commodities like any other. Indeed, according to Jameson, writing in the early 1990s, one of the distinctive features of postmodernity (or late capitalism) is that the realm of culture has lost its relative autonomy, or become instrumentalized, as the Frankfurt School's culture industry thesis predicted.[49]

At the same time, the economy continues to be dominated either by the oil and auto industries (which account for thirteen of the top twenty companies in the Fortune *Global 500*); or by finance, as the volume of money circulated in financial speculation now dwarfs money invested in the 'real' economy. (Note that Time-Warner, the world's largest entertainment company, ranks 159th in the *Global 500*, with revenues barely one-tenth those of number one ranked Royal Dutch Shell or number two ranked Exxon-Mobil).[50] Even in the 1940s, however, Horkheimer and Adorno had singled out the culture industry, though at that time, too, it was 'weak and dependent by comparison'[51] with other industrial sectors. For Horkheimer and Adorno, the colonization of culture by capital exemplifies the unprecedented depths to which instrumental rationality has penetrated, comparable to the rationalization of morality in their analysis of de Sade. At the same time, however, insofar as (for Adorno in particular) aesthetic practices remain a locus of resistance to instrumental rationality, the (always necessarily incomplete) industrialization of culture also represents a limit to the rule of universalizing reason.

For Fredric Jameson, the strategic importance of culture and the culture industry is slightly different. Jameson understands postmodernity to be a phase in which the cultural realm not only has lost its autonomy but also has simultaneously expanded 'to the point at which everything in our social life – from economic value and state power to practices and to the very structure of the psyche itself – can be said to be cultural in some original and as yet untheorized sense.'[52] Jameson follows the Frankfurt School thinkers at least in this sense: while the culture industry is relatively insignificant in the context of a 'purely' political economic analysis, culture itself – and its fate as it is increasingly industrialized – provides an important benchmark for diagnosing societal irrationality. The quotation from Jameson that opens this chapter suggests that in a society dominated by the image, the world is delivered to us as alien object for 'rapt, mindless, fascination': *this* is the metanarrative of visual media and of our increasingly visual culture. Jameson's penchant for quoting Guy Debord's line about the image being 'the final form of commodity reification'[53] helps cement the connection between the dominance of visual media (experienced even more intensely with moving images) and societal irrationality.

In a more recent essay, Jameson hints at a somewhat more precise meaning of this totalizing expansion of culture, observing that 'no society has ever been quite so addictive, quite so inseparable from the condition of addictiveness as this one, which did not invent gambling, to be sure, but which did invent compulsive consumption. The postmodern, or late capitalism, has at least brought the epistemological benefit of revealing the ultimate structure of the commodity to be that of addiction itself.'[54]

Jameson makes this claim in the context of a discussion of utopia, in which divergent utopian visions (full employment versus the abolition of labour, city versus country, etc.) are shown to exist in a 'negative dialectic[al]'[55] relationship. The generation of these apparently contradictory visions of utopia is then linked to Adorno's insistence on the impossibility of a positive representation of 'an emancipated society,' and Adorno's further claim that 'Utopia will then be characterized by the falling away of that imperious drive towards self-preservation, now rendered unnecessary.'[56] It is just at this point that Jameson invokes the figure of the addict (as well as sexuality), maintaining that utopia confronts us with anxiety, insofar as its realization might entail the loss of identity, of desire, and of 'the features I have mentioned, addictiveness and sexuality, [that] are the very emblems of human culture as such, the very supplements that define us as something other than mere animals.'[57]

Elsewhere, Jameson describes film as 'an addiction that leaves its traces on the body itself.'[58] The claim appears similar to the Frankfurt School's insistence that our very senses are restructured by the experience of living in a society dominated by the moving image. But Jameson goes further, to say that 'for the addict to desire a cure [would] be only this or that form of bad faith or self-deception.'[59] Curing the addiction would entail a crisis of identity, and recognition of this crisis 'is then to all intents and purposes the same as the fear of death, and it is not for nothing that Adorno evoked self-preservation … In matters of existential experience there can be no picking and choosing, no separation of the wheat from the chaff.'[60] For Jameson, then, it is something like the self-preservation instinct itself that pulls us away from the realization of utopian visions. Or more to the point for us here, it is what fuels our compulsive consumption, even as we know that it is destroying the basis for our long-term survival. Somewhat similarly, Marcuse once wrote that under advanced capitalism, the rule of capital sinks right down to the biological level, conditioning us instinctually for the perpetual of toil: even the false and destructive pleasures, 'racing the outboard motor, pushing the power lawn mower, and speeding the automobile are fun.'[61] And it is in this deep sense of the very constitution of subjectivity, as I have suggested above, that we can understand Horkheimer and Adorno's observation that 'the triumph of invested capital … is the meaningful content of every film, whatever plot the production team may have selected.'[62]

'Climate Porn'

What then is the fate of attempts to communicate problems of environmental sustainability in an industrialized culture? The title of this section is a term coined in a 2006 report titled 'Warm Words,' written by Gil Ereaut and Nat Singer for the British Institute for Public Policy Research, which analyses the public discourse on climate change in the United Kingdom.[63] In that report, one of three identified dominant strains of discourse identifies climate change as a societal challenge of unprecedented scope and complexity. While recent IPCC reports suggest that such a diagnosis is likely to be substantially correct, Ereaut and Singer suggest that this discourse presents the magnitude of the problem as overwhelming and 'effectively counsels despair.' But what is more, the authors argue, this pessimistic discourse, by presenting disastrous scenarios to come, is also 'secretly thrilling.' Because it presents the obscene possibilities of catastrophic climate change as little more than a spectacle to be passively consumed (because it is too late and/or too difficult to do anything to forestall it), Ereaut and Singer refer to this type of discourse as 'climate porn.' Rather than encouraging action, climate porn promotes political disengagement, as climatological crisis becomes just another form of spectacular commodity consumption, and anthropogenic global warming becomes a vehicle for the further accumulation of economic value.[64] Such a view seems to be supported, for example, by Doyle's critical analysis of early Greenpeace climate change campaigns, which 'resort to cataclysmic images that render the viewer powerless in terms of agency.'[65]

Using the Frankfurt School's analysis of the culture industry allows us to see climate porn as a significantly broader phenomenon in environmental communication than Ereaut and Singer suggest. Recall here Marcuse's notion of 'repressive desublimation,' which can be used to understand sexual pornography. If the harm caused by the distribution and consumption of pornography lies in its creation of a more or less generalized social environment in which sexual objectification is routinized or seen as acceptable, then a greater degree of sexual liberalization does not necessarily entail greater human liberation, and indeed may even be an obstacle to it. 'Repressive desublimation,' or 'the mobilization and administration of libido,' is, Marcuse notes, 'gratifying to the managed individuals,' but at the same time it represses the desire to seek change to more broadly repressive societal institutions: 'The range of socially permissible and desirable satisfaction is greatly enlarged, but through this satisfaction, the Pleasure Principle is reduced – deprived of the claims which are irreconcilable with the established society.'[66]

In a similar fashion, climate porn describes the scope of the problem of global warming[67] even while discouraging those receiving the information from taking action to deal with that problem: as spectacle it can only be passively consumed. But agreeing on what constitutes climate porn would mean agreeing on what in fact does (or does not) constitute appropriate action to deal with climate change. As Michael Maniates (among others) has suggested, the dominant tendency to posit individualized solutions to environmental problems actually undermines the capacity to achieve the sorts of societal changes that are in fact required if we are to mitigate environmental changes such as global warming.[68] If this diagnosis is correct, then the disabling features of climate porn are found not just in the ('secretly thrilling') pessimistic discourses on climate change, but also in the other two discourses that Ereaut and Singer identify as dominating climate change communications. 'Optimistic but non-pragmatic discourses,' which suggest that climate change is not a serious problem, by definition do not aim to induce change at all. And what they refer to as the 'small changes' discourse – that relatively small or painless incremental changes will be enough to solve the problem – similarly allows people to feel as if they are doing something worthwhile by switching to energy-efficient light bulbs, but does not challenge existing societal structures (i.e., an economic system predicated on limitless growth).

Indeed, the same could be said for Ereaut and Singer's own prescriptions, which take the problem largely to be one of 'issue framing.'[69] Their report concludes that activists should 'treat climate-change communications in the same way as brand communications: we have to approach positive climate behaviours in the same way as marketers approach acts of buying and consuming ... *It amounts to treating climate-friendly everyday activity as a brand that can be sold.*'[70]

Like Michael Shellenberger and Ted Nordhaus with their call to 'tap into the creative worlds of myth-making,'[71] Ereaut and Singer seek to move environmentalism away from an overly rationalized view of human nature. And while their attempt to steer clear of an excessively earnest scientific or policy wonkish approach (not to mention a reductive view of human nature) – in Adorno's terms, their attempt to recall 'historical beings' (putatively rational actors) as at the same time also 'natural' (subject to non-rational appeals) – may well be commendable, the dangers on the other side should also be apparent. The means of corporate branding language risk undermining the desired ends. More precisely, the use of advertising and branding as discursive strategies risks foreclosing the very possibility of a substantive debate over desired ends. And in fact it is quite clear that a focus on rhetorical tactics leads the report authors to lower expectations with respect to where change can occur: 'The challenge is to make climate-friendly behaviours feel normal, natural, right and "ours" to large numbers of people who are currently unengaged, and on whose emotional radar the issue does not figure. *The answer is not to try to change their radar but to change the issue*, so it becomes something they willingly pick up, because it means something valuable in their own terms.'[72]

The shift to a post-carbon economy – which will happen sooner or later, be it smoothly or abruptly, because of an increased public desire to curb global warming or for some other reason – will surely constitute a momentous societal transformation. And previous societal transformations on this scale have had profound impacts on human subjectivity. But unless the focus is on laying bare and collectively challenging our fundamental values ('emotional radar'), the possibility of consciously reflecting on how this transformation might be managed will be lost. In other words, the transition will, like previous societal transitions, be experienced as a kind of 'second nature.'

Breaking the Gaze

If the transcendence of consumerist identity is the task of contemporary environmentalism, this is made more complicated by the fact that claims about impending scarcity appeal to precisely the self-preservation instinct that brought us to 'a mode of human conduct adapted to production as an end in itself'[73] in the first place. While a reimposition of terror in the face of first nature remains a real possibility, it can only be seen as historically retrogressive. An intervention that would contribute to historical progress instead must emphasize the possibility of reshaping our identity; or of developing a new form of culture that is not driven either by the biological imperatives of consumption and reproduction (addictiveness and sexuality) or by the natural historic cares that we share with beetles. This would, to be sure, be a radical departure. If Jameson is correct, such breaks are deeply resisted. Is such a break even possible? Or must we arrive at the following deeply pessimistic conclusion: that there is no escape from the dialectic of enlightenment or from an unshakeable consumerist culture *cum* biology?

Jameson's recourse to the figure of addiction is instructive here, and not only insofar as it is also invoked in discussions of the unsustainable trajectory of contemporary consumerism. In the opening pages of *One-Dimensional Man*, in speaking of the needs that are unnecessarily introjected by repressive civilization, Marcuse writes: 'Their satisfaction might be most gratifying to the individual, but this happiness is not a condition which has to be maintained and protected if it serves to arrest the development of the ability (his own and others) to recognize the disease of the whole and grasp the chances of curing the disease.'[74] Marcuse thus helpfully reminds us that addiction can be understood as a disease and that its treatment might involve cold, calculating reason – 'keeping one's distance' from seemingly immediate desires – for the purposes of achieving a more humane end. But Marcuse never satisfactorily resolved the issue of the political subject who might allow us to develop these abilities: Who are the doctors, and how will they be empowered to (in Rousseau's terms) force us to be free?

For Adorno, for whom the 'seductive power of sensuality' always threatened to overwhelm critical thought,[75] the abolition of the culture industry holds out the promise of achieving some greater degree of reflection on the 'mediated immediacy' of the senses. The possibility of escape is posited; though as with Marcuse, the problem of agency looms large. The following passage is notable more for emphasizing that our enjoyment (or not) of the products of the culture industry is not rooted *solely* in the structure of the senses:

> If most of the radio stations and movie theaters were closed down, the consumers would probably not lose so very much. To walk from the street into the movie theater is no longer to enter a world of dream; as soon as the very existence of these institutions no longer made it obligatory to use them, there would be no great urge to do so. Such closures would not be reactionary machine wrecking. The disappointment would be felt not so much by the enthusiasts as by the slow-witted, who are the ones who suffer for everything anyhow.[76]

Odysseus (via Horkheimer and Adorno) taught us that it is spectatorship that defines our humanity, but also that spectatorship demands a cold-bloodedness that is the antithesis of humane values. Jameson's confession of film's addictive qualities comes just before the quotation cited at the outset of this paper: 'The visual is *essentially* pornographic, which is to say that it has its end in mindless, rapt fascination ... Pornographic films are thus only the potentiation of films in general, which ask us to stare at the world as though it were a naked body.' He then adds: 'Other kinds of thought have to replace the act of seeing by something else.'[77] In other words, the production of a sustainable and humane society, on the other side of the climate crisis, will require environmental communication that is geared toward the expression and realization of self-consciously humane values. Anything else, as Walter Benjamin reminds us, is the experience of our self-destruction as a source of aesthetic pleasure.[78]

NOTES

1 Walter Benjamin, 'The Work of Art in an Age of Mechanical Reproduction,' in *Illuminations*, ed. Hannah Arendt, trans. Harry Zohn (New York: Schocken, 1964), 242.

2 Herbert Marcuse, *One-Dimensional Man: Studies in the Ideology of Advanced Industrial Society* (Boston: Beacon, 1964), 68.

3 Fredric Jameson, *Signatures of the Visible* (New York: Routledge, 1992), 1.

4 Nigel Gibson and Andrew Rubin, 'Introduction: Adorno and the Autonomous Intellectual,' in *Adorno: A Critical Reader*, ed. Nigel Gibson and Andrew Rubin. (Oxford: Blackwell, 2002), 1.

5 Ibid., 1–2.

6 See Shane Gunster, *Capitalizing on Culture: Critical Theory for Cultural Studies* (Toronto: University of Toronto Press, 2004).

7 While there are of course important exceptions, this 'Americanization' is broadly true of the geographic origin of mass cultural products, and formally in the sense that many cultural products that originate elsewhere are in line with American ('Hollywood') conventions. On the former point, see Dal Yong Jin, 'Neoliberal Restructuring of the Global Communication System: Mergers and Acquisitions,' *Media, Culture, and Society* 30, no. 3 (2008).

8 Fredric Jameson, *Late Marxism: Adorno, or, The Persistence of the Dialectic* (New York: Verso, 1990), 5.

9 Fredric Jameson, 'Periodizing the Sixties,' in *The Ideologies of Theory*, vol. 2, *Syntax of History*, by Fredric Jameson (Minneapolis: University of Minnesota Press, 1988), 207.

10 See http://www.millenniumassessment.org.

11 See http://www.ipcc.ch.

12 Box office receipts (in U.S. dollars) from http://boxofficemojo.com/movies/?id=avatar.htm.

13 Theodor W. Adorno, 'The Idea of Natural History,' trans. Robert Hullot-Kentor, *Telos* 60 (1985): 117, emphasis in original.

14 Theodor W. Adorno, 'Culture Industry Reconsidered,' trans. Anson G. Rabinbach, *New German Critique* 6 (1976): 18–19.

15 Max Horkheimer and Theodor W. Adorno, *Dialectic of Enlightenment*, trans. John Cumming (New York: Continuum, 1987), xiii.

16 William Leiss, *The Domination of Nature* (Montreal and Kingston: McGill-Queen's University Press, 1994), 167–98.

17 Ibid., 171, 177.

18 Ibid., 169.

19 Bill Devall and George Sessions, *Deep Ecology: Living as if Nature Mattered* (Salt Lake City: Peregrine Smith, 1985), ix. For a trenchant critique of this view, see Timothy W. Luke, *Ecocritique: Contesting the Politics of Nature, Economy, and Culture* (Minneapolis: University of Minnesota Press, 1997), especially chapter 1, 'Deep Ecology as Political Philosophy,' as well as the essays by Colin Campbell and Bruce Martin in this volume.

20 Andrew Dobson, 'Critical Theory and Green Politics,' in *Politics of Nature: Explorations in Green Political Theory*, ed. Andrew Dobson and Paul Lucardie (New York: Routledge, 1995), 190.

21 Horkheimer and Adorno, *Dialectic of Enlightenment*, 124.

22 Ibid. Herbert Marcuse takes this even further, arguing that even our preconscious sense perception is determined by social forces, such that 'in a society based on alienated labour, human sensibility is *blunted* … Thus, the existing society is *reproduced* not only in the mind, the consciousness of men, but *also in their senses*.' Marcuse, *Counterrevolution and Revolt* (Boston: Beacon, 1972), 71; emphases in original.

23 Horkheimer and Adorno, *Dialectic of Enlightenment*, 126. See also the essays by Shane Gunster and Michael Lipscomb in this volume.

24 Ibid., 129.

25 Adorno, 'Culture Industry Reconsidered,' 14.

26 Horkheimer and Adorno, *Dialectic of Enlightenment*, 137.

27 Ibid., 124–5.

28 See the essays in part 2 of this volume for the concerns raised by critical theory about the move away from anthropocentrism.

29 Herbert Marcuse, *Eros and Civilization: A Philosophical Inquiry into Freud* (London: Ark, 1987); *An Essay on Liberation* (Boston: Beacon, 1969).

30 Marcuse, *Counterrevolution and Revolt*, 60.

31 Andrew Dobson, 'Critical Theory and Green Politics,' 204; the internal quotation is from Marcuse, *Counterrevolution and Revolt*, 64.

32 See, for example, William Cronon, 'The Trouble with Wilderness, or, Getting Back to the Wrong Nature,' in *Uncommon Ground: Toward Reinventing Nature*, ed. William Cronon (New York: Norton, 1995).

33 See the essay by Steven Vogel in this volume; and Vogel, 'Environmental Philosophy after the End of Nature,' *Environmental Ethics* 24, no. 1 (2002).

34 Vogel, 'Environmental Philosophy,' 38.

35 See also ibid., 37; and Steven Vogel, *Against Nature: The Concept of Nature in Critical Theory* (Albany: SUNY Press, 1996).

36 See ibid., 134–43; and Andrew Biro, *Denaturalizing Ecological Politics: Alienation from Nature from Rousseau to the Frankfurt School and Beyond* (Toronto: University of Toronto Press, 2005), 182–90.

37 Marcuse, *Counterrevolution and Revolt*, 68; emphasis in original

39 Theodor W. Adorno, *Negative Dialectics*, trans. E.B. Ashton (New York: Continuum, 1992), 389.

40 Theodor W. Adorno, *Minima Moralia: Reflections from a Damaged Life*, trans. E.F.N. Jephcott (London: New Left, 1974), 156.

41 See Rainer Nagele, 'The Scene of the Other: Theodor W. Adorno's Negative Dialectic in the Context of Poststructuralism,' *Boundary 2* 11, nos. 1–2 (1983), for a similar discussion of *Negative Dialectics*.

42 Adorno, *Minima Moralia*, 156.

43 Adorno, *Negative Dialectics*, 363.

44 Ibid. It is also, of course, associated with Odysseus' encounter with the Sirens. See Horkheimer and Adorno, *Dialectic of Enlightenment*, 32–5.

45 Horkheimer and Adorno, *Dialectic of Enlightenment*, 126.

46 Guy Debord, *The Society of the Spectacle*, trans. Donald Nicholson-Smith (New York: Zone, 1995).

47 Anders Huyssen, 'Introduction to Adorno,' *New German Critique* 6 (1976): 7.

48 Jin, 'Neoliberal Restructuring.'

49 Fredric Jameson, *Postmodernism, or, the Cultural Logic of Late Capitalism* (Durham: Duke University Press, 1992), 48.

50 'Fortune Global 500, 2009,' *Fortune Magazine*, http://money.cnn.com/ magazines/fortune/global500/2009/full_list/index.html.

51 Horkheimer and Adorno, *Dialectic of Enlightenment*, 122.

52 Fredric Jameson, *Postmodernism*, 48.

54 Fredric Jameson, 'The Politics of Utopia,' *New Left Review* 25 (2004): 52. Gordon Coonfield has recently noted that the spread of the idea of addiction from a relationship with particular kinds of drugs to a world in which 'apparently, one can be addicted to nearly everything' is a particularly contemporary phenomenon, one that is connected to a specific mode in which subjectivity is constituted – indeed, corresponding to 'the apogee of subjection,' given that addiction is only intelligible 'as an *individual* problem.' Gordon Coonfield, 'Mapping Addicted Subjection: Toward a

Cartography of the Addiction Epidemic,' *Cultural Studies* 22, no. 1 (2008): 80, 100, emphasis in original.

55 Jameson, 'The Politics of Utopia,' 50.

56 Ibid., 51.

57 Ibid., 53.

58 Jameson, *Signatures of the Visible*, 1.

59 Jameson, 'Politics of Utopia,' 52.

60 Ibid.

61 Marcuse, *One-Dimensional Man*, 75.

62 Horkheimer and Adorno, *Dialectic of Enlightenment*, 124.

63 Gil Ereaut and Nat Singer, *Warm Words: How Are We Telling the Climate Story and Can We Tell It Better?* (London: Institute for Public Policy Research, 2006).

64 For a somewhat similar analysis, see Ingolfur Blühdorn, 'Sustaining the Unsustainable: Symbolic Politics and the Politics of Simulation,' *Environmental Politics* 16, no. 2 (2007).

65 Julie Doyle, 'Picturing the Clima(c)tic: Greenpeace and the Representational Politics of Climate Change Communication,' *Science as Culture* 16, no. 2 (2007): 138.

66 Marcuse, *One-Dimensional Man*, 75.

67 Ereaut and Singer suggest, however, that one of the problems with this kind of discourse is that 'it allows for no complexity or middle ground – it is simply extreme.' Ereaut and Singer, *Warm Words*, 13.

68 Michael Maniates, 'Individualization: Plant a Tree, Buy a Bike, Save the World?' in *Confronting Consumption*, ed. Thomas Princen, Michael Maniates, and Ken Conca (Cambridge, MA: MIT Press, 2002). See also Tom Crompton, *Weathercocks and Signposts: The Environment Movement at a Crossroads* (Godalming: World Wildlife Fund–UK, 2008).

69 While Ereaut and Singer do not specifically use the term 'issue framing,' their analysis shares a great deal with that developed in Michael Shellenberger and Ted Nordhaus, *The Death of Environmentalism: Global Warming Politics in a Post-Environmental World* (Oakland: Breakthrough Institute, 2004). Shellenberger and Nordhaus do use this term, popularized by linguistic analyst (and US Democratic Party strategist) George Lakoff.

70 Ereaut and Singer, *Warm Words*, 28, emphasis in original.

71 Shellenberger and Nordhaus, 'The Death of Environmentalism,' 34.

72 Ibid., 28, emphasis added.

73 Adorno, *Minima Moralia*, 156. See also Jameson's connection of ecological calls for restraint with 'contemporary authoritarianism.' Fredric Jameson, *The Seeds of Time* (New York: Columbia University Press, 1994), 47–8.

74 Marcuse, *One-Dimensional Man*, 5.
75 Horkheimer and Adorno, *Dialectic of Enlightenment*, 194; see also Vogel, *Against Nature*, 65–7.
76 Horkheimer and Adorno, *Dialectic of Enlightenment*, 139.
77 Jameson, *Signatures of the Visible*, 1.
78 Benjamin, 'The Work of Art,' 242. The connection between Benjamin's comment (about fascist art) and contemporary overconsumption is made by Stuart Ewen in the video 'The Ad and the Ego' (Parallax, 2000).

BIBLIOGRAPHY

Adorno, Theodor W. 'Culture Industry Reconsidered.' Translated by Anson G. Rabinbach. *New German Critique* 6 (1976): 12–19.
– 'The Idea of Natural History.' Translated by Robert Hullot-Kentor. *Telos* 60 (1984): 111–24.
– *Minima Moralia: Reflections from a Damaged Life*. Translated by E.F.N. Jephcott. London: New Left, 1974.
– *Negative Dialectics*. Translated by E.B. Ashton. New York: Continuum, 1992.
Benjamin, Walter. 'The Work of Art in an Age of Mechanical Reproduction.' In *Illuminations*, edited by Hannah Arendt, translated by Harry Zohn. New York: Schocken, 1964.
Biro, Andrew. *Denaturalizing Ecological Politics: Alienation from Nature from Rousseau to the Frankfurt School and Beyond*. Toronto: University of Toronto Press, 2005.
Bluhdorn, Ingolfur. 'Sustaining the Unsustainable: Symbolic Politics and the Politics of Simulation.' *Environmental Politics* 16, no. 2 (2007): 251–75.
Coonfield, Gordon. 'Mapping Addicted Subjection: Toward a Cartography of the Addiction Epidemic.' *Cultural Studies* 22, no. 1 (January 2008): 80–113.
Crompton, Tom. *Weathercocks and Signposts: The Environment Movement at a Crossroads*. Godalming: World Wildlife Fund–UK, 2008.
Cronon, William. 'The Trouble with Wilderness, or, Getting Back to the Wrong Nature.' In *Uncommon Ground: Toward Reinventing Nature*, edited by William Cronon. New York: Norton, 1995.
Debord, Guy. *The Society of the Spectacle*. Translated by Donald Nicholson-Smith. New York: Zone, 1995.
Devall, Bill, and George Sessions. *Deep Ecology: Living as if Nature Mattered*. Salt Lake City: Peregrine Smith, 1985.
Dobson, Andrew. 'Critical Theory and Green Politics.' In *Politics of Nature: Explorations in Green Political Theory*, edited by Andrew Dobson and Paul Lucardie. New York: Routledge, 1995.

Doyle, Julie. 'Picturing the Clima(c)tic: Greenpeace and the Representational Politics of Climate Change Communication.' *Science as Culture* 16, no. 2 (June 2007): 129–50.

Ereaut, Gil, and Nat Singer. *Warm Words: How Are We Telling the Climate Story and Can We Tell It Better?* London: Institute for Public Policy Research, 2006.

Gibson, Nigel, and Andrew Rubin. 'Introduction: Adorno and the Autonomous Intellectual.' In *Adorno: A Critical Reader*, edited Nigel Gibson and Andrew Rubin. Oxford: Blackwell, 2002.

Gunster, Shane. *Capitalizing on Culture: Critical Theory for Cultural Studies.* Toronto: University of Toronto Press, 2004.

Horkheimer, Max, and Theodor W. Adorno. *Dialectic of Enlightenment.* Translated by John Cumming. New York: Continuum, 1987.

Huyssen, Anders. 'Introduction to Adorno.' *New German Critique* 6 (1976): 3–11.

Jameson, Fredric. *Late Marxism: Adorno, or, The Persistence of the Dialectic.* New York: Verso, 1990.

– 'Periodizing the Sixties.' In *The Ideologies of Theory: Essays 1971-86*, vol. 2, *Syntax of History*, by Fredric Jameson. Minneapolis: University of Minnesota Press, 1988.

– 'The Politics of Utopia.' *New Left Review* 25 (January–February 2004): 35–54.

– *Postmodernism, or, the Cultural Logic of Late Capitalism.* Durham: Duke University Press, 1992.

– *The Seeds of Time.* New York: Columbia University Press, 1994.

– *Signatures of the Visible.* New York: Routledge, 1992.

Jin, Dal Yong. 'Neoliberal Restructuring of the Global Communication System: Mergers and Acquisitions.' *Media, Culture, and Society* 30, no. 3 (2008): 357–73.

Leiss, William. *The Domination of Nature.* Montreal and Kingston: McGill-Queen's University Press, 1994.

Luke, Timothy W. *Ecocritique: Contesting the Politics of Nature, Economy, and Culture.* Minneapolis: University of Minnesota Press, 1997.

Maniates, Michael. 'Individualization: Plant a Tree, Buy a Bike, Save the World?' In *Confronting Consumption*, edited by Thomas Princen, Michael Maniates, and Ken Conca. Cambridge, MA: MIT Press, 2002.

Marcuse, Herbert. *Counterrevolution and Revolt.* Boston: Beacon, 1972.

– *Eros and Civilisation: A Philosophical Inquiry into Freud.* London: Ark, 1987.

– *An Essay on Liberation.* Boston: Beacon, 1969.

– *One-Dimensional Man: Studies in the Ideology of Advanced Industrial Society.* Boston: Beacon, 1964.

Nagele, Rainer. 'The Scene of the Other: Theodor W. Adorno's Negative

Dialectic in the Context of Poststructuralism.' *Boundary 2* 11, nos. 1–2 (1983): 59–79.

Shellenberger, Michael, and Ted Nordhaus. 'The Death of Environmentalism: Global Warming Politics in a Post-Environmental World.' Oakland: The Breakthrough Institute, 2004. http://www.thebreakthrough.org/images/Death_of_Environmentalism.pdf.

Vogel, Steven. *Against Nature: The Concept of Nature in Critical Theory.* Albany: SUNY Press, 1996.

– 'Environmental Philosophy after the End of Nature.' *Environmental Ethics* 24, no. 1 (2002): 23–39.

PART FOUR

Critical Theory's Moment

10 Natural History, Sovereign Power, and Global Warming

JONATHAN SHORT

In our times the signs of environmental crisis are everywhere. The most urgent among these at the moment, global climate change, shows with particular relief the deeply troubled relationship that humanity maintains with the natural world on which it ultimately depends. Despite decades of warnings about the likely impact of climate warming, and despite the undeniable effects of this warming as they enter the daily experiences of millions of people, there has been relatively little in the way of substantive action at the international level to reduce the production of greenhouse gases; nor are the prospects of substantial reductions likely.[1] Even with the urgency of the crisis strikingly apparent, the most recent round of talks failed to produce anything close to the binding targets that will be necessary to begin stabilizing global temperatures and quite literally save millions of lives, both human and non-human.

With the situation now so dire, it seems worthwhile to think about the nature of this crisis, which will eventually affect all living beings to some degree. Its global scope seems to impose a course of action that addresses the global collective good. Yet it is noteworthy that *this* kind of crisis, which cannot be resolved by bigger military budgets or through more security measures taken against enemies real or imagined, seems to be of the sort that cannot be resolved by the economically and politically dominant social formations of the late-modern world. The much-touted global civilization in which humanity (admittedly to differing degrees) now resides seems to function, much as always, in such a way that competitive struggle, rather than cooperative or coordinated action, is visualized as the solution to the problems confronting it.

In this chapter I analyse the relationship between, on the one hand, the state's demonstrated inability to address an ecological problem whose solution requires collaboration rather than competition (i.e., the partial sacrifice of narrowly construed interests in the broader interests of the greater good); and on the other hand, the mode of enforcement of the system of narrowly conceived interests. Instead of confining myself to a highly specific analysis of the various actors who must define their interests either in concert with or in opposition to the majority interest of humanity in dealing effectively with global warming, my emphasis will be on the broader social and philosophical factors that underlie the current crisis. Investigating the latter will lead me to look at two quite specific bodies of thought. The first is the work of Theodor W. Adorno (partly in concert with Max Horkheimer), whose thought attempts to articulate the historical relationship between (a) a mode of rationality and subjectivity (summed up by the term 'occidental reason'), and (b) the kinds of social formations this mode constitutes internally and with the natural world more broadly. The second body of work is that of the philosopher Giorgio Agamben, whose relatively recent work on sovereign power allows us to comprehend what I will argue here is the close link between a historically produced and socially mediated 'mode of reason' and the techniques of political domination that follow from it. Looking at these forms promotes an understanding of how those very social structures once allowing for survival not only become unserviceable for that goal, but constitute the greatest substantive obstacle to it. In other words, in drawing from the theoretical resources offered by Adorno and Agamben, I seek to expose the connection between the kind of obstruction on display on the part of some of the more powerful Western nations on the environmental front and the equally dismaying commitment to a renewal of sovereign power and militarism in the domain of global politics.

To get at the theoretical connection between what Adorno and Horkheimer call the domination of nature and Agamben's discussion of sovereign power, I will begin by examining the diagnosis of 'occidental rationality' and Western civilization outlined in *Dialectic of Enlightenment*, and then turn to some of Adorno's other texts to see how this diagnosis is built up in subsequent work. After this, I will turn to the idea of the domination of nature as the domination of both inner and outer nature by examining Agamben's theorization of sovereign power in Western politics in light of the analysis provided by Adorno. Finally, I will draw some conclusions from this link for the discussion of global warming and sovereign power, arguing that though the analysis remains sombre, it does not leave us entirely without hope.

Adorno and the Dialectics of 'Survivalism'

With an austerity that would impress any contemporary advocate of a strictly naturalistic understanding of the development of human rational faculties, Adorno maintains that human reason evolved as a tool of survival. In *Negative Dialectics*, for instance, Adorno insists that even (or especially) the most rarefied uses of reason have their 'primal history in the pre-mental, the animal life of the species'; in this regard, human reason is quite literally an example of the 'belly turned mind.'[2] Yet despite the uncompromising quality of this assertion, which is used repeatedly against idealist modes of thought, Adorno maintains that understood consistently, survival cannot be simply a matter of adaptation to ready-made circumstances. If it were, human intelligence, with its variegated capacities and its remarkable plasticity, would be denying its most characteristic feature – that is, its capacity to change, to engage in freely self-transformative activities. Thus in Adorno's complex view of human evolution, a reductive conception that restricts human intelligence to the reproduction of narrowly pre-given conditions of survival, however much creativity this involves, is insufficient and posits an irrational concept of reason. For human reason to be thought with sufficient rationality, it must be seen as thoroughly historical. Following a materialist line of thinking initiated by Marx, Adorno argues that what distinguishes the human species is that its nature is not written in biological stone, but is thoroughly mediated by its history. It follows that history is not a mere temporal repetition of variable adaptation to the initial conditions it began with – it must be understood as including the transformation of those initial conditions.[3]

When Adorno and Horkheimer attempted to assay the catastrophic situation of world war from their vantage point as émigrés to 1940s America, what was unmistakably manifest to them was 'the compulsive character of self-preservation' central to modern life, a compulsion 'constantly magnified into the choice between survival and doom.' This characterization is remarkably cogent as a descriptor of the circumstances confronting humanity with global warming; indeed, the sentence's continuation exposes neatly what is at stake in the present day: 'a choice [i.e. between survival and doom] which is reflected even in the principle that, of two contrary propositions, only one can be true and the other false' (*DE* 23). Thinking in contrary or oppositional terms, they add, is symptomatic of social irrationality reflected in thought: 'The formalism of this principle and the entire logic established around it stem from the opacity and entanglement of interests in a society in which the maintenance of forms and the preservation of individuals only fortuitously coincide' (*DE* 23). It would not be too difficult to hear these lines echoed in the repeated insistence of climate warming deniers or obstructionists that it all comes down to a choice between the economy *or* the environment, that of the two only one can be the 'realistic' choice, with that 'realism' coinciding with a kind of crude survivalist doctrine in which short-term interests and adaptation to chaotic circumstances trump everything else. Yet, as Adorno and Horkheimer seem to be warning us, the single-minded pursuit of this form of survival – of 'our way of life' come what may – marks the dialectical inversion of survival strategies into their opposites. Furthermore, that pursuit only fortuitously results in actual survival, in the maintenance of life for flesh-and-blood individuals.

The contradictory situation that Adorno and Horkheimer are describing stems from the fact that while human nature is indeed historical, humans tend not to recognize this fact, instead regarding their immediately historical circumstances *as* nature – that is, as the repetition of something naturally given that is thus fated to self-identical continuance over time.

Paradoxically, this non-recognition seems especially prevalent in those conditions that are *also* held to be historical, such as with the culturally canonical idea that technology is inherently progressive, new, and ever changing. If Adorno and Horkheimer are right, the recognition of the ever-changing nature of technology has been misconstrued to be the repetition of a certain naturally given (ahistorical) fact: the pursuit of improved means to master (naturally) pre-given (hence unchanging and unchangeable) ends. Most people recognize that history and nature are different; the problem is that they fail to see that they are also (dialectically) related and that there is a natural–historical dynamic wherein the opposite poles continually change places.

This failure to grasp the dialectical character of the opposition turns on misconstruing nature. Nature, according to an ancient cultural prejudice, is that which does not change or move, except perhaps through endlessly repeating cycles. Nature, accordingly, cannot really be substantially altered by history – it cannot truly *be* historical – so (human) history must remain a kind of epiphenomenon of underlying natural regularity. Yet this is not to say that people don't desire change. Most modern people would find a version of natural fatality intolerable, so they pin utopian hopes on things such as technology or ever-changing consumer goods that might make their lives better or at least more interesting. For Adorno this constitutes misrecognition of the fact of historical nature, that nature is actually and actively historical. When we do not recognize this historical dimension of the natural, then as long as nature is thought of as being transcended in the utopian moment of novelty, and as long as this moment is conceived in opposition to a static nature, there will be no choice but to reidentify technological change as a mere adaptation to unchanging nature. This idea accounts for Adorno's intention to present 'history, where it seems to be most historical ... as a sign for nature.'[5] Presenting the innovative as simply the archaic repetition of naturally imposed fate amounts to an attempt to jolt historical consciousness into awareness that its perpetual desire to be free of nature – insofar as it is perpetual – is a symptom of a nature statically conceived.

From this perspective, what makes *Dialectic of Enlightenment* such an important text is the way it develops Adorno's dialectic of natural–history into a speculative diagnosis of the development of human cognitive faculties under the pressure of their misconception of nature as the 'ever same.' Identity thinking as a particular mode of cognitive comportment is linked to the broader theme of the cultural misapprehension of static nature. In this regard, the discussion of identity thinking in the *Dialectic* brings into relief the most persistent feature of Western rationality – the idea of equivalence, which 'makes dissimilar things comparable by reducing them to abstract qualities' (*DE* 5). Adorno concedes that within limits, this form of thinking is entirely necessary for both historical and logical reasons.[6] As he writes in *Negative Dialectics*, 'the appearance of identity is inherent in thought itself, in its pure form. To think is to identify' (*ND* 5). At the same time, however, this appearance of identity is not *merely* a pure form but is historically conditioned, 'because concepts on their part are moments of the reality that requires their formation, primarily for the control of nature' (*ND* 11). Indeed, the principle of equivalence or identity thinking is for human beings a necessary element of their survival. But to the extent that identity thinking is necessary, it also becomes a trap. Once established, the principle of equivalence constantly renders diverse things and events identical for purposes of control; reason becomes subject to the 'principle of immanence, the explanation of every event as repetition,' the hallmark of the misapprehension of nature as static (*DE* 5).

Adorno and Horkheimer argue that because identity thinking was a key stage in the development of human rationality, the earliest cosmological myths were forms of enlightenment, the historical outgrowth and development of human reason. The ancient mythical cosmologies featured cyclical repetition of elements and thus advanced survival by placing everything within an order where the unique or different was cast as but an instance of the ever recurring and underlying same (*DE* 8). With the explanation of nature as a cycle of immanent recurrence, of birth, death, and rebirth, mythical thought was already enlightened, already a form of reason. But in this regard, Adorno and Horkheimer establish a circuit, rather than a linear development, between myth and enlightenment; the advance of reason is predestined to lapse back into its mythical preconditions when it fails to question the doctrine of equivalence which underwrites that very advance. Consequently, Adorno and Horkheimer propose that even the most modern forms of thinking are closer to mythical doctrines than such forms can admit. Present-day economics, for instance, embraces the calculus of rationality according to which 'human beings are defined by self-preservation through adaptation' (*DE* 8). Behind this calculus lurks the 'barren wisdom' of the mythical 'sanction of fate which, through retribution, incessantly reinstates what always was' (*DE* 8). This is because the 'principle of immanence, the explanation of every event as repetition, which the enlightenment held up against mythical imagination, is that of myth itself' (*DE* 8). With every step away from myth, myth is reconstituted in a new and updated guise. Rational thought has been incapable of ridding itself of the principle of equivalence, which conditions both mythical and enlightened thinking.

Under such conditions, Adorno and Horkheimer argue, it is inevitable that social relations between people systematically reflect the drive toward equivalence. In identity thinking, 'not merely are qualities dissolved in thought, but human beings are forced into real conformity' (*DE* 9). But such a claim should not be misunderstood as the suggestion that it is thought *per se* that determines the features of society, since 'power in the sphere of the concept is built on the foundation of power in reality' (*DE* 10). One of the features of identity thinking that makes it so compelling is precisely that it 'gets the job done,' that its procedures produce results. But as Adorno points out in *Negative Dialectics*, such 'mastery' perpetuates the illusion that reality is actually known, when in fact 'conceptual order is content to screen what thinking seeks to comprehend' (*ND* 5). The ability to ensure survival through identity thinking, the latter's ability to harness and control the forces of nature, is the reason why 'the control of internal and external nature has been made the absolute purpose of life,' to the point that those who live 'without any rational reference to self-preservation' are thought to 'revert to the realm of prehistory,' to the altogether pre-rational and possibly to the pre-human as well (*DE* 24, 22). This equation encompassing reason, identity thinking, and survival helps secure a vision of society and of human life that is plainly mythical: humans are fated by the grinding necessity of ahistorical nature to employ their rational faculties in ever more cunning ways for purposes of self-mastery and self-preservation. The definition of survival is always given as the necessity to control nature, so that no amount of control can be too much. If, as Adorno and Horkheimer contend, industrial capitalism represents the pinnacle of identity thinking in service to self-preservation, it is no wonder that most North Americans easily accept the political rhetoric that environmental protection can only come at the cost of economic security, where the perpetuation of the latter is taken as an unconditional good.

To return to the 'survival or doom' thesis with which we began, the problem with a fixed and limited definition of survival or self-preservation is that it inevitably leads to crisis conditions that jeopardize survival itself. Many of the environmental crises faced by 'advanced' industrial societies are precisely of this type: global warming, chronic pollution, depletion of resources, despoiling of natural habitats ... the list goes on. If we were able to recognize the one-sided conception of survival for what it is, we might develop a reconceived notion of survival, one that would substitute cooperation and solidarity for limitless accumulation and competition at the expense of others.[7] Absent this, 'the taboo encroaches upon the power imposing it, enlightenment on mind, which it itself is' (*DE* 23). The irrationality of narrowly conceived reason ensures that 'nature as true self-preservation is thereby unleashed, in the individual as in the collective fate of crisis and war, by the process which promised to extirpate it' (*DE* 23). Perversely, the very forces of irrationally understood preservation that lead to crisis reinforce that same irrationality. The ideal of preservation is held to be necessary, given the 'reality' of the situation of crisis, as though that crisis had nothing to do with the ethos of preservation that led up to it in the first place. One can clearly see this kind of thinking in the global warming impasse, where instead of working cooperatively to decrease carbon emissions, the worst offenders utilize their existing (and remaining) economic advantage to perpetuate a situation that has dire consequences for other nations and, in the long run, most likely for the advantaged ones as well.

These previous considerations of the cognitive dimension of the myopic conception of survival, however, leave out the affective character that drives it. Adorno and Horkheimer argue that the myopic conception of survival based in identity thinking or equivalence in turn has its roots not in rationality as such, but in the affective dimension of the 'noonday panic fear in which nature suddenly appeared to humans as an all-encompassing power' (*DE* 22). At some point in their evolution, human beings must have become aware of their own helplessness relative to other animals when faced with natural forces such as disease, injury, predators, and the elements. At that point, furthermore, the sense of self-identity, which had emerged out of the various psychic states, was immediately menaced with the prospect of its own de-differentiation and return to primordial chaos. Primal or undifferentiated chaos, itself unknowable, was a source of terror; and so, it follows, were those identifiable forces of nature that were hastening the return of the undifferentiated. Hence, according to Adorno and Horkheimer, the 'cry of terror called forth by the unfamiliar becomes its name' (*DE* 10). In the course of the development of human rational faculties, the mythic name – which 'springs from human fear' – becomes expressed as explanation in the forms of equivalence and identification that we considered above. But this does not solve the basic problem, since such explanation 'remains powerless as long as it emerges from the cry of terror, which is the doubling, the mere tautology, of terror itself' (*DE* 11). The drive for all-encompassing explanation takes off because humans falsely 'believe themselves free from fear when there is no longer anything unknown,' that is, anything remaining outside explanation, since 'the mere idea of the "outside" is the real source of fear' (*DE* 11).[8]

If fear of the power of nature – in turn an aspect of the fear of returning to undifferentiated chaos – is the real sticking point in the persistence of the narrow conception of survival, we have a basis for understanding much more clearly the role played by nature in human culture. The failure to conceive of human nature as historical, and hence the failure to understand that survival might be more than the simple application of identity thinking to nature, derives ultimately from a real and traumatic *historical* experience of nature that has been culturally preserved. At a certain moment in time, humans had an experience of nature as overpowering and terrifying, as a kind of opponent that had to be defeated, not by being propitiated, and not by being bought off by ritualized appeasement, but rather through mastery derived from rational cunning.[9] Rationality of this kind, however, is still very much connected to what it seeks to take distance from through its mastery. To dominate the nature that once dominated the subject, the subject had to orient itself toward domination, to internalize what it had once experienced as external. This necessitates two modifications of human nature: first, the self must dominate and control its own impulses; and second, society must be organized in such a way as to impose domination on its constitutive members so as to subdue external threats. The domination of the self in order to dominate nature also entails the domination of the nature that comprises the self. But the attempted expulsion of everything not consistent with the pursuit of domination and mastery ultimately stems from fear. Humans can see neither their own nor external nature as historical because they remain trapped by the past. Occidental (and now global) civilization continues to confront an ancient enemy that has in substantial ways already been defeated but whose threat is still internally felt, even perpetuated, by a culture of fear. Under these conditions, the behaviours learned in order to struggle against nature, both internal and external, are desperately perpetuated, no matter what their contemporary consequences. To let these behaviours go would require facing up to the fear that makes them continue to appear necessary; and it is this facing up that is too terrifying to contemplate because it would imply non-mastery, the opening and exposure to that which is not like the self.

Agamben and the Problem of Sovereignty

Adorno's work provides an insight into the development of human rational faculties under the sway of a distorted vision of survival, a development that I have been arguing affects the ability to respond to serious environmental problems like global warming. Yet what Adorno tends to neglect is reference to an institution that seems especially important to the current governmental inaction on global warming – namely, state or sovereign power. This section explores the possibility that Agamben's work on sovereign power can provide an avenue for examining this institution that is largely compatible with Adorno's analysis, while providing some additional insight of its own.

At first glance, it might seem that Agamben's work on sovereign power is an unlikely place to look for confirmation or advancement of Adorno's conception of the dialectic of enlightenment and the natural–historical. To begin with, Agamben's work remains intimately bound up with Heidegger's philosophical trajectory, one to which Adorno remained resolutely hostile throughout his life.[10] More directly, Agamben's work on sovereign power does not concern itself with the historical development of reason as such; it is likely that Agamben would consider the focus on reason's development to be unduly cognitive. Agamben's focus on the state of exception as the social practice of sovereignty rather than on identity thinking as a mode of cognitive comportment seems to indicate at least a different philosophical focus if not a very different set of concerns.

Yet these appearances are deceiving. Very much like Adorno, Agamben maintains that there is an intimate relationship between Western social and cultural practices and forms of thought. Even if Agamben is not as convinced as Adorno is that modes of thought reflect material conditions, he still posits an undeniable symmetry between them. What Agamben calls the Western *logos* – in which 'pure existence' is 'the ultimate metaphysical stakes' of thought – parallels sovereign power's obsession with 'pure violence as the extreme political object.'[11] Thought seeks to capture pure existence in its grasp, since only then will it be able to claim total comprehension and mastery of the totality of beings; by the same token, only if the sovereign is able to claim uncontested disposition over pure violence will it be assured that no entity can claim to be outside its purview. Without naming it in so many words, by identifying sovereign power as the immemorial practice of laying hold of pure violence as an exclusive prerogative, Agamben is already bringing the obscure lineage of sovereignty into contact with Adorno's notion of mythic fear that demands nothing be allowed to subsist outside sovereignty's jurisdiction.

Sovereignty's need to secure exclusive access to pure violence in order to exercise dominion over beings also accounts for Agamben's turn to Carl Schmitt's theory of sovereignty as the state of exception. The relationship between sovereign power and the legal order of the state is an intimate one, because, as Agamben points out, 'what is at issue in the sovereign exception is, according to Schmitt, the very condition of possibility of juridical rule, and along with it, the very meaning of State authority.'[12] The requirement that sovereign power be able to fix the condition of possibility of juridical rule demands that the sovereign entity not be straightforwardly subject to the law. The importance of Schmitt's understanding of the state of exception is, accordingly, that 'the sovereign, having the legal power to suspend the validity of the law, legally places himself outside the law' (*HS* 15). The sovereign who lays exclusive claim to pure violence must suspend the normal rule of law in order to exercise this claim in conditions where the sovereign's survival is at stake; however, according to Schmitt, the threatening situation cannot be specified in advance without violating the principle of sovereignty itself, since a sovereign whose conditions of survival are dictated from without would be no sovereign at all.

For Agamben, the exception is the key to the structure of sovereignty because it both affirms and denies the principle of the sovereign's claim to exclusivity. In the exception, 'what is excluded from the general rule is an individual case. But the most proper characteristic of the exception is that what is excluded is not, on account of being excluded, absolutely without relation to the rule' (*HS* 18). On the contrary, by declaring that the individual case (the situation that puts survival at stake) does not conform to the general rule (the law), the sovereign is also declaring that the rule maintains a relationship – one of exclusion – to that case. 'In this sense,' Agamben writes, 'the exception is truly, according to its etymological root, *taken outside* (*ex-capere*), and not simply excluded' (*HS* 18). Though seemingly unrelated, there is a strong resemblance between identity thinking as the subsuming of the different under the same (the individual under the identifying concept) and the exception as the removal to the outside of what does not belong to the normal order. In both cases, what is denied is the specificity or singularity of the particular in its particularity: identity thinking by excluding those features of the particular that are irrelevant to the classificatory concept; and the exception by isolating through its removal what does not fit under the general rule of normal law.

In the case of the exception, the symmetry with identifying logic becomes sharper when it is remembered that what is at stake in the exclusion of the particular is the ability of the rule to claim general validity, 'not so much [in] the control or neutralization of an excess as [in] the creation and definition of the very space in which the juridico-political order can have validity' (*HS* 19). In this sense Agamben can argue that sovereign violence 'does not limit itself to distinguishing between what is inside from what is outside but instead traces a threshold (the state of exception) between the two' (*HS* 19). The purpose of this tracing, as we have seen, is not simply to banish the threatening excess by pushing it outside. If sovereign power remained content to push the threatening particular outside, it would at least nominally respect both the existence of the outside as an already constituted location, and the distinct character of the threatening particular. Instead, in constituting the rule as general, the sovereign exception consists primarily of the 'taking of the outside' as such, the exclusion or banishment of the outside (*HS* 19). Though in banishing the outside the sovereign must appear to be simultaneously inside and outside the normal or general order, its actions are taken with an interest in the general rule; hence the 'sovereign exception ... is the presupposition of the juridical reference in the form of its suspension' (*HS* 21, original de-emphasized). The pure violence of the state of exception is nothing other than the sovereign's 'force of law,' whereby, Agamben tells us, 'acts that do not have the value of law acquire its "force"' (*SE* 38). The sovereign's violence, while not strictly lawful, takes on the legitimacy of law, its sense of the law's being in force even though suspended or inactive. From this perspective it appears that the sovereign's violence, like identity thinking, encounters something beyond its own activity, but nonetheless regards this otherness as though it were simply nothing – nothing, that is, except a feature of its own activity. To this extent, then, the exception is closely aligned with the identity thinking outlined by Adorno.

If so, it is not surprising that for Agamben the purpose of taking the outside lies in 'ruling out the existence of a sphere of human action that is entirely removed from law,' from the order of general validity (*SE* 11). The need to rule out the possibility of human action divorced from law accounts for the 'immemorial' role of sovereign power in establishing and maintaining the boundaries of the human community. One of Agamben's well-known claims is that sovereign boundary setting consists in separating and excluding *zoē* from *bios*, the mere natural fact of living from the qualified life of human communities. The exercise of sovereign power is in this sense one of the most ancient of human practices, since in demarcating the line separating the properly human from the merely living, sovereign power also establishes and patrols the boundary between culture and nature, *nomos* and *physis* (*HS* 34).[13] To draw these boundaries, sovereign power must presuppose 'the anteriority of *physis*' as pure natural violence; this in turn 'justifies the violence of the strongest' as sovereign within the community (*HS* 35). The conclusion suggested by this is that *physis* is in fact already in a complex relationship with cultural *nomos* so that what was presupposed as external (the state of nature) now reappears, as in a Möbius strip or a Leyden jar, in the inside (as state of exception), and the sovereign power is this very impossibility of distinguishing between outside and inside, nature and exception (*HS* 37). Not unlike Adorno's claim that the ancient cyclical cosmologies trace the cultural need to dominate nature and are thus already nature's culturally mediated receptions, Agamben's unpacking of the indistinction between nature and culture strongly implies that the idea of irreducible and hence ahistorical 'natural violence' is already social ideology in its most primitive and perhaps most undetectable form. Sovereign power, justifying its actions by appeal to an outside that is never truly outside, seeks to get those living on the inside of the political community to acquiesce to the use of violent power as the means to – and in exchange for – communal security.

As an ancient means of separating culture from nature, inside from outside, sovereign power underwrites a form of life in which the human being 'separates and opposes himself to his own bare life and, at the same time, maintains himself in relation to that bare life in an inclusive exclusion' characteristic of the state of exception (*HS* 8). On the threshold of the political community, through the inclusive exclusion of bare life, 'the humanity of living man is decided' (*HS* 8). Human life is included within the political order through its capture and abandoned exposure to sovereign violence, and this marks human life with an original political guilt. Guilt in this sense refers to a situation of being in debt, 'of being in relation to something from which one is excluded or which one cannot fully assume' by virtue of being the potential object of sovereign violence, exposed to the pure force of law that both decides on and makes indistinguishable the difference between fact and law (*HS* 27).

According to Agamben, it is not by accident that one of the best examples of sovereign guilt is also one of the most contemporary. President Bush's 'military order' of 13 November 2001 illustrates strikingly well the sovereign exception as 'the original structure in which law encompasses living beings by means of its own suspension' (*SE* 3). 'What is new about President Bush's order,' compared to agreements such as the Geneva Convention, Agamben notes, 'is that it radically erases any legal status of the individual, thus producing a legally unnameable and unclassifiable being ... Neither prisoners nor persons accused, but simply "detainees," they are the object of a pure de facto rule' (*SE* 3). The 'enemy combatants' captured in the 'war on terror' are reduced completely to their bare life and to the bare status of being detained; the only thing that they retain in common with other human beings is their biology; legally speaking, they are not human beings, so that whatever happens to them while in custody cannot be considered a crime.[14] The detainees are reduced to a pure identity – so pure, in fact, that the category under which they are classified has no actual content. There is no recognized external fact that applies to them, nor does their designation carry with it any legal status. It is not surprising, therefore, that Agamben writes that the only circumstance to which these detainees of Guantanamo 'could possibly be compared is the legal situation of the Jews in the Nazi *Lager*' (*SE* 4). Such a statement could easily be an echo of Adorno's in *Negative Dialectics* that 'in the concentration camps it was no longer an individual who died but a specimen' – a situation confirming 'pure identity as death,' the category of identity having no content, constituting but a bare logical form of sameness whose only correspondence in extramental reality would be the dead (*ND* 362).[15]

Nor does Agamben give us any reason to think that Bush's actions constitute an isolated incident; rather, they are part of a renewed tendency toward the use of sovereign power more broadly. Like Adorno with his supposition that mythical thought finds an updated counterpart in enlightened reason, Agamben suggests that the ancient practice of sovereign violence has now become 'a paradigm of government' (*SE* 2). Examining the history of the modern nation-state, Agamben makes the case that 'the voluntary creation of a permanent state of emergency … has become one of the essential practices of contemporary states, including so-called democratic ones' (*SE* 2). The sovereign exception, once a truly exceptional measure used to establish the boundaries of the city or the political community, now finds itself transformed 'into a technique of government' regularly employed; under the contemporary conditions of what Agamben calls 'global civil war,' the crises generated by the complexities of the contemporary world are met with permanent or repeatedly invoked states of exception (*SE* 2–3). It is as if, faced with the impossibility of traditional sovereignty in a complex and interdependent world, sovereign power increasingly and desperately resorts to this venerable tactic in order to cope.

Before we address possible ways out of this bind, it might be useful to retrace the lines of affinity between the thought of Agamben and Adorno that we have explored to this point. Adorno and Agamben present an image of human culture in which certain activities are compulsively repeated. For Adorno, the denial by identity thinking of anything beyond its categories used to control nature results in repetition, even while these categories present themselves as simple reflections of a world 'out there'; for Agamben, the denial on the part of sovereign power that there is anything outside the boundaries of the sovereign decision that might be independent of it is what mandates the constant redrawing of those very boundaries. Both these structures of thought and action portend a world in which humans become increasingly alienated from the historical–natural world they inhabit, unable to respond originally to the exigencies that arise as a result of their very activities.

In the context of global warming, Agamben's work on sovereignty can be used to supplement Adorno's discussion of the distorted evolution of human reason. If human reason develops in a one-sided, self-misrecognizing way, sovereign power can be seen to be one of its most prototypical manifestations. Sovereign power, like identifying reason, compulsively repeats the domination of nature through the domination of human life, capturing it in the order underwritten by sovereign power; we have seen how the capture of life in the sovereign exception is simultaneously the imposition upon human life of a compulsively repeated order, an injunction to humans to fit themselves into an order whose parameters have already been disclosed and whose boundaries are fixed by violence. What such violence disallows is the possibility that human life might do something unprecedented, that there could be a creative response to the world's problems outside the terms imposed on that response by sovereign power. If we combine Adorno's insights about identity thinking with Agamben's concerning sovereign power, the plausible suggestion emerges that the kind of obstructionist behaviour witnessed at the international level on the part of certain states with respect to global warming is a fairly direct extension of a well-established coercive approach to ordering human life more generally. From this perspective, while nothing prevents people from organizing locally – perhaps even regionally – to do things to ameliorate global warming, sovereign power intervenes to impose its monocular priorities on global society, as created and ordered by the 'realism' of the inter-state system.[16] It is not incidental that these obstructionist priorities are the same ones that manifest themselves in the global security order – access to fossil fuel supplies being chief among them. What must be avoided at all costs from this perspective is the admission that a certain age-old strategy for survival, one involving a coercive relationship to human nature and the natural world, has finally encountered its limits.

The picture that has been painted here seems especially gloomy. One of the ways to begin to pick away at the gloom is by way of an insight provided by this exploration of Adorno and Agamben. What seems clear from the perspective presented by both of them is that the real problem is not alienation from the external environment, but rather alienation from our historical nature. For Adorno this follows directly from the claim that human beings are historical beings; if they are, and if this is denied, then a very important part of human nature is denied as well. Agamben's assertion leads in a similar direction: in Western societies – which at least for the moment dominate global society – human life must be politicized and captured within the sovereign exception in order to become 'properly' human. The main reason that humans still deny their historical nature has more to do with coercively established and engrained cultural categories – grounded, as we have seen, in fear of the unknown – than it does with the necessities imposed by external nature.

Beyond Denying / Taking the Outside

The advantage of seeing the problem of nature as an 'internal' or cultural one, and not as a question of alienation from a supposedly primordial nature, is that such nature is itself a symptom of seeing nature ahistorically.[17] Primordial nature, as should by now be fairly obvious, is another way of thinking about nature ahistorically – as a great, unchanging set of conditions from which humans have become estranged by being the changeable beings that we are. Suggestions about 'going back' to nature as a solution to environmental crises are simply the mirror image of the view that humans are the Other of nature and hence are fated to struggle eternally against it. These two views are united in the sense that they understand humans as simply what nature is not. Yet human culture is not simply the Other of nature: it is also an outgrowth of the natural world. Therefore what happens in human culture is important not only for human nature but also for the natural world beyond, especially in an era during which our cultural activities wield immense power over nature as a whole. This is why it is especially important to understand that what our cultural attitudes tell us *about nature* reflects primarily the historical state of our *internal nature*, and is therefore not anything like a simple objective fact about which we can do nothing.

For Adorno and Horkheimer in *Dialectic of Enlightenment*, the way out of our defective relationship to nature – both internal and external – is precisely a matter of understanding identifying reason to be the cultural trace of an ancient historical relation of human beings to their own natural existence:

> Although unable to escape the entanglement in which it was trapped in prehistory, that thinking is nevertheless capable of recognizing the logic of either/or, of consequence and antimony, by means of which it emancipated itself radically from nature, as that same nature, unreconciled and self-estranged. (*DE* 31)[18]

Only in self-reflection is human nature capable of glimpsing an image of itself as nature translated into the categories of thought and alienated because of the character of those categories. Thought is able to grasp that through the compulsive 'mastery of nature, without which mind does not exist, enslavement to nature persists' in the form of a-historical reason (*DE* 31).

As we have seen, such enslavement reveals itself as the blind urge to dominate and overpower. But Adorno and Horkheimer suggest that in an age in which the pre-historical need to master nature 'has been fulfilled on a telluric scale,' humans have a chance to grasp the irrationality of the continuation of the project of mastery (*DE* 33). This chance comes precisely because the human mind, which has developed out of the necessity to control nature, is itself also nature, seeking by means of that very control an end to the need for domination. Thus, according to Adorno and Horkheimer, in 'modestly confessing itself to be power and thus being taken back into nature, mind rids itself of the very claim to mastery which had enslaved it to nature' (*DE* 31). This self-confession of mind to be power is enabled because, 'as nature divided from itself,' human nature 'is calling to itself, but no longer directly by its supposed name ... omnipotence, but as something blind and mutilated' (*DE* 31). In other words, having succeeded in dominating nature on a massive scale, humans may now find it possible to recognize the extent of the damage inflicted on nature, both internal and external, by reflecting on the state of their internal nature. Perhaps, Adorno and Horkheimer suggest, this is possible today because nature is no longer experienced as the intractable external foe it once was, and this may allow a glimpse of the non-identical, historical nature of nature – both human and otherwise.

In the midst of the crisis of global warming, of course, this idea may have to be modified. If nature is once again becoming an intractable foe, this is not simply a continuation of the pre-historical relationship between humans and nature, but is a result of the very triumph of the ethic of power and survival. The tragedy this time is that if nature once again becomes a virulent foe, it will do so because of our own inability to relinquish domination, to move to a way of life that does not depend on the blind destruction of the natural world through a competitive politics equally dedicated to the blind pursuit of power.

Agamben would likely express a quite similar thought. To the extent that sovereign power dominates human life in the state of exception, and this domination becomes more and more comprehensive as a paradigm of government, the non-identity comprising such life becomes apparent. In reducing life to its bareness, in attempting to isolate a pure instance of *zoē* completely cut off from *bios*, sovereign power ends up exposing a certain contingent but irreducible excess in life that evades the attempts of power to impose on it a particular form.[19] Agamben argues toward the conclusion of *Homo Sacer* that if the fundamental task of Western metaphysical thought has been to 'isolate pure Being (*on haplos*) from the many meanings of the term "Being,"' in Western politics what is 'at stake is the separation of bare life from the many forms of concrete life' (*HS* 182). But precisely on the occasions where this separation seems to have been enacted with inescapable finality, the Western project seems to 'run up against an unthinkable limit' because 'reason cannot think bare life except as it thinks pure Being, in stupor and astonishment' (*HS* 182). Even though bare life appears 'as indeterminate and impenetrable' to the categories of the *logos*, its very indeterminacy allows it to exceed and elude the 'bareness' imposed upon it by sovereign power (*HS* 182). What this portends is the impossible and untenable nature of the sovereign project. Beyond this project, Agamben suggests, 'bare life must itself instead be transformed into the site for the constitution of a form of life that is wholly exhausted in bare life and a *bios* that is only its own *zoē*' (*HS* 188). The form of life that would be exhausted in or at one with its bare life would be incapable of being reduced, so that the attempt to separate life from its forms would be given up (*HS* 188). In this sense, much as in Adorno, life would be inseparable from its nature, where nature is no longer conceivable as a static and unchangeable essence, but has instead become one with its historical and social possibilities. From this perspective, calls from the environmental movement for a 'permanent state of emergency' to deal with environmental crises must be rejected as inadequate. Conceiving the human relationship to nature simply as one of permanent crisis also preserves the opposition between them. Adorno and Agamben would instead advocate abolishing the concept of 'emergency' (or the choice between survival and doom) by using the current crisis as the opportunity to rethink our relationship to human life, and through it, to nature itself.

It is quite obvious even from this relatively brief canvassing of alternatives to identity thinking and sovereign power that Adorno and Agamben share a similar understanding of self-transcendence. For both thinkers, it cannot be a question of simply transcending the given toward some other reality, for whatever other reality becomes possible does so only because of the historical trajectory that has been traversed. Agamben puts this point well in *The Coming Community*, in which he writes that 'ethics begins only when the good is revealed to consist in nothing other than a grasping of evil and when the authentic and the proper have no other content than the inauthentic and the improper.'[20] What this passage entails is that transcendence can be achieved by no other means than by immanence, than by 'a self-grasping of evil' that allows the latter's overcoming toward the good.[21] This, however, also implies that the nature of things is resolutely historical, that all things – nature and life included – not only are subject to temporality but also find their 'essence' through time. Agamben and Adorno both acknowledge that human beings are fundamentally shaped by the conditions of their historical formation – in this case, their separation from non-sentient nature. The development of human beings under the twin imperatives of survival and domination, revealed in both identity thinking and the political form of sovereignty, suggests that most of humanity is today still living out its prehistory. But this situation does not constitute a simple and unchanging natural fact. Instead it points to both the intolerability of this situation and the possibility that it might be different. Human nature, here reflected through the collective crisis of global warming, is being again assigned the same task as in its prehistory: of becoming what it is, a historical existence.

NOTES

1 See Richard Black, 'Climate Change Treaty "More Urgent Than Ever,"' http://news.bbc.co.uk/2/hi/science/nature/8611811.stm, for a discussion of how the Copenhagen summit not only failed to produce a binding treaty, but also was strong-armed by the United States and several other heavy-emitting countries to establish a 'voluntary' system favoured by

themselves. Many environmental groups fear that the outcome of Copenhagen sets a dangerous precedent in which the non-binding regime favoured by the U.S. and its allies will be the new precondition for seats at the table in future talks.

2 Theodor W. Adorno, *Negative Dialectics*, trans. E.B. Ashton (New York: Continuum, 1973 [1966]), 22–3. Hereafter ND.

3 Adorno is expanding on Marx's well-known claim in the *German Ideology* that 'men can be distinguished from animals by consciousness, by religion or anything else you like. They themselves begin to distinguish themselves from animals as soon as they begin to *produce* their means of subsistence, a step which is conditioned by their physical organization. By producing their means of subsistence men are indirectly producing their material life'; Karl Marx and Friedrich Engels, *The German Ideology* (New York: Prometheus, 1998[1845]), 37. In the text of a lecture given early in his career, Adorno puts the thought quoted above this way: 'The elements of nature and history are not fused with each other, rather they break apart and interweave at the same time in such a fashion that the natural appears as a sign for history and history, where it seems to be most historical, appears as a sign for nature'; Theodor W. Adorno, 'The Idea of Natural History,' trans. Robert Hullot-Kentor, *Telos* 60 (1984): 121. This conception of 'natural history', where history and nature are at all points dialectically interwoven, turned out to be remarkably consistent throughout Adorno's career.

4 Horkheimer and Adorno, *Dialectic of Enlightenment*, trans. Edmund Jephcott (Stanford: Stanford University Press, 2002[1944/1947]), 23. Hereafter DE.

5 See n4 above.

6 Adorno does not want to separate the historical and the logical, as modern philosophical thought is generally wont to do.

7 I am deliberately discounting here the classical liberal economic thesis – along with its neoliberal updating – that competition ultimately works for the good of everyone, as ideological baggage. This does not mean that artificial mechanisms cannot sometimes be set up so that narrowly individual interests produce a beneficial collective outcome. But these circumstances are indeed contrived and designed precisely to bend self-seeking behaviour toward ends that are not part of their initial intent. Yet doctrinaire economic liberalism maintains that markets are not artificial, but natural, and hence that they should be left to function with as little 'interference' as possible. This view can only be sustained by referring to an 'invisible hand' as a kind pseudo-scientific homeostatic mechanism – or more likely, a thinly disguised stand-in for divine beneficence.

8 Again, this dynamic of historical development yields increasingly totalizing explanations that act as a 'universal taboo' in relationship to earlier explanations, which now appear as mere superstitions requiring liquidation (DE 11). Despite the veneer of progress this creates, enlightenment's course of development is thus ultimately self-destructive, since its 'mythic terror springs from a horror of myth' of earlier times that still made room for experiences outside the context of narrowly construed survival (DE 22). Advancing irrationally, enlightenment 'detects myth' in 'any human utterance which has no place in the functional context of self-preservation' (DE 22). J.M. Bernstein has systematically developed this aspect of Adorno's thought with the concept of 'rationalized reason' in his *Disenchantment and Ethics* (Cambridge: Cambridge University Press, 2001); see especially chapter 2, 75–133.

9 For Adorno, the Greek hero Odysseus is the paradigm case of this shift from an earlier, magic-based form of appeasement to the rational pursuit of mastery through cunning; from this perspective, Adorno argues, Odysseus is the prototype of the bourgeois individual.

10 It is interesting to note that 'The Idea of Natural History' lecture we considered at the beginning of this essay took shape as a critical challenge to Heidegger's concept of 'historicity' as articulated in *Being and Time*. Unfortunately, this essay cannot explore the complexities of Adorno's view of Heidegger, even less undertake an assessment of its cogency. Recent scholarship has questioned the distance that Adorno sought to put between himself and Heidegger, suggesting that it was at least in part a matter of rhetoric. For an interesting collection of essays on this topic, see Iain Macdonald and Krzysztof Ziarek, eds., *Adorno and Heidegger: Philosophical Questions* (Stanford: Stanford University Press, 2008).

11 Giorgio Agamben, *State of Exception*, trans. Kevin Attell (Cambridge: Cambridge University Press, 2005), 59. Hereafter SE.

12 Giorgio Agamben, *Homo Sacer: Sovereign Power and Bare Life*, trans. Daniel Heller-Roazan (Stanford: Stanford University Press, 1995), 17. Hereafter HS.

13 I would suggest that just as Adorno attempts to trace identity-thinking back to its earliest historical documentation in the *Odyssey*, Agamben's discussion of Pindar's 'Fragment' and Plato's *Laws* plays a similar role in establishing the ancient pedigree of the sovereign obsession with distinguishing between nature and culture.

14 This is, of course, not to claim that they cease being human simply because the law does not regard them as such.

15 The law of identity can be written A = A: whatever the content of A, it

contains nothing but what is equal to itself; it therefore has no content. But as Hegel points out in the *Science of Logic*, the law of identity cannot have the last (or even the first) word for thinking. As Hegel notes, those who rigidly adhere to this law of identity 'do not see that in this very assertion they are themselves saying that *identity is different*; for they are saying that *identity is different* from difference ... their assertion implies that identity, not externally, but in its own self, in its very nature, is this, to be different'; Georg W.F. Hegel, *Science of Logic*, trans. A.V. Miller (New York: Humanity, 1969[1841]), 413. As we will see, Adorno and Agamben each have similar views about the ultimate vacuity of the law of identity.

16 This might well be another way to understand Agamben's use of the term 'global civil war.' The United States and its allies, as a block, appear strong enough to impose a particular order, not just on a group of countries, but on a world scale. But this block creates a crisis for the whole that must be resisted.

17 I am thus expressing my agreement in principle with the thesis of Steven Vogel's essay in this volume.

18 It might be tempting to see this statement as a claim of human alienation from nature in the sense of a static state of affairs that humans have moved away from. But I think it is also possible to read this passage as saying that as long as humans repeat a particular mode of relation to nature – the ways of domination and mastery – they indeed remain enslaved to and alienated from nature, nature that is conceived as ahistorical. Adorno and Horkheimer on this reading are not committing the fallacy of appeal to nature as a direct unmediated category. Rather, to the extent that humans are outgrowths of nature, recognition of their proper historicity is also recognition of external nature's historicity. Human self-emancipation is thus revolutionary in that it would also allow the recognition of the historicity proper to the non-human natural world.

19 Agamben's book *Remnants of Auschwitz*, trans. Daniel Heller-Roazan (New York: Zone, 1999), details this aspect of his work. The details and scope of that work exceed the concerns of my discussion here.

20 Giorgio Agamben, *The Coming Community*, trans. Michael Hardt (Minneapolis: University of Minnesota Press, 1993), 13.

21 Ibid., 15.

BIBLIOGRAPHY

Adorno, Theodor W. 'The Idea of Natural History' (1932). Translated by Robert Hullot-Kentor. *Telos* 60 (Summer 1984): 111–24 .

- *Negative Dialectics.* Translated by E.B. Ashton. New York: Continuum, 1973[1966].
Agamben, Giorgio. *The Coming Community.* Translated by Michael Hardt. Minneapolis: University of Minnesota Press, 1993.
- *Homo Sacer: Sovereign Power and Bare Life.* Translated by Daniel Heller-Roazan. Stanford: Stanford University Press, 1995.
- *Remnants of Auschwitz.* Translated by Daniel Heller-Roazan. New York: Zone, 1999.
- *State of Exception.* Translated by Kevin Attell. Cambridge: Cambridge University Press, 2005.
Bernstein, J.M. *Disenchantment and Ethics.* Cambridge: Cambridge University Press, 2001.
Hegel, Georg W.F. *Science of Logic.* Translated by A.V. Miller. New York: Humanity, 1969[1841].
Horkheimer, Max, and Theodor W. Adorno. *Dialectic of Enlightenment.* Translated by Edmund Jephcott. Stanford: Stanford University Press, 2002[1944/1947].
Macdonald, Iain, and Krzysztof Ziarek, eds. *Adorno and Heidegger: Philosophical Questions.* Stanford: Stanford University Press, 2008.
Marx, Karl, and Friedrich Engels. *The German Ideology.* New York: Prometheus, 1998[1845].

11 Adorno's Historical and Temporal Consciousness: Towards a Critical Theoretical Environmental Imagination

MICHAEL LIPSCOMB

I

What time is it for environmental politics? What historical time does such a politics inhabit? What characterizes this time? Thus, what is the time of this time, or the tempo, of this historical moment and its unfolding? What are the effects of these temporal imperatives on the range of our political imaginations and on our capacity for autonomy, particularly in response to the environmental crises we face? This chapter proceeds from an assumption that these kinds of temporal questions, and the polyvocality of 'time' that they begin to reveal, are important concerns for the health of a critical environmental politics. Though these kinds of questions threaten a drift toward mere philosophical abstraction, they also seem unavoidably central to any concrete environmental political position. It is fair to say, in fact, that such temporal questions maintain and productively complicate the link between any environmental politics and its material referents; and that to think along the register of time, at the intersection of its different meanings and emphases, entails an elaboration of the material conditions in which we find ourselves situated.

If one looks across the field of competing voices that make up environmental political discourse, one can clearly see that concerns about time are central to the core logics of several different environmental political perspectives. For the theorists and activists who have articulated these perspectives, time – thematized in a variety of different ways – is a very real concern. And given that time is a central concern of almost every environmental political discourse, unpacking the preconceptions of our typical time-consciousness opens up a wide-ranging practical and normative discussion about what kind (or kinds) of time-consciousness can and should inform a coherent environmental politics.

When we survey a variety of environmental perspectives, we discover a repeated sense that time has almost dwindled away, that it is late in the game. Since at least the 1960s, an organizing trope of many environmental political discourses has been the idea that human population and human consumption, which have tended to expand at exponential rates, will overtake the carrying capacity of important earth ecosystems. We continue to hear these kinds of dire warnings about reaching tipping points regarding continued degradation, but also as a concern about the depletion of valuable resources and the threat of global warming.[1] At the same time, wildlife conservationists and scientists warn about a catastrophic wave of extinction that we seem to be helplessly overseeing in our era.[2]

A sense of urgency informs these temporal self-understandings, and that urgency undoubtedly informs the strategies and tactics of some environmental political actors. Driven by such a desperate time-consciousness, revolutionary environmental groups have emerged, such as the Earth Liberation Front (ELF) and the Animal Liberation Front (ALF), which operate outside the normal channels of the political system and which turn to a 'politics of the deed' that seeks to use the symbolic value of direct action to interrupt and thereby mark, for its mostly slumbering audience, the destructive impacts of our productive and consumptive habits.[3] But even less radical political responses, such as the turn toward sustainability, often entail rethinking the time-consciousness of production and consumption that is destroying the environment; at the metagoverning level, such approaches seek to somehow regulate or productively harness our sped-up drive for consumption in order to maintain a more rational pace of interaction with the non-human environment. A concern about the seemingly inescapable rapidity of environmental degradation and resource depletions thus lurks within a broad cross-section of our environmentally concerned, historically situated self-understandings.

This chapter turns to Theodor Adorno's treatment of 'time' as an exemplar of how a critical environmental politics might begin orienting itself toward our pervasive, inescapable temporal concerns. In the context of these appraisals of how environmentalism should understand itself in relation to the temporal paces of environmental degradation and rehabilitation, Adorno's attentiveness to temporal themes turns our attention to another important dimension of temporal concern: it focuses our thinking on how beings like us, inculcated within and by the temporal rhythms of our material experience, might be capable of living in more ecologically responsible ways. Given how those temporal imperatives work to mask that responsibility, and how those imperatives are intertwined with the destructive effects of overarching systems of consumption and production, Adorno's response to the materially imposed, subject-shaping tempo of our historical circumstances, his interruption of and alternative to that tempo, can have a salutary critical effect. Adorno cultivates a critical historical consciousness that is attuned to the historically specific tempo of our times.

Given his inattention to the practical problems of an environmental politics (not to mention his initially forbidding prose), his contribution to such a politics will be too oblique for some. From another perspective, however, Adorno's preoccupation with the kind of individuals that we are and that we could be in our specific historical circumstances remains instructive for many *democratically committed* environmental political orientations. Though Adorno's critique of a totalizing reason lacks the conceptual resources necessary for clarifying our intersubjective potential for action coordination,[4] his critical appraisal of the kinds of people produced within the cultural/technological/economic milieux in which he was living remains an instructive complement to the procedural and consensual drift of deliberative and discursive democratic approaches.[5] In repeatedly returning to the question of our subjective potential within the temporal dictates of the contemporary material world, his work contributes to the cultivation of an affirmative temporal ethos,[6] a glimpse of how an autonomous and morally responsive life might be imagined despite the objective tendencies of our age.

Adorno's work, then, is important for a critical environmental politics because he engages the question of the 'new human being' on which the radical edge of any critical theory of society is premised. Given the material, mnemotechnic forces – such as the tempo of our times – that powerfully and thoroughly shape who we are, and that reproduce us as the malleable, fatuous, consuming mass that we are, Adorno's work helps us ask: How can we become the different kind of people whom we want to become, the people who would inhabit and sustain the social and environmental world that we want to bring into being? From the perspective of a critical environmental politics, that question can be sharpened: How can we become the kind of people who are capable of realizing and sustaining the environmental future that we want to bring into being? But Adorno's work also asks us whether and how such subjective transformations, despite the urgency of environmental degradation and the stubbornly colonizing effects of liberal capitalist assumptions, might be achieved democratically.

Adorno's thinking is explicitly germane to the cultivation of this environmental–democratic orientation, in that it explores the question of the human relationship to non-human nature within a thinking that troubles the enshrinement of that dichotomy; he considers both *how* that relationship has been produced and deracinated by an ascendant instrumental reason and *what* our proper comportment toward that non-human nature should look like. For Adorno, as we shall see, our capacity to admirably relate to a non-human nature, in the material–temporal historical contexts in which we are ensconced, is very much a matter of temporal responsibility.

For some leftist readers, Adorno's insistently intellectual – even aristocratic – response to the historically specific problems of time has merely signalled the intellectual abdication of practice; but for Adorno his response was a crucial and historically timely form of practice – the check on an actionism incapable of opposing its totalitarian, authoritarian, or administrative masters.[7] If, in the name of an end that is now cordoned off from critical appraisal, human beings are reduced to means, the revolution is left to reproduce the general structure of unfreedom that a progressive humanity is seeking to transcend. Adorno, however, emphasizes an autonomous subjectivity that opposes both the inculcative forces of an informationalized and commodified exchange economy and the use of state-sponsored force to re-educate and rehabilitate the recalcitrant. Though Adorno decries the stubbornly inscribed, physiologically experienced hold that mass culture has over modern man, he expressly rejects the direct route of forcing other humans to be free through an overt counterviolence – that is, he rejects the justification that this violence is the only realistic means of fighting the reified, embodied habits of capitalist man. He pursues a way of thinking that fights this impulse, offering instead a set of resources for describing a more admirable human being affirmatively, for realizing him or her performatively in terms of his or her autonomous, democratic potential.

At the very least, that work on the individual subject gestures toward an increasingly anachronistic slowness within the accelerating tempos of our work, play, and consumption, and within the temporal imperatives of environmental crises. Such work on the individual subject seems to take more time than many seem to have and – in any case – to entail a rationally chosen rehabituation of our practices and desires that defies instant gratification. To put it bluntly, Adorno's commitment to an antifascist thinking, to both democratic forms of governance and a democratic mode of thinking, may be too slow, given the material facts of the environmental crises that beset us. Even if something like the critical autonomy that Adorno belabours could be produced in any kind of political way, the *way* he belabours it – through his strange, highly intellectual, dialectical method of patiently or peturbedly rehearsing the cultural productions that shape and reflect the kind of people we are – is not a realistic or a germane response to a world imploding around us.

Certainly, Adorno's commitment to a temporally prolonged critical reflexivity reveals a central paradox within the kind of historically sensitive responsibility that he endorses: in a circumstance that demands speed, that imposes it as a rule of the game, Adorno endorses a qualitatively richer slowness, a prolongation of focus and encounter that seems out of step with the culturally predominant, technologically sped-up tempo of our times. Though he recognizes the profound difficulties in realizing this kind of temporal reorientation, and though any efficacious politics must take pragmatic advantage of the temporal achievements of our late capitalist technological order,[8] Adorno insists that the cultivation of this temporal alternative has a central political importance.

For Adorno, the stakes of this historically situated temporal drama are high: from his perspective there is a connection between the subject-shaping temporal imperatives of late capitalist production and consumption and the fascist, authoritarian impulses that continue to lurk within post-Holocaust society. To the degree that these different formations – capitalism and fascism – are reinforced by a particular mode of temporal expectation, unpacking the logic of that expected tempo would be fundamental to resisting their heteronomous imposition of barbarity.

The potential for fascism is encoded, Adorno argues, in inscribed patterns of temporal expectation, a desire for an immediate, presentizing, uncritical, and personal gratification. Within the simulacra of the culture industry, advertising prepares the individual subject for the realization of his or her fascist potential through the rapid deployment and spread of superficially new and instantaneously delivered products. In that context, the word's

character as sign is reinforced by the speed with which linguistic models are put into circulation from above. Whether folksongs are rightly or wrongly called upper-class culture which has come down in the world, their elements have at least taken on their popular form in a long, highly mediated process of experience. The dissemination of popular songs, by contrast, is practically instantaneous. The American term 'fad' for fashions which catch on epidemically – inflamed by the action of highly concentrated economic powers – referred to this phenomenon long before totalitarian advertising bosses had laid down the general lines in their countries. If the German fascists launch a word like 'intolerable' [*Untaghar*] over the loudspeakers one day, the whole nation is saying 'intolerable' the next. On the same pattern, the nations against which the German *Blitzkrieg* was directed have adopted it in their own jargon. The universal repetition of the denoting of such measures makes the measures, too, familiar, just as, at the time of the free market, the brand name on everyone's lips increased sales. The blind and rapidly spreading repetition of the designated words links advertising to the totalitarian slogan.[9]

As the above quote suggests, Adorno and Horkheimer are interested in how the speed of repeated consummation made possible by modern technologies deflates the possibility of a reflective autonomy, always closing down the temporal space in which that reflection could occur. A certain richness made possible by 'a long, highly mediated experience' is replaced by the impoverishment of 'a blind and rapidly spreading repetition.' In the technologically mediated simulacra in which we swim, we have lost 'the layer of experience which made words human like those who spoke them.'[10]

It is in the context of this rapid repetition of advertising and propaganda imagery – which is perhaps even less escapable in our current First World circumstances – that Adorno sketches his affirmative temporal response, his commitment to a dialectic mode of comportment that responds to the object of its concern(s) by carefully situating and resituating that object in terms of the other objects with which it is constellated – a movement that seems to practise an impractical slowness, to hover when it should be moving directly forward. Adorno's thinking, however, need not lead to an inactionable, idealist 'time out of time.' In remaining dialectically responsive to the material realities in which it proceeds, Adorno offers us a theoretical account of a subjectivity conditioned by the primacy of the object. Such an orientation actually returns the focus of our environmental political thinking to the material reality of time and thus to the varying temporal frameworks that intersect at the point of our environmental concerns. In the window in which we work now, when the final throes of crises have not overtaken us, and when democratic forms of political comportment remain possible, Adorno's form of theoretical intervention can help democrats articulate the basis of their environmental commitment. The material anchor of his thinking, in fact, grounds the concrete encounter with a natural world under siege within the historically specific material conditions of twenty-first century global capitalism, framing a demand for immediate action and long-term patience, which are central temporal concerns for any kind of environmental politics.[11] In interrupting the seamless flow of our capitalist–bureaucratic experience of time, the demands of environmentalist concern open up the possibilities and necessities of being able to think along different temporal registers.

The slowness that reading Adorno engenders remains germane, then, for important epistemological and strategic–tactical reasons; but it also seems a prerequisite for our moral consideration of the others whom we encounter.[12] One can get some sense of how slowness opens toward these different directions by considering the Hegelian scenography that frames much of his thinking,[13] in which a distinct 'subject' and 'object' are set off against each other in the world in a posture of encounter. Though the hope of overcoming this distance can never be abandoned, Adorno insists that this hope is never a matter of a finally pleasing resolution. Thus, rather than suggesting an immediate conflation of the natural and the human, Adorno suggests that attending to our received relationship to 'nature' is a crucial moment of engagement for those who seek, rightly, to overcome that duality. For a critical environmental politics, Adorno's constellative, negative dialectical approach to the question of the human relationship to nature offers a fascinating flexibility, suggesting a way of thinking that is capable of recognizing moments of our direct entwinement with nature – of how we *are* nature – in juxtaposition to moments when the other of non-human nature, and of other concrete others, disrupt those moments of seamless connection.

This trajectory of Adorno's thinking as it travels through the subject/object relationship grounds his analysis in a material register, revealing the ways in which the historical development of subject/object epistemologies have – in their very pretensions of universality – covered over the partial and thus oppressive effects that they reflect and enable. For environmentalists, Adorno's thinking thus offers a useful critique of the atomistic, rational-actor model of the subject that centres capitalist ideology. Adorno helps us see the unfreedoms, both material and psychological, of this regime of knowledge by dramatizing the struggle for subjective actualization and achievement within the temporal realities that predominantly contour the horizons of our historical self-understanding. This historical–temporal emphasis allows us some insight into how a range of interrelated processes – the acceleration of experience as it is mediated through increasingly powerful and expansive informational and travel technologies; the emphasis on the speed-up of productivity and on the new in an emerging media simulacrum; the cultivation of a certain tempo of expectation and fulfilment in the products of the culture industry – increasingly threaten to engulf us in the totalizing logic of an instrumental modernity.

Tracking back along the sociological and philosophical understandings of the subject/object relationship, Adorno rereads that relationship, showing how an irreducible dimension of non-identity persists in our ability to know the world. Thus, for Adorno, thinking in the register of 'subject' and 'object' is necessary because 'the separation of subject and object is both real and semblance.'[14] It is real because 'it lends expression to the real separation, the rivenness of the human condition, the result of a coercive historical process.' On the other hand, this separation 'must not be hypostatized, not magically transformed into an invariant.'[15] Emerging out of an originary pragmatics of consciousness, the subject/object split has hardened into an unassailable assumption that fatally locks our thought into a logic of identity; we forget that this state of affairs is historical rather than eternal and inevitable.

Thus, this critical posture toward the distinction between subject and object is crucial, according to Adorno, because of the totalizing understanding of this relationship, in which 'mind then arrogates to itself the status of being absolutely independent – which it is not: mind's claim to independence announces its claim to domination. Once radically separated from the object, subject reduces the object to itself; subject swallows object, forgetting how much it is object itself.'[16]

Despite the logic of domination that necessarily accompanies the historical enactment of this epistemological staging – how the distancing that provides human beings' subjective capacity for knowledge also underwrites the subject's mastery of the objects it confronts – Adorno's mimetic inflection of this staging gives critical environmental political theory pause about abandoning its sense of 'nature' as the external object of its concern, as the Other of the rationalizing imperatives of modernity. For Adorno, this travelling through the mutually dislocating relationship of the subject and the object, as the activity of thinking, provides the opportunity for enacting the moral–practical ethos that resists the fascist, the totalitarian, and – environmental political theorists would add – the ecologically destructive trends of an increasingly rationalized modern world that simply posits the Other as that which is to be mastered.

Against that backdrop, the possibility of an affirmative, critical subjectivity is the story of resisting the triggers of fulfilment that we are trained to press, imposed upon us by the systematic dictates of the whole we participate in reproducing. This is a semiomaterial whole, where the conditions of production are mediated by the simulacra in which we make the meaning of our lives. Adorno's work resonates with our current concerns, in part, because he recognizes the strong connection between thinking and habitual, embodied practice, and how, moreover, capitalist forms of production are mediated by logics of cultural production and consumption, reaching into our bodies through the habituating repetition of our work and our play. His work thus suggests that thinking of our sociopolitical world as this kind of semiomaterial whole is a fundamental step in achieving any kind of autonomous subjective potential.

Adorno's negative dialectical thinking, however, enacts something different. The thinking that he advocates does not resign itself to the dictates of the totalizing field it inhabits; rather, it countersigns that totality in a way that reveals the falseness of that totality. Within the totalizing tendencies of an age that colonizes our bodies and our minds, the question of what constitutes a proper countersignature becomes a matter of central importance. On the one hand, any effective countersignature must somehow capture the affective dimension of experience that, in the form commanded by the social totality, is a fundamental promise that reproduces the logic of that totality. On the other hand, there would not seem to be, strictly speaking, any available language for this countersignature within the totalizing space from which it must proceed. In the context of these demands, the possibility of a meaningful refusal of the dictates of the system as a whole hinges on a difficult language that challenges the warm sense of fulfilled expectation that we are taught and that we internalize throughout our lives. In this sense, Adorno's various foci – such as his critical response to the predominant compositional forms of Western music and his embrace of Schoenberg's atonalism; or his effort to find alternative forms of philosophical and conceptual presentation, such as the paratactical approach of *Aesthetic Theory*[17] – are united by a critique of the predominant temporal sensibilities (and the uncritical comfort they inspire) of a historically ascendant instrumental reason.

II

What is the object, then, of this essay, which Adorno's thinking is meant to bring into play? In part, it is the way in which 'time' operates as a concept within environmental political self-understandings – understandings that are at least sometimes articulated by environmental political activists and theorists. But the object must also be the material reality of time that contours who we are. This material dimension of time can itself be understood in reference to each individual's inescapable mortality, in terms of the ultimate finitude of the earth itself and the likely finitude of the human species, but also in terms of the technologically mediated tempos of our times, which will undoubtedly be mediated differently and take on different forms across historical and socioeconomic circumstances. Adorno's thinking remains relevant to our historical moment because the temporal trends to which he responded have only been amplified by recent technological achievements. Adorno thus continues to offer resources for responding to a technologically mediated acceleration of experience that is moving beyond the technologies he experienced.

The slide in the description of our object – time as it is conceived by different strands of environmental theory and the way time is understood in its specific material contexts, for example – reflects how 'time' is a pivot, with the various dimensions of how we understand the phenomenon of time partially overlapping even as they move along their own trajectories. But this slide in what time *means* in our discussion reflects something of Adorno's broader insistence that the very logic of naming demands that we take up the object of our concern from a variety of angles, in terms of a constellation of concepts.[18] Following that general method, we can best approximate the truth of an object, but we are also ongoingly reminded of the disruption of our ability to know the final truth of the thing-in-itself.

The object itself, time, might seem particularly suited for this kind of approach. From at least Augustine onward, philosophers have grappled with the paradoxical nature of time and our human efforts to represent what it is. It is something we mark but that by its very definition is that which unmarks, that which undoes through its movement any effort to say, conclusively, what it is. In seeking to arrest in a word that which cannot be stopped, efforts to conceptualize 'time' specifically 'capture' a central insight of Adorno's theory of meaning: his insistence on the non-identity that inheres within the very logic of identity; the misnaming that necessarily occurs when we name; the interdependence of truth and lie.[19] This theory of meaning, as we will see, is not incidental to the ethical, moral, and aesthetic dimensions of Adorno's overarching project, all of which reflect a certain nobility of comportment. All language, as the bearer of meaning, entails a response to the question of time, the drawing of a boundary within time; Adorno's work can be understood largely as an effort to show, through language, a more noble relationship to time than that enacted by the quickly creeping, immediately consumptive progress of an instrumental, capitalist/bureaucratic reason exploding through, and thus being shaped by, its technological achievements. That nobility is a fundamental dimension of the affirmative democratic–environmental ethos that might be drawn out of Adorno's work.

As we have clearly seen, looking across the field of competing voices that make up environmental political discourse, concerns about time are central to the core logics of several different environmental political perspectives. For the theorists and activists who have articulated these perspectives, time is a very real concern. In nearly all of these stories, we find humans as both subject and object, battling both with themselves and with their own behaviours that are leading to the destruction of nature. Those behaviours have long been highly productive; and thus, from certain perspectives, they are perfectly rational and desirable ways of living. People enjoy the pleasures they have come to know in the technological panorama of contemporary life. We like the speed of exchange, variation, and encounter that is possible in our late-modern, technologically mediated lives. Little bits of power, knowledge, and pleasure seem endlessly available through these networked technologies. Yet at the same time, many of us are dismayed by the ecological destruction that is the inevitable by-product of those behaviours. The natural things that are being destroyed are things that many human beings claim to want, things that we need to preserve as important parts of the public good.

Famously, even our celebrations of 'natural' disruptions of the day-to-day contribute to the destruction of what we want to preserve. When we drive through Yosemite, for example, we see a wide range of natural wonders in a day that we could never reach so quickly by hiking into the park from a central point; but that convenience, even while it affords us a 'connection' to nature, is destroying the very habitats we have come to see. That same impulse for an unfettered time outside of time afforded by nature can be sold to us as the SUV that allows us to reach the untrammelled places that we unthinkingly seek to trammel. We might be convinced, indeed, that the ways we habitually act lead to outcomes we might not consciously choose, outcomes that are contrary to the common good[20] and that are prohibitive of the kind of world that we *want* to preserve for our individual and collective enjoyment and edification, or that we *should* preserve out of respect for the integrity of the non-human world that we inhabit and for the generations to follow.

This central social fact – that human beings might persistently act in ways that are contrary to their true interests or obligations, rightly understood or remembered – remains a central challenge for the broader aims of a democratically committed environmental political theory. As we have seen, however, reading Adorno suggests that this irrational outcome, at a self-interested, means–ends level, is related to how human beings have learned, at an epistemological–ideological level, to understand nature as a resource to be used by them according to their preferences. It would seem that environmental political theory not only must be concerned with delineating our true interests and obligations, but also must combat the 'Matrix-like' dream-world of our inherited anthropocentrism, as a result of which our productive and consumptive habits have taken on the veneer of a seamless necessity and the possibility of an alternative mode of comportment in the larger world we inhabit is unimaginable.[21] Within that inherited dream, we are literally blind to the full scope of the natural world that we necessarily inhabit. We tend to be blind to our own entwinement with the natural world; indeed, we take up our estrangement as a basis for forgetting the irreducible moments of non-identity in our relationship to nature. As a consequence, we are ultimately unable to respond to a moment of moral integrity that is introduced and sustained by this moment of non-identity.

The moral dimension of Adorno's negative dialectical, constellative method is central to his contribution to a critical and democratically informed environmental politics. Given how our behaviours are produced by the economic and highly mediatized culture we inhabit, and given the environmental degradation that can be connected to those behaviours, many directions in contemporary environmental political practice and theory are centred – more or less consciously – around the possibility of a 'new man,' of a different kind of person who would live in a more morally and spiritually sound relationship with nature. In a society almost entirely colonized by the hegemonic forces of modernity, however, the space for this kind of autonomous response will remain difficult and elusive. Our organism is saturated with the systematic forces of the social apparatus, and this influences not only how we think but also how we feel about and act within the world. Adorno's sensitivity to the ways in which capitalist–bureaucratic systems and their manifestations in the culture industry have transformed our time-consciousness, the ways in which we experience the world in particular temporal terms, is one avenue open for us to remain focused on how our self-understandings are inculcated at a material, corporeal level. We are beings who are produced by the materially driven tempos we inhabit; as such, the tempo of our comportment is a legitimate site of political contestation; and as our turn to Adorno suggests, finding the right time, a countertime, will be central to becoming the different kinds of people who will be necessary for a successful environmental politics. In a world in which time is rationalized by both our labour and our experience of free time, and where time itself – like the entirety of nature with which it is necessarily entwined – is regularly turned into a consumable commodity, the possibilities for autonomy seem wedded to strategies for finding the contrapuntal spaces where, and the times when, a critical thinking might still take place.

The particular form of consciousness we experience is both true in terms of its factual existence and false in relation to our better human potentials. This reflects the particular unfolding of a rapidly changing world – a world in which, indeed, the rapidity of change has become a norm. The awesomely productive but irrational power of capitalism that Marx and Engels noted in the *Communist Manifesto* has shown little sign of slackening. Yet for all the undeniable force of these ongoing changes, their overall effect has been to maintain the basic structures of global capitalism. These status quo structures continue to govern the lives that people born in different parts of the world are likely to live. Work remains structured around boring, repetitive tasks for certain populations, who tend to work for the benefit of others. Even within the cocoon of First World consumerism, the dialectical relationship between technological development and the development and proliferation of markets continues to shape our behaviour.[22]

The critique of the human domination of nature – an analysis of its historical development and its ideological manifestations – was at the heart of Adorno's larger critical project, especially as he began to respond to the rise of Nazism and the horrors of the Holocaust. Those lessons no doubt solidified the defiant and reverberating impact that Adorno continues to have on Marxist thinking. In that tradition, he thematizes how capitalism, with its ultimately counterfeit promises, functions as a heteronomous force that defines the unfreedom of modern human beings. He never abandons the basic materialist tenet that economic conditions contour our subjectivity; in fact, he *extends* that tenet, and he does so in ways that complicate and enrich Marxism's critical orientation.[23] Adorno elaborates on how ideology is mediated by cultural production; and in that broad site – philosophy, literature, popular culture – he finds a place to maintain a critically responsive ethos of principled resistance to the colonizing force of the instrumental reason to which we modern humans find ourselves committed.

That resistance is a form of a particular *techné*, what Michel Foucault would call 'the undefined work of freedom.'[24] Adorno's thinking, as a form of praxis, can be linked to a central thrust of Foucault's work in that it thematizes the subject as a site of material and political contestation; in this way it iterates, within the idiom of a different but overlapping lineage of thinkers, our work on ourselves as a necessary part of the democratic and emancipatory thrusts of the Marxist tradition. Adorno crafts a picture of the subject capable of both critiquing the mutilating effects of technically mediated global capitalism *and* resisting the totalitarian impulses that emerge when a radical politics seeks to effect its aims in the context of a realpolitik. Adorno's effort to sustain the question of freedom in relationship to our mastery of and dependence on the environment we inhabit emphasizes a view of autonomy – as the cardinal prerequisite and outcome of a democratic society – that does not understand itself as being separate from either the society or the natural worlds with which it is entwined, and that is thus more capable of responding to the 'others' from whom we delineate ourselves. Only a response that is grounded in the alienation of subject and object, and that reflects the historical reality of our inherited condition, and that recognizes how this logical structure underwrites the success of instrumental–scientific–technological reason, can realistically assess our circumstances and thereby preserve the critical possibility of transforming those circumstances.

Fundamental to those historical circumstances is a technologically mediated acceleration that constantly and increasingly diffracts the ways in which we modern human beings experience the world, even as it mockingly transforms our subjectivity into the predictable gestures of lifeless repetition. Electronic communications and information technologies promise an infinitely pluralist and pluralizing space; but what they actually deliver is a levelling down, a narrowing, a banal typecasting of human possibilities that discourages the autonomy necessary for true self-governance. As Tim Luke points out elsewhere in this volume, despite enthusiasts' claims that digitizing technology is creating a new space in which 'post-human' subjects 'are busy at work and happy at play on the Net, their desires seeming to have found adequate expression in eBay, MySpace, Facebook, YouTube, Second Life, America Online or just Google,'[25] it is more the case that

> the properties of post-human being are those of rapid capitalist commerce at its neoliberal nadir mistaken as the freedoms of the electronic frontier by the machinic monads of deluded individual clients linked into occluded systems of servers. Of course, some elements of this social formation clash for the individual and for the whole; but these fragmented networks of posthuman being with regard to their balance of power and powerlessness actually realize a regimen of command, control, and communication far beyond what 'the state dictators dream of.'[26]

From the perspective of a critical environmental political theory, a central problem would be the ways in which these technologies and their functions within an overarching economic totality reproduce the attitudes and habits of human beings, who through their behaviour participate in the reproduction of the environmental barbarity of the system as a whole. More specifically, any environmental political theory that would bring environmental concerns to the centre of political thinking necessarily faces a materially inscribed set of economic realities and social understandings that run counter to, and move at a different tempo than, a serious revaluation of the natural world.

This encounter with the social–technological–economic imperative of our times reflects the effort of Adorno (and his Frankfurt School compatriots) to build on the emancipatory thrust of Marx's critique of capitalism. For this group of thinkers, it was necessary, however, to go beyond Marx by linking his critique to Max Weber's diagnosis of the increasingly pervasive reach of instrumental reason. The triumph of that instrumental reason, and its concomitant devaluation of the natural world as a thing to be dominated, informed the rise of bureaucratic divisions of labour and the organization of a totally administered life in the free market economies of the West *and* in the central command economies of the East. Like Weber, the Frankfurt School thinkers saw an increasingly rationalized world that was disenchanting nature and turning it into a mere thing to be mastered – a process that would mutilate human beings to the point that they would be unable to critically question their deracinated relationship to their natural and social worlds.

Moving beyond Weber, critical theory focused more and more on how individuals were being turned into particular kinds of subjects in the increasingly administered world of the twentieth century. Adorno made it abundantly clear that this focus on the formation and possibilities of the individual subject was really the only game in town in the aftermath of Stalin's crimes, the Nazi Holocaust, and the movement toward the totalizing tendencies of capitalism and bureaucracy. As he wrote in 'Education after Auschwitz': 'Since the possibility of changing the objective – namely societal and political – conditions is extremely limited today, attempts to work against the repetition of Auschwitz are necessarily restricted to the subjective dimension.'[27] This observation may be even truer today, when the totalizing triumph of post–Cold War global liberal capitalism has only heightened our sense of the importance of cultivating the subjective dimension within an emancipatory politics.

Despite his enormous respect for the contouring effects of the sociopolitical system, Adorno works within the Socratic lineage that connects a demystifying self-knowledge with the possibilities of a critical autonomy. In intervening at the level of subjectivity in the fight against the always recurring threat of a collective inhumanity, Adorno maintains that most important of all, 'one must come to know the mechanisms that render people capable of such deeds, must reveal these mechanisms to them, and strive, by awakening a general awareness of those mechanisms, to prevent people from becoming so again.'[28] Education, the real practical activity of the theorist,[29] must 'labor against this lack of reflection, must dissuade people from striking outward without reflecting upon themselves. The only education that has any sense at all is an education toward critical self-reflection.'[30] What is central, then, is a form of temporal comportment – a temporally responsive ethos – that resists the trained compulsion of 'striking outward without reflecting upon' ourselves.

A critical political question, then, is whether the time of our time, the tempo of our time, can allow for this interruption of its systematically determined rhythms. Those rhythms, experienced in the repetitive hum of the assembly line, or in the routine in the cubicle, but also in the predictable outcomes of the sit-com plot and the crescendo of the clichéd pop song, unerringly prepare us to become certain kinds of individuals. Those rhythms not only reinforce the substantive outcome of our lives, preparing us to smilingly accept their deadening sameness, but also reach into our bodies, habituating our very pre-rational sensibilities to the pace and the narrative sense prefigured by the demands of commodity capitalism. Rhythm's colonizing effects always threaten to pre-empt the reflective space of critical theory.

Critical theory, as it is understood here, necessarily entails an interruption of the way things are, of a prescribed, prefigured temporal unfolding. Critical theory, this suggests, entails a temporal gesture that seeks a pause in the seamless reproduction of the way things are. In a sense, the language of environmental crisis, as an appeal to an ineffable material fact, introduces a moment of non-identity that would, literally, give pause to this seamless reproduction of the way things are. Adorno, however, in the constellating movement of the dialectical labour of his thinking, also allows us to draw out the affirmative dimensions of the interrupting movement of non-identity, giving us glimpses into how such a non-identity might be positively affirmed.

Adorno impels us to think about the falseness of the ways in which we typically uncritically inhabit time; moreover, he suggests ways of recognizing the untruth of the totalizing natural aesthetic that inspires certain radical and/or quietist environmental political responses. By demonstrating the pervasive ways in which that ideal moment of awe before nature is merely a moment, and by drawing that legitimate moment of experience into a negative dialectical relationship with material–instrumental concerns about human survival and normative–ethical concerns about justice and about what constitutes a well-lived life, Adorno's thinking suggests a way of responding to the mystifying lure of some radical environmentalisms' jargons of authenticity. Such a thinking, by breaking up the 'presentism' of the reverential moment of the natural whole, renews the temporal demands of thinking, bringing the critical movement of thought into contact with the material elements that constitute the fullest account of the object. Adorno, in this sense, is suggesting a radical politics capable of considering the full range of material implications for human beings who necessarily coproduce the environment they inhabit – not just to the pure nature they/we are destroying or have already destroyed. Working in terms of a countertempo to the accelerated world that both empowers and delimits us, Adorno's negative dialectical approach practisesthe slowness necessary for democratic reflection rather than the partial certainty that informs radical actionism.

III

A systematic tracking of where, how, and why the theme of time drifts in and out of Adorno's writing, how the notion or trope of time most fully functions within his work, is certainly worth scholarly interest. That more exhaustive kind of account cannot be pursued here. But at this stage of the encounter between Adorno's temporal sensibilities and the time-consciousness of environmental political theory, we can mark at least three interrelated ways in which the theme of time circulates through his work. Ultimately, these different conceptualizations of the problem of time raise concerns that are central to the kind of human being that a critical, democratic environmental politics hopes to cultivate.

First, Adorno is attentive to time's experiential content, to the question of human meaning in relationship to a world of flux and mortality, and he frames his philosophical/aristocratic insistence about what constitutes the good life within this temporal drama of the human struggle for meaning. In typically negative fashion, his encounter with the question of meaning is framed in part by a critique of existentialism's return to a pure presence of meaning,[31] which, like the return to immediacy in Bergson,[32] is merely the inverted form of the old bourgeois dream of a timeless security against the erosive forces of an ever changing world. Both the bourgeois dream of stasis and the vitalogical and romantic celebrations of immediacy conjure a space where time ceases to be a part of how we experience the world, even as the rapidity of exchange accelerates under the possibilities of modern technologies. Adorno seeks a more mature perspective, one that does not abdicate its posture of critique when faced with those moments of immediacy that escape the ratio of language and calculation. Nonetheless, his thinking gains much of its force as an effort to live rightly, as an effort to judge and act in an exemplary way, in the temporal contexts in which we are enmeshed; in doing so, it enacts a specific temporal attitude, ethos, or orientation.[33]

A second important way in which Adorno treats the theme of time follows his recognition that questions about the good life are experienced within particular, semiomaterial understandings of time. We are produced within certain identifiable tempos, habituated to the discipline of particular rhythms. We think the way that we think as bodies moving to these internalized rhythms. Adorno articulates a critical theory that must respond to these tempos, offering tactics of resistance, countertempos, that show us the way to the temporal imaginary he endorses. We can see in this concern one reason why the gestures of Adorno's political and social theory are connected to his musical composition and criticism. Music, as a site of semiomaterial enculturation, helps us understand a specific way in which our temporal expectations are shaped by cultural production; but it also offers a sense of how the possibility of acting rightly might find its more admirable temporal response.

Third, Adorno is always attentive to the problem of time as the problem of the political future. Especially for a leftist politics that had already seen the totalitarian implications of its Stalinist misrealization, and especially in the aftermath of the Nazi rise to power, Adorno's insistence on the diremptive power of the negative takes on an important normative function, serving as a vigilant philosophical gesture against the totalizing power of both capitalist–bureaucratic rationality and the totalizing responses it inspires.

Along all three of these dimensions, Adorno's post-Holocaust thinking responds to the increasing speeds of consummation that our semiomaterial realities impose on us. By demystifying the mechanisms that produce us in certain ways, and by showing us how our thinking and behaviour tend to reproduce the system, Adorno's critical form of thinking opens the possibility of an autonomous subjectivity that is capable of responding to those forces and limits, however difficult that work might continue to be.

Reading Adorno is important for a critical, democratic, environmental political theory if for no other reason than that he demonstrates the true difficulty involved in moving toward the future it could endorse. The demands placed on readers by Adorno's writing, by its very form, interrupt the economic and technological imposition of immediacy. The experience of reading his prose prepares the kind of engaged patience that energizes the kind of critical subjectivity that he seeks to model.

That patience is necessary in a world in which we are thoroughly the products of an increasingly pervasive historical self-understanding generated by our economic and technological circumstances. Adorno's thought is famous for its insistence on our inability, in any complete way, to transcend the totalizing grip of an instrumental reason that has defined and continues to impel the development of human beings. As the overcoming of myth, enlightenment is particularly convincing when it works, when it demonstrates an ability to translate nature into something of value. Ironically, the colonizing force of this mentality converts enlightenment back into myth, as a coherent, totalizing narrative that masks the irrationalities that it continues – more or less secretly – to convey.[34] Following Marx, Adorno refuses a cheap utopianism by insisting that thinking proceed from where it must begin, in the world that has always already contoured the possibilities of who we are; and he seeks to present his thinking within the space of this colonizing thought, to go through this thought in an effort to imagine a way beyond its grip. By depicting some of the machinations by which material practices are translated into psychic realities, especially as those material realities are transformed by informational technologies that directly affect how individuals experience the world, Adorno allows us to imagine alternative forms of comportment that, in their enactment, turn the legacy of the Enlightenment toward its more noble possibilities.

Taken in its proper measure, Adorno's insistence on the insidious, inescapable reach of these processes of reification is a virtue. For a critical environmental political theory, Adorno's thinking, through its hyperbolic description as an administered totality, gives us a clearer picture of how thoroughly our sense of selves – as the self is determined on both conscious and unconscious levels – is invested in a set of stories that are ongoingly repeated by the media productions that we constantly see, hear, smell, and taste, as well as within the systems of reward and punishment that we inhabit. In repeatedly and hyperbolically formulating thinking in reference to such an inescapable totality, Adorno at least orients us toward thinking about how the mediatized productions of the culture industry function in a totalizing kind of way, creating a field of affective coherence that is capable of robbing human beings (who experience the world in terms of these productions) of their autonomy. This rhetorical insistence, in other words, has the substantive import of communicating something still true – cognitively, psychically, corporeally, materially – about the stubbornly reified world in which environmental politics, and any environmental political theory that would distil that politics' voice, necessarily operates. Adorno's thinking, as his treatment of the theme of time demonstrates, seeks to do more than trade on a superior critical perspective; it also forces us to approximate more realistically the difficulties of seeking a reconciliation with nature within the movement of a productivist, consumerist economy's gripping and seemingly totalizing power.

One way in which Adorno captures this seemingly totalizing force and the reach of this administered world as it manifests itself in a temporal register is in his treatment of 'free time.' Adorno, again following Marx, recognized the segmented, repetitive, dehumanizing ways in which productive labour time was structured in the modern world. Adorno argues, however, that the rationalization of time extends beyond the schedules and plans of officially administered labour time. The putatively free time, where 'people are at least subjectively convinced that they are acting of their own will, this will itself is fashioned by precisely what they want to shake off during their time outside of work.'[35] Free time, of course, is crucial for a productivist system based on human toil; it is during free time that we replenish ourselves so that we can be all the more productive with our labour time. As Adorno points out, within the functional logic of a productivist/consumerist system, 'organized free time is compulsory.'[36]

Free time, as it functions within this totality, is ultimately colonized by the logic of that totality even while offering a space for resisting its logic. Camping, for example, emerged as 'a protest against the tedium and conventionalism of bourgeois life,' but it has since become, even to the degree that it might allow for an important kind of contact with the natural world and with different modes of living, 'institutionalized by the camping industry.'[37] Camping, 'sleeping under the open sky,' remains a legitimate need, 'but business functionalizes, extends, and reproduces the campers' "need for freedom."'[38] That need, in being commodified, seems destined to be transformed into something quite contrary to its original, animating motivation, which by definition entails escaping the demands of usefulness imposed by the social totality in which they are pursued.

The reach of a colonizing rationality, modulated by and in the service of the demands of capitalism, is driven along by the empowering appeal of its own technological achievements. Campers and tents filled with electronic devices, to give one example of this process, reunite us with the totality that camping trips legitimately seek to escape. Campers loaded with MP3s, cell phones, televisions, Blackberries, GPS systems, bike computers, and digital maps, Adorno would argue, further reinforce the imperatives of the overall administered system. Those technologies continue to plug us into the broader imperatives of the informational matrix we inhabit. On the one hand, this 'plugging in' reinforces our habit of reducing non-human nature to a set of measurable quantities understandable in terms of an instrumentalized ratio, though much of that use, like our day-to-day expectation of electricity, almost seems invisible (until, at least, the electric bill arrives). On the other hand, this 'plugging in' reinforces an incessantly repeated temporal expectation that banalizes what counts as good, occluding the kinds of temporal variation that might be cultivated through an at least less mediated encounter with non-human nature.

Listening to our iPods when we take a walk on the beach or through the woods, we find ourselves at least doubly alienated from a less mediated nature, both separated by a wall of intervening sound, and trapped again within the deadening repetition of the culture industry's products. Even though the variety of musical genres from which we are able to choose seems to suggest an ever expanding variety, there remains something remarkable about the limited range of the products that most of us crave. Adorno's denigration of jazz, whether or not we agree with his analysis of the form, captures something of how we continue to experience a variety of popular musical styles; he asserts that 'jazz fans, short for fanatics, sense this [boring repetition of the same] and therefore prefer to emphasize the music's improvisational features. But these are mere frills. Any precocious American teenager knows that the routine today scarcely leaves any room for improvisation, and what appears as spontaneity is in fact carefully planned out in advance with machinelike precision.'[39] Likewise, on the television show that relaxes us and amuses us, 'the performance flits by,' moving at a speed that covers the effects 'specifically designed for the unconscious.'[40] In both these cases, media inscribe a time sense of ongoing change, elaboration, and differentiation; but in both cases, the ultimate effect of this superficial flurry of elaboration merely reproduces the structural effects of the overall system, locking us back into the overall logic of that system and alienating us from the moments of connection or immediacy that we putatively seek.

For Adorno, these effects of the culture industry, as a particular example of the insidious reach of an always advancing instrumental reason, are a crisis for advocates of enlightenment. As we continue to accelerate in the Information Age, we should maintain a critical attentiveness to our propensity to fetishize technology. For Adorno, that propensity creates people 'who cannot love.'[41] Writing in 'Education after Auschwitz' in reference to the comment by a test subject from *Authoritarian Personality* that 'I like nice equipment,' Adorno sees our ability to love being 'absorbed by things, machines as such.'[42] The alarming thing about the pervasive net cast by the routinizing, mechanizing, and consumerist logics of modernity is that 'this trend goes hand in hand with that of the entire civilization. To struggle against it means as much to stand against the world spirit.'[43] And to the degree that the degradation of nature is rooted in the same dominating impulse that informed the very possibility of Auschwitz, the battle Adorno enjoins against the tendency toward totalitarianism is directly relevant to the maintenance of a critical environmental ethos.

In its insistence on underlining the difficult terrain in which democrats fight for an ecological or environmental orientation within political thinking, Adorno's work can be discouraging. Most pessimistically, Adorno's insistence on the creeping totality of administered thought can give the impression that there is no way out, leading to either a political quietism or a shrill (re)actionism. Adorno's thinking, however, fights these impulses by cultivating the outwardly opening possibilities of an autonomous, reflexive picture of the subject, morally oriented toward the others it encounters.[44] For an environmental political theory that is interested in refashioning the ways in which we relate to nature and the ways in which we inhabit it, Adorno's effort to reopen this space of moral possibility through an attentiveness to the problems and questions of tempo spawned by late capitalism may suggest a maturing form of environmental critical theory.

Adorno recognizes an explicit relation between the temporal realities of a capitalist order and the moral capacity of human beings. Toward the conclusion of Part I of *Minima Moralia*, in section 49, Adorno intensely scrutinizes the links among time's existential content, the tempo of our time, and our moral autonomy: 'The irreversibility of time constitutes an objective moral criterion. But it is one intimately related to myth like abstract time itself. The exclusiveness implicit in time gives rise, by its inherent law, to the exclusive domination of hermetically sealed groups, finally to that of big business.'[45] Thus our very being, as our experience of time, reflects our internalization of our response to that temporal experience, our entirely understandable desire to find a kind of permanence amidst the flux of experience. The very possibility of language, to which Adorno's work is obviously committed, entails this proprietary movement. That impulse, however, culminates in the extended structures of domination that rule modern capitalist society, which in turn recoil on the humanity from which it arose.

Adorno argues that the representational thinking, and by extension the instrumental reason, in which we are enmeshed gathers its metaphysical ballast from the illusory, unenlightened answer it gives to the existential problem of time: 'Historically, the notion of time is itself formed on the basis of the order of ownership. But the desire to possess reflects time as a fear of losing, of the irrecoverable. Whatever is, is experienced in relation to its possible non-being.'[46] The great irony, of course, is that the existential–temporal logic that underwrites the idea of ownership gives rise to a logic of exchange that erects a further barrier to sustaining a more qualitatively rich relationship to time. To turn time and all that it bears into a thing to be used for specific ends, 'this alone makes it fully a possession and, thus petrified, something functional that can be exchanged for other, equivalent possessions.'[47] Echoing the Marxist insight that capitalist relations turn people into things for one another, Adorno reminds us how this capitalist/bureaucratic/consumerist re-evaluation of the qualitative experience of time has undercut the realization of our Kantian moral sensibilities, for 'such possessiveness loses its hold on its object precisely through turning it into an object, and forfeits the person whom it debases to "mine."'[48]

Adorno recognizes that the ethos we inherit reflects the materially dictated tempo of our times, but he also posits an ethos of critical response to those temporal imperatives. The ethos we inherit impoverishes our ability to love others; the ethos he cultivates is a precondition for that love. The negative on which Adorno always insists can never be understood as a rejection; indeed, it is quite the opposite: it is the *positive* basis for true human interaction. 'If people were no longer possessions,' he writes, 'they could no longer be exchanged. True affection would be one that speaks specifically to the other, and becomes attached to beloved features and not to the idol of personality, the reflected image of possession.'[49] For Adorno, the very possibility of a binding affection for the other is grounded in an ability to speak specifically to that other. That kind of speaking, which Adorno's writing puts into practice, recognizes the paradox of its task: to speak *to* the other and *of* the other in a way that preserves the other *as* other, so as to somehow enact an affection or a solidarity for the other that does not mutilate the object of affection and respect.

To the degree that our experience of time, enmeshed in the logic of private property and thus in the ideology of exchange, directly impoverishes our cognitive, moral, and aesthetic orientations to the world, the necessity of countertempo becomes increasingly apparent. Inscribed as we are by and within the tempos of immediate gratification and the proliferating images of our late-capitalist, technically mediated world, our tendency to turn the other – whether we are referring to an*other* concrete individual, or a group of individuals, or to non-human nature – into a thing to be used for our own advantage insinuates itself into the deepest recesses of our psyche. Given the normalization of exchange, and the fascination with the new that this inspires,[50] even our most intimate and seemingly organic relationships always face the risk of falling back into the logic of our prevailing social norms. In this faster world, in which 'all that is solid melts into air,' the fate of all genuine solidarity is always at risk; the tendency, in fact, is for such solidarity to fracture and dissolve, only flitting by on the screen as it passes into oblivion, or when its genuine impulse, conscious of its own impotence under existing social conditions, explodes in the horrific pseudo-solutions of totalitarian political reactions to material hardship or catastrophe. The possibility, then, of the kind of democratically imagined environmental politics that might be drawn from Adorno's work entails living in a different temporal relationship to the others (human and/or non-human) on whom we depend and who, after all, are part and parcel of the idiosyncratic individual that each of us is.

But what would that countertempo look like, or feel like? It would be a tempo that disturbs the tempos of our time. Where the tempo of our time demands speed – the speed of immediate gratification – such a tempo would seek to conserve space for reflection. Where the tempo of our time imposes rhythms of monotonous repetition – of a machinelike task, of the message of advertisements, of the reactionary plots of the typical sit-com, of the now utterly predictable gestures of classic rock or auto-tune – a countertempo, by definition, would preserve the possibility of difference. But the cultivation of countertempos would also entail an appreciation of non-human tempos – the tempos of cosmic time, geological time, the life cycle time of different species (and the interactions of these life cycle times), evolutionary time, and the time of post-degradation or post-catastrophe environmental rehabilitation. Working out when and how these different tempos should be negotiated and deployed, and thinking more systematically about how those suggestions are applicable in our concrete circumstances, are both necessary tasks for a more fully coherent environmental politics. In thematizing the centrality of temporal concerns for realizing our critical, autonomous potentials, Adorno offers an important impetus to a fuller consideration of the questions of time that frame our specific historical circumstances. And certainly, if there were time, or when there is time, more clearly connecting Adorno's aesthetic preoccupations with his political and sociological interests is an important part of understanding the notion of an *affirmative countertempo* that might be drawn from his work.[51]

The affirmative countertempo that Adorno's work suggests environmental politics must preserve, at the heart of its critical spirit, is always this tempo of the paradox of speaking specifically to the other. This other, which for Adorno would always include the other to which we refer when we speak and the other (or others) to whom we speak, has an integrity, within the negative dialectical approach to which Adorno is committed, that precedes and exceeds our ability to know the other. As Romand Coles has made this point, 'Adorno's thinking was, from early on, quintessentially ethical – whatever else it may have been at the same time. Adorno's critique of epistemology as "first philosophy" opened the possibility of understanding philosophy essentially as an ethical movement beyond ourselves toward engagements with non-identity.'[52]

That epistemological/ontological commitment can thus underwrite the fundamentally ethical, interruptive tempo of Adorno's work. His insistence on the primacy of the object as something best understood through a constellation of its descriptive concepts communicates an ethical attitude toward the concrete others we encounter; it suggests, in fact, the ethical/moral dimension that inheres in our orientation toward knowing the world. As Adorno notes, the primacy of the object, the negative, reveals the temporal reality of being. This kind of critical approach 'dissolves the fetish of the irrevocability of things in being' by demonstrating 'that things are not simply so and not otherwise, that they have come to be under certain conditions.'[53] For Adorno, that insight demands an optics that challenges modes of knowing 'enthralled by the idol of a pure present.'[54] The predominant forms of knowledge that govern who we are would conjure a timeless moment that secures, fitfully, for the bourgeois imagination we inhabit, a kind of security that the totality of our bourgeois behaviours would tear asunder. Those moments in time that we pursue, that we seek to memorialize as part of the specific story we seek to give to the meaning of our lives, throw us back under the repetitious yoke of the ways things have always been, the same old circle that remains unbroken. Such a knowledge, 'wholly conforming to the idol of that purity, of total timelessness – a knowledge coincident with formal logic – would become a tautology; there would be no more room in it even for transcendental logic. Timelessness, the goal of which the bourgeois mind may be pursuing in order to compensate for its own mortality, is the acme of its delusion.'[55]

Adorno saw the conditions of bourgeois consciousness as creating the desperation behind the geopolitical irrationality of the Nazis' drive for world domination. The ideological veneer of meaning that sustains bourgeois psychic stability (the meanings provided by the culture industry and its consumerist logics, all of those bits of 'time out of time'), collapses under the threat of economic deprivation. Losing power and status, in discovering the degree to which they are not autonomous individuals, the mass seeks to craft its identity through the illusory empowerment of a collective force. Ironically, the material conditions that give rise to the critical and progressive notion of the free individual were thwarted by the increasing rationalization of economic processes throughout the twentieth century, which split off individuals from the kind of cultivated insight and foresight that might have forestalled the tragedy of the Holocaust, turning them instead into its prosecutors.

The analogous question that Adorno poses for environmental political theory is whether or not we are in a similar situation in relation to those environmental holocausts that we continue, as part of the overall machinery, to prosecute. Adorno's work situates the critical work we perform on ourselves within the socioeconomic machinery that continues to destroy species and ecosystems, threatening global ecosystem catastrophe; but he also suggests a form of environmental critical theory capable of recognizing and criticizing those broader economic and cultural forces that, in their subject-forming effects, continue to bedevil the progress of our human ability to live more rightly and rationally with the broader natural and social world we inhabit. But in anchoring his thinking in that material register, thereby opening up an understanding of our relationship to the broader environment, he insists on maintaining the rational promise of a democratic ideal, where the possibility of realizing everyone's autonomous capacity to participate in his or her own self-governance has not faded from our memory and where that possibility is not contrary to a politics that recognizes its responsibility to build a sounder socioenvironmental future.

NOTES

1 See, for example, Paul Roberts, *The End of Oil: On the Edge of a Perilous New World* (New York: Mariner, 2005).
2 See, for example, Edward O. Wilson, *The Future of Life* (New York: Vintage, 2002); and David Foreman, *Rewilding North America: A Vision for Conservation in the 21st Century* (Washington: Island, 2004).

3 See Steven Best and Anthony J. Nocella, eds., *Igniting a Revolution: Voices in Defense of the Earth* (Oakland: AK, 2006), for various articulations of this movement.

4 See Jürgen Habermas, *The Philosophical Discourse of Modernity: Twelve Lectures*, trans. Frederick Lawrence (Cambridge, MA: MIT Press, 1990), particularly chapter 5, 'The Entwinement of Myth and Enlightenment: Max Horkheimer and Theodor Adorno,' 106–30.

5 For a discussion of how an aesthetic orientation derived from the work of Nietzsche, Foucault, and Connolly productively complements the emancipator thrust of Habermas's project, see Michael E. Lipscomb, 'The Theory of Communicative Action and the Aesthetic Moment: Jürgen Habermas and the Neo-Nietzschean Challenge,' *New German Critique* 86 (2002): 135–58.

6 For a discussion of the subtleties of affirmative, 'weak' ontologies across a range of contemporary critical thinkers, see Stephen K. White, *Sustaining Affirmation: The Strengths of Weak Ontology* (Princeton: Princeton University Press, 2000).

7 Theodor Adorno, 'Resignation,' in *Critical Models: Interventions and Catchwords*, trans. Henry W. Pickford (New York: Columbia University Press, 1998), 289–93.

8 William Connolly, for example, has thoughtfully articulated a pluralist ethos capable of flourishing within and taking advantage of the technological capacities for speed that characterize our late capitalist circumstances. See Connolly, *The Ethos of Pluralization* (Minneapolis: University of Minnesota Press, 1995); *Neuropolitics: Thinking, Culture, Speed* (Minneapolis: University of Minnesota Press, 2002); *Pluralism* (Durham: Duke University Press, 2005); and *Capitalism and Christianity, American Style* (Durham: Duke University Press, 2008). This last text, in particular, seeks to apply his temporally reoriented pluralist ethos to the motivational and practical challenges that characterize multigenerational environmental tasks and goals, such as possible political responses to global warming.

9 Max Horkheimer and Theodor Adorno, *Dialectic of Enlightenment: Philosophical Fragments*, ed. Gunzelin Schmid Noerr, trans. Edmund Jephcott (Stanford: Stanford University Press, 2002), 134–5.

10 Ibid., 135.

11 See Connolly, *Capitalism and Christianity*, particularly chapter 4, for an effort to imagine and pursue a progressive environmental politics within the horizon of an 'interim future.'

12 For a more filigree (and quite funny) analysis of the rhetorical effects of the variable speeds of Adorno's writing in *Minima Moralia*, see Jeff Nealon, 'Maximum Immoralia? Speed and Slowness in Adorno's *Minima Moralia*,' *Theory and Event* 4 (2000).

13 Judith Butler's observations on the rhetorical effects of Hegel's sentences are relevant to the experience of reading Adorno's negative dialectical approach: 'Because Hegel's rhetoric defies our expectations of a linear and definite philosophical presentation, it initially obstructs us (no one reads Hegel quickly), but once we have reflected upon the assumptions that Hegel wants to release us from, the rhetoric initiates us into a consciousness of irreducibly multiple meanings which continuously determine each other.' Judith Butler, *Subjects of Desire: Hegelian Reflections in Twentieth Century France* (New York: Columbia University Press, 1987), 19.

14 Adorno, 'On Subject and Object,' in *Critical Models: Interventions and Catchwords*, trans. Henry W. Pickford (New York: Columbia University Press, 1998), 246.

15 Ibid., 246.

16 Ibid.

17 Robert Hullot-Kentor, translator's introduction to *Aesthetic Theory*, by Theodor W. Adorno (Minneapolis: University of Minnesota Press, 1997), xiv–xix.

18 'The determinable flaw in every concept makes it necessary to cite others; this is the font of the only constellations which inherited some hope of the name. The language of philosophy approaches that name by denying it. The claim of immediate truth for which it chides the words is almost always the ideology of a positive, existent identity of word and thing.' Theodor W. Adorno, *Negative Dialectics* (New York: Continuum, 2004), 53.

19 This central thesis of Adorno's thinking echoes Nietzsche's analysis of language in 'Truth and Lie in an Extra-Moral Sense.' See also Karin Bauer, *Adorno's Nietzschean Narratives: Critiques of Ideology, Readings of Wagner* (Albany: SUNY Press, 1999), 81–5.

20 For an extended discussion of how we make judgments within competing preference schedules, as consumers oriented toward individual utilities and as citizens oriented toward the common good, see Mark Sagoff, *The Economy of the Earth* (New York: Cambridge University Press, 1988), 50–73.

21 Paul Watson uses the imagery of humans 'living in a Matrix-like dream called anthropocentrism' in the film *Testify! Eco-Defense and the Politics of Violence*; Michael Becker and Stephen Gamboa, *Green Theory and Praxis: Journal of Ecopedagogy* 3, no. 1 (2007), http://www.youtube.com/watch?v=7OgCqWS2yhc.

22 New informational, communications, and surveillance technologies, for example, have radically transformed our behaviours and important parts of our social self-understandings over the past fifteen years. Though he wrote prior to many of these informational technologies that we now take

for granted, Adorno's early responses to the rise of new informational
technologies such as print media, radio, and television continue to have
salience in the late modern world we inhabit, even when we can point to
ways in which his work may mischaracterize contemporary conditions.
See Tim Luke's chapter in this volume for a thoughtful effort to update the
kind of totalizing, assimilating understanding of the culture industry that
emerges out of the first generation of the Frankfurt School.

23 See, for example, Simon Jarvis, 'Adorno, Marx, Materialism,' in *The
Cambridge Companion to Adorno*, ed. Tom Huhn (Cambridge: Cambridge
University Press, 2004), 79–100.

24 'And this critique will be genealogical in the sense that it will not deduce
from the form of what we are what it is impossible for us to do and to
know; but it will separate out, from the contingency that has made us
what we are, the possibility of no longer being, doing, or thinking what we
arc, do, or think. It is not seeking to make possible a metaphysics that has
finally become a science; it is seeking to give new impetus, as far and wide
as possible, to the undefined work of freedom.' Michel Foucault, 'What Is
Enlightenment?' in *Ethics: Subjectivity, and Truth*, ed. Paul Rabinow, trans.
Robert Hurley and others (New York: New Press, 1997), 315–16.

25 Tim Luke in this volume, 321.

26 Ibid., 328. The quote is from Max Horkheimer, *Critique of Instrumental Reason* (New York: Seabury, 1974), 27.

27 Theodor W. Adorno, 'Education after Auschwitz,' in *Critical Models: Interventions and Catchwords*, trans. Henry W. Pickford (New York: Columbia
University Press, 1998), 192. For an extended defence of this investment
in the subjective dimension, see the 'Dedication' to *Minima Moralia*, where
Adorno argues that this focus reflects the germane site of contestation in
current contexts. In contemporary society, Hegel's emphasis on totality of
the system and his neglect of the individual subject, while an understandable response of a liberal political theory seeking to reconcile its emphasis
on individuation with claims about the harmonious working of the whole,
is ultimately misleading. Where philosophy has denigrated the individual,
the entire social apparatus now seeks to confirm that nullity. Fighting
against that nullity and recapturing the best promises of autonomy is a
central focus of Adorno's project. Adorno, *Minima Moralia: Reflections from
a Damaged Life*, trans. E.F.N. Jephcott (New York: Verso, 1978), 15–18.

28 Adorno, 'Education after Auschwitz,' 193.

29 In the Introduction to *Negative Dialectics*, Adorno combatively begins
his case that philosophy is the most germane form of practice. Directly
invoking Marx's *11th Thesis on Feurebach*, Adorno declares: 'Philosophy,

which once seemed obsolete, lives on because the moment to realize it was missed. The summary judgment that it had merely interpreted the world, that resignation had crippled it in itself, becomes a defeatism of reason after the attempt to change the world had miscarried.' A materialism disconnected from philosophy, disconnected from a thinking that could not be reduced to any preconceived ends – not even the ends of the revolution – devolves into a mere actionism. Such a materialism, in the end, could never reflect upon the moral content of its means and its aims. Without, however, the transformative promise of violent, instantaneous, or anarchic change, critical theory needs to be able to give some reason for its activity, some sense of how its work is germane to the struggle against the heteronomous injustice that it combats. For Adorno, the very articulation of this injustice and the alternative subjective position that it might make possible becomes the heroic necessity of its justification. Adorno, *Negative Dialectics*, 3.

30 Adorno, 'Education after Auschwitz,' 193.
31 '[H]is procedure is to isolate the factual moment, to conceive it, in Hegel's terminology, as abstractly as idealism conceives the synthetic moment. Hypostatized, it ceases to be a moment and comes to be what ontology in its pretext against the split between concept and entity would least like it to be: it becomes a thing.' Adorno, *Negative Dialectics*, 80.
32 Adorno, *Negative Dialectics*, 333–4.
33 For an elaboration of this assertion, see Adorno's 'Dedication' to *Minima Moralia*, 15–18.
34 'Myth is already enlightenment, and enlightenment reverts to mythology.' Horkheimer and Adorno, *Dialectic of Enlightenment*, xviii. For a treatment of the dialectical implications of this statement, see Andrew Biro, *Denaturalizing Ecological Politics: Alienation from Rousseau to the Frankfurt School and Beyond* (Toronto: University of Toronto Press, 2005), 118–29.
35 Theodor W. Adorno, 'Free Time,' in *Critical Models: Interventions and Catchwords*, trans. Henry W. Pickford (New York: Columbia University Press, 1998), 168.
36 Ibid., 170.
37 Ibid.
38 Ibid.
39 Theodor W. Adorno, 'Perennial Fashion – Jazz,' in *Prisms*, trans. Samuel Weber and Shierry Weber (Cambridge, MA: MIT Press, 1997), 123.
40 Theodor W. Adorno, 'Television as Ideology,' in *Critical Models: Interventions and Catchwords*, trans. Henry W. Pickford (New York: Columbia University Press, 1998), 59.

41 Adorno, 'Education after Auschwitz,' 200.

42 Ibid., 201.

43 Ibid.

44 'It [Negative Dialectics] attempts by means of logical consistency to substitute for the unity principle, and for the paramountcy of the supra-ordinated concept, the idea of what would be outside the sway of such unity. To see the strength of the subject to break through the fallacy of constitutive subjectivity – this is what the author felt to be his task ever since he came to trust his own mental impulses.' Adorno, *Negative Dialectics*, xx.

45 Adorno, *Minima Moralia*, 78.

46 Ibid., 79.

47 Ibid.

48 Ibid.

49 Ibid.

50 Within our world of hyperproduction and hyperconsumption, society begins to fetishize the 'new' in a way that prepares the ground for fascism. The speed of the world, the ongoing demand for production and public presentation, disintegrates our subjective integrity, leaving us homeless, insecure, alienated. The same forces of neoliberal capitalism that emphasize individualism are at the same time de-emphasizing social connectivity in terms of everything from housing to culture. The individuality that is promised by the totality thus provides the basis of disconnection, fear, and loneliness that underwrites a desire for the deindividualizing force of the collective. 'If one does not take part, and that means, if one does not swim bodily in the human stream, one fears, as when delaying too long to join a totalitarian party, missing the bus and bringing on oneself the vengeance of the collective.' And the feeling of fear, commingled with the longing for home and security, act as an inchoate motivating force in our lives, driving us inexorably toward our totalitarian conclusion as subjects without subjectivity, lacking the integrity of autonomy: 'The unconscious interventions which, beyond thought processes, attune individual existence to historical rhythms, sense the approach of the collectivization of the world.' Adorno, *Minima Moralia*, 139.

At a different point in *Minima Moralia*, Adorno has found indications of this perverse rush toward the 'new' as the rush toward a fascist destiny in the imagery of modern literature, such as the figure of the novel in Poe's image of maelstrom and Baudelaire's 'the depths of the unknown.' Adorno, *Minima Moralia*, 235–8.

51 For one such consideration, see Donald Burke's chapter in this volume.

52 Romand Coles, *Rethinking Generosity: Critical Theory and the Politics of Cari-*

tas (Ithaca: Cornell University Press, 1997), 83. Samir Gandesha also makes
this connection between Adorno's and Levinas's thinking; Gandesha,
'Leaving Home: On Adorno and Heidegger,' in *The Cambridge Companion
to Adorno* (Cambridge: Cambridge University Press, 2004), 122.
53 Adorno, *Negative Dialectics*, 52.
54 Ibid., 53.
55 Ibid., 54.

BIBLIOGRAPHY

Adorno, Theodor W. 'Education after Auschwitz.' In *Critical Models: Interven-
tions and Catchwords*, translated by Henry W. Pickford. New York: Columbia
University Press, 1998.
– 'Free Time.' In *Critical Models: Interventions and Catchwords*, translated by
Henry W. Pickford. New York: Columbia University Press, 1998.
– *Minima Moralia: Reflections from a Damaged Life*, translated by E.F.N. Jephcott.
New York: Verso, 1978.
– *Negative Dialectics*. New York: Continuum, 2004.
– 'On Subject and Object.' In *Critical Models: Interventions and Catchwords*,
translated by Henry W. Pickford. New York: Columbia University Press,
1998.
– 'Perennial Fashion – Jazz.' In *Prisms*, translated by Samuel Weber and
Shierry Weber. Cambridge, MA: MIT Press, 1997.
– 'Resignation.' In *Critical Models: Interventions and Catchwords*, translated by
Henry W. Pickford. New York: Columbia University Press, 1998.
– 'Television as Ideology.' In *Critical Models: Interventions and Catchwords*,
translated by Henry W. Pickford. New York: Columbia University Press,
1998.
Bauer, Karin. *Adorno's Nietzschean Narratives: Critiques of Ideology, Readings of
Wagner*. Albany: SUNY Press, 1999.
Becker, Michael, and Stephen Gamboa. 'Testify! Eco-Defense and the Politics
of Violence.' *Green Theory and Praxis: Journal of Ecopedagogy* 3, no. 1 (2007).
Best, Steven, and Anthony J. Nocella, eds. *Igniting a Revolution: Voices in De-
fense of the Earth*. Oakland: AK, 2006.
Biro, Andrew. *Denaturalizing Ecological Politics: Alienation from Rousseau to the
Frankfurt School and Beyond*. Toronto: University of Toronto Press, 2005.
Butler, Judith. *Subjects of Desire: Hegelian Reflections in Twentieth Century France*.
New York: Columbia University Press, 1987.
Coles, Romand. *Rethinking Generosity: Critical Theory and the Politics of Caritas*.
Ithaca: Cornell University Press, 1997.

Connolly, William. *Capitalism and Christianity, American Style*. Durham: Duke University Press, 2008.

– *The Ethos of Pluralization*. Minneapolis: University of Minnesota Press, 1995.

– *Neuropolitics: Thinking, Culture, Speed*. Minneapolis: University of Minnesota Press, 2002.

– *Pluralism*. Durham: Duke University Press, 2005.

Foreman, David. *Rewilding North America: A Vision for Conservation in the 21st Century*. Washington: Island, 2004.

Foucault, Michel. 'What Is Enlightenment?' In *Ethics: Subjectivity, and Truth*, edited by Paul Rabinow, translated by Robert Hurley and others. New York: New Press, 1997.

Gandesha, Samir. 'Leaving Home: On Adorno and Heidegger.' In *The Cambridge Companion to Adorno*. Edited by Tom Huhn. Cambridge: Cambridge University Press, 2004.

Habermas, Jürgen. *The Philosophical Discourse of Modernity: Twelve Lectures*. Translated by Frederick Lawrence. Cambridge, MA: MIT Press, 1990.

Horkheimer, Max. *Critique of Instrumental Reason*. New York: Seabury, 1974.

Horkheimer, Max, and Theodor Adorno. *Dialectic of Enlightenment: Philosophical Fragments*. Edited by Gunzelin Schmid Noerr, translated by Edmund Jephcott. Stanford: Stanford University Press, 2002.

Hullot-Kentor, Robert. Translator's introduction to *Aesthetic Theory*, by Theodor W. Adorno. Minneapolis: University of Minnesota Press, 1997.

Jarvis, Simon. 'Adorno, Marx, Materialism.' In *The Cambridge Companion to Adorno*. Edited by Tom Huhn. Cambridge: Cambridge University Press, 2004.

Lipscomb, Michael E. 'The Theory of Communicative Action and the Aesthetic Moment: Jürgen Habermas and the Neo-Nietzschean Challenge.' *New German Critique* 86 (Spring–Summer 2002): 135–58.

Nealon, Jeff. 'Maximum Immoralia? Speed and Slowness in Adorno's *Minima Moralia*.' *Theory and Event* 4, no. 3 (2000).

Roberts, Paul. *The End of Oil: On the Edge of a Perilous New World*. New York: Mariner, 2005.

Sagoff, Mark. *The Economy of the Earth*. New York: Cambridge University Press, 1988.

White, Stephen K. *Sustaining Affirmation: The Strengths of Weak Ontology*. Princeton: Princeton University Press, 2000.

Wilson, Edward O. *The Future of Life*. New York: Vintage, 2002.

12 Towards a Critique of Post-Human Reason: Revisiting 'Nature' and 'Humanity' in Horkheimer's 'The Concept of Man'*

In this study of critical ecology, I revisit the Frankfurt School and critically examine 'the concept of man' as it was articulated in the analytical interventions of Max Horkheimer. I make this move because men and women still desire, as Horkheimer asserts, 'to draw conclusions for political action from the critical theory' first articulated in essays in the *Zeitschrift für Sozialforschung*.[1] Those essays, however, appeared decades ago, so we must bear in mind our own responsibility for how we arrive at political conclusions today. As Horkheimer warns, a 'thoughtless and dogmatic application of the critical theory to practice in changed historical circumstances can only accelerate the very process which the theory aimed at denouncing.' His warning should be heeded.[2]

When speaking of critical ecology, there are dangers in dogmatically mapping the Frankfurt School critique onto today's changed historical circumstances. Still, the increasingly common fixation on 'the post-human'[3] in today's high-tech economy and society – as inevitable, empowering, even desirable – opens those of us who are intent today on advancing effective political change, to charges of a thoughtlessness beyond belief if we make no effort at all toward critique. These techno-science-driven developments have intrigued me for years, especially with regard to the politics, or 'subpolitics,' implied by cyborg subjectivity or post-human identity in planetarian eco-managerialism, digitized informationalization, and commercial bioengineering.[4] The challenge here is to avoid the threat of dehumanization or subhumanization that rests undetected in the processes of post-humanization. Whether it is cybertheorists pushing the idea of bodies-in-code, networked subjectivity, and power to the computing platform protocols; or Earth Firsters' calls to 'Return to the Pleistocene'; Animal Liberation Front activists privileging of white lab rats' lives over those of people; or eco-anarchists' desire to embrace the wild in whatever form, all of these developments pose the prospect that we will soon be stumbling down the path of dehumanization. These adverse outcomes must be resisted, because far too much ecological criticism and post-humanist thought is easily adapted to propping up the existing disorder of everyday life.[5]

Indeed, pious moralizing about 'the end of nature' or 'earth in the balance' typically leads to meliorist manifestos about becoming 'geo-green' on a planet where once again 'the world is flat.'[6] Green critics of this sort arguably have done little to alter today's oppressive political circumstances; indeed, many such critics today are busily reducing human beings to post-human subjects defined mainly by their carbon footprints or greenhouse gas emissions. The rich are allowed to remain rich by lessening their carbonized subjectivity; the poor are told to embrace the virtues of almost subhuman poverty when it has no carbon footprint. Again, Horkheimer should be heeded: 'To protect, preserve, and, where possible, extend the limited and ephemeral freedom of the individual in the face of the growing threat to it is far more urgent a task than to issue abstract denunciations of it or to endanger it by actions that have no hope of success.'[7] Yet few critical thinkers among today's ecologists hear his vital warnings about preserving individual liberty, opportunity, or rationality. And some excellent examples of the implications of ignoring his warnings about such inequalities are to be found in today's discourses and practices of 'the post-human.'

Fighting for new ways to free individuals, perhaps by putting the 'earth first,' is certainly important; but it is clear that Earth Firsters' resistance actions on this front have not enhanced individual freedom, nor have they succeeded in protecting the earth. The critical theory of Frankfurt School critics from the 1940s or 1950s is helpful in the here and now, because it encourages us to face this performative shortcoming – as Horkheimer suggested, 'to judge the so-called free world by its own concept of itself, to take a critical attitude towards it and yet stand by its ideas.'[8] As we develop a critical ecology for the present that is grounded in today's dire circumstances, exploring what is meant by 'the concept of man' is one place to begin.[9]

On 'the Concept of Man' and Prior Passes at the Problem

This analysis tracks a lead from 'The Concept of Man' – one that was examined with eloquence in a critical essay by Max Horkheimer fifty years ago.[10] That essay is five decades old, yet it sets the stage for a critique of 'post-human reason' far more effectively than other contemporary efforts by the Frankfurt School. Recently, Jürgen Habermas has tried to follow this same trail in *The Future of Human Nature*. There he pokes at post-human concerns by asking, 'What is the good life?' as humanity faces designer embryology, cosmetic neurology, and pharmaceutical pediatrics at the start of life as well as genetic engineering, orthopedic robotics, and nutriceutical dietetics across the lifespan.[11] Habermas recognizes that developments in nanotech, informatics, genetics, and biotech all are placing 'human nature' in danger on many levels, but he seems only to rehearse commonplace ethical qualms and political concerns that have been expressed by many thinkers since the 1950s.

Habermas asserts that 'our own weal and woe arise in the context of a *particular* life history or a *unique* form of life.' For him, ethical considerations of human identity in today's rapidly shifting technological contexts must address 'how we should understand ourselves, who we are and want to be.'[12] Yet he never emerges from the snarled tangles of agency and identity to ask clearly who 'we' are and how 'we' should understand ourselves, nor does he articulate what 'we' want to be. This leaves us with the usual image of Habermas becoming this 'we,' accompanied by a few devotees who will stomach sitting through another unfocused disquisition about such vital matters without reaching closure. More significantly in this short book, Habermas pointedly asserts: 'The new technologies make a public discourse on the right understanding of cultural forms of life an urgent matter. And philosophers no longer have any good reasons for leaving such a dispute to biologists and engineers intoxicated by science fiction.'[13] Of course, many philosophers, from Lewis Mumford to Jean Baudrillard, from Michael Foucault to C.S. Lewis, and even from Herbert Marcuse to Murray Bookchin, had reached similar conclusions years before. More to the point, Horkheimer was working directly at this task by 1957.

Horkheimer's 'concept of man' essentially highlights the characteristics and values of 'man the concept' as gripped by the larger forces of post-humanizing operationality, instrumentality, or activity (forces that Habermas in his musings only vaguely depicts). Humanity, when placed in a certain scriptural economy, permits critical theory to outline the 'concept of man,' which 'can be dealt with as a unity' determined by some humanistic *ratio* that sees 'the concept itself' as what 'gives rise to a particular figure of history.'[14] Habermas usually privileges the communicative interactions spun forth by that history, but his recent reading of human nature only probes the physiological, somatic, and therapeutic realms in shaping this more technoscientific 'man of the concept.'

Habermas calls our attention briefly to how technical interventions in human reproduction, disease, and aging are lessening 'the element of natural uncontrollability' that has been essential for 'normative self-understanding.'[15] Nature always has provided a certain content and a fixed context for human thought and action. But as such thoughts and actions are set against an accelerating technological event horizon, they appear, intentionally and unintentionally, to sublate the content and context of nature in new technics that make nature more uncertain and unfixed.[16] Indeed, technified forms of life appear to be remapping, remaking, and remediating nature as well as human nature so rapidly and so thoroughly that human understanding now must resort to post-human tropes to disclose what is developing.[17]

Older understandings cannot now account for the concurrence of a lessened element of natural controllability (such as genetic engineering or medical technology) with the heightened *un*controllability of natural elements (such as global warming and resource overshoot). Very articulate warnings have been raised repeatedly to challenge scientists, owners, engineers, and bureaucrats over these developments, and those alerts coming from radical environmentalists are among the strongest and most persistent. The Frankfurt School project can be useful to those engaged in these urgent disputes over 'the right understanding' of 'the cultural forms of life' needed to navigate today's admixtures of greater predictability and unpredictability in ethico-political deliberation. Yet this context will remain an unstable amalgam of choices inasmuch as the seemingly predictable – such as nanoscale technologies and genetic engineering – will have many unforeseen and unpredictable consequences that further disrupt nature's pattern; and inasmuch as the apparently unpredictable – such as rapid resource depletion and global climate change – may soon have unanticipated or unintended regularities amid Nature's turbulence.[18]

Other Views of the Question

Habermas is to be applauded for his concern about 'the future of human nature.' Even so, we can only wonder whether he is merely restating the dangers in modernity that Horkheimer marked in *Critique of Instrumental Reason*. That is, 'the rule of freedom, once brought to pass, necessarily turns into its opposite: the automatizing of society and human behavior,'[19] even when – as critical ecologists often do – we seek refuge in nature and in forms of resistance rooted in environmental alternatives. Horkheimer foresaw that nature itself is being transformed by men and women, who are gripped so tightly by automatized social behaviour that the natural turns into another 'deceitful image of the supposedly authentic and real' – an image that leads men and women to believe they have 'insight into relations as they really are, by [their] awareness of the unity of all living things, and by the desire that everything should turn out right.'[20] Seized by such abstractions, automatized subjects can appear in images of a more ecological, natural, or sustainable authenticity. Horkheimer, in this regard, reminds us how often these constructs are nothing but 'an empty well from which those who cannot achieve their own private life, their own decisions, and inner power, fill up their dreams.'[21]

Horkheimer worries openly that whether their dreams are full of deep ecology, animal liberation, sustainable development, or green spirituality,[22] those who put earth first, who front for animal liberation, or who simply defend wildlife, will draw false solace from nature as 'the promising symbol of authentic reality' in order to fulfil 'the need that there be *being*.'[23] Plainly, he is questioning those who fetishize empty abstractions of being, authenticity, or nature, like Gabriel Marcel or Martin Heidegger. He contends that any belief, green or not, 'which declares the abstract concepts of being and man to be concrete reality depends for its existence on decadence in education.'[24]

Taken up by the supposed authenticity of nature, and convinced by fables of being as natural authenticity revitalizing abstract man, this decadence in education evinces itself whenever men and women 'turn attention away from the real totality with its injustice and from the diversified interaction, overt and covert, between society and individuals who are determined by society and determine it in turn.'[25] Theoretical reflection must help individuals attain liberation from social injustice and existential inauthenticity by tending to the particularity of such concrete but also contingent materialities.[26] Critical reasoning can attain this goal by undercutting and eliminating the instrumental reason of liberal social individuality, which – as Horkheimer observes – Hegel effectively indicted in his *Logic* and *Phenomenology of Mind*, for its surrender to 'the superstition of the isolated, independent being and the absolutization of independent experiences as well as of being and all that claims to be being.'[27]

A good case in point is deep ecology, whose proponents, who include Bill Devall and George Sessions, surrender willingly to such abstract mystifications. On the one hand, they fabricate a concept of man in which humans are lost souls beset by 'the dominant worldview of technocratic-industrial societies which regards humans as isolated and fundamentally separate from the rest of Nature.'[28] On the other hand, they espouse the merits of another concept of man, one that supposedly is cognizant that 'we may not need something new, but need to reawaken something very old, to reawaken our understanding of Earth wisdom.'[29] And they work their way to this conclusion by endorsing Gary Snyder's vague devotion to the 'real work' of 'being,'[30] whose existential qualities 'cannot be grasped intellectually but are ultimately experiential.'[31] This abstract man of experiential real work, however, is a self-defeating figure who eschews hard rational criticism and real material freedom in resorting to some blissed-out experiential being of nature itself. By hugging the experiential wild, the deep ecologist acts 'as though he were the one to avert the evil that lurks behind all out economic miracles, sounds like both a referral and an appeasement.'[32]

Here, critique could not be more correct. The deep ecologists first appease the totally administered society by whipping up their followers as social actors to either settle into a holistic green quietism or spin up into an ecotaging green rage.[33] 'Philosophers, sociologists, economists, and not least, the representatives of the economy and government,' as Horkheimer notes, tell everyone that 'everything depends on the individual.'[34] So too does deep ecology. Neither quietist philosophy nor monkey-wrenching politics, however, do much to stop environmental destruction, even though deep ecologists might get their followers in the news or perhaps ease their individual consciences a bit. Also, deep ecologists' weak acknowledgment of this abstract man only hangs all of the conflicts and crises of technocratic–industrial societies on the figure of 'man'; yet that notion 'no longer expresses the power of the subject who can resist the status quo, however heavily it may weigh upon him.'[35]

Both quietism and activism in these deep green manoeuvres by radical ecologists fail to reduce the physical and psychic suffering caused by environmental degradation, because the difficulties and insecurities of existence are 'fobbed off' with the conclusion that 'the important thing is personality' or with calls for 'models and examples and, all too easily, for leaders and fathers.'[36] The concept of man deployed by deep ecology springs from what Horkheimer would regard as 'the dark overtones of talk about being and from exaggerated, rootless ideas about supposed authenticity' rather than from a truly critical effort 'to understand the influential forces that shape and move men for good or for ill'[37] – forces such as spirituality, ethics, or the transcendent.

In trying to act effectively with radical self-awareness, we cannot dismiss the spiritual. Critical theory must retain a knowledge of theological traditions, their conflicted but still crucial grasp of 'human freedom and its conditionings' within 'the contradiction-filled whole which is body and spirit, and the interconnection between society and individual of which that whole is a part.'[38] No education is complete without a vision of the spiritual and the mundane. Their confluence in nature provides a key intersection to occupy politically and ethically. Moreover, a solid education allows for these productive tensions, since Horkheimer believed 'it is impossible to oppose falsity without falling prey to it, unless knowledge won by past and present generations is kept alive.'[39]

Regrettably, modernity's dangers are all too real here; they even tend to be increasing, because the productive negations made possible by 'personal views and convictions, and a general yet differentiated education are losing their usefulness' in the drift of so much inconclusive discourse and deadlocked democracy.[40] In their place, the empty rule of reason in automatized society, beset by decadent education and an abstract inauthenticity embedded in its mythos of being, dessicates the autonomous interiority Horkheimer saw as required for true *Bildung* with its associated 'joy of making personal decisions, of cultural development, and of the free exercise of imagination.'[41]

False fear of, and a false faith in, the individual weakens some strings in critical ecology. The individual either is reduced to a derivative and/ or integer of transnational production in the networked totality of administered society, as Gore or Friedman assert; or is the beautiful soul awaiting, if not yearning for, a return to the garden of nature, as Devall and Sessions claim. Long before post-structuralists and radical environmentalists were bringing forward 'man' to be pilloried for logocentrism, ethnocentrism, phallocentrism, and (ultimately) anthropocentrism, Horkheimer expressed major doubts. Does 'man,' as the rational master of nature, truly exist, and can the 'mankind' of today ever still 'stand for a theory of reason such as once was based on the unshakable belief that just world could be brought into existence'?[42]

In this vacuum, many of today's geo-greens float around with visions of a new natural capitalism.[43] Likewise, communitarian ecologists tout their imaginative return to nearly subhuman ecological simplicities, voicing second and third thoughts about Horkheimer's figure of man in their respective programs for a strange, individual-driven environmental transformation.[44] Our doubts should be more intense with regard to post-humanist schools of thinking that accede to easy (con)fusions of the natural and artificial as an always already given to a new environmental order on the earth, one that integrates its biospheres, technospheres, and cyberspheres into the new green model of terrestrial governmentality.[45]

Human Reason and Nature

A more critical ecology, one that would rest on the Frankfurt School's theoretical project, must probe into how scientific knowledge and technical acumen shape all ecological practices and environmental policies today. Since the nineteenth century, the development of instrumental knowledge and collective action around the thematics of 'ecology' has required a special politics of scientific knowledge – a politics capable of organizing rational collaboration around 'the concept of man' among many disciplinary discourses to the degree that those in authority, and those who resist authority, can track who knows what, where, when, how, and from whom with regard to environments, ecology, or nature, which are new social formations tied to environmentality.[46] All of these practices are entangled with the Enlightenment and its forms of rational subjectivity.[47] As Foucault notes, Kant in 'What is Enlightenment?' 'is looking for a difference: What difference does today introduce with regard to yesterday.'[48] Foucault saw Kant believing that a decisive difference arises for modern humanity, or 'Man,' when all come to realize 'knowing as empowering.' From the unfolding Enlightenment, Kant's assigned enlightenment is 'an instruction that one gives oneself and proposes to others. What, then, is this instruction? *Aude Sapere:* "dare to know," have the courage, the audacity to know.'[49]

Such daring, courage, and audacity are qualities that often are 'all too human,' and they are not found everywhere in equal measure: acquiring them takes a great many trials and quite considerable tribulations.[50] During the Enlightenment, Paul Henri d'Holbach in *The System of Nature* enjoined human beings to 'Let Man study this Nature, let him learn her laws, contemplate her energies.'[51] The general appeal to 'Man' by d'Holbach and Kant to study nature and master its laws and energies, however, raises a flag over 'the concept of man,' which Horkheimer closely interrogates. Does daring to know become a limited licence for only those few who are capable enough actually to learn these natural laws, overcome natural ignorance, and divert rational energies into nature? In modern economies, freedom for a few can soon lead to *unfreedom* for the many elsewhere, since the material demands of surpassing necessity for a few privileged humans probably will leave many of the rest at the threshold of accepting a lesser 'post-human'[52] condition.

In the current context, d'Holbach's invitation to study nature, to learn her laws, and to contemplate her energies fulfils Kant's evocation of modernity to fulfil 'enlightenment' by turning knowledge of, and power over, nature to the tasks of 'improvement.' Modern reason, in turn, rests on making improvements, but many forms of countermodernity supposedly spark doubts about, or only see injuries from, those who go about making such 'improvements.' Both modernity and countermodernity express 'attitude' and 'daring' by shaping an audacious 'era of history,' one during which having 'the courage to know' leads to different forms of post-humanity purely through the quest for greater rational knowledge. The scientific and technical experts needed for 'improvements' – or what nowadays is usually labelled endless 'development' – clearly stand in the vanguard of modernizing enlightenment because nature is to be improved to the point that it is now the setting, or even the raw material, for the making of post-human being.[53]

While they are adapted to the political agendas of the present, these permanent programs for improvement, along with this odd dialectic of enlightenment, infect many believers among the ecological resistance. These programs' viral force comes at 'the strange limits of human development,' or the ultimate excess (which Nietzsche foresaw) of how 'those who command and are independent' soon prove to suffer 'from a bad conscience' and then 'find it necessary to deceive themselves before they could command – as if they, too, merely obeyed' as they pose 'as the executors of more ancient or higher commands (of ancestors, the constitution, of right, the laws, or even of God).'[54] Technical expertise and moral probity supposedly allow those 'in the know' about the world's barbarous realities to frame who knows what, where, when, how, and from whom, as they make enlightened improvements in the systems of waste behind 'environment policy.' It follows that such quasi-aristocratic knowledge of the savvy few is rationalized as natural right, the rightful modern constitution, or the market's most right equilibrium.[55]

Civic awareness and unawareness, scientific knowledge and ignorance, therefore, never can be easily disentangled in any conventional environmental policy or resistant critical ecology. Their politics determine who is encircled by what, and how and why, in a world of ecological overshoot, shortage, and perhaps even collapse as the manufactured 'man of the concept' occupies and inhabits the 'nature of domination.' Here perhaps is where one of Nietzsche's notions of living 'beyond good and evil' arises in an era of post-human reason. As a result, too many face their future with only mystifications, such as 'sustainable development' or 'collaborative governance,' even while the material dynamics of inequality are spinning up the disturbing sites of sustainable degradation and directive design as the endpoints for post-human being amidst a planet beset by spreading brownfields, dying ecosystems, and changing climates.[56]

Post-Human Reason, Digitalization, and a Processed World

The full sweep of radical technicized change in contemporary economies and societies, as it compounds its effects in global time-space compression, is often attributed to even newer environments beyond 'the big outdoors' of nature – that is, environments inside 'the closed world' of the telematic technics for computer networks.[57] One intellectual response to seeing telematic technics emerging everywhere has been a foundational shift in some thinkers' philosophical anthropology. The remediation of cultural meaning and political power by such interactions in postmodernity is sometimes recast in terms approximating some sort of 'post-humanism' by examining the growing numbers of individuals living as much 'online' as 'offline.'

More than any other contemporary technology, digitalization reaffirms Ihab Hassan's anticipation of 'post-humanism.' Caught up in the online environments of the Internet, as digital beings whose agency expresses itself in photons or electrons, humans supposedly are becoming 'different.' Hassan asserts: 'We need to understand that the human form – including human desire and all its external representations may be changing radically ... Five hundred years of humanism may be coming to an end as humanism transforms itself into something we must helplessly call posthumanism.'[58] Hayles informs us that with nature conquered – or even gone and forgotten for many – these post-humans are busy at work and happy at play on the Net, their desires seeming to have found adequate expression in eBay, MySpace, Facebook, YouTube, Second Life, America Online, or just Google. For Hayles, that we have become post-human traces with virtual bodies can be attributed mainly to the remodernizing work of machine intelligence, social chaos, telematic networks, and decentred individuality.[59] Of course, these supposedly weightless electronic beings are in many ways among the more rapacious resource users on the planet.

Rushkoff typifies the root perspectives of many post-humanism proponents, who have cast computer-mediated communication, or the contested idea of cyberspace, as a new ontological standpoint: 'Now that PCs are linked through networks that cover the globe and beyond, many people spend real time out there in "cyberspace" – the territory of digital information. This apparently boundless universe of data breaks all of the rules of physical reality. People can interact regardless of time and location ... through new technologies such as virtual reality. All of this and more can happen in cyberspace.'[60]

In such rhetoric, technification becomes much more than the mere operational effects of apparatuses and agents and their interactivities; it mushrooms into fresh domains of absolute immanence, Hayles tells us, with their own network-rooted metanational rules of postmodern embodiment, extraterritorial engagement, and hyperreal enlightenment.[61] Because everything changes, including the old rules for cultural, economic, and political action, the fields of force and cognition structuring 'the concept of man' also loosen, and new post-human beings with their own special forms of association begin developing. Rushkoff sees these informatic individuals as 'the cyberians, who are characterized primarily by faith in their ability to consciously rechoose their own reality – to design their experience of life' with post-human bodies, presences, and mentalities.[62] The unawareness of real ecological degradation that accompanies this mindset is hard to ignore.

The cyberspaces upon, within, or around which Hayles rests her vision of post-humanity evolve into flexibly networked concretizations of an even more fluid and totally administered society. That there are discourses of post-humanities that struggle to find meaning in the contingency, factuality, or seriality of digitization follows from – as Horkheimer would argue – 'the meaning which accrued to every action in life from the thought of eternity' being eroded and then displaced 'by an absolutizing of the collective, into which the individual feels himself incorporated.'[63] Digitalization accelerates everyday life, exchange, and communication on orders of magnitude far exceeding those of Futurism's wildest dreams after the First World War, or Situationists' greatest fancies after the Second World War.

Instead of recognizing how these elaborate ensembles of electronic action are interoperating much more perniciously as cyberspatial modes of political economy, international relations, and cultural community for exploited human beings, Hayles argues that post-humanism brings people and machines to another existential – if not ethical – level of being. All must accept machines as being more than merely machines; all must accede that technoscience is now creating new subjectivity-formatting principles of the post-human for us. Oddly enough, it seems that post-human reason is (con)fusing instrumental and substantive rationality together. Hayles maintains that those who cling inflexibly to the ontopolitical writs of liberal humanist values will experience panic in technified virtual and actual environments, because they will immediately recognize the degree to which 'the system' itself, rather than some human master controller somewhere in a network sysops centre, finds ends–means solutions in these digital environments even while it self-valorizes its tasks. She invites us all to accept the post-human – to give up those fictive human selves, which we inherited from seventeenth- and eighteenth-century liberal 'state of nature' stories. That is, she invites us to enter into conscious covenants – corporeal and intellectual – as contractual equals in order to create civic order among ourselves. The prospect of living with – or even better, living *inside* – intelligent machines as desiring post-human bodies illuminated by the light of flickering signifiers is for Hayles a truly awesome promise. But while real, this set of beliefs is neither universal or universalizable. Whether it is affluent people living in Saint Augustine, Dubai, Sao Paulo, Davos, or Santa Barbara, what underpins the post-human 'life of the screen' is an immense environmental disaster rising out of severely distorted human lives and badly degraded ecosystems.

As an enthusiast of post-human rationality, Hayles suggests that humans have never been 'in control' of the emergent chaotic processes constituting most amalgams of nature and society found in environments and technologies, be these offline or online. Post-humanism does not need to refer to sci-fi fantasies to find truly post-human practices; it need merely assert that even today's neural networks, intelligent bots, and expert programs exercise judgment that is equal or even superior to human decision making and action taking when it comes to evaluating questions of instrumental ends–means and substantive values.

Of course, digitalization drives media convergence as well as time-space compression. Places of work, modes of leisure, and forms of order all are brought down to earth as 'devices' via 'iTouching' to the desktop; or they are pushed into laptops, crammed into notebooks, or reworked as personal digital assistants. Wireless mobile devices, or 'WMDs,' against and amidst people, are turning the wheels of post-humanization by means of mass digitalization. When and how these WMDs and 'the person' then start/stop, begin/end, exist/terminate fuzzes indefinitely into 'the post-human.' For post-human beings, then, 'escape to a slower-paced style of life is closed off,' and digitalization ensures, as Horkheimer wrote a half-century ago,

> the machinery of mass opinion – newspapers, radio, cinema, television – must provide guidance for men as they relax from their duties, and must carry for them the burden of all decisions not connected with their work. The very nature of each individual's work accustoms him to react ever more surely to signs, and signs are his guide in every situation. Men need directives, and their need increases the more they obey these directives; consequently they disaccustom themselves increasingly to spontaneous reactions. If the dream of machines doing men's work has now come true, it is also true that men are acting more and more like machines.[64]

Notwithstanding the delusions of digital self-determination that post-humanism fosters out there in the network, Horkheimer is anticipating that this post-human reason will be rooted in the buzz of bits. As nothing more than swirling swarms of ones-and-zeros simulating social and personal activity, post-humanity ironically shows how signs constitute dehumanizing normalization routines and why society evaporates into clouds of fragmented nodes.

The domination of nature, which worried Horkheimer, now crystallizes 'the Nature of domination' as it points toward how post-human reason, as humanity's first nature in the wild and as second nature in the machine, is being blended together by technified action and machinic thought to become a third nature on the Net. Artefacticity displaces facticity as intentional artifice captures and contains autochthonous existence. The once human root set of rational theory and intentional practice melds into post-human recursive sets of code and conduit, explanation and event, society and culture, control and chaos. Quite clearly, Horkheimer even now would maintain that 'mastery of Nature has not brought man to self-realization; on the contrary, the status quo continues to exert its objective compulsion.'[65]

Post-humanists, therefore, argue that by applying another kind of reason, artificial aggregates of animal and apparatus can enhance and expand what had been mere humanity's unaugmented awareness and unmediated embodiment. Hayles asserts that 'in this account, emergence replaces teleology; reflexive epistemology replaces objectivism; distributed cognition replaces autonomous will; embodiment replaces a body screen as a support system for the mind; and a dynamic partnership between humans and intelligent machines replaces the liberal humanist subject's manifest destiny to dominate and control nature.'[66] These chaotic complexities exist; even so, post-humanist principles plainly read like positive referrals to the dehumanizing performativity of integrated systems as well as another appeasement of the dynamic partnership of networks and people in 'friction-free capitalism' as it articulates post-human reason.

Post-human development is never 'friction-free.' In this regard, consider the materiality behind 'the concept of man,' which Horkheimer explored by tracking down 'the man of concept,' which itself echoes Lyotard's notion of performativity. For post-human ecologies, as Lyotard hints, 'economic powers have reached the point of imperiling the stability of the State through new forms of the circulation of capital that go by the generic name of *multinational corporations*'; furthermore, such new modes of revalorizing exchange 'imply that investment decisions have, at least in part, passed beyond the control of the nation-states.'[67] This raw political economy probably was not what Hayles envisioned; nevertheless, post-human corporate agents fit her definition of post-humanism as that condition in which no organism can be entirely differentiated from its environment, no self is separate from society, and no agency lacks structure. And these agents' powers are growing so pervasive that raw information, DNA, nanoscale tech, and culture code are all capable of being monetized. Here again, post-human reason (con)fuses instrumental and substantive rationality. Emergent knowledges framed as bits begin

circulating along the same lines as money, instead of for its 'educational' value or political (administrative, diplomatic, military) importance; the pertinent distinction would no longer be between knowledge and ignorance, but rather, as is the case with money, between 'payment knowledge' and 'investment knowledge' – in other words, between units of knowledge exchange in a daily maintenance framework (the reconstitution of the work force, 'survival') versus funds of knowledge dedicated to optimizing the performance of a project.[68]

By fabricating digital domains and then continuously working to master their telemetrical terrains, post-humans concretize in thought and action Lyotard's prognoses about 'the postmodern condition.' That is, 'knowledge in the form of an informational commodity indispensable to productive power is already, and will continue to be, a major – perhaps *the* major – stake in the worldwide competition for power.' Indeed, the struggle over bits transnationally perhaps illustrates how relentlessly the machinic residents of nation-states will need to tussle around while the post-human subjects of remediated artificial electronic environments make multinational corporate space for 'control of information, just as they battled in the past for control over territory, and afterwards for control of access to and exploitation of raw materials and cheap labor.'[69] Third nature rather than first nature will be the object of control. Mediations of post-human being work through rational data/information/knowledge constructs in accordance with familiar liberal humanist goals that drift just above their abstract being. The nature of domination here is plain and simple: information 'is and will be produced in order to be sold, it is and will be consumed in order to be valorized in a new production: in both cases, the goal is exchange.'[70]

In this regard, everything in society, the marketplace, and culture rests upon a rationality that

> is made conditional on performativity. The redefinition of the norms of life consists in enhancing the system's competence for power. That this is the case is particularly evident in the introduction of telematic technology: the technocrats see in telematics a promise of liberalization and enrichment in the interactions between interlocutors; but what makes this process attractive for them is that it will result in new tensions in the system, and these will lead to an improvement in its performativity.[71]

The torrent of funds that sustains digitized capital, and labour's battle to survive in such knowledge economies, are actually, in Hayles's view, a material basis for why 'the posthuman becomes us.' After excoriating stable societies and states for decades over their efforts to regulate, tax, and administer, transnational corporate authorities stumbled into cyberspace during their anti-government neoliberal campaigns in the 1970s and 1980s, only to find that its unstable network environments had perfectly anticipated the widespread acceptance of a mystified individual subjectivity that had been presumed to exist in the *mythos* of neoliberal market culture draped over the matrix of controls, codes, and commodities. Quite clearly, post-human networks resonate with, as Horkheimer argues, how much 'the greater man's power, the greater the tension between what is and what ought to be, between the existing situation and reason.'[72]

This close embrace of the post-human, therefore, is yet another marker of today's empty situational acceptance of reason. Here, Horkheimer would regard reason as having no status other than 'simply as a tool [in which] it is not only the business but the essential work of reason to find means for the goals one adopts at any given time.'[73] In a more totally administered world, among those who inhabit the cells and corridors of cybernetic normality, post-humanity is imagined to be the height of contemporary subjectivity. Digital beings are post-humanized agents attuned to accede 24/7 to electronic and machinic environments in which, Horkheimer would fear, 'progress imposes stricter limitations on life and regulates behavior more fully, imagination is replaced by purposive systematic procedures, active emotions by reliable reactions, and feeling by reason.'[74] While Hayles need not retain the idea of the soul – of conscience or transcendence – it is clear that for Horkheimer, this construction of post-human being would fail to 'keep alive the doubt which is a conscious element in serious thinking today.'[75]

Post-human being, it follows, is plainly a disposition for, or a representation of, or a reduction to, surrendering to new sites and structures for automatizing action in matrices of matrices shaping 'man's character.' Yet, as Horkheimer might argue, post-human reason directly 'mirrors the changes in a society which has not yet achieved peace with itself,' because the flexibilization, financialization, and fungibilization of individual life under neoliberalism leads to a society that 'is forced constantly to change its form and adapt to new conditions.'[76] Strangely, the post-human paens to pulses of laserlight switching on and off bits of code as determinate material praxis bring to a higher level of abstract technification the raw alienation that Adorno decried fifty years ago.

Reflecting on the mutually assured destruction of free society and liberated individuals in the anomic relations of contemporary corporate commerce in 'the free world,' Adorno made an observation that captures the essence of Hayles's post-human being:

> The isolated individual, the pure subject of self-preservation embodies the inner-most principle of society, but does so in unqualified contrast to society. The elements that are united in him, the elements that clash in him – his properties – are simultaneous elements of the social whole. The iso-

328   Critical Ecologies

lated individual is a monad in the strict sense, that is, it reflects the whole
with all of its contradictions but it is not aware of the whole.[77]

The properties of post-human being are those of rapid capitalist commerce at its neoliberal nadir mistaken as the freedoms of the electronic
frontier by the machinic monads of deluded individual clients linked
into occluded systems of servers. Of course, some elements of this social formation clash for the individual and for the whole; but these fragmented networks of post-human being with regard to their balance of
power and powerlessness actually realize a regimen of command, control, and communication far beyond what 'the state dictators dream of,'
as Horkheimer mused.[78]

Even if modern science has not attained full technical control over
nature, many suspect that it has sufficient power to force all of us to
recognize that human control over external environments, inner nature, and built environments approaches, if it does not already exceed,
a post-human condition. Whether one points to nuclear weapons, nanoscale technologies, genetic engineering, geophysical surveillance, or
applied bioinformatics, there now exists a real capability to transform,
or deform, human nature as well as non-human nature. A critique of
post-human reason – or a reconsideration of a (con)fused instrumental
and value rationality – in the context of today's conjuncture of events
must take into account, first, the ends and means used for creating
these post-human conditions for non-human nature; and second, the
command and control over the ethical engagement, social formation,
and political organization of post-human agents and structures. The
domination of nature engendered by attaining greater operational sophistication in the life, physical, and social sciences, remains according
to Adorno and Horkheimer the hallmark of modernity. Even so, for
Horkheimer, 'all of these developments are what they are now because
of deficiencies at earlier points in the process, and they have, of themselves the power to liberate as well as to fetter.' So, for critical theory
today it matters that 'perhaps an accurate grasp of what is false in the
situation will enable what is true and valid to force its way through.'[79]

(In)Conclusions: Continuous Critique?

Fifty years ago, when Horkheimer addressed 'the concept of man,' he
noted how contemporary philosophers were exploring 'the problem of
being as such [as] inseparable from the problem of man,' especially giv-

en that 'the doctrine of being as such arises [only after] the process of reflection' mounts a sustained effort 'to win insight into man.'[80] Asking about the concept of man, therefore, leads one to the man (or woman) of the concept, who always remains caught inextricably in particular social, political, and economic circumstances when critics or philosophers begin raising this more universal philosophical question. Ontological philosophy cannot escape historical materialities, and those limiting conditions turn any explorations of the concept of man into starkly ontopolitical events.

The classical German idealism that Horkheimer takes as his benchmark holds its metaphysical answers up to the critique of reason and reality, asking with Kant what can be known, what ought to be done, and what can be hoped for out this entire activity. For the critical theory of the Frankfurt School, one might claim faith in a transcendent world, clear judgment in the immanent world, and hopeful rational life. This faith would mediate between these two planes of being, animated by the ideas of the highest good, absolute justice, and effective action. In the service of these planes would be what can be hoped for, what must be done, and what can possibly be known by human beings.

Yet any exercise in critical philosophy on the themes of ontology is a challenge. It leads to the ground under, around, and for 'man'; and the concept of man consequently must seek the ground that 'supplies direction, in the endless quest for an image of man that will provide orientation and guidance.'[81] Such practices are unavoidably ontopolitical, and their ontopolitics often must test this ground of ontic finality with their critique of reason, a concept of man, and moral conscience. Upon such systems of truth, Horkheimer is certain that much depends: 'the difference between good and evil' as each critical thinker or agent 'rebels against the thought that the present state of reality is final and that undeserved misfortune and wrong-doing, open or hidden, and not the self-sacrificing deeds of men, are to have the last word.'[82] Thus, the critical theory of man and society should maintain that 'an essential role belongs to the idea of a moral order and the conception of a world in which human merit and happiness are not simply juxtaposed but necessarily connected and in which injustice has disappeared.'[83] In the 1950s this militant vision of the German Enlightenment might have created embarrassment, because ethical reflection by that time had sunk to levels of superficial glibness that all too well served positivistic projects of domination and/or existential excuses for resignation. Today's crises, however, are so sweeping that one must always push ontological reflection to remain faithful to its founding critical warrants, so that it too does not become prey to misuse, drift, or capitulation within the injustices of the existing order.

The 'domination of Nature' examined by Horkheimer and Adorno is important to reconsider, because third nature cooks its own 'Nature of domination' from recipes for performativity as domination. In turn, post-humanity constitutes its own fields of programmed, regulated, or technified operations in the always alreadyness of alienated agency. Following de Certeau, then, domination produces its own space – a 'Nature of domination' – as 'rational organization' sets to work to 'repress all the physical, mental and political pollutions that would compromise its networks of networks.'[84] This nature of domination can then substitute a 'now when,' or 'a synchronic system for the indeterminable and stubborn resistances offered by traditions,' using 'univocal scientific strategies, made possible by the flattening out of all the data in a plane projection.'[85] Finally, in de Certeau's reasoning, the nature of domination implied by global sets of technified activities behind 'the domination of Nature,' traces the workings of 'a *universal* and anonymous *subject*,' such as one caught up in the dominant paradigm of instrumental rationality who provides 'a way of conceiving and constructing space on the basis of a limited number of stable, isolatable, and interconnected properties.'[86] Thus the domination of nature is a concept sited, embedded in, or derived from strategic action by a strategic actor to materialize strategic sites for the nature of domination.[87]

In some measure, this highly engineered outcome is constantly being sought; yet as Ulrich Beck observes, it may be unattainable.[88] As this critical revisitation of 'the concept of man' indicates, some very definite material points about 'the domination of Nature' today must be remembered: economic abundance is being realized for some, but not everyone; control over Nature is becoming tangible, but not truly total; unintended consequences of instrumentally rational action are exposing the structural inequities of abundance, even while leaving many unsustainable practices in the exertion of this control; and the unanticipated rise of constant risk – both old familiar threats and new unknown dangers – is lessening the emancipatory promise made by the domination of nature, while leaving us with even newer perils as we coevolve under essentially post-human terms within the networks of machinic collectivities, non-human actants, engineered organisms, and degraded ecosystems constituting 'the Nature of domination.'[89]

With the dialectic of enlightenment, the wager to conquer nature by means of instrumental reason was won, but the payout has required all to embrace the consequent substantive rationality that threatens the concept of man.[90] We are constantly making the same bet, even while realizing that what is being paid out is not the payoff that first brought everyone to the game. Moreover, the game's probable ongoing benefits are as contested as its anticipated costs because the game changes itself, its players, the stakes, and its rules merely by triggering play.[91] Whether this is postmodernity, second modernity, third nature, or some other condition yet to be named but still being endured, it is unclear whether the dialectic of enlightenment easily, or even ever, will illuminate fully for us these deeper, darker details in the concept of man.

NOTES

* This paper draws from a larger book-length project still in progress, 'The Poverty of Practice,' and earlier arguments for a North American critical theory that I have been developing in *Alternatives* since 1995, *Capitalism Nature Socialism* since 2001, and *Telos* since 1983.

1 Max Horkheimer, *Critical Theory: Selected Essays*, ed. Matthew J. O'Connell and others (New York: Herder and Herder, 1972), v.

2 Ibid.

3 Ihab Hassan, 'Prometheus as Performer: Towards a Posthumanist Culture,' in *Performance in Modern Change*, ed. Michael Benamov and Charles Carmella (Madison: Coda, 1977); Katherine N. Hayles, *How We Became Posthuman: Virtual Bodies in Cybernetics, Literature, and Infromatics* (Chicago: University of Chicago Press, 1999).

4 Timothy W. Luke, 'Environmentalism as Globalization from Above and Below: Can World Watchers Truly Represent the Earth?' in *Confronting Globalization: Humanity, Justice, and the Renewal of Politics*, ed. Patrick Hayden and Ramsy El-Ojeili (New York: Palgrave Macmillan, 2005); 'Ideology and Globalization: From Globalism and Environmentalism to Ecoglobalism,' in *Rethinking Globalism*, ed. Manfred Steger (Lanham: Rowman and Littlefield, 2004).

5 Timothy W. Luke, 'Training Eco-Managerialists: Academic Environmental Studies as a Power/Knowledge Formation,' in *Living with Nature: Environmental Discourses as Cultural Politics*, ed. Frank Fischer and Maarten Hajer (Oxford: Oxford University Press, 1999).

6 Thomas Friedman, *The World Is Flat*, rev. ed. (New York: Farrar Strauss

Giroux, 2006); Al Gore, *An Inconvenient Truth: The Planetary Emergency of Global Warming and What We Can Do About It* (Emmaus: Rodale, 2006); Bill McKibben, *The End of Nature* (New York: Random House, 1990).

7 Horkheimer, *Critical Theory*, viii.

8 Ibid., ix.

9 Andrew Biro, *Denaturalizing Ecological Politics: Alienation from Rousseau to the Frankfurt School and Beyond* (Toronto: University of Toronto Press, 2005); Catriona Sandilands, *The Good-Natural Feminist: Ecofeminism and the Quest for Democracy* (Minneapolis: University of Minnesota Press, 1999); William Leiss, *The Domination of Nature* (Boston: Beacon, 1974).

10 Max Horkheimer, *Critique of Instrumental Reason* (New York: Seabury, 1974). In this essay, Horkheimer uses the term 'man' quite generically, and this chapter will follow his generic use without implying a gender bias.

11 Jürgen Habermas, *The Future of Human Nature* (Oxford: Oxford University Press, 2003), 1–5.

12 Ibid., 3.

13 Ibid., 15.

14 Michel de Certeau, *The Practice of Everyday Life* (Berkeley: University of California Press, 1988).

15 Habermas, *The Future of Human Nature*, 15.

16 Barry Commoner, *Making Peace with the Planet* (New York: Pantheon, 1990).

17 Timothy W. Luke, 'Codes, Collectives, and Commodities: Rethinking Global Cities as Metalogistical Spaces,' in *Global Cities: Cinema, Architecture, and Urbanism in a Global Age*, ed. Linda Krause and Patrice Petro (New Brunswick: Rutgers University Press, 2003).

18 Timothy W. Luke, 'Globalisierung als plantetarisches Oekomamangement: Eine Kritik globaler Biokomplexitaetsmodelle,' in *Welt-Raeume: Geschichte, Geographie und Globaliserung seit 1900*, ed. Iris Schroeder und Sabine Hoehler, (Frankfurt: Campus Verlag, 2005).

19 Horkheimer, *Critique of Instrumental Reason*, ix–x.

20 Ibid., 5.

21 Ibid., 6.

22 Timothy W. Luke, *Ecocritique: Contesting the Politics of Nature, Economy, and Culture* (Minneapolis: University of Minnesota Press, 1997).

23 Horkheimer, *Critique of Instrumental Reason*, 6; Gabriel Marcel, *Presence and Immortality* (Pittsburgh: Duquesne University Press, 1967), 139.

24 Horkheimer, *Critique of Instrumental Reason*, 7.

25 Ibid., 6.

26 Timothy W. Luke, *Capitalism, Democracy, and Ecology: Departing from Marx* (Urbana: University of Illinois Press, 1999).

27 Horkheimer, *Critique of Instrumental Reason*, 6–7.
28 Bill Devall and George Sessions, *Deep Ecology* (Salt Lake City: Peregrine Smith, 1983), 65.
29 Ibid., ix.
30 See, for example, Gary Snyder, *Turtle Island* (New York: New Directions, 1974).
31 Devall and Sessions, *Deep Ecology*, 67.
32 Horkheimer, *Critique of Instrumental Reason*, 5.
33 Arne Naess, *Ecology, Community, and Lifestyle: Outline of an Ecosophy* (New York: Cambridge University Press, 1989); Christopher Manes, *Green Rage: Radical Environmentalism and the Unmaking of Civilization* (Boston: Little, Brown, 1990).
34 Horkheimer, *Critique of Instrumental Reason*, 4.
35 Ibid.
36 Ibid., 5.
37 Ibid., 7.
38 Ibid.
39 Ibid.
40 Ibid., 13.
41 Ibid., 12.
42 Ibid., 4.
43 See Paul Hawken, Amory Lovins, and L. Hunter Lovins, *Natural Capitalism: The Next Industrial Revolution* (Boston: Little, Brown 1999); James C. Briden and Thomas E. Downing, *Managing the Earth: The Linacre Lectures* (Oxford: Oxford University Press, 2002); Frances Cairncross, *Costing the Earth* (Boston: Harvard Business School Press, 1992).
44 Doug Torgerson, *The Promise of Green Politics: Environmentalism and the Public Sphere* (Durham: Duke University Press, 1999).
45 See Timothy W. Luke, 'Cyborg Enchantments: Commodity Fetishism and Human/Machine Interactions,' *Strategies* 13, no. 1 (2000); *Capitalism, Democracy, and Ecology.*
46 Timothy W. Luke, '"Environmentality" as Green Governmentality,' in *Discourses of the Environment*, ed. Eric Darier (Oxford: Blackwell, 1999).
47 See Michel Foucault, *The Foucault Effect: Studies in Governmentality*, ed. Graham Burchell, Colin Gordon, and Peter Miller, trans. Colin Gordon, Leo Marshall, John Mepham, and Kate Soper (Chicago: University of Chicago Press, 1991).
48 Michel Foucault, *Power/Knowledge: Selected Interviews and Other Writings, 1972–1977*, ed. Colin Gordon (New York: Pantheon, 1984), 34.
49 Ibid., 34–5.

50 See Edmund Husserl, *The Crisis of European Science and Transcendental Phenomenology* (Evanston: Northwestern University Press, 1970).

51 Paul Henri d'Holbach, *The System of Nature* (Whitefish: Kessinger, 2004), 1.

52 See David Harvey, *Spaces of Global Capitalism: Towards a Theory of Uneven Geographical Development* (New York: Verso, 2005); Frederic Jameson, *Postmodernism, or the Cultural Logic of Late Capitalism* (Durham: Duke University Press, 1992); Don Ihde, *Technology and the Lifeworld: From Garden to Earth* (Bloomington: Indiana University Press, 1990).

53 See Kate Soper, *What Is Nature?* (Oxford: Blackwell, 1997).

54 Friederich Nietzsche, *Beyond Good and Evil: Prelude to a Philosophy of the Future* (New York: Random House, 1966), 10–11.

55 See Jean-François Lyotard, *The Postmodern Condition: A Report on Knowledge* (Minneapolis: University of Minnesota Press, 1989).

56 See Timothy W. Luke, 'The System of Sustainable Degradation,' *Capitalism Nature Socialism* 17, no. 1 (2006); 'Neither Sustainable nor Developmental: Reconsidering Sustainability in Development,' *Sustainable Development* 13, no. 4 (2005).

57 See David Harvey, *The Condition of Postmodernity* (Oxford: Blackwell, 1989).

58 Hassan, 'Prometheus as Performer,' 212.

59 See Michael Heim, *Virtual Realism* (Oxford: Oxford University Press, 1998); Sherry Turkle, *Life on the Screen: Identity in the Age of the Internet* (New York: Touchstone, 1997); Kevin Kelly, *Out of Control: The Rise of Neo-Biological Civilization* (Reading: Addison-Wesley, 1994).

60 Douglas Rushkoff, *Cyberia: Life in the Trenches of Hyperspace* (San Francisco: HarperCollins, 1994), 2.

61 See Hayles, *How We Became Posthuman.*

62 Rushkoff, *Cyberia,* 4.

63 Horkheimer, *Critique of Instrumental Reason,* 152.

64 Ibid., 26.

65 Ibid., 4.

66 Hayles, *How We Became Postmodern,* 288.

67 Lyotard, *The Postmodern Condition,* 5.

68 Ibid., 6.

69 Ibid., 5.

70 Ibid., 4.

71 Ibid., 64.

72 Horkheimer, *Critique of Instrumental Reason,* 29.

73 Ibid., vii.

74 Ibid., 60.

75 Ibid., 62.

76 Ibid., 27.
77 Theodor Adorno, 'Zum *Verhältnis* von Soziologie und Psychologie,' in *Sociologica: Reden und Vorträge*, vol. 1, ed. Max Horkheimer und Theodor Adorno (Frankfurt: Europäische Verlaganstalt, 1995), 21.
78 Horkheimer, *Critique of Instrumental Reason*, 27.
79 Ibid., 33.
80 Ibid., 1.
81 Ibid., 4.
82 Ibid., 2.
83 Ibid., 3.
84 De Certeau, *The Practice of Everyday Life*, 94.
85 Ibid.
86 Ibid.
87 Ibid., xix.
88 See Ulrich Beck, *The Risk Society* (London: Sage, 1992).
89 On these points, see James O'Connor, 'Capitalism, Nature, Socialism: A Theoretical Introduction,' *Capitalism, Nature, Socialism* 1 (1988); Timothy W. Luke, 'Informationalism and Ecology,' *Telos* 56 (1983); 'Radical Ecology and the Crisis of Political Economy,' *Telos* 46 (1980–1).
90 Max Horkheimer and Theodor Adorno, *Dialectic of Enlightenment*, trans. John Cumming (New York: Seabury, 1972).
91 Timothy W. Luke, 'Liberal Society and Cyborg Subjectivity: The Political of Environments, Bodies, and Nature,' *Alternatives: A Journal of World Policy* · 21, no. 1 (1996).

BIBLIOGRAPHY

Adorno, Theodor W. 'Zum *Verhältnis* von Soziologie und Psychologie.' In *Sociologica: Reden und Vorträge*, vol. 1, edited by Max Horkheimer und Theodor Adorno. Frankfurt: Europäische Verlaganstalt, 1995.
Beck, Ulrich. *The Risk Society*. London: Sage, 1992.
Biro, Andrew. *Denaturalizing Ecological Politics: Alienation from Rousseau to the Frankfurt School and Beyond*. Toronto: University of Toronto Press, 2005.
Briden, James C., and Thomas E. Downing. *Managing the Earth: The Linacre Lectures*. Oxford: Oxford University Press, 2002.
Cairncross, Frances. *Costing the Earth*. Boston: Harvard Business School Press, 1992.
Commoner, Barry. *Making Peace with the Planet*. New York: Pantheon, 1990.
de Certeau, Michel. *The Practice of Everyday Life*. Berkeley: University of California Press, 1988.

Devall, Bill, and George Sessions. *Deep Ecology*. Salt Lake City: Peregrine Smith, 1983.

d'Holbach, Paul Henri. *The System of Nature*. Whitefish: Kessinger, 2004.

Foucault, Michel. *The Foucault Effect: Studies in Governmentality*. Edited by Graham Burchell, Colin Gordon, and Peter Miller, translated by Colin Gordon, Leo Marshall, John Mepham, and Kate Soper. Chicago: University of Chicago Press, 1991.

– *Power/Knowledge: Selected Interviews and Other Writings, 1972–1977*. Edited by Colin Gordon. New York: Pantheon, 1984.

Friedman, Thomas. *The World Is Flat*, rev. ed. New York: Farrar Strauss Giroux, 2006.

Gore, Al. *An Inconvenient Truth: The Planetary Emergency of Global Warming and What We Can Do about It*. Emmaus: Rodale, 2006.

Habermas, Jürgen. *The Future of Human Nature*. Oxford: Oxford University Press, 2003.

Harvey, David. *The Condition of Postmodernity*. Oxford: Blackwell, 1989.

– *Spaces of Global Capitalism: Towards a Theory of Uneven Geographical Development*. New York: Verso, 2005.

Hassan, Ihab. 'Prometheus as Performer: Towards a Posthumanist Culture.' In *Performance in Modern Change*, edited by Michael Benamov and Charles Carmella. Madison: Coda, 1977.

Hawken, Paul, Amory Lovins, and L. Hunter Lovins. *Natural Capitalism: The Next Industrial Revolution*. Boston: Little, Brown, 1999.

Hayles, Katherine N. *How We Became Posthuman: Virtual Bodies in Cybernetics, Literature, and Informatics*. Chicago: University of Chicago Press, 1999.

Heim, Michael. *Virtual Realism*. Oxford: Oxford University Press, 1998.

Horkheimer, Max. *Critical Theory: Selected Essays*. Translated by Matthew J. O'Connell and others. New York: Herder and Herder, 1972.

– *Critique of Instrumental Reason*. New York: Seabury, 1974.

Horkheimer, Max, and Theodor Adorno. *Dialectic of Enlightenment*. Translated by John Cumming. New York: Seabury, 1972.

Husserl, Edmund. *The Crisis of European Science and Transcendental Phenomenology*. Evanston: Northwestern University Press, 1970.

Ihde, Don. *Technology and the Lifeworld: From Garden to Earth*. Bloomington: Indiana University Press, 1990.

Jameson, Fredric. *Postmodernism, or the Cultural Logic of Late Capitalism*. Durham: Duke University Press, 1992.

Kelly, Kevin. *Out of Control: The Rise of Neo-Biological Civilization*. Reading: Addison-Wesley, 1994.

Leiss, William. *The Domination of Nature*. Boston: Beacon, 1974.
Luke, Timothy W. *Capitalism, Democracy, and Ecology: Departing from Marx.* Urbana: University of Illinois Press, 1999.
– 'Codes, Collectives, and Commodities: Rethinking Global Cities as Metalogistical Spaces.' In *Global Cities: Cinema, Architecture, and Urbanism in a Global Age*, edited by Linda Krause and Patrice Petro, 157–74. New Brunswick: Rutgers University Press, 2003.
– 'Cyborg Enchantments: Commodity Fetishism and Human/Machine Interactions.' *Strategies* 13, no. 1 (2000): 39–62.
– *Ecocritique: Contesting the Politics of Nature, Economy, and Culture.* Minneapolis: University of Minnesota Press, 1997.
– 'Environmentalism as Globalization from Above and Below: Can World Watchers Truly Represent the Earth?' In *Confronting Globalization: Humanity, Justice and the Renewal of Politics*, edited by Patrick Hayden and Ramsy El-Ojeili, 154–71. New York: Palgrave Macmillan, 2005.
– '"Environmentality" as Green Governmentality.' In *Discourses of the Environment*, edited by Eric Darier, 121–51. Oxford: Blackwell, 1999.
– 'Globalisierung als planetarisches Oekomamangement: Eine Kritik globaler Biokomplexitaetsmodelle.' In *Welt-Raeume: Geschichte, Geographie, und Globaliserung seit 1900*, edited by Iris Schroeder und Sabine Hoehler, 282–302. Frankfurt: Campus Verlag, 2005.
– 'Ideology and Globalization: From Globalism and Environmentalism to Ecoglobalism.' In *Rethinking Globalism*, edited by Manfred Steger, 67–77. Lanham: Rowman and Littlefield, 2004.
– 'Informationalism and Ecology.' *Telos* 56 (Summer 1983): 59–73.
– 'Liberal Society and Cyborg Subjectivity: The Political of Environments, Bodies, and Nature.' *Alternatives: A Journal of World Policy* 21, no. 1 (1996): 1–30.
– 'Neither Sustainable nor Developmental: Reconsidering Sustainability in Development.' *Sustainable Development* 13, no. 4 (October 2005): 228–38.
– 'Radical Ecology and the Crisis of Political Economy.' *Telos* 46 (Winter 1980–1): 63–72.
– 'The System of Sustainable Degradation.' *Capitalism, Nature, Socialism* 17, no. 1 (March 2006): 99–112.
– 'Training Eco-Managerialists: Academic Environmental Studies as a Power/Knowledge Formation.' In *Living with Nature: Environmental Discourses as Cultural Politics*, edited by Frank Fischer and Maarten Hajer, 103–120. Oxford: Oxford University Press, 1999.
Lyotard, Jean-François. *The Postmodern Condition: A Report on Knowledge*. Minneapolis: University of Minnesota Press, 1989.

Manes, Christopher. *Green Rage: Radical Environmentalism and the Unmaking of Civilization*. Boston: Little, Brown, 1990.

Marcel, Gabriel. *Presence and Immortality*. Pittsburgh: Duquesne University Press, 1967.

McKibben, Bill. *The End of Nature*. New York: Random House, 1990.

Naess, Arne. *Ecology, Community, and Lifestyle: Outline of an Ecosophy*. New York: Cambridge University Press, 1989.

Nietzsche, Friedrich. *Beyond Good and Evil: Prelude to a Philosophy of the Future*. New York: Random House, 1966.

O'Connor, James. 'Capitalism, Nature, Socialism: A Theoretical Introduction.' *Capitalism, Nature, Socialism* 1 (Fall 1988): 11–39.

Rushkoff, Douglas. *Cyberia: Life in the Trenches of Hyperspace*. San Francisco: HarperCollins, 1994.

Sandilands, Catriona. *The Good-Natural Feminist: Ecofeminism and the Quest for Democracy*. Minneapolis: University of Minnesota Press, 1999.

Snyder, Gary. *Turtle Island*. New York: New Directions, 1974.

Soper, Kate. *What Is Nature?* Oxford: Blackwell, 1997.

Torgerson, Doug. *The Promise of Green Politics: Environmentalism and the Public Sphere*. Durham: Duke University Press, 1999.

Turkle, Sherry. *Life on the Screen: Identity in the Age of the Internet*. New York: Touchstone, 1997.

Afterword:
The Liberation of Nature?

ANDREW FEENBERG

Walter Benjamin's eleventh thesis on the philosophy of history contrasts exploitative labour with liberating labour. The contrast is familiar except that Benjamin refers not to the exploitation and liberation of human beings but to that of nature. He does not hesitate to give this unexpected application of Marxist categories its full utopian force. He writes that the Social Democratic

> conception of labor amounts to the exploitation of nature, which with naïve complacency is contrasted with the exploitation of the proletariat. Compared with this positivistic conception, Fourier's fantasies, which have so often been ridiculed, prove to be surprisingly sound. According to Fourier, as a result of efficient cooperative labor, four moons would illuminate the earthly night, the ice would recede from the poles, sea water would no longer taste salty, and beasts of prey would do man's bidding. All this illustrates a kind of labor which, far from exploiting nature, is capable of delivering her of the creations which lie dormant in her womb as potentials.[1]

The early Frankfurt School placed nature more and more at the centre of its reflections as it lost hope in a socialist transformation. The publication of *Dialectic of Enlightenment* marked a turning point. Thereafter the question of nature played a major role in the work of Adorno, Horkheimer, and Marcuse, only to disappear once Habermas and his followers again focused on the possibilities of progressive social change.

It seems to be a question of the priority of human relations versus the relation of human beings and things. Adorno says something like this in 'On Subject and Object.' He criticizes as 'shameful' the concept of communication as 'imparting information between subjects' 'because it betrays what is best – the potential for agreement between human beings and things.' This is peculiar: in what sense can human beings and things 'agree'? Adorno goes on to explain that 'peace is the state of differentiation without domination, with the differentiated participating in each other.'[2] So, the sought after agreement is to be understood as a kind of mutual participation.

These passages occur in a speculative ellipsis that Adorno 'allows' himself exceptionally. He moves on quickly to other subjects without explaining properly what he means. When scattered passages throughout his work are pulled together, certain ideas come through that help interpret his intent. Nature and history are not independent of each other and must be understood in their inseparable connection. Human beings are not merely spectators on nature; as natural beings, they themselves belong to it. In modern societies a historically sedimented 'second nature' of dead conventions and institutions occupies the place of mythic fate that unmastered nature once signified for primitive peoples. Natural beauty, especially where human artefacts have been harmoniously integrated with it, prefigures a redemptive future in which the 'wounds' of nature will be healed and life will flourish in peace. Nature, in one of Adorno's interpretations, thus holds a utopian promise.[3]

Adorno never related this promise to environmental issues, which only entered postwar public discussion toward the end of his life. However, Marcuse did address ecology explicitly in terms that appear to flow directly from Adorno's elliptical remarks. As usual, Marcuse enthusiastically breaches Adorno's self-imposed limits, and this makes for a more explicit and decisive presentation. In a 1972 speech he wrote that nature 'has a dimension *beyond* labor, a symbol of beauty, of tranquility, of a non-repressive order.' Yet this nature is being destroyed by capitalism. 'The power of capital is extended over the space for release and escape represented by nature. This is the totalitarian tendency of monopoly capitalism: in nature, the individual must find only a repetition of his own society; a dangerous dimension of escape and contestation must be closed off.'[4] The revolution must therefore liberate not only human beings but nature as well. I want to discuss this notion of a 'liberation of nature' here in the conclusion to this book and consider briefly how this aspect of the Frankfurt School's reflections might be continued today.

Marcuse knew that the utopian conception of nature he shared with

Adorno appears remarkably unscientific, even regressive. Yet these were resolutely modern thinkers who resisted theoretical backsliding. They were not looking to re-enchant nature or to merge with it in a romantic unity. Yet Marcuse linked his argument directly to several surprising comments in Adorno's *Aesthetic Theory* that appear to contradict the modern view. There Adorno had claimed that human beings are called 'to help nature "to open its eyes," to help it "on the poor earth to become what perhaps it would like to be."'[5] Marcuse sought a non-teleological interpretation of such notions, a third term beyond premodern essentialism and the idealistic kitsch of a 'new age.'

He found his answer in an aspect of Kant's aesthetics, the definition of natural beauty as 'purposiveness without purpose.' Nature exhibits characteristics of an object constructed to achieve a purpose without actually having been so constructed and without actually having a purpose. Marcuse interpreted purposiveness in this sense as a purely formal property of self-organizing objects. It arises from freedom, from the self-production of the object according to its own intrinsic nature, its growth potential. Presumably, we can distinguish the freely developed living thing from the mutilated product of a constricted growth process. The distinction manifests itself in formal properties we associate with health and beauty. Here is a non-teleological concept that can support a normative understanding of nature and its tendencies.

But exactly how is this supposed to work? Adorno considered this idea and drew utopian conclusions from it but stopped short of accepting its literal truth. He wrote that natural beauty 'recollects a world without domination, one that probably never existed.'[6] Natural beauty hints at the idea of freedom that corresponds to such a world. But, Adorno concluded, nature is in reality a realm of *un*freedom, so the aesthetic appreciation of nature is deceptive, a suggestive misapprehension.

Marcuse took a different tack. Natural beauty and its purposeless purposiveness express the flourishing of life. This is a value that humans share in different ways with all of life. But unlike other living things, humans are able to conceive the potentialities of things and of themselves. They can, in Marx's astonishing phrase, 'form things in accordance with the laws of beauty.'[7]

Marcuse developed Marx's brief mention of beauty as an objective characteristic of the real – it has 'laws' – in terms of a quasi-Freudian theory of the erotic. He argued that the erotic impulse is directed toward the preservation and furtherance of life. That impulse is not merely an instinct or drive; rather, it operates in the sensuous encounter with the world that reveals it in its beauty, the objective correlate of the erotic. But this impulse is repressed by society, partially sublimated, partially confined to sexuality. The loss of immediate sensory access to the beautiful gives rise to art as a specialized enclave in which we perceive the trace of erotic life affirmation.

Marcuse argued that human beings can favour the life-enhancing forces in nature and bring about the harmonious coexistence of human and natural life. But he did not carry this argument to a naive 'biocentric' *reductio ad absurdum*. He recognized that human flourishing harms many other living things, but he believed that in favouring life insofar as possible, human beings also create a favourable environment for their own flourishing.

Concepts such as these have an intuitive appeal. It is obvious that strip mining wounds nature in Adorno's sense; by contrast, the architecture of Frank Lloyd Wright is far more compatible with the unfolding of the potentialities of its living setting. But is this more than a sentimental preference? 'Nature' in one form or another goes on regardless of what human beings feel and do. Why single out its flourishing around a renaissance palace neatly tucked into the landscape, or Wright's Falling Water? Nature 'flourishes' in a garbage can too, especially one uncollected for a week, but this is not the affirmation of life we recognize as normatively valid. Does this mean that our intuitive understanding of life affirmation is an arbitrary and subjective opinion without normative force? Not necessarily.

There is a difference between our intuitions and the counterexample insofar as the former seem to be rooted in our nature and are generally shared while the latter is a mere intellectual construction set up for the sake of argument. To call the multiplication of bacteria in a garbage can an example of flourishing is to mistake the emphatic meaning we normally give the term. What 'flourishes' is not simply a mass of cells but the realization of such values as vitality and grace through the free development of living things in which we recognize a certain family resemblance or affinity. The concept necessarily reflects the kind of being we are if it is to have any force at all. A garden or a child 'flourish'; bugs merely multiply.

Marcuse assumed this distinction in arguing that a liberated human 'sensibility' recognizes the 'existential ... truth in things, in nature.'[8] This 'truth' is existential in the sense that it is experiential rather than scientific. The fact that experience is always *our* experience and not that of an imaginary pure rationality means that its anthropocentric character is unsurpassable. But this does not refute its cognitive value. Rather, it is the condition of another kind of knowledge. Experience in this sense offers a non-scientific truth.

This truth is not just an idea but is 'existential,' manifest in the inherently normative character of experience itself. We do not perceive the world as scientific reason apprehends it, as a meaningless order of primary qualities in abstract space and time. The 'secondary qualities' belong essentially to the sensed world, and these include the objects of lived 'judgments' of good and bad, beautiful and ugly experienced directly in the act of sensation. According to Marcuse, a concrete 'libidinal' attachment to the world underlies this normative dimension of sensation. This attachment is historically variable, restricted by scarcity in the past, and suffering a peculiar reduction to sexuality in the present. Its full realization as a mode of presence awaits a liberated society.[9] Pleasure in beauty would then express a generally life affirming sensibility. Beauty would relate the given to its potentialities in sensation, rather than serving as a temporary escape from competitive strife.

In one of his last speeches, in 1979, Marcuse developed this conception in its implications for environmental struggle. He argued that ecological devastation is an effect of capitalist productivity against which the 'life instincts' rebel:

> What we have is a politicization of erotic energy. This, I suggest, is the distinguishing mark of the most radical movements today. These movements do not ... constitute a struggle to replace one power structure by another. Rather, these radical movements are existential revolts against an obsolete reality principle. They are a revolt carried by the mind and body of individuals themselves ... A revolt in which the whole organism, the very soul of the human being, becomes political. A revolt of the life instincts against organized and socialized destruction.[10]

Disgust and rage at the abuse of human beings is an 'aesthetic' expression of our sensitivity to the value of suppressed potentialities. It articulates that value at the existential level. At that level the subject does more than observe the given state of affairs; she participates in it vicariously. This is the other side of the coin of mutual participation in which Adorno found the meaning of peace. On Marcuse's account, participation is experienced as solidarity. A similar disgust and rage at harm to the environment would inspire the environment's less destructive appropriation within the human world. He argued that the emergence of such a sensibility in the New Left foreshadowed the possibility of a different relation to nature.

I believe that here we are at the core of what the early Frankfurt School can contribute to contemporary environmental debates. It has nothing to say about the important technical questions we now face, but it offers a unique approach to such issues in environmental philosophy as the value of nature. By reorienting the question around the normative dimensions of aesthetic experience of nature, it suggests a way of transcending the antinomy of objectivism and subjectivism, fact and value. On this basis it conceives a utopian vision of a life-affirming form of individuality and the corresponding politics and society. And a vision is certainly needed as modern societies head straight for environmental disaster along the old familiar paths of productionism and consumerism.

But we cannot conclude this discussion without also noting the limitations of this approach. I want to mention three of these limitations briefly. They have to do with the Frankfurt School's evaluation of the media and technology and its concept of experience.

The Frankfurt School is identified with a theory of media manipulation. It would be foolish to deny the partial truth of this very negative assessment of the media. Certainly, for men who witnessed Hitler's use of the techniques of modern propaganda, much of the contemporary reflection on the agency of shoppers and television viewers would have seemed ridiculous. But there are certainly problems with the Frankfurt School approach. The dismissal of all mass cultural products as pure expressions of capitalism not only smacks of mandarin elitism – a commonplace charge – but also makes for difficulties interpreting progressive movements.

As a result, there is a lack of mediation in Marcuse's theory of the new sensibility. He seems to have believed that the contrast between the potential and the reality of advanced societies is obvious and that the media are responsible for the widespread failure to recognize this fact. But even at the time he was writing, there were mass cultural products that stimulated the critical consciousness of the 1960s radicals. I can recall a veritable flowering of dystopianism, especially in the European cinema. Films such as La Dolce Vita and Alphaville denounced the technological society that was coming into being in the postwar world. A subversive counterculture was emerging around jazz, poetry, and folk music, and this counterculture gradually reached the mainstream.

What tensions within the mass culture opened the breach through which the New Left was able to march and grow? What are the similar tensions today that spread environmental awareness and prepare a response to the environmental crisis? Questions such as these require more nuanced media theories. New approaches have been proposed by theorists who draw from the Frankfurt School for inspiration without following slavishly in its footsteps.[11]

Next consider the question of technology. The atmosphere surrounding the critique of technology in Adorno, Horkheimer, and Marcuse is heavy with dystopian *Angst*. But they were not technophobes. Rather, they blamed capitalism for the disastrous development of technology. There are occasional passages in the works of Adorno and Horkheimer in which they hint at the possibility of a non-dominating technology. For example, Adorno writes:

> It is not technology which is calamitous, but its entanglement with societal conditions in which it is fettered … Considerations of the interests of profit and dominance have channeled technical development: by now it coincides fatally with the needs of control. Not by accident has the invention of means of destruction become the prototype of the new quality of technology. By contrast, those of its potentials which diverge from dominance, centralism and violence against nature, and which might well allow much of the damage done literally and figuratively by technology to be healed, have withered.[12]

Similar ideas were given fuller development by Marcuse, particularly in *One-Dimensional Man*. There Marcuse called for a new science and technology of liberation based on a new mode of experience of nature in a free society. He offered interesting suggestions concerning the role of the imagination in the reconstruction of technological rationality and the technical base. But none of these positive suggestions were elaborated to the point where they carry conviction. The implausibility of the positive in the Frankfurt School's evaluation of technology simply reinforces the impression that only its negative critique was seriously meant.

Marcuse claimed that the problem with modern technology stemmed from its value neutrality. He argued that the formalistic, quantitative rationality of modern science was incompatible with the concept of potentiality or essence. Without some such concept, furthermore, all value is expelled from the scientific conception of nature. Values appear as

merely subjective, and no difference of principle distinguishes a preference for wealth and power from the needs of the mass of humanity.
Modern scientific–technical rationality is thus adjusted in some sense to
its destiny as the basis for the domination of human beings and nature,
the intrinsic potentialities of which it ignores.

This critique was derived explicitly from phenomenological considerations in Husserl and Heidegger. Those two argued that scientific–
technical reason is abstracted from the lifeworld and hence from the
secondary qualities present in immediate experience. Marcuse took up
this argument and extended it by considering its implications for technology under capitalism. In this he comes perilously close to Heidegger,
whose critique of technology also derives practical consequences from
the structure of scientific–technical rationality. Both draw dystopian
conclusions from the triumph of modern reason.

But Marcuse's argument is historically grounded on the alternative
of capitalism and socialism. An early essay on Max Weber pointed out
that Weber's concept of rationality depended on the separation of ownership and labour characteristic of capitalism.[13] But what is rational
from the standpoint of capitalist management constitutes a very narrow cross-section of existence. The life process of workers responds
also to essential human potentials that are irrelevant to profit making.
This broader reality is the basis for a very different dialectical concept
of rationality, one that would be realized in a socialist organization of
society oriented toward life-affirming values.

These arguments are suggestive, but we can do better today. Very
radical changes in both the experience of technology and its understanding in the academic world open new and more concrete paths. Environmentalism, the Internet, and many struggles around a variety of
technologies have broken the dystopian spell and restored confidence
in human agency in ways unanticipated by the Frankfurt School. We
must draw from these experiences to situate its important contribution
in the context of a satisfactory philosophy of technology able to address
the environmental crisis.[14]

Marcuse's critique of value neutrality is not entirely compatible with
contemporary views, but it can be reformulated in a way that preserves
his essential point. Recent study of technology shows that it does in fact
incorporate values despite its appearance of neutrality. But these values
are 'translated' into technical specifications and can only be identified
in a social context or through historical reconstruction of the process of
technical development in which various social actors determined de-

sign in accordance with their preferences. In this respect, modern technology is no different from earlier craft technology. There is, however, a difference of another kind.

Consider value neutrality not as an achieved state of purity but as a tendency with a history. Indeed, the development of modern technology has been accompanied by the gradual elimination of traditional values from technical practice. Those values were deeply rooted in a culture; by contrast, the new valuative translations that characterize modern technology are rootless results of calculative economic strategies. The imperatives of the capitalist market underlie this tendency to free technology from craft values, whose place is taken by developments oriented exclusively toward profit. Technical disciplines are made possible by this reduction, which eliminates most ethical and aesthetic mediations and orients practical knowledge toward a purely quantitative treatment of processes and materials.

Naturally, the pursuit of profit mediates real demands that continue to shape technical designs. To some extent these demands appear in the technical disciplines as well, as constraints or choices among technically underdetermined options. No complete value neutrality is ever achieved, but the tendency is toward a simplification of the valuative constraints on design. The less technology is invested with culturally secured values, the more easily it can be adapted to the changing conditions of the market. Hence the appearance of value neutrality of modern production, with its purified technical disciplines to which correspond standardized parts available for combination in many different patterns with different value implications.

Reformulated in these terms, Marcuse's argument suggests a quite definite future for technology under socialism. Technical disciplines and technologies would translate values related not just to profitability but more broadly to human and natural needs recognized in political debate. These values would be incorporated into the disciplines as principles guiding choices among possible designs, much as the healing mission of medicine guides it toward a value-based selection among the possibilities opened by knowledge of human biology.

The emergence of these new constraints should be conceived not as obstacles but as opportunities. The capacity for innovation would be challenged by these political demands, much as it is challenged today by market demands. The situation that Marcuse foresaw is anticipated by the regulation of technology where it imposes life-affirming standards independent of the market. We see the beginnings of something like this in relation to environmental standards. As these standards are internalized by the disciplines, what Marcuse called the 'technological rationality' of the society is transformed. A new technology responds to valuative considerations that it 'materializes' in procedures and devices. Marcuse thus imagined a reformed science and technology that would respond to human and natural needs on the basis of its own standard of rationality.

The most philosophically problematic limitation of the early Frankfurt School has to do with its concept of experience. This limitation is less obvious in Adorno and Horkheimer, who studiously avoid direct engagement with politics. They deplore the decline of experience in modern societies without offering a political alternative. It is thus easy to dismiss statements about nature such as Adorno's as metaphors or aphoristic exaggerations.

But there is something right about this complaint. Benjamin distinguished two types of experience, *Erlebnis* from *Erfahrung*. The difference has to do with time. *Erlebnis* refers to fleeting and superficial reactions to the rapidly changing urban environment, what Benjamin called 'shock.' *Erhfahrung* describes an experience that is more deeply assimilated by the subject. It presupposes a slowness of life, even a state of boredom, that allows the salient features of the object to stand out and undergo reflection or transformation in the mind of the subject. On the terms of this distinction, one could agree with Adorno that experience is in 'decline' in modern societies.

However, Marcuse and Benjamin go further than Adorno. The distinction in types of experience is related to the utopian content of the idea of nature as it enters consciousness and shapes a progressive experience of the world. This leads Marcuse to the notion of aestheticized sensation. But he left us with only fragments of a theory, and some of these fragments – the Freudian ones – are less plausible today than they were when he first proposed them. The suspicion remains that the ideas of a 'new sensibility' and a 'liberation of nature' merely describe ordinary political views and sentimental attitudes in overblown metaphors. From the standpoint of this critique, the Frankfurt School's idea of nature is not a historically and philosophically significant alternative.

To counter that conclusion one would need to distinguish experienced nature from nature as an object of natural science and from purely cultural objects. Experienced nature would have to have an ontological status, but exactly what sort remains to be determined. I have argued that Marcuse was blocked from addressing this problem by the Frankfurt School's rejection of the heritage of phenomenological ontology.[15] This blockage had historical motives that resulted in Marcuse making a sharp break with his own early attempt at a synthesis of Heidegger's fundamental ontology and the early Marx. The concept of experience that Adorno borrowed from Benjamin and then modified cannot do this work outside the realm of art, and Marcuse, who violated the restriction to art, never developed a viable alternative.[16]

Marcuse's Freudian concept of libidinal attachment to reality was supposed to make the leap beyond art to politics. But this appears to be a psychological concept occupying the place of a philosophical justification for the utopian idea of participation in things, to which Adorno referred in the passage cited at the beginning of this discussion. If the recognition of life by life is nothing more than a 'positive attitude' toward nature, it is not an 'existential truth' and is of no special interest to philosophy, however significant it might be for encouraging sound environmental policy.

The key problem is thus the ontological status of lived experience. Natural science is, by nature, totally disenchanted. It has no room for teleology, for the erotic, for any preference for life over death. Like Melville's white whale, it is bleached of value and so invites subjective projections of every sort in the form of ever more powerful technologies serving ever more violent ends. Against this background, lived experience is increasingly devalued in modern times. It appears to be without epistemic credentials or ontological significance.

Marcuse rejected the privilege of nature in this scientific sense. Lived experience is not a subjective overlay on nature as natural science understands it. Rather, it reveals dimensions of reality that science cannot apprehend in its present form. These dimensions, beauty, potentialities, essences, life as a value, are just as real as electrons and tectonic plates. The imagination that projects these dimensions is thus not merely a subjective faculty; it also reveals aspects of the real.

But there is an ambiguity in Marcuse's approach that shows up particularly in his rather vague demand for a new science that would discover value in the very structure of its objects. Did he wish to reenchant natural science, to attribute qualities such as beauty to it that contemporary science does not recognize? This is the most contentious interpretation of Marcuse's thought, but it is not entirely justified by the texts.

There is a more plausible interpretation. According to this alternative, experience is valorized not in opposition to modern science but as an alternative ontological field coexisting with science and claiming its own rights and significance. This seems to be the implication of Marcuse's rejection of any return to a 'qualitative physics.' On this account, science might very well evolve in new directions through genuine discoveries stimulated by life in a liberated society. But no one can anticipate, much less dictate, the science of the future. More significant for Marcuse's theory would be the evolution of experience, reshaped by resistance and ultimately by freedom. This evolution would release the aesthetic imagination from its marginal role under capitalism so that it could take a central place in the reconstruction of the technology and the world it supports. The philosophical task – regrettably, one that Marcuse did not undertake – would be to delimit the spheres of science and experience so as to avoid confusion between the two different kinds of truth.

This alternative corresponds to the phenomenological approach as it is explained in thinkers such as Gadamer and Merleau-Ponty. They did not endorse a regressive re-enchantment of nature; rather, they defended the multiplicity of points of view on reality. This operation requires a critique of the 'view from nowhere' in order to validate the specifically engaged perceptions of a finite being in the world, an embodied being that belongs to a community.

Interpreted in this way, it makes sense to claim that the perceived potentialities of objects have a kind of reality. As I argued earlier, there are important domains of experience to which we bring a normative awareness quite apart from opinions and intellectual constructions. Lived experience of the real is not confined to the empirically given but often refers beyond it to essential potentialities that it more or less fulfils. Things are given 'in' a form that is attuned to the subject's disposition and vice versa, and not as indifferent physical objects 'invested' with subjective associations by a psychological subject. The phenomenological correlation of subject and object preserves their distinctness while testifying to their mutual implication. This 'two-dimensional' nature of experience could be extended to form the basis of the political discrimination that Marcuse substitutes for the traditional Marxist notion of class consciousness.

Both Adorno and Marcuse rejected phenomenology as incompatible with their historical standpoint; yet I find buried, perhaps unconscious, links to phenomenology in their attempts to grant the experience of nature a philosophical role.[17] Because they failed to develop these links, they fell between two stools, psychology and philosophy. Adorno seems to have been content with the ambiguity. Marcuse found a very unorthodox interpretation of Freud useful for linking his concept of nature with his political theory. But we may prefer to pursue the Frankfurt School's insight into nature by a different path. For this purpose, I believe it worth looking again at the contribution of phenomenology.

In recent years the concept of experience has been largely purged from philosophy under the influence of post-structuralism and Habermas's communication theory. These approaches triumphed in a period of relative social peace in which reforms appeared possible. But the rejection of experience they presuppose rests on a straw man: the notion that experience as a category necessarily involves romantic immediacy. An alternative conception would recognize the social mediation of experience without eliminating its existential weight in the 'vapourware' of language and culture. The program for developing such a concept was announced by the early Frankfurt School but was not carried out.

Unfortunately, the most influential inheritors of the Frankfurt School today have dropped this program, which is so important for linking its original contribution to the politics of the environment. When the most influential later critical theorists turned away from the problematic of nature to exclusively social concerns they lost the ability to address environmental issues. The disappearance of any reference to technology stripped the theory of the resources it needed for this purpose. But in the age of environmental crisis it is becoming increasingly clear that these three terms are mutually implicated: no *society* without *technology* and no *technology* without *nature*. Perhaps the further development of the early Frankfurt School's concept of nature undertaken here can provide a basis for a synthesis.

NOTES

1 Walter Benjamin, *Illuminations*, ed. H. Arendt, trans. H. Zohn (New York: Schocken, 1968), 259.
2 Theodor W. Adorno, *Aesthetic Theory*, trans. R. Hullot-Kentor (New York: Continuum, 1997), 247.
3 See Burke in this volume.
4 Herbert Marcuse, *The New Left and the 1960s*, ed. D. Kellner (New York: Routledge, 2005), 174.
5 Herbert Marcuse, *Counterrevolution and Revolt* (Boston: Beacon, 1972), 66; Adorno, *Aesthetic Theory*, 100, 107.

6 Adorno, *Aesthetic Theory*, 66.
7 Quoted in Marcuse, *Counterrevolution and Revolt*, 67.
8 Ibid., 69.
9 Herbert Marcuse, *One-Dimensional Man* (Boston: Beacon, 1964), 73.
10 Herbert Marcuse, 'Ecology and the Critique of Modern Society,' *Capitalism, Nature, Socialism* 3, no. 3 (1992): 9.
11 See, for example, Shane Gunster's chapter in this volume; Douglas Kellner, *Media Culture: Cultural Studies, Identity, and Politics between the Modern and the Postmodern* (New York: Routledge, 1995); and Shane Gunster, *Capitalizing on Culture: Critical Theory for Cultural Studies* (Toronto: University of Toronto Press, 2004).
12 Theodor Adorno, *Introduction to Sociology*, trans. E. Jephcott (Cambridge: Polity, 2000), 161–2n15.
13 Herbert Marcuse, *Negations*, trans. J. Shapiro (Boston: Beacon, 1968).
14 See, for example, Christoph Görg in this volume; Andrew Feenberg, *Questioning Technology* (New York: Routledge, 1999).
15 Andrew Feenberg, *Heidegger and Marcuse: The Catastrophe and Redemption of History* (New York: Routledge, 2005).
16 Martin Jay, *Songs of Experience: Modern American and European Variations on a Universal Theme* (Berkeley: University of California Press, 2005), chapter 8.
17 Brian O'Connor, *Adorno's Negative Dialectic* (Cambridge, MA: MIT Press, 2004), 147, 157–8.

BIBLIOGRAPHY

Adorno, Theodor. *Aesthetic Theory*. Translated by R. Hullot-Kentor. New York: Continuum, 1997.
– *Introduction to Sociology*. Translated by E. Jephcott. Cambridge: Polity, 2000.
Benjamin, Walter. *Illuminations*. Edited by H. Arendt, translated by H. Zohn. New York: Schocken, 1968.
Feenberg, Andrew. *Heidegger and Marcuse: The Catastrophe and Redemption of History*. New York: Routledge, 2005.
– *Questioning Technology*. New York: Routledge, 1999.
Gunster, Shane. *Capitalizing on Culture: Critical Theory for Cultural Studies*. Toronto: University of Toronto Press, 2004.
Jay, Martin. *Songs of Experience: Modern American and European Variations on a Universal Theme*. Berkeley: University of California Press, 2005.
Kellner, Douglas. *Media Culture: Cultural Studies, Identity, and Politics between the Modern and the Postmodern*. New York: Routledge, 1995.

Marcuse, Herbert. *Counterrevolution and Revolt*. Boston: Beacon, 1972.
– 'Ecology and the Critique of Modern Society.' *Capitalism, Nature, Socialism* 3, no. 3 (1992): 29–38.
– *Negations*. Translated by J. Shapiro. Boston: Beacon, 1968.
– *The New Left and the 1960s*. Edited by D. Kellner. New York: Routledge, 2005.
– *One-Dimensional Man*. Boston: Beacon, 1964.
O'Connor, Brian. *Adorno's Negative Dialectic*. Cambridge, MA: MIT Press, 2004.

Contributors

Andrew Biro is Canada Research Chair in Political Ecology and Environmental Political Theory and is an Associate Professor in the Department of Political Science at Acadia University. He is the author of *Denaturalizing Ecological Politics* (Toronto: University of Toronto Press, 2005), as well as a number of articles in the areas of political theory, environmental politics, and cultural studies.

Donald A. Burke is a doctoral candidate in the Graduate Program in Social and Political Thought at York University in Toronto. He is also a sessional instructor in the Faculty of Liberal Studies at OCAD University. He is co-editor (with Colin J. Campbell, Kathy Kiloh, Michael K. Palamarek, and Jonathan Short) of *Adorno and the Need in Thinking* (University of Toronto Press, 2007). His current research centres on aesthetic philosophy in the traditions of German idealism and the Frankfurt School.

Colin Campbell recently finished a doctorate in Social and Political Thought at York University, with a dissertation focusing on Georges Bataille, Rene Girard, and Jean-Jacques Rousseau. His current research focuses on the deep religious and anthropological roots of the ecological-political crisis.

Katharine N. Farrell is an Ecological Economist and Political Theorist. Her work focuses on the political economy of knowledge in international environmental governance, with concentrations in the areas of green constitutional theory; institutional aspects of ecosystem services valuation; legitimacy of environmental policies; the role of science (and scientists) in sustainable development; and the role of time and tradition in processes and principles of ecological economic production. After completing her PhD studies in 2006 she was awarded a two-year Marie Curie Fellowship to conduct a dedicated empirical research project at the Helmholtz Centre for Environmental Research–UFZ in Leipzig, Germany. She is currently affiliated with the Institute of Environmental Science and Technology at the Autonomous University of Barcelona, the Department of Resource Economics at the Humboldt University of Berlin, and the Department of Environmental Science and Policy at the Central European University in Budapest, and has worked as a senior researcher with the Danish National Environmental Research Institute (NERI) at the University of Aarhus.

Andrew Feenberg is Canada Research Chair in Philosophy of Technology at the School of Communication of Simon Fraser University. His recent books include *Heidegger and Marcuse, The Essential Marcuse,* and *Reason and Experience: Essays in Technology and Modernity.*

Christoph Görg is Professor of Environmental Governance at the University of Kassel, Department of Social Sciences. At the Helmholtz Centre for Environmental Research–UFZ in Leipzig, he is head of the Department for Environmental Politics and speaker of the research cluster on 'Governance and Integrated Strategies for Adaptation.' He has published widely on a critical theory of societal relationships with nature, on global environmental politics and biodiversity policy, and on state transformation.

Shane Gunster teaches Media Studies and Critical Theory at the School of Communication at Simon Fraser University. He is the author of *Capitalizing on Culture: Critical Theory for Cultural Studies* (University of Toronto Press, 2004). His current research interests include conservative political discourse and environmental communication about climate change.

William Leiss is a Fellow and Past President (1999–2001) of the Royal Society of Canada and an Officer in the Order of Canada. He was the NSERC/SSHRC Research Chair in Risk Communication and Public Policy at the Haskayne School of Business, University of Calgary (1999–2005), and the Eco-Research Chair in Environmental Policy at Queen's University (1994–9). He is author, collaborator, or editor of fifteen books and numerous articles and reports and is currently writing a trilogy in the genre of utopian fiction, the first two volumes of which are *Hera, or Empathy* (2006) and *The Priesthood of Science* (2008). His website is http://www.leiss.ca.

Michael Lipscomb is an Associate Professor of Political Science at Winthrop University, where he teaches Political Theory and Environmental Politics. He is currently working on a book about the relationship between the constructed tempos of modern life and the experiential sensibilities that underwrite various commitments to environmental politics. His work has appeared in *New German Critique* and *Administrative Theory and Praxis*. He is also co-author of *Breastfeeding Rights in the United States* (Praeger, 2007) with Karen M. Kedrowski.

Timothy W. Luke is University Distinguished Professor of Political Science at Virginia Polytechnic Institute and State University in Blacksburg, Virginia. He also is the Program Chair for Government and International Affairs in the School of Public and International Affairs and Director of the Center for Digital Discourse and Culture (CDDC) at the College of Liberal Arts and Human Sciences at Virginia Tech.

D. Bruce Martin is an administrator at New Mexico State University at Alamogordo responsible for institutional research, assessment, and strategic planning. He also teaches political science courses and has been a long-time environmental and peace activist in New Mexico.

Jonathan Short holds a doctorate from the Social and Political Thought Program at York University and teaches in the Department of Communication Studies at Wilfrid Laurier University. He is the co-editor of *Adorno and the Need in Thinking*. Currently he is preparing a book manuscript on the political theory of Giorgio Agamben.

Steven Vogel is the Brickman-Shannon Professor of Philosophy at Denison University. He is the author of *Against Nature* (SUNY Press, 1996), and of numerous articles in Environmental Philosophy that have appeared in *Environmental Ethics*, *Environmental Values*, and elsewhere.

Index